Aristotle, Kant, and the Stoics

Aristotle, Kant, and the Stoics

Rethinking Happiness and Duty

Edited by

STEPHEN ENGSTROM
University of Pittsburgh

JENNIFER WHITING
Cornell University

CAMBRIDGE
UNIVERSITY PRESS

CAMBRIDGE UNIVERSITY PRESS
Cambridge, New York, Melbourne, Madrid, Cape Town,
Singapore, São Paulo, Delhi, Tokyo, Mexico City

Cambridge University Press
The Edinburgh Building, Cambridge CB2 8RU, UK

Published in the United States of America by
Cambridge University Press, New York

www.cambridge.org
Information on this title: www.cambridge.org/9780521624978

© Cambridge University Press 1996

First published 1996
First paperback edition 1998

A catalogue record for this publication is available from the British Library

Library of Congress Cataloguing in Publication data

ISBN 978-0-521-55312-4 Hardback
ISBN 978-0-521-62497-8 Paperback

Contents

CONTENTS

Contributors

JULIA ANNAS is Regents Professor of Philosophy at the University of Arizona.

JOHN M. COOPER is Professor of Philosophy at Princeton University.

STEPHEN ENGSTROM is Assistant Professor of Philosophy at the University of Pittsburgh.

BARBARA HERMAN is Griffin Professor of Philosophy at the University of California, Los Angeles.

T. H. IRWIN is Susan Linn Sage Professor of Philosophy at Cornell University.

CHRISTINE M. KORSGAARD is Professor of Philosophy at Harvard University.

JOHN MCDOWELL is University Professor of Philosophy at the University of Pittsburgh.

J. B. SCHNEEWIND is Professor of Philosophy at Johns Hopkins University.

JENNIFER WHITING is Associate Professor of Philosophy at Cornell University.

ALLEN W. WOOD is Professor of Philosophy at Yale University.

Acknowledgments

The essays in this volume were originally prepared for a conference entitled "Duty, Interest, and Practical Reason: Aristotle, Kant, and the Stoics," held at the University of Pittsburgh in March 1994 under the auspices of the Joint Program in Classics, Philosophy, and Ancient Science. We thank all of those, in addition to the authors, who contributed to the success of the conference. We are especially grateful to the National Endowment for the Humanities, an independent federal agency, and the Department of Philosophy at the University of Pittsburgh for generous financial assistance. We also thank the Department of Classics and the Department of the History and Philosophy of Science for their support. Peter Koehler, dean of our Faculty of Arts and Sciences, deserves special mention for covering our last-minute deficit.

Other institutions also gave their support. We thank those who agreed to serve as session chairs and the universities that provided funds for them to attend: Nancy Sherman and Henry Richardson of Georgetown University; Andrews Reath of North Carolina State University; Thomas Hill, Jr., of the University of North Carolina, Chapel Hill; and Brad Inwood of the University of Toronto. We are also grateful to Terence Moore of Cambridge University Press for his support from the very start, as well as to the Center for Advanced Study in the Behavioral Sciences for secretarial and other assistance provided (with support from the Andrew W. Mellon Foundation) while we were completing this volume.

Finally, we thank our colleagues and, above all, our graduate students for all of their assistance – from the intellectual stimulation they provided in our year-long seminar on Aristotle and Kant to their willingness to house visitors and provide transportation for the speakers to and from the airport. We are most grateful to Thomas Berry for his assistance in all phases of the project – from preparing the grant application and designing the brochures to taking care of every last detail before, during, and after the conference. We could not have done it without him.

Introduction

STEPHEN ENGSTROM AND JENNIFER WHITING

There is a venerable tradition according to which ancient ethical thought and modern ethical thought are sharply opposed. The outlines of this view are clear in Sidgwick, and it has figured prominently in work of contemporary writers such as G. E. M. Anscombe and Alasdair MacIntyre. The differences between ancient and modern ethics are, according to this tradition, due largely to the influence of Christianity and its conception of morality as based on divine law. The story runs roughly as follows.

The ancients took as their starting point the idea of the good, particularly the human good, which they identified with *eudaimonia*, or happiness. Because they tended to view the good of a being as determined by its natural end or function, and to regard the capacities whose exercise enables a being to perform its function *well* as its characteristic excellences or virtues, they tended to view a being's good as achieved in or through the exercise of its characteristic virtues. But in spite of their emphasis on the human end and characteristic human virtues, the ancients were sensitive to the fact that this end must be sought and these virtues exercised in different ways in different circumstances. Right action is determined not by general rules but by the virtuous agent's perception of what the circumstances require. Ancient ethics is thus teleological and particularist: the end determines what sort of action is appropriate given the agent's particular circumstances.

The moderns, on the other hand, took as their starting point the moral code they inherited from medieval Christianity, which consisted roughly in a system of rules or commands grounded in divine law. But as a result of the religious disputes of the Reformation and the rise of modern science and secular society, the specific content of this code could no longer be justified by appeal to revelation. The central project of modern ethics thus came to be one of providing an alternative foundation. Though some sought a basis in human sentiments, the legalistic character of the code encouraged most

1

Enlightenment moralists to seek a foundation for our duties in universal laws of nature ascertainable by natural reason. Modern ethics thus tends to be deontological and universalist: since the rules of duty are based on laws prescribed by reason alone, they bind all agents absolutely, without regard to their private interests.

This historical sketch no doubt captures some important differences between ancient and modern ethics, but proponents of the traditional view tend to regard these differences as symptomatic of a fundamental opposition, one thought to be most clearly exemplified by the paradigmatic representatives of ancient and modern ethics – namely, Aristotle and Kant. According to this line of thought, Aristotle is a teleologist who insists that all action be done for the sake of eudaimonia, while Kant is a deontologist who insists that moral action be done for the sake of duty alone; Aristotle's conception of practical reason is monistic insofar as he justifies all action by appeal to the single end of eudaimonia, while Kant's conception is dualistic insofar as his distinction between categorical and hypothetical imperatives reflects a sharp distinction between moral and nonmoral reasoning; and Aristotle sees right action as determined by the virtuous agent's perception of what is required by particular circumstances, while Kant sees duties as rules prescribed by reason alone.

This tradition exercises a pervasive influence on contemporary ethics. Many thinkers take the traditional opposition for granted, and thus see only a restricted range of options. Viewing their choice as one between ancient and modern, they overlook the possibility that there are important respects in which these outlooks are compatible and perhaps even complementary. Bernard Williams and Alasdair MacIntyre, for example, regard modern ethics, both Kantian and utilitarian, as products of an Enlightenment conception of rationality that is hopelessly flawed by its reliance on impartial and ahistorical universal principles. Because they take the traditional opposition for granted, Williams and MacIntyre think it necessary, in order to recover ancient insights about virtue and happiness, to reject features of modern ethical thought. Many theorists, however, continue to find some of these features, such as the emphasis on impartiality, attractive. If we value both the ancient insights and also such features of modern ethical thought, then we have good reason to reexamine the traditional assumption that ancient and modern ethics are irreconcilably opposed.

Moreover, the traditional view begins to look less plausible when we turn to the Stoics, who combine elements of these allegedly opposed ways of thought. Like Aristotle and other ancient ethicists, the Stoics are eudaimonists: they take eudaimonia to be the ultimate source of moral motivation and justification. This should, on the traditional view, distinguish the Stoics from Kant, who is supposed to focus on duty and to reject the eudaimonist's appeal

2

to happiness. Nevertheless, the Stoics, with their emphasis on universal reason, articulate a conception of moral duty, based on natural law, that exercises a profound influence on Enlightenment ethics in general and Kant in particular. The Stoics thus provide not only a historical link between Aristotle and Kant, but also an illustration of how putatively ancient and modern ethical thought might be coherently integrated.

There are further challenges to the traditional view surfacing in contemporary work on Aristotle and Kant. Some commentators – for example, John McDowell and Jennifer Whiting – are now interpreting Aristotle in strikingly "Kantian" ways, while others – for example, Barbara Herman and Christine Korsgaard – are reading Kant in highly "Aristotelian" ways. There is thus emerging a convergence of interpretations of Aristotle and Kant, though one not yet widely appreciated because these Aristotelian and Kantian commentators have been working largely independently of one another. This independence is of significant evidential value since it renders their conclusions mutually supporting. Taken together, these interpretations pose a formidable challenge to the traditional view.

This emerging challenge, combined with that posed by recent work on the Stoics, suggests that the time is ripe to reevaluate the traditional view. To promote such reevaluation, we invited the authors of the essays collected here to participate in a conference entitled "Duty, Interest, and Practical Reason: Aristotle, Kant, and the Stoics," at the University of Pittsburgh in March 1994. We sought out scholars, some more and some less sympathetic to the traditional view, whose recent work suggested that they could be fruitfully paired with one another. Each session included one speaker working primarily on Aristotle or the Stoics, and one working primarily on Kant. In arranging the essays for this volume we have retained the original session topics and pairings of speakers, as indicated in the following synopses.

I. Deliberation and Moral Development

The striking similarities between John McDowell's Aristotle and Barbara Herman's Kant provided the original inspiration for both the theme and the format of the conference. Both reject standard classifications of Aristotelian and Kantian moral theories as, respectively, teleological and deontological. Herman even recommends that we read Kant's ethics as focused, like Aristotle's, on the good rather than, as traditionally claimed, on duty. And McDowell's Aristotelian conception of practical reason is explicitly Kantian insofar as he denies that practical reason stands in need of external, or extraethical, validation. Both emphasize upbringing and perception rather than rules, and both reject elucidations of practical reasoning that reduce it to a weighing of the relative costs and benefits of competing alternatives.

McDowell's contribution to this volume attacks what he regards as the dominant tradition, according to which Aristotle adopts a "blueprint picture" of the sort of deliberation involved in exercising *phronēsis* (practical wisdom). Deliberation proceeds, according to this picture, in two stages. One first formulates, in universal terms, an explicit blueprint for eudaimonia, or living well in general. Once explicit, this blueprint can then be applied to particular circumstances in a straightforward, perhaps even mechanical, way. McDowell rejects the blueprint picture because he believes that it can accommodate neither Aristotle's hostility to the idea of universal ethical truths nor Aristotle's association of practical wisdom with responsiveness to the details of particular practical predicaments.

McDowell claims that the blueprint picture is motivated, in spite of its patently non-Aristotelian rigorism, by a deductivistic prejudice of relatively recent vintage: modern moralists – because they tend to seek external foundations for ethical conclusions – tend to think that in cases of noninstrumental or specificatory reasoning, they can secure the sort of correctness required for "getting things right" only if they can represent the conclusion of deliberation as *deductively* warranted on the basis of independently acceptable starting points. McDowell's Aristotle is happily innocent of any such tendencies. In this respect, he resembles Kant: he takes the goodness of *eu prattein* (i.e., of good-willing-in-action) to be unconditioned and feels no need to ground it in the goodness of other goods whose value is independently accessible to those without a proper upbringing. McDowell concludes that categorical imperatives are not entirely alien to Aristotle's ethics.

McDowell believes that the blueprint picture fails because Aristotle's conception of eudaimonia is not such that it is clear in abstraction from particular practical predicaments what it would be for eudaimonia to have been achieved. Although he allows that the agent's conception of eudaimonia is a universal that gets applied in particular circumstances, McDowell claims that the content of this universal cannot be detached from the concrete psychological state, involving situation-specific perception, that constitutes its grasp. This state, which is the product of habituation, is simultaneously intellectual and desiderative: in learning to see certain actions as worth undertaking because they are noble (*kalon*), the agent acquires the concept of the noble *along with* the propensity to be motivated by its application. And this, according to McDowell, is all that we need in order for the concept of correctness to get a grip within the sphere of practical reason.

Though she doesn't herself put it this way, Herman's contribution can be described similarly. She rejects the idea that Kantian moral theory is committed to the blueprint picture. Given the traditional contrasts, it is less sur-

4

prising to find the blueprint picture here, and more surprising to find it rejected here, than in the case of Aristotle, where its appearance may be due to the influence of Aristotle's Kantian and other "deontomaniac" interpreters. Herman nevertheless seeks explicitly to accommodate within the Kantian framework a perception-based account of moral judgment similar to that developed by McDowell. This, she claims, requires us to rethink traditional accounts of the relation between desire and motive in Kantian moral theory.

Because Kant views pure practical reason as the determining ground of the will, commentators have traditionally ignored the shape and content of the Kantian agent's desires. Kantian moral development tends to be viewed as the cultivation of a kind of "rational musculature" sufficient to yield morally correct action, even in the face of recalcitrant desires. Herman, however, takes Kant's claim that pure practical reason is the determining ground of the will to be acceptable only if it is interpreted as a claim about the *authority*, and not about the *efficacy*, of the moral law. And she denies that it follows from this that our motivating understanding of the moral law, what she calls our "effective moral motive," must be pure.

Herman claims that there is room within Kantian moral theory for something like the view Aristotle expresses when he speaks of the nonrational part of the soul as sharing in reason. On her view, Kantians can allow that it is a natural fact about us as rational beings that our desires are *reason-responsive* in the sense that their shape and content can – given the right sort of development – be affected by our appreciation of the evaluative situations in which we find ourselves, and indeed by our appreciation of the moral law itself. As Herman puts it, the desires of a mature human agent have been brought within the scope of reason, or rationalized, in the sense that they normally contain not only a conception of an object, but also a conception of the object's value – not only for itself and as determined by its fit with other valued objects, but also as its satisfaction comports with the principles of practical reason. The motive of duty can thus function in the virtuous agent not as a separate motive to be weighed against others, nor as something added to independent incentives to act, but as dispersed throughout the motives that satisfy the requisite constraints.

Herman concludes with the suggestion that the Kantian framework may have advantages that the tradition-bound Aristotelian framework lacks, especially in dealing with the sort of moral perplexity that arises as a result of encountering new and unfamiliar moral phenomena.

II. Eudaimonism

T. H. Irwin's essay examines in detail Kant's well-known criticisms of ancient Greek eudaimonism. Kant criticizes the ancients on the ground that they commit the general error of regarding the highest good, or eudaimonia, as the basis of morality. Some of Kant's criticisms seem to rest on the assumption that all rational action, except for action on the moral motive, rests on a desire for pleasure. These criticisms thus amount to the objection that ancient attempts to base moral principles on eudaimonia subordinate morality to pleasure. But since some Greek eudaimonists, such as the Stoics, do not share this hedonist assumption, and since it is in any case a questionable one, this objection is not convincing. Kant has further objections, however, which do not depend on this assumption. He argues that any attempt to base morality on some prior conception of the good must treat moral principles as hypothetical imperatives and hence make moral agency heteronomous. Since Kant supposes that a hypothetical imperative based on our eudaimonia cannot provide a sufficient justification for an action unless we have a sufficiently strong inclination for our eudaimonia and for the specific elements within it that will be promoted by the action, he thinks that eudaimonia cannot provide any reasons for action that are independent of the inclinations of the subject, so that any attempt to base morality on eudaimonia subordinates moral principles to inclination.

Irwin argues, however, that Aristotle and the Stoics do not accept Kant's supposition that we have no sufficient justification for pursuing our eudaimonia that is not inclination-based. Aristotle and the Stoics hold that we have reason to pursue our eudaimonia not because we desire it, but because it is our ultimate good, which depends on the sort of being we are, not on what we happen to desire. There is thus a sense in which for Aristotle and the Stoics there can be *categorical* imperatives of prudence. To forestall the misleading impression that this disagreement with Kant reflects a division between ancient and modern views, however, Irwin points out that Butler and Reid agree with Aristotle and the Stoics on this point. Irwin also suggests that Kant fails to identify any difference between prudence and morality that would warrant his idea that imperatives of prudence can only be hypothetical, and that Kant's failure to free himself from this idea leads to certain inconsistencies in his understanding of the Stoics. Irwin concludes by noting that if imperatives of prudence can indeed have a categorical and autonomous status, then there may be a sense in which a justification of morality requires an appeal to eudaimonia, and that a correction of the mistakes in Kant's criticisms of Greek eudaimonism ought to result in a salutary reconstruction of his moral theory.

Stephen Engstrom begins his essay by noting that Aristotle's ethics has an attractive feature that Kant's is often thought to lack. By taking happiness, or eudaimonia, as his starting point, Aristotle ensures that his ethics is grounded in a conception that gives unity to practical life and whose content has some claim to be our natural end. Kant, on the other hand, while he speaks of happiness, or *Glückseligkeit,* as a natural end, sharply opposes the pursuit of this end to the practice of duty and virtue. Engstrom argues, however, that the fact that Aristotle conceives of eudaimonia as an end that includes virtuous activity, whereas Kant conceives of Glückseligkeit as an end from which such activity is excluded, indicates that their conceptions of eudaimonia and Glückseligkeit are fundamentally distinct and hence not appropriate reference points for comparison. Engstrom proposes that there is another concept in Kant's ethics that does provide the sort of unity that the conception of eudaimonia provides in Aristotle's, namely, the idea of the highest good.

But there is an apparent obstacle to this proposal. Kant explicitly criticizes the ancients for taking the highest good, which Aristotle identifies with eudaimonia, as the starting point for their ethical reflection. Consequently, he and Aristotle appear to differ in their understanding of the highest good. Engstrom argues, however, that attention to the nature of Kant's criticism and to the manner in which Aristotle articulates his conception of eudaimonia reveals that, as Irwin suggests, Kant's criticism does not in fact apply to Aristotle (though Engstrom and Irwin have quite different readings of that criticism). Kant requires that the specification of the highest good be, not the basis for, but rather something that depends on, the specification of virtue. And Aristotle seems to honor this requirement in his account of the lives of contemplation and of ethical virtue.

Engstrom goes on to argue that there is considerable agreement between Kant's and Aristotle's substantive conceptions of the highest good. Kant's conception provides a distinctive kind of unity for practical life through its systematic ordering of goods and its specification of an internal (causal) connection between them: virtue is both the basis for the goodness of Glückseligkeit and the cause of its realization in the highest good. Through an examination of Aristotle's accounts of eudaimonia, virtue, and the goods of fortune, Engstrom tries to show that Aristotle's conception of the highest good involves a similar ordering and connection of goods.

III. Self-Love and Self-Worth

Allen Wood argues that the main difference between Aristotle and Kant on the issue of self-love lies in a difference in their "empirical conceptions of human nature." Both find the topic of self-love to be morally important owing to the tendency people have in loving themselves to employ the wrong conception of self. But Aristotle thinks the error can be corrected, yielding a rationally satisfactory conception of self-love, while Kant holds that that self-love is in itself morally problematic and indeed fundamentally irrational, riddled with psychic conflict and self-alienation, so that love is not an attitude that clear-sighted and rational people will have toward themselves.

Wood argues that Kant takes our self-love to involve a rationally based desire for happiness that is essentially comparative: we want to think of ourselves as better than our neighbors, and this leads us to compete for status in their eyes and always to measure our own happiness by comparing ourselves with others. This "unsociable sociability" has a natural purpose, which lies in the development of our capacities, but it achieves this end by producing discontent: competitive desires, in making us unhappy, spur us to perfect ourselves, but they are nevertheless bound ultimately to leave us unhappy.

A further aspect of self-love, as Kant understands it, is that self-love involves the claim that one's happiness is objectively good, which it founds on a presumption of self-worth. Wood notes that in this respect Kant's view has affinities with Aristotle's view as interpreted by Whiting: both Kant and Aristotle take the value we place in our happiness to be grounded in judgments of self-worth. Wood argues, however, that Aristotle and Kant differ in that Aristotle allows that one person can be worth more than another, while Kant bases worth in the dignity of rational nature itself and thus holds that all rational beings have a worth that is absolute and radically equal.

Kant does allow for moral self-esteem and self-contempt, but maintains, in opposition to a long ethical tradition, that these attitudes are self-deceptive unless based on a comparison of oneself, not with others, but with the moral law alone. But Kant also holds that human nature includes a radical propensity to evil, or to self-conceit, which leads us self-deceptively to persuade ourselves of our absolute superiority over others. Thus, our nature dooms us to a conflict between two irreconcilable standpoints toward our self-worth. Nature's plan is that our reason should develop through self-deceptive antagonism with others, but through this development we become aware that our true worth lies only in a rational nature that we all share.

Wood concludes that despite the fact that Aristotle and Kant agree on such important points as that our true self is rational nature, and that rational self-benevolence follows upon rational self-esteem, the inference that Aristotle quite naturally draws from these points – namely, that good people will be friends to themselves – is one that Kant's empirical conception of human nature leads him to reject.

Jennifer Whiting questions Wood's suggestion that Aristotle's conception of good self-love is essentially competitive or comparative, and suggests that Aristotle may allow the virtuous agent's conception of self-worth to be based on something like the sort of comparison of himself with the moral law that Wood claims to find in Kant. Relying on a passage in the *Politics* where Aristotle associates *nous* (reason) not only with God but also with (impartial) law, Whiting reads the good self-lover's identification with his nous (as opposed to his desire) as an identification not only with something divine, but also with the impartial principle that natural goods should be distributed, both to himself and to others, according to worth. Because Aristotle views God as maximally self-determined and maximally independent of fortune, the good self-lover, in taking God as the standard by which to measure himself, aims at a kind of self-determination and independence of fortune reminiscent of Kantian autonomy.

Whiting's contribution is essentially a commentary on *Eudemian Ethics* viii 3, a text whose remarkably Kantian tone she attributes to the Socratic legacy common to Aristotle and Kant. This text distinguishes (1) the *kaloskagathos* (or fine-and-good) man, for whom natural goods (like wealth and power) are both good and fine, both from (2) the merely *agathos* (or good) man, for whom the natural goods are good but not fine, and also from (3) the non-agathos (or nongood) man, for whom natural goods are neither good (because he is prone to misuse them) nor fine. Aristotle seems here to rely on the Socratic view that wisdom (or virtue) is the only unconditional good – a view echoed in Kant's claim that the good will is the only thing that is good without qualification.

Whiting focuses on Aristotle's distinction between the kaloskagathos and the merely agathos. She takes Aristotle's view that the natural goods become fine for the kaloskagathos because he chooses them for the sake of something fine as structurally similar to the Kantian view (according to Wood and Korsgaard) that rational choice is a "value-conferring property." Relying partly on the connection between something's being fine and its being a suitable object of praise, Whiting suggests that the kaloskagathos, who is a good self-lover, deserves praise or honor in a way in which the merely agathos does not, because the kaloskagathos, having made the transition from natural to authoritative virtue, has shed as far as possible the effects of constitutive luck and is thus responsible for who he is in a way in which the merely agathos is not. Whiting compares the merely agathos, who performs virtuous actions "coincidentally," to the Kantian agent whom fortune has endowed with a sympathetic temperament, and whose actions in conformity with duty (though not *from* duty) are said to deserve "praise and encouragement but not esteem." Whiting concludes that Aristotle shares many of Kant's concerns, including his concern with autonomy, a point taken further by Korsgaard (who also compares the merely agathos to Kant's person of sympathetic temperament).

9

IV. Practical Reason and Moral Psychology

Christine Korsgaard examines an important question on which Aristotle and Kant are widely thought to be in sharp opposition. Whereas Aristotle holds it to be the mark of a good person to take pleasure in moral action, Kant seems to maintain that it is the person who acts from the motive of duty in the teeth of contrary inclination who shows an especially high degree of moral worth. But Korsgaard, like Wood, finds the real disagreement between Aristotle and Kant to lie not in ethics but in psychology. Ultimately, she traces the disagreement to different understandings of pleasure and pain.

Korsgaard argues that Aristotle and Kant share the following view of human action in general and morally good action in particular. What is distinctive about human action in general is that it is not driven by inclination or instinct, but governed by reason: such action is chosen and thereby endorsed by the agent's reason and conceived as good. What is distinctive about morally good action in particular is that such action – including its purpose – is chosen because it is *intrinsically* good. As Kant expresses this point, morally good action is done "from duty," which means that it is chosen because it has the intrinsic form of a law; for Aristotle, similarly, morally good action is done "for the sake of the noble [*kalon*]," which means that it is chosen for its own sake and moreover because it is in accordance with the right rule of reason. Both thus agree that the moral value of action is determined by considering action just as action (as *praxis*) and not as the production or making of something. In addition, both think that the exercise of choice involved in morally good action constitutes a kind of rational self-command whereby we give shape to our own characters and identities. Kant calls this autonomy; Aristotle calls it nobility. And both take the presence of this self-command to distinguish someone with true virtue from someone, such as the naturally sympathetic person, who chooses morally good action for its own sake but without quite grasping the reason why it is good.

The difference between Aristotle and Kant lies in their attitudes toward the feelings of the naturally sympathetic person; in particular, about whether the presence of such feelings could contribute any moral character to actions. Korsgaard points out that the disagreement about whether and when such feelings are likely to be present is not as great as is often thought: Kant recognizes that we must cultivate virtues, which will lead us to be pleased when we achieve our morally obligatory ends, and Aristotle's remarks about courage reveal that he does in fact recognize that virtuous action can involve considerable pain and may even, when unsuccessful, fail to involve pleasure. The difference shows up, however, in the one case about which they do seem to disagree. Unlike Aristotle, Kant holds that the cold person who acts from duty is not any less good, morally speaking, than the person who acts from duty and enjoys it. Korsgaard traces this difference to a difference in their views of what inclination is and ultimately in their views of what pleasure and pain are: Aristotle thinks of pleasure and pain as something like perceptions of the reasons for actions, whereas Kant does not. For Kant, therefore, feelings serve only as external aids to the performance of virtuous actions. Thus, while Aristotle and Kant agree that ethics concerns our capacity to choose our actions and thus to transcend mere reactivity in our relationship to the world, they differ in their understanding of the receptive part of our nature.

Julia Annas argues that Kant's account of practical reason differs significantly from Aristotle's in that Kant's account is dualistic in a way in which Aristotle's is not: Kant recognizes a sharp distinction, foreign to Aristotle's eudaimonism, between moral and nonmoral reasoning. This might appear to constitute a defense of the traditional view according to which ancient eudaimonism is monistic in a way in which modern ethics is not. But Annas explicitly disavows the traditional view on the ground that the Stoics drew a sharp distinction between moral and nonmoral reasoning within an indisputably eudaimonist framework. Because she takes this to demonstrate that a dualistic version of eudaimonism was conceptually available to Aristotle, Annas concludes that it is not Aristotle's commitment to eudaimonism that explains his monistic conception of practical reason. In her view, the monism stems instead from Aristotle's methodological deference to the common sense of his contemporaries, which tended to blur the distinction between moral and nonmoral reasoning.

Proponents of the traditional view often take eudaimonism's alleged failure to distinguish moral from nonmoral reasoning as evidence that eudaimonism cannot accommodate genuinely moral (as distinct from merely prudential) reasoning, and this is often associated with the charge that eudaimonist theories are objectionably egoistic. Annas rightly resists these aspects of the traditional view by appealing to Aristotle's requirement that virtuous agents choose virtuous actions for a "distinctive kind of reason" – namely, because they are *kalon* – which Aristotle represents both as ultimate and as excluding ulterior reasons. Annas takes this to show that Aristotle's theory is one *we* would recognize as moral (as distinct from prudential). But she goes on to point out two characteristics of his view that she takes as evidence that he – unlike Kant and the Stoics – did not draw a sharp distinction between moral and nonmoral considerations. First, Aristotle classifies together with recognizably moral virtues (such as justice) dispositions like magnificence, tact, and social friendliness, which are not recognizably moral. And second, Aristotle – unlike the Stoics – attaches significant value to a virtuous agent's *success* in achieving the external ends at which he aims.

11

Annas claims that this too tends to blur the distinction between moral and nonmoral reasoning. Here Aristotle differs significantly from the Stoics, who seem to anticipate the Kantian view that a good will "has its full value in itself" and not in what it effects or accomplishes.

To the extent that Annas takes Aristotle to recognize the kalon as providing a distinctive kind of reason for action, she might seem to weaken the case for saying that Aristotle's conception of practical reason is monistic. But she would resist this charge on the ground that it reflects the overly narrow interpretation of eudaimonism characteristic of the traditional view. Moreover, she emphasizes that Aristotle is significantly different from the Stoics in that he recognizes three kinds of *goods* – goods of soul, goods of body, and external goods – while the Stoics claim that virtue is the *only* genuine good and reduce everything else (including so-called goods of soul other than virtue) to the status of "indifferents." Here the Stoics, unlike Aristotle, are willing to part company with common sense, with the result that for them the Aristotelian distinction between goods of soul on the one hand, and bodily and external goods on the other, is not a sharp one. On this point, at least, the Stoics are closer to Kant than they are to Aristotle. And Annas, like Irwin, though seeing important differences between ancient and modern ethics, wants to warn against facile contrasts.

V. Stoicism

John Cooper tackles head-on the central issue of the compatibility of eudaimonism with a "deontological" conception of moral duty as consisting in conformity to universal law. Cooper defends their compatibility by defending the philosophical respectability of three theses, each central to Stoic accounts of "living virtuously": virtuous persons always (1) act for the sake of their own happiness; (2) choose virtuous actions for their own sakes, as parts of happiness; and (3) choose virtuous actions as conforming to the universal law (i.e., to the will of Zeus). Cooper is especially concerned to explain (3), not simply because he is interested in possible anticipations of Kantian deontology, but also because understanding the role played by the appeal to universal law is crucial to understanding Stoic eudaimonism.

Greek eudaimonists, from Socrates on, struggle to show that living virtuously is necessary, if not also sufficient, for living happily, typically by revising received views about the nature of happiness and virtue. Stoic revisionism is especially severe, for the Stoics secure the *identity* of happiness with virtue by denying the eudaimonic value of most things ordinarily recognized as good: on their view, so-called goods like health and wealth – although they are to-be-pursued and their opposites to-be-avoided – do not themselves contribute to the agent's happiness.

Cooper argues that the construction and plausibility of this Stoic view depends significantly on the Stoics' appeal to nature. This appeal goes beyond Aristotle's in the following way. Although Aristotle allows that nature is capable of providing extraethical confirmation of the *value* of virtuous living, it does not occur to him to think, as the Stoics think, that nature might provide extraethical confirmation of the substantive *content* of the various virtues. But the Stoics' belief that nature is a benevolent *reasoning* agent entitles them to take the natural development of an organism of any kind as a guide to the sort of behavior organisms of that kind ought to exhibit – that is, as a guide to the sort of acts appropriate to, or "incumbent" upon, organisms of that kind. The natural instincts of rational and nonrational creatures alike reveal material objectives – like health and the welfare of their offspring – that are "in accordance with nature." But it belongs to the nature of rational beings as such – even if experience suggests that many of us may not actually do so – to develop a peculiar and counterintuitive attitude toward these objectives: rational creatures come naturally to value the *rational pursuit* of material objectives *for itself*, in ways such that the value attached to this pursuit does not derive from the value attached to these objectives. Indeed, rational creatures come – again, "naturally" – to regard so highly the value of this rational pursuit that they attach no value at all to the actual achievement of these material objectives.

Cooper's central thesis is that the Stoics' appeal to universal nature plays a crucial role in establishing the coherence of this counterintuitive view. It is only because the virtuous person views his nature and life as nothing but parts of the (rational and benevolent) nature and life of the universe as a whole that it is reasonable for him to measure his "local" advantage with reference to the needs of the universe as a whole. Cooper sees no way of arriving at this conclusion simply from within "ethical reflection," so he claims that extraethical argument plays a crucial role in establishing the Stoic identification of virtue not only with happiness but also with obedience to universal law. This conception of universal law differs, of course, from the Kantian conception, most notably in leaving no room for individual rational beings to set their own ends. But the differences are peripheral to Cooper's central task of showing how obedience to universal law can in principle be incorporated within the eudaimonist point of view.

While Cooper defends the compatibility of eudaimonism and a deontological conception of duty in the Stoic view, J. B. Schneewind maintains that the distinction between teleology and deontology can still be used to mark significant differences between the Stoics and Kant. Defending the traditional view on two fronts, Schneewind both rejects the position of Kantian revisionists who deny that Kant is a deontologist and also argues against students of ancient ethics who deny that Stoic ethics is teleological in any sense that contrasts meaningfully with deontology. Schneewind begins by criticizing the recent interpretations of Kant by Paul Guyer and Barbara Herman, who deny that Kant subordinates all considerations of value to formal principles of duty and claim to find in his ethics a theory of value that provides an intelligible rationale for moral constraints. Against Guyer's suggestion that the foundation of Kant's moral philosophy is the intrinsic and absolute value of freedom, Schneewind counters that Kant does not permit any value that is "intrinsic" in a sense that would imply its priority to all rational principles governing the will. And against Herman's suggestion that acting according to principles of rational willing has value for us because it sustains our sense of ourselves as rational agents, Schneewind argues that this idea, though in some ways attractive, implies that our freedom and rational agency are vulnerable possessions, and hence it does not accurately capture Kant's position. Schneewind also argues that since the categorical imperative always requires the presence of nonrational desires in order to yield specific directives, it is not by itself a complete source of reasons and hence cannot play the role that, by Herman's own account, a conception of value plays in human agency.

Though Schneewind appreciates many of the commonalities that Annas claims to find in Stoic and Kantian ethics, he maintains that there are still deep differences separating Kant from Stoic doctrines. The Stoics assume that it is by perceiving the divine rational order of the universe that we introduce rational order into our own souls and thereby perfect ourselves and achieve happiness. This Stoic picture of moral motivation as grounded in perception of the good leads Schneewind to doubt Annas's suggestion that something like respect for the moral law is a central moral motive for the Stoics. Kant rejects the idea that perception of the good is the basis of desire and action; respect is not the perception of some good, but rather a unique feeling produced in us by the moral law. Schneewind also points out a further difference. Whereas the Stoics take the attainment of happiness to be their aim in philosophy and regard nature as the guide we should follow, Kant does not think happiness is the proper concern of philosophy, and he has a quite modern lack of confidence in the natural world. Thus, even the Stoics are teleologists in a sense in which Kant is not, and so the contrast between Kantian deontology and ancient teleology remains significant.

Schneewind concludes with the observation that Kant's loss of confidence in the rational order of nature confronted him with a question that is of enormous importance to us today but that the Stoics could not even have raised – the question of how we are to shape our lives and society in the absence of constraints imposed by nature. Although we may sometimes assume that all philosophers throughout the history of ethics have attempted to answer the same basic questions, it is more useful to ask whether different

14

historical circumstances have led philosophers in different ages to ask different questions; otherwise we may fail to see differences that are more revealing than the similarities.

As the foregoing synopses reveal, the contributors to this volume present a wide variety of perspectives on the relation between ancient and modern ethics. But together their essays illustrate that our understanding of Aristotle, Kant, and the Stoics is significantly enriched through a careful comparison of them and further that contemporary ethics can profit substantially from the exploration of its ancient and modern antecedents.

I
Deliberation and Moral Development

1

Deliberation and Moral Development in Aristotle's Ethics

JOHN MCDOWELL

I

In this essay, I try to set out an understanding of a distinctively ethical application that Aristotle evidently wants to make of the notion of deliberation (*bouleusis*). The main obstacle in the path of the reading I want to recommend is the temptation to give an overly "intellectualistic" cast to the idea of a correct conception of doing well – the conception that is put into practice in actions that, in manifesting excellences of character in the strict sense, manifest the intellectual excellence of practical wisdom. I think Aristotle's view is that it is the moral development effected by upbringing that puts us in a position to undertake ethical deliberation. His account of the habituation that sets up states of character already contains enough to display states of character as having the intellectual aspect that he insists on. If the content of a correct conception of doing well is fixed by proper upbringing, that renders it superfluous to credit that role to an autonomous operation of the practical intellect, or to look to the intellect for a foundation for the claim that this rather than that conception of doing well is correct. I think those ideas figure in interpretations of Aristotle only because he is read in a modern, and hence alien, framework. Ironically enough, if we clear those ideas away, and equip ourselves with a different understanding of the sense in which practical wisdom is an intellectual excellence, we make it possible to see a certain convergence, in a context of undeniable divergence, between Aristotle and Kant.

II

Nicomachean Ethics III.3 discusses deliberation in general. The topic is thinking that starts from a proposed end and, when successful, arrives at something the agent can simply do with a view to that end – a project that he can put

19

into effect without further thought. The idea is that it is only across a gap that the end, as proposed, casts a favorable light on doing something in particular, and it takes an exercise of the intellect to bridge the gap.

This schema fits most straightforwardly where the thinking needed to bridge the gap between end and action is instrumental or technical. In this kind of case, there is no problem about what it would be for the end to have been achieved: say, for the agent to possess a winter covering. But proposing an end to oneself in such terms does not by itself single out an immediately practicable course of action. So a task is set for the intellect: to arrive at a course of action such that undertaking it will, if all goes well, result in achieving the end proposed. Perhaps there are several such actions; in that case comparisons in terms of efficacy, and perhaps other dimensions of desirability, come into play in selecting among the competing options.[1]

Now Aristotle uses the concept of deliberation when he characterizes an intellectual excellence that is specifically ethical. He says excellence in deliberation with a view to living well in general is characteristic of the person who possesses practical wisdom (the *phronimos;* 1140a25–8). Practical wisdom is operative in actions that display the excellences of character – courage, temperance, and so forth. It is the involvement of practical wisdom that distinguishes the excellences of character, strictly so called, from mindless behavioral propensities that might (perhaps only roughly) correspond with them in behavioral output (VI.13).

Here we have a different sort of gap between end and action undertaken with a view to it. The end is living well or doing well, which Aristotle tells us is the same as *eudaimonein* (1095a18–20). Here we cannot say it is clear, in a particular practical predicament, what it would be for the end to have been achieved. In fact it seems plausible that that is exactly the problem for thought directed at bridging this kind of gap between end and action. The agent has to determine which (perhaps we should add "if any"), from among the actions that he can directly set about performing, would here and now, in these circumstances, *amount to* doing well.

What might an exercise of the intellect, directed at this other kind of practical question, look like? And what is the content of the idea of deliberating excellently in this kind of case? Reflecting on technical or instrumental deliberation does not help with these questions. Where the problem is technical or instrumental, we can understand deliberation as working toward something immediately practicable, if necessary through intermediate means, with what figures at each stage being singled out by the intellect as *conducive* to what figures at the preceding stage. And for these cases, we can begin to explain the idea that one person deliberates better than another by saying that good deliberation is such as to be *effective*: acting on its deliverances tends to achieve the proposed end.[2] But in the kind of deliberation that displays practical wisdom, the problem is precisely that it is not clear what it would be to have achieved the proposed end. We cannot exploit the idea of effectiveness to explain excellence in deliberation of this kind.

Some commentators have supposed that Aristotle hoped to use technical deliberation to cast light on this other kind of deliberation, at least when he wrote Book III.[3] I have been urging that this idea is unpromising. And there is really no reason to saddle Aristotle with it. When he talks about deliberation in general, he is not addressing the question what it is for exercises of the practical intellect to be correct. It is an indication of this that even when his discussion suggests a focus on the technical case, he shows no special concern with efficacy, as opposed to other sorts of desirability in action. What the general account of deliberation is supposed to give us is just the idea of using the intellect to bridge a gap between proposed end and action. It is true that technical problems provide the easiest illustrations of this idea. But that by itself leaves Aristotle's options open, when he comes to consider cases where the gap between end and action is of a different kind.[4]

III

In the kind of deliberation excellence at which is characteristic of practical wisdom, the question addressed is "What action here and now would *be* doing well?"[5] The end proposed – doing well – is, logically speaking, a universal, and the problem is to arrive at an instance of it. That can suggest that deliberation of this sort requires arriving at, or otherwise availing oneself of, a blueprint, in universal terms, for doing well, and applying it to the circumstances at hand. This has perhaps been the main alternative, in modern readings of Aristotle, to the idea that he hopes to illuminate this kind of deliberation somehow by exploiting a technical model.[6]

But it is increasingly familiar that this picture does not fit Aristotle. He repeatedly denies that ethical truth is stateable in universal terms. (See, e.g., 1094b11–27, 1109b12–23, among many similar passages.) And there is a connected point about how he conceives bringing the universal end, doing well, to bear on the details of a situation. If one had a blueprint for doing well, applying it should be straightforward, perhaps even mechanical. The blueprint would suit actions to types of situation, and applying it would require scanning the circumstances to see if they bring the situation under one of the specified types. That might be laborious, but it would not call for anything special in the way of an excellence of the *practical* intellect. On this picture, having one's practical intellect in good order, in the relevant respect, would be a matter of having the right blueprint; applying the blueprint would require only general capacities for gathering information, and the capacity for logical inference. But this is difficult to square with a strong suggestion, in various passages, that practical wisdom – excellence at the relevant kind of deliberation – at least includes, and perhaps is even to be identified with, a proper responsiveness to the details of situations – something Aristotle is willing to conceive as like, and even as a kind of, perception (see especially 1142a23–30, 1143a5–b5).

The idea of the "blueprint" picture is that the content of a conception of the universal, doing well, is in principle available, and assessable for correctness, in abstraction from the judgments or actions, in particular circumstances, that we want to see as applications of it. We could make the universal explicit in context-independent words; they would pin down its content, in a way that should in principle be intelligible from outside the actualizations, in particular circumstances, of a propensity to make just such judgments or engage in just such actions (a propensity that would be possessed only by someone who had the corresponding end as his own). Whether some particular judgment or action was a correct application of the universal would be a question of what followed from the universal's content together with the facts of the situation. So the question whether some conception of doing well was correctly applied in some particular case would be separable from the question whether doing well so conceived was the right end to pursue. Correctness of application would be recognizable, in principle, from a stance that was neutral with respect to the corresponding end. And for a deliberator to be getting things right, arriving at what really is an instance of doing well, both conception and application would need to be correct.

But when Aristotle stresses discernment of the specifics of a situation, he seems to be pointing to a different way of keeping in place the notion of getting things right. A discerning view of a situation is one that reads the significance of the situation's features correctly. If we can get correctness into the picture on these lines, that might leave the idea that we must conceive application in terms of deduction, and must see questions about the correctness of applications as presupposing a separately established correctness in the universal conception of the end that is applied, looking like a mere prejudice – we might call it "rationalistic" – about the nature of this kind of exercise of rationality, perhaps reflecting a prejudice about rationality as such.

IV

We are considering deliberation with a view to doing well. Early in the *Nicomachean Ethics* Aristotle explains that "well," in that specification of an end, is to be understood as "in accordance with excellence" (1098a16–18). That is the pretext for the discussion of excellence and the particular excellences that starts at the end of Book I (1102a5–6). Aristotle deals with the excellences of character mostly by giving character sketches of those who possess them, and one thing he thereby achieves is to put into place in his lectures a somewhat determinate picture of the content of the end that is constituted by doing well in general, as correctly conceived (by his lights, of course).[7] Doing well is acting in the sort of way that is characteristic of people such as he describes. This indirection is just what we ought to expect, if he thinks the content of a correct conception of doing well cannot be captured in a deductively applicable blueprint for a life.

Aristotle evidently does not mean it to be possibly contentious, as between him and his audience, that the excellences are just the states of character that he lists, or that those who possess the particular excellences are just the sorts of people he describes in his character sketches. The ethical substance, the content of the conception of doing well that he puts into place by going through the particular excellences, is meant to be already shared between him and the audience, because they have been properly brought up (1095b4–6). They have been habituated into a propensity to admire and delight in the actions that are characteristic of the excellences. They see those actions as fine or noble (*kalon*); the concept of the noble organizes the evaluative outlook of one who possesses excellence (see, e.g., 1120a23–4).

This picture of habituation, in which it institutes a conceptual capacity – possession of the concept of the noble – in the course of shaping motivations, is helpful in bringing out how arriving at what really are instances of doing well need not be understood as applying a blueprint. There is nothing wrong with saying that one who possesses excellence grasps the content of the universal, doing well. But we need not conceive that grasp as separable, even in principle, from the state, one aspect of which is a motivational propensity, that results from having been properly brought up. Someone who has been properly brought up has been habituated into seeing the appropriate actions as worth going in for in the specific way that is expressed by bringing them under the concept of the noble. According to the ''blueprint'' picture, the content of the correct conception of doing well can be abstracted away from this psychological state, the result of habituating evaluative and motivational propensities into shape. The idea is that the content of practical wisdom's universal end could in principle be grasped in an act of pure intellect. But if we juxtapose Aristotle's stress on discernment with his picture of how the correct conception of doing well is acquired, we have the essentials of a contrasting picture, in which the content of the end cannot be pinned down in abstraction from the ability to put it into practice in recognizing specific occasions for action. In this contrasting picture, there is nothing for grasp of the content of the universal end to be except a capacity to read the details of situations in the light of a way of valuing actions into which proper upbringing has habituated one.

V

Even commentators who see that the "blueprint" picture is not Aristotle's can be influenced by the idea that applying a practical universal would have to conform to a deductive model. There is an instructive example of this in Sarah Broadie's reading of Aristotle's ethics.

Rightly in my view, Broadie rejects the "blueprint" picture, which she calls "the Grand End theory," as a reading of Aristotle.[8] But she concludes that deliberation that displays practical wisdom cannot, in Aristotle's view, be thinking directed at bridging a version of the gap between end and action that figures in the account of deliberation in general, with doing well as the end. In her reading, deliberation that displays practical wisdom must be directed not toward doing well in general as its end, but toward this or that particular end – for instance, the safety of one's *polis* or the well-being of one's friends. This is because she cannot find anything but the "blueprint" picture in the idea of doing well as an end needing to be brought to bear on action in a way that would fit Aristotle's general picture of deliberation.

Some commentators try to register Aristotle's hostility to the leading idea of the "Grand End theory," the idea that the shape of the good life can be specified in universal terms, while retaining the idea that the deliberation characteristic of practical wisdom is deliberation with a view to doing well. Broadie hears this combination as keeping the Grand End in play, and merely denying that it is, and perhaps that it could be, explicit in the minds of agents.[9] As she understands this combination, just because there is supposed to be deliberation toward the end of doing well, that end must have the logical character envisaged in the "blueprint" picture. It is just that the universal that is applied in this kind of deliberation, which involves movements of thought that could be made explicit in deductions, is only implicit in the mind of the deliberator.

I think this reflects a deductivistic prejudice about the very idea of applying a universal. Broadie does not see the possibility I have been urging: that grasp of the universal that forms the content of a correct conception of doing well need not be isolable, even in principle, as a component in the propensity to put that end into practice in specific situations, so that exercises of the propensity could be reconstructed as deductive steps from an autonomous object of the practical intellect, whether explicitly or only implicitly in view. We can suppose that grasp of the universal is not thus isolable, and still have grasp of the universal in our picture. We can still conceive exercises of the propensity as applications of a universal, and we can still conceive the resulting actions as products of deliberation with a view to doing well. That need not be bound up with the idea of a Grand End.

Broadie is surely not wrong to insist that on particular occasions on which

24

practical wisdom is operative, the agent will be pursuing ends that are narrower than doing well in general – ends such as the well-being of a friend
or the safety of one's *polis*. But we would not have a satisfactory picture of
practical wisdom if we left it at that, without providing for any conception
of how these pursuings of narrower ends hang together. Action directed at
the well-being of a friend may display practical wisdom on an occasion, but
there may be other occasions on which the well-being of a friend could be
pursued (the situation affords that opportunity), but that is not what one who
possesses practical wisdom would do; the right reading of the situation would
focus on an opportunity it presents to pursue a different particular end. Why
would that different reading of the situation be the right one? There must be
room for an answer on these lines: "Because a correct conception of doing
well, as brought to bear on this situation, dictates acting with a view to the
different particular end. Although actions of the type, acting with a view to
the well-being of a friend, can amount to doing well, and although an action
of that type is available as an option in these circumstances, that is not what
doing well would amount to here and now." Right readings of situations are
not isolated from one another. They are such that the actions that result from
them are all indeed instances of a universal, doing well.

It can be tempting to suppose we cannot have a thought like that, consistently with the multiplicity of the more specific ends that may be pursued in
acting on right readings of situations, unless we take the content of the universal to embody principles that rank the various particular ends that might
be pursued on the relevant occasions; perhaps the rankings would be relative
to different sorts of situation.[10] This is just a version of the "blueprint"
picture, and I think Broadie is right to set her face against that. But when
we discard the "blueprint" picture, we do not discard all forms of the thought
that we can find a unity in actions that involve a multiplicity of particular
ends, by seeing them as all undertaken with a view to doing well. It is just
that the unity would not be discernible, any more than the rightness of a
particular action is, apart from the specifics of particular situations.

Of course, it would be implausible to suppose that a person of practical
wisdom arrives at immediately practicable intentions by proposing a general
end, doing well, and looking around for an action that might constitute doing
that. But this is not damaging. It is anyway questionable to what extent
Aristotle thinks that the actions that manifest excellence – even excellence
in the strict sense, which requires practical wisdom – issue from actual
courses of thinking, the sort of thing one might call "deliberation." He remarks that appropriate actions are better indicators of courage if they are
produced in emergencies, when there is no time to work out what to do
(1117a17–22).[11] The point surely generalizes: actions that manifest excellence, and so display practical wisdom in operation, need not result from

25

actual courses of deliberative thought. However, even when someone who possesses excellence does not work out what to do, starting from an explicitly proposed end of doing well, his choice and action reveal a correct reading of the situation, one that centers on its being an opportunity for this action rather than any of the other actions for which it might be taken to present an occasion. My suggestion has been that there is nothing for a correct conception of doing well to be apart from this capacity to read situations correctly. We might gloss "reading situations correctly" as: seeing them in the light of the correct conception of doing well. The conceptual apparatus of universal end and application to the circumstances at hand still fits, even in the absence of any course of thinking that constitutes arriving at the application. So the structure of deliberation as Aristotle conceives it – thought that bridges a gap between end and action – can get a purchase in our understanding of an action, even if there is no train of thinking that actually moves from universal end to application. Actions can reveal the shape of a way of seeing situations in the light of the end. It is precisely by doing that that they display the character of their agent.

VI

I have been urging that we should not try to see having the right conception of the end as separable from a capacity to read predicaments correctly – the intelligible upshot of being habituated into delighting in the sorts of actions that exemplify the excellences of character.

There may seem to be a problem for this reading in Aristotle's distinction between excellences of character and intellectual excellences. When he embarks on the topic of excellence and the excellences, he singles out the excellences of character as the results of habituation and postpones the intellectual excellences for later treatment. Practical wisdom is an intellectual excellence. It may seem that in linking its ethical content, the universal end it pursues, so closely to the intelligible upshot of habituation, I am not separating it sharply enough from the excellences of character.

This objection fits a picture in which the ethical content of practical wisdom is established, independently of habituation, by an autonomous exercise of the practical intellect. On this view, habituation yields only nonrational motivational propensities. Habituation sees to it that the nonrational elements in the perfected ethical agent are obediently receptive to independent prescriptions issued by his practical intellect. A consequence that makes the shape of the picture vivid is that a reflective ethical agent has a double motivation for an action that displays an excellence of character: one motivation issuing from a nonrational motivational propensity, a result of habituation, and another independently generated by an exercise of the intellect.[12]

26

But must the intellectual excellences in general be so sharply separated from the excellences of character? I do not think this is required by the way Aristotle organizes his treatment of the excellences.

He introduces the distinction between intellectual excellences and excellences of character in terms of a partitioning of the soul. The main division is into a rational part, the seat of the intellectual excellences, and a desiderative part, the *orektikon*. We are given to understand that the orektikon is the seat of the excellences of character, and Aristotle says that it is not rational in the sense of being capable of issuing directives, but it is not utterly non-rational, in that it is capable of being persuaded (see 1102b31–4). Now this seems quite consistent with supposing, as I have urged, that the directively rational excellence, practical wisdom, is not separable from the product of habituating the orektikon – that the content of that intellectual state is formed by molding the orektikon.

Aristotle says that the desiderative element is not directively rational. Well, of course the desiderative element, as such, is not directively rational; if it were, then, for instance, mere animal appetites would be directively rational. But this leaves it open that some region, as it were, of the desiderative element is nevertheless the seat of directive rationality.

The claim that the desiderative element is capable of being persuaded might seem to suggest the picture I am questioning, in which excellence of character is a state of the desiderative element, by virtue of which the agent's nonrational inclinations are obedient to the autonomously generated prescriptions of his practical intellect. But when Aristotle talks of persuasion, he need not be alluding to the structure of a *formed* state of character and intellect. The persuasion he is talking about can be what takes place, not in the generation of action that displays a certain formed state of character, with an independently shaped practical intellect persuading the agent's nonrational inclinations, but in the *formation* of states of character. Here is an alternative gloss on the claim that the orektikon is open to persuasion: a directive-issuing state can be constituted (by "persuasion") out of psychic materials that, before the formation of character, are not a source of rational prescriptions.

Aristotle is strikingly casual about the precise significance of the partitioning of the soul that structures his treatment of the excellences (see 1102a28–32). The division into excellences of character and intellectual excellences looks like a mere expository convenience. There is no reason not to suppose that he means a more complex picture of the relation between character and intellect to emerge, as his account takes shape. By the time practical wisdom is prominently on the scene, it is clear that the excellences of character, in a strict sense that can now be made explicit, involve the intellectual state that is practical wisdom, not a mere nonrational desiderative propensity (see VI.13). And we need not take the intellectual and desiderative aspects of excellence of character, in the strict sense, to be even notionally separable components of a composite state, as they are in the picture I am disputing. Already in Books II–IV, where the division of excellences of character from intellectual excellences is as much in force as it ever is, and discussion of the intellectual excellences is still officially postponed to a later point in the exposition, it is clear that the habituation that produces excellences of character is not supposed to produce motivational propensities that are merely obedient to an extraneous exercise of reason, like those of a trained animal. The relevant habituation includes the imparting of conceptual apparatus, centrally the concept of the noble. That concept crystallizes the pleasure that an agent has learned to take in certain actions into the form of a reason for undertaking them. The ability to see actions as noble is already a perhaps primitive form of the prescriptive intellectual excellence, practical wisdom, with its content intelligibly put in place by habituation.

VII

Talk of responsiveness to the specifics of situations, in the reading of Aristotle that I am urging, functions instead of a certain kind of generality that modern commentators tend to hanker after, in an account of how deliberation with a view to doing well might work: perhaps something modeled on the role of effectiveness in a general account of instrumental deliberation, or something on the lines of the "blueprint" picture. I think it is a strength of Aristotle's thought on these matters that he says so little in general terms about the workings of deliberation with a view to doing well. It shows his immunity to the temptation to suppose there ought to be something on the lines of a *method* for arriving at right answers to deliberative questions of the interesting kind.

Not that more could not be said, in a quite Aristotelian spirit. The concept of the noble comes into play when deliberation of the interesting kind has reached its goal, but other concepts must be operative en route to the goal, in capturing the potential significance of features of situations for what to do, and so bringing those features into view for the exercise of discernment. Some of the concepts that figure in Aristotle's character sketches of those who possess the particular excellences can be seen as playing this role, and this would be the place for some of those more explicitly ethical concepts that have figured in recent discussion under the head of "thick" ethical concepts. Elaborating a battery of concepts of this kind could surely illuminate the general shape of an ethical outlook, a conception of doing well.

This elaboration might include registering an ethical direction in which such a concept generally points, by saying such things as this: "Other things being equal, an unpaid debt (say) should be paid." What that says is that if

28

a situation has no other potentially significant feature, the presence of an unpaid debt is decisive for deliberation. I think it is harmless to acknowledge the availability of truths with that shape, so long as we are clear that the acknowledgment is no concession to the idea of a method – since (obviously enough) whether other things are equal will always depend on whether there are other potentially significant features and, if there are, what importance they should be accorded in the case at hand.

VIII

In the "blueprint" picture, there is nothing in the way one arrives at instances of the universal, doing well, that looks as if it might be special to the *practical* intellect. So if we want something interesting for the practical intellect to do in this area, it is natural to credit it, rather than proper upbringing, with establishing the content of the universal. This is another basis, deeper than Aristotle's expository division of intellectual excellences from excellences of character, for the idea that, in his view, good upbringing merely institutes a propensity to obey prescriptions that originate in reason, conceived as external to a well-shaped character.

A closely related thought is that if it is habituation that determines the content of a correct conception of doing well (by Aristotle's lights), that leaves it mysterious how the notion of correctness can be in place at all – since other modes of upbringing would presumably issue in different conceptions of doing well. This can suggest that the intellect must play a grounding role. The idea is that the intellect must be able to stand outside the ethical outlook Aristotle takes for granted in his audience, the result of their having been well brought up (by his lights), and produce a justification of the outlook. (That would justify the claim that being brought up into that outlook is being well brought up.)

How is this to be done? Many commentators credit Aristotle with the idea that a justification of his ethical outlook can be based on goods whose status as such is indisputable even while the ethical outlook is in suspense. The justification would validate the outlook's distinctive conception of doing well, on the ground that it amounts to a plan for a life that would be optimal by the lights of such independent goods.[13] Presumably the idea is that the justificatory argument can be given in a general way, in abstraction from particular circumstances to which one applies the conception of doing well that it justifies. So the envisaged target of the justificatory argument would be a blueprint for doing well, in something like the sense I have been considering.

Now it is striking that Aristotle seems to be immune to the sort of anxiety that might be alleviated by this kind of external validation. He simply assumes that in being brought up into the ethical outlook that he sketches by giving his inventory of excellences of character, the members of his audience have been brought up as they should be. There is no sign that he thinks this conviction of correctness stands in need of grounding from outside.

And it would be wrong to suggest that this leaves the conviction of correctness looking merely mysterious, unless an external grounding is available. As I insisted, Aristotle does not see the product of habituation into the excellences of character as a collection of mindless behavioral tendencies. The result of habituation is a motivational tendency, but one with a conceptual and hence rational aspect. People with a properly formed character have learned to see certain actions as worth undertaking on the ground that they are noble; they have acquired that reason-giving concept, in a way that is inextricably bound up with acquiring the propensity to be motivated by thoughts in which it is applied. The question of correctness is the question whether the actions they see as worth going in for in that specific way are really worth going in for in that way. We can resolve it into a series of piecemeal questions, whether this or that action is correctly seen as noble. And these piecemeal questions arise *within* the conceptual and motivational outlook that, according to Aristotle, ethical upbringing imparts. They can be perfectly adequately settled from that standpoint.

It is undeniable that, to many modern readers, there seems to be a question of correctness that such an approach cannot address, precisely because the approach does not seek a foundation for the outlook as a whole. But I think the very idea of such a question reflects a kind of anxiety that is distinctively modern. In that case, it is anachronistic to suppose that Aristotle thinks he has an answer to it. Moreover, it is disputable whether the question is anything but confused. If the question is confused, we do Aristotle no favor by reading a foundational thought into him – any more than we do by crediting him with the deductivistic prejudice about the very idea of applying a universal that we are now equipped to see as partly sustained, in this application, by the wish for a foundation for ethical thinking.[14]

Aristotle says that the end of the deliberation that is characteristic of practical wisdom is living well *in general*, and that may seem to point to the sort of thing I am rejecting: an exercise of the intellect that might serve a validating function, starting from some totality of indisputable goods and reasoning toward a conception of a way of living that combines them optimally. But this would be a misreading. The formulation "living well in general" merely contrasts the relevant kind of deliberation with deliberation directed at a narrower end than a life plan (such as health; 1140a27). The presence of the phrase "in general" does not dislodge the earlier glossing of "well," in a similar formulation of "the" end, as "in accordance with excellence" (1098a16–18). Aristotle is not talking about an "all things considered" kind of reasoning, in which some weight is given to all the independent goods that are in the offing, and a verdict is reached that somehow combines all their claims. What he calls "deliberation with a view to living well in general" is controlled by the value of nobility, the value that guides action in accordance with excellence; it is not deflected by the claims of other goods. (It is worth remarking that the Greek word *bouleusis* does not have the link to the idea of weighing possessed by the English 'deliberation,' which is the best we can do for an equivalent.)

IX

I said that the result of habituation, properly conceived, can be seen to be already a perhaps primitive form of practical wisdom. Why primitive? Because Aristotle depicts the ethical thinking of members of his audience, at least to begin with, as an unquestioning acceptance of the ethical outlook (or its piecemeal deliverances) that they find themselves with because of their upbringing. They have the "that" but not the "because" (see 1095b4–9). Moving to the "because" would presumably come with reflection.

It would naturally belong with the conception that I am questioning to take it that the "because" is the supposed external foundation for the ethical outlook. But nothing in Aristotle requires this reading; and if I am right, it is actually excluded, on pain of anachronism. It is not as if there is nothing else he could mean by the difference between the "that" and the "because." Here is an alternative: moving beyond the "that" to the "because" is moving from unreflective satisfaction with piecemeal applications of the outlook to a concern with how they hang together, so that intelligibility accrues to the parts from their linkage into a whole.

As far as that goes, moving beyond the "that" to the "because" might leave the "that" undisturbed. In fact I do not believe Aristotle suggests otherwise. He proceeds as if the content of a conception of doing well is fixed once and for all, in the minds of the sort of people he assumes his audience to be, by their upbringing; as if moral development for such a person is over and done with at the point when his parents send him out into the world to make his own life. There is no suggestion that an increase in reflectiveness and explicitness will alter the substance of the conception. Even so, there is nothing to prevent us from seeing the result of habituation as a genuinely intellectual excellence, even if only in a primitive form so long as the concept of the noble is applied unreflectively.

However, even if it is not explicitly part of Aristotle's own picture, it seems consistent with the spirit of Aristotelian ethics to allow for further moral development. It is open to us to suppose that reflection toward the "because," aimed at an accrual of intelligibility from seeing how elements of the "that" hang together, might issue in a reasoned modification of an

31

inherited outlook. Elements of what has hitherto passed for the "that" might not hang together satisfactorily, on reflective consideration in which one tries to integrate them so as to equip them with a "because." And situations might turn up that one cannot read, with one's present repertoire of thick concepts, as warranting any satisfying judgment as to what to do – satisfying in that one can see how it could be integrated with other such judgments, to make up a plurality of expressions of what one can regard as a coherent conception of doing well.[15] One way or another, setting out to apply a conception of doing well in a reflective way can throw up reasons – according to the conception's own more or less inchoate lights – to modify its content, even to the extent of forming new thick concepts for dealing with novel kinds of predicament.[16]

This makes it even less problematic to combine the conviction of correctness (at least in the main, we would now have to say) with not envisaging an external grounding for an ethical outlook. Reflection toward the "because" can put what has hitherto passed for grasp of the "that" at risk. In that case, if some putative grasp of the "that" survives the test, that is some ground for supposing that it is correct.

X

There is an Aristotelian idea that we can capture, misleadingly but appropriately for purposes of comparison with Kant, by saying that good willing has a value that is unconditioned. Of course Aristotle has nothing like a Kantian conception of the will. For Aristotle, what has the unconditioned value I want to point to is *doing* well, and that is not something that is in place independently of what happens in the objective world. Aristotle's analogue to the unconditioned value of the good will is not something that is actual no matter what favors are afforded to an agent by stepmotherly nature. Nevertheless, there is a point of resemblance to Kantian thinking, and that is what I want to bring out by saying that the value of doing well is unconditioned. In Aristotle's thinking, the goodness of doing well is self-standing; it is not owed to the goodness of some other goods, in a relation of dependence that would be traced by the sort of external validation of Aristotle's own conception of doing well that I have been urging that Aristotle does not envisage. We might say that when one sees an action as an instance of doing well, one takes it to be dictated by an imperative that is not hypothetical.

This stands in opposition to a common reading of Aristotle, according to which it is a task for the intellect to ground the correctness of one specific conception of the end, and the intellect can execute that task by exploiting the idea of an optimal combination of goods, with their goodness, and the goodness implicit in 'optimal,' available independently of any specifically ethical convictions. I have suggested that such readings are partly motivated by a distinctively modern thought, that ethical thinking stands in need of a foundation. If the very idea of this kind of foundation is distinctively modern, it is out of place in a reading of Aristotle.

There is an irony here. Reading Aristotle in the framework of a modern anxiety, one that he cannot have felt if I am right, blots out a similarity between his ethical thinking and Kant's. This is not to play down the dissimilarities. In the context of what I have been urging in this essay, the main divergence can be put like this: about Aristotle, it cannot even be a question, as it notoriously is about Kant, whether his ethical thinking can genuinely make provision for substantive content. Aristotle has no inkling of the idea that one might squeeze content out of formal conditions for there to be such a thing as the good will. For Aristotle, substantive ethical content is in place already, the product of habituation, before philosophical ethics begins. Ethical reflection is controlled by substantive convictions that predate it and shape its course; reflection brings them into question only piecemeal, and when one is questioned, that is only on the basis of others. The very idea of ethical theory takes on a different look in this context. But if we frame the contrast correctly, we can hold on to the idea that something like categorical imperatives are not alien to Aristotelian ethics.

NOTES

1. At 1112b17 *kallista* seems to indicate a ranking by something other than efficacy. (All references will be to the *Nicomachean Ethics*.)
2. This is not the whole of an explanation. "Such as to" and "tends to" accommodate the fact that good technical deliberation may fail, and bad deliberation succeed, by luck. But we would still need to complicate the story in order to take account of the other dimensions of desirability in solutions, over and above efficacy (see n. 1).
3. For a version of this suggestion (coupled with the idea that Book VI introduces a new doctrine, in which correctness in nontechnical deliberation is a matter of bringing cases under rules), see the essays by D. J. Allan, "Aristotle's Account of the Origin of Moral Principles," in *Proceedings of the XIth International Congress of Philosophy*, vol. 12 (Amsterdam: North Holland, 1953), pp. 120–7, and "The Practical Syllogism," in *Autour d'Aristote* (Louvain: Publications Universitaires de Louvain, 1955), pp. 325–40. See the discussion by David Wiggins, "Deliberation and Practical Reason," in Amélie O. Rorty, ed., *Essays on Aristotle's Ethics* (Berkeley and Los Angeles: University of California Press, 1980), pp. 221–40.
4. In chap. 4 of *Ethics with Aristotle* (New York: Oxford University Press, 1991), Sarah Broadie seems to me to make more fuss than is warranted about dangers that she thinks are posed for Aristotle's conception of ethical deliberation by the role of crafts in his thinking about deliberation in general.

5. No doubt the end of doing well can also figure in practical problems of a broadly technical kind. It may be that an action is undertaken, not as an instance of doing well, but as required to put the agent in a position to engage in other actions that will be instances of doing well. See G. E. M. Anscombe, "Thought and Action in Aristotle," in Renford Bambrough, ed., *New Essays on Plato and Aristotle* (London: Routledge & Kegan Paul, 1965), pp. 143–58, at pp. 149–50.

6. See, e.g., Allan, "The Practical Syllogism."

7. I shall ignore the exercise of the excellence of the theoretical intellect, which turns out in Book X to be (in some sense) the highest kind of doing well; I am concerned with the kind of doing well in which *practical* wisdom is operative.

8. Broadie, *Ethics with Aristotle*, chap. 5.

9. Ibid., p. 236.

10. See John M. Cooper, *Reason and Human Good in Aristotle* (Cambridge, Mass.: Harvard University Press, 1975), pp. 94–6. For the idea that a conception of *eudaimonia* must embody a decision procedure, on pain of leaving out the unity in the succession of actions that constitute acting it out, cf. Terence Irwin, *Plato's Moral Theory* (Oxford: Clarendon Press, 1977), pp. 264–5.

11. This passage is most naturally read as saying that when an occasion for a courageous action is sprung on him, a courageous person *chooses* the courageous action in accordance with his character, rather than as a result of calculation. This need not conflict with 1111b9–10; there the point is only that acts whose occasions are sprung on one are not *in general* chosen. Choice (*prohairesis*) is the main point of contact between Aristotle's discussions of the excellences of character and practical wisdom, the associated intellectual excellence; see 1105a31–2, 1139b4–5.

12. For a clear formulation of a picture of this kind, see John M. Cooper, "Some Remarks on Aristotle's Moral Psychology," *Southern Journal of Philosophy* 27, supplementary volume (1988): 25–42. T. H. Irwin suggests a similar view in "Some Rational Aspects of Incontinence," ibid., 49–88. See especially p. 83, where he concludes, "Non-cognitive training is necessary . . . because we need some non-cognitive preparation if we are to be able to listen carefully and without distortion or distraction to what practical reason tells us."

13. For a version of this idea, see Cooper, *Reason and Human Good in Aristotle*, pp. 124–5.

14. I do not mean to suggest that the goodness of other goods is irrelevant to the shape taken by a correct conception of The Good. (A fortiori, I do not mean to credit Aristotle with a "Stoicizing" devaluation of the goodness of other goods.) But there can be relevance without the sort of rational derivativeness that would be required for a relation of grounding.

15. Perhaps the case is a tragic one, and no available action can count as doing well by the lights of one's conception of doing well. (There is no reason to saddle Aristotle with thinking that practical wisdom can find an instance of doing well in any predicament whatever.) If the problem is in the situation, rather than the ethical outlook, there is no need to modify the outlook. But the judgment that

the problem is in the situation rather than the outlook would itself have to stand up to critical reflection.

16. Barbara Herman suggests that the place of tradition in an Aristotelian ethic precludes this kind of flexibility, but I see no ground for that. I think it is a deep truth that all thinking, just as such, is anchored in traditions. Reflection has nothing to go on, anywhere, but a putative grasp of the "that," which (at least to begin with) is merely inherited. This cannot condemn reflection to inflexibility.

2

Making Room for Character

BARBARA HERMAN

In the course of the very productive encounter between Aristotelian and Kantian ethics, some things seem to have been established. In particular, from the Aristotelian side, it has been argued and is now widely accepted that moral judgment is not a practice of applying fixed rules to particulars in the manner of a legal system.[1] There is, on the one hand, the recognition that what is right to do *here* is often, if not typically, a function of what is specific to a given situation,[2] and on the other, the requirement of salience – much of the work of moral judgment takes place prior to any possible application of rules in the eliciting of the relevant moral facts from particular circumstances. Indeed, one of the great successes of revitalized virtue theory has been to shift philosophical attention away from the mechanics of a rule-based practical syllogism to the ways in which the conditions for moral judgment involve the complexities of a developed moral character.[3] Having a virtuous character, we see different things, or see them in ways that have different practical significance, than we would if our character were vicious or in some lesser way defective. And because of the way we come to see what we see, we are moved to act.

This seems to me exactly right, and to present a feature of moral judgment that *any* sound moral theory must be able to accommodate. Establishing the place within Kantian moral theory for such an account is the first and major object of this essay. The central difficulty for Kantian theory comes from the identification of the aspect of character that makes moral judgment possible with a capacity that involves, or requires for its development, the nonrational faculties. But if we are ever to have a Kantian ethics liberated from its noumenal baggage, this is just the sort of fact that must be accommodated. It is one thing to reject the idea that moral perception flows directly from a nonrational faculty – the sophisticated virtue theorist rejects this too – and quite another to resist the role of the nonrational in our capacities for judgment

36

and action. I believe that the key to getting this right involves rethinking the basic relation between desire and motive: the way desires are or can be the occasion for motives and the way rational motives in turn affect the structure or natural history of desire.[4] Mistakes here open an unnecessary chasm between reason and character in Kantian ethics.

The other topic I want to touch on comes from a concern that a conception of judgment that relies on the notion of character may have a tendency to be normatively static, especially when it involves the development of special perceptual capacities. Character-based judgment is good at explaining how an agent "gets it right" and why, in getting it right, there is no separate question of motivation. But the task of moral judgment often requires the resolution of practical perplexity in circumstances where part of getting it right requires being able to recognize and evaluate unfamiliar moral phenomena. Here, I think, the initial advantage may go the other way: certain features of a Kantian conception of moral judgment make room for moral perplexity and its practical resolution, especially in changing circumstances of judgment. Classical virtue theory seems to me less flexible – not inflexible, but in its nature less open to the tumult of competing values and ways of life that characterize the contemporary moral scene. This may be more a legacy of its historical origins than any permanent defect. That will be for others to say. My ambitions here are limited to describing some of the resources that might be drawn on to develop a Kantian idea of character and to indicate, briefly, some of its advantages for moral judgment.

I

The first step to take in introducing a robust conception of character into Kantian theory involves a rethinking of the place of desire in the *naturalistic* story of moral motivation. This is because much of the problem about desire for Kantian ethics comes from ways that desire is thought about elsewhere. When it is taken that desire, or some other original (unmediated or noncognitive) spring of activity, lies behind action as a cause, the resulting story of motivation in a rational agent is one of direction or redirection of an activity-producing force.[5] An agent's practical rationality – her access to motivating reasons – extends the array of actions that are possible for her, given a set of desires (or desire-like states). She expresses her rationality in action by doing what she does out of a sense of its fit with something she wants. She may desire food; she may desire pistachio ice cream. How she should act is a function of judgment and circumstantial orientation: what is at hand; how she might proceed to acquire an object not presently available. No very special explanation is required for the possibility of acquiring a taste for pistachio ice cream; no explanation of any sort is required for the reason-giving force of hunger. Nor do we require explanation of the move to means: we define a rational agent as one who can act via a representation of an object of desire *as* a possible effect of her acting. What does require special explanation according to this story, what appears to be most strange, is a moral motive that is not tied to natural desires (such as self-interest or sympathy). To the extent that the moral motive seems to come from nowhere, it calls not for explanation, but to be explained away, or reduced to something else. That is why the standard Kantian account of moral motivation seems so unhelpful. It asserts as true just the thing that does not seem possible.

Most reductive strategies for explaining moral motivation orient themselves to providing an account of reliable causes of moral outcomes. Knowing what moral agents are to do (treat strangers with honesty and respect, honor agreements, etc.), and what "natural" materials a theory may draw on, the task is to explain how the moral concern of the normal agent is assembled from these nonmoral materials. Where the cause of our moral interest is itself not obscure – suppose it is sympathy – its relative priority and limited scope require correction (sympathy is neither strong nor general; it does not reach to justice). If there are no natural desires that can support a moral motive directly, one posits various mechanisms to account for the transformation of a morally indifferent affective state into a moral motive (reflective self-interest, for example). The emergent motive may require correction so that its independently defined (moral) object is more reliably and predictably its output. But lack of fit is of no grave concern to the theory since the point was to show the possibility of motivating moral action at all.[6]

Not every naturalistic account of moral motivation looks to independently defined moral outcomes in its explanation of moral motivation. For example, Samuel Scheffler has explored psychoanalytic theory as a possible explanatory framework because it includes the moral capacity as one of the emergent mechanisms by which a young child resolves what is perceived to be a life-threatening parental response to the aggressive and sexual desires of the Oedipal situation.[7] But though this story can account for the emergence of a capacity for moral action and concern, it leaves the moral character of the individual shrouded by the obscurity of its prerational development. For Freud, the hidden origins of moral character had explanatory power. Once uncovered, they could explain a subject's (possibly correct) perception that her moral convictions were not good for her.[8] However, what is an advantage to psychoanalytic treatment may not be advantageous for moral theory. This is especially so given the fact that the deep structure of personality dictates no more than the form of the moral: cost-sensitive rules and ideals relevant to negotiating intimacy and separation. The range of normal development does not thereby rule out morally noxious content.[9]

It is most likely because reductive theories are prompted by the perceived strangeness of the moral motive – by the need, in effect, to explain it away – that they have a high toleration for indirect or self-effacing solutions. It is thought not to matter if our interest in morality is the inscrutable product of a complex process or a mask for other, themselves unexamined, interests. What counts is that our having a moral disposition is explained, and in that limited sense, justified. I think this is a mistake. It very much does matter that the moral motive have some available transparency with regard to its origins. This is not to say that we must be able to recover and endorse all the developmental steps that produce our character. But the structure of character that is the product of this process should have reflexive connection with moral content. It is not neutral. When subjected to reflective pressure, the conditions of our caring about morality affect the resources we have available for moral response.

If the range of "moral outcomes" is uncertain, if new facts or changed circumstances can require changes in the way the moral agent responds and acts, the lack of available connection between the roots of moral attachment and the moral motive can be the occasion of serious moral failure. We tend to mistake the nature of the motivational stability that morality requires. It may not be so much a matter of steadfastness in the face of temptation to transgress as it is openness to continuity of development in response to new demands. In this sense, an agent's reflective self-understanding can be a vital component of an agent's moral character.[10]

Support for this mistake comes from the acceptance of two views that are often connected: skepticism about the possibility of a nonreductive (or pure) moral motive and a contemporary version of motivational internalism – one that makes the defining issue for morality, for the range of moral reasons, depend on what can be motivating for an individual at a time. The sites of contention are then restricted to the range of possible causal links that practical reason can deliberatively make available, and the possibility of some nondeliberative, yet rational transformation that is nonetheless anchored in an agent's current motivating interests.[11]

It seems to me that one should be able to accept that a moral theory must be constrained by the facts of human motivation without also having to hold that moral reasons must be capable of motivating each individual within their scope at all relevant times through a connection, however attenuated, with the agent's interests. This last is such an implausible position that the most steadfast internalist almost always supplements the connection, adding full information, clear deliberative connections, absence of distraction, depression, and so on. The real puzzle is why such a form of internalism has a lock on moral theory. If, as McDowell suggests, it is in part to stave off a kind

39

of predatory move by the partisans of universal, denatured Reason, then as a strategy its cost to the claims that morality would make on human character may be unacceptably high.[12]

Suppose, instead, we divided the question of reasons that an agent has or could have here and now from the question of the possibility conditions for morality. We might then think there is an internalism requirement for moral theory that is different from the requirement when addressed to an agent's reasons for action. The area of concern for theory internalism would be the nature and point of different possible directions of human development. Morality as a normative enterprise is then not restricted to what an individual at a time is capable of doing. It can be, indeed it often ought to be, subjectively transforming, not just with respect to its demands at a particular moment, but about the kind of person one comes to be. It will be consistent with this sort of internalism to view the facts of human nature as constraining the shape of a moral life, without determining it. We should even be able to talk of possible directions for moral growth and development without having to argue for any strong teleological idea of human flourishing. Experiences, especially moral experiences, create possibilities of character.[13] I believe that Kantian ethics can not only help itself to this idea; it can contribute the next bit through the conception of character it offers, based on the transformative role of the moral motive in the structure of agents' intentions and maxims.

II

I want to return now to the claim I made earlier: that the key to a Kantian account of moral development and moral character is in the relation between motive and desire. Let us take desire, in the most general sense, to refer to those states of an organism that dispose it to activity. This includes desires in the colloquial sense (for drink, fame, companionship), as well as what we think of as instincts (governing flight, reproduction, etc.). The defining Kantian claim is that desires, in this general sense, do not directly support reasons for action. Desires may move us to activity; they may provide the occasion for reasons for action (and for reasoning about action). They are nonetheless not reasons, and they do not on their own give agents reasons to act.

The Kantian claim is about what there is: in a world without rational agents whose reason is effectively practical, there could be active beings, even beings who select means for their ends, but no reasons for action. Reasons are evaluative. An agent has a reason when she judges that acting (in a particular way) is in some sense good. She acts for a reason when her activity is governed by such a judgment. Judgment about reasons for action need not involve deliberation or ratiocination. It necessarily involves evalu-

40

ating an action or possible action, under a description, as it is or promotes something itself judged to be of value.

In Kant-speak, to say that an agent has and acts on a reason is to say that she acts on a maxim. It is to present the agent as having a practically effective evaluative attitude toward the sources of activity she encounters – within and outside herself.[14]

That said, there is nonetheless something right in the view that a full account of human actions must include desires – indeed, that the presence of desire is in some sense a condition for its being the case that an agent has an effective reason for action. We are that sort of organism. The question is, What follows from such a concession? I want to explore the thesis that there is some primitive desire or desire-connected state in the genealogy of what moves us, even when we act for Kantian reasons. Such complex desire-connected states are the normal product of human development; they are also, I believe, the natural solution to the Kantian problem with desire.

It is important to be clear about what I do and do not want to claim. My acceptance of a "priority of desire" account is not nominal: it is not a case of merely widening the range of things to be called "desire" to "whatever moves us." In speaking of desire-connected states I mean affective, practical states derived in some way from such primary desires as those for nourishment, erotic bonding, and so forth. (It will matter, though not now, just what we imagine the cast of original desires to be.) I want to accept *both* that there is a difference between reason and desire and that even rational action depends on desire. However, I also want to argue that a full explanation of what moves us to action in a given instance need not appeal to primary desires. Not only may there be no recognizable traces of these desires in our motives, the content and object of what moves us may be "from reason."

Kant is often saddled with the view that all action based (in any way) on desire is both mechanistic in its structure and pleasure or satisfaction seeking in its end. This is not Kant's view.[15] As rational agents, we take the presence of desires to be occasions (or grounds) for reasons to act. To say that our action is to yield satisfaction (of desire) is not to mark the single end of all action-on-desire, but to say something about what desire is (we have acted successfully when our desire is satisfied). Since Kant's primary concern is to distinguish autonomous from heteronomous willing, the fact about desire that he attends to is that reasons that look to desires are ultimately derived from contingent facts alien to the rational will. He can ignore the fact that the relations between reason and desire in a person are quite complex. But if our interest is in developing a Kantian conception of character, we cannot.

Consider a possible Kantian thesis about reason and desire. What it means for us to be practically rational beings is that we are by nature disposed to develop and modify desires in accordance with the requirements of practical

41

reason. Normal human development is reason-responsive. This is not to say that we have an original desire to conform to rational principle. I think we could have no such original desire. Where it seems reasonable to expect such a desire is in a mature and moderately reflective person whose life has proceeded in a roughly normal – that is, noncatastrophic – way. We take it to be normal that a person come to recognize the value not only of acting according to reason, but also of having rational desires; we expect the development of a general (or second-order) desire to conform to reason. There is neither inevitable completeness nor developmental necessity in this. One might come to value rationality in some areas of one's life and not in others, and to value some aspects of rationality, not others.

The claim that our development is originally reason-responsive, as opposed to reason-following, is a claim about what it is to be a rational-being-with-desires. It involves, among other things, the idea that we have a distinctive kind of mechanism for learning, one such that at least some of the information acquired in our earliest stages is archived in a way that is available to emerging cognitive function. That is, the potential for rationality in us must be expressed in prerational structures of perception, recognition, memory, and the like. One might further speculate that such structured information contributes to the epigenetic causes of the emergence of higher cognitive function. We should then think of the defining features of rational agency – self-consciousness, judgment, rule-following – as later stages in a complex process of development. Other sorts of creatures with desires will have different learning and development mechanisms. Instinct in animals, we might suppose, will play a greater role, more tightly constraining the form of information acquired and the possible development of desires.

The *principles* of rationality are thus descriptive of our kind of activity and development; they are also normative (in a reflexive sense) for our success as the kind of being we are. Whether they are effective guides for our individual flourishing or well-being is a contingent and local matter, depending on circumstances (personal, physical, and institutional) and, of course, good fortune. They are nonetheless the tools we possess; no other principles can be systematically normative for us.[16]

What I am trying to do here should be plain. I want to describe – in a lightly speculative way – a natural fact about us as rational beings that is resonant with both a Kantian view of practical reason and an Aristotelian view of the nonrational part of the soul that "shares in reason." I would continue in an Aristotelian vein this way: Obedience to reason is possible for some desires because they *can* develop in certain reason-related ways, though they need not do so. That is why a child needs guidance based in the reason of others: when desires are to be satisfied and when frustration is tolerable; when there is a range of substitution for objects of desires and for which desires this is so; and so on. Such instruction is possible because the system of desires already has a certain structure – one that places (some) desires on a developmental track that leaves them open to transformation through the effects of training and new knowledge carried on the threads of intimacy and early bonding.[17]

Now some will surely think that such a claim of resonance for a naturalistic account of reason with the Kantian project is impossible to support – perhaps even showing the Kantian project's fatal weakness. In this mood, if there is any concession to a story of moral development, it is of the emergence of a kind of rational musculature, a special power capable of providing sufficient motivation for the morally correct action, even in the face of recalcitrant desires. Moral learning is a matter of refinement of judgment: the capacity to discern morally salient features of one's circumstances. What happens in the system of desires is of no deep moment: the moral life will be easy if desires are cooperative, hard if they are not. Nothing that could happen in the system of desires could be deeply relevant to the moral project. The fundamental Kantian moral fact is, after all, that the ground of obligation in us cannot involve desires. However, the inference from the foundational argument to the developmental conclusion – to the practice of moral judgment and action – is not valid.

The question comes to this: Must it follow from the fact that the foundations of morality – the determining ground of the will – can only be in pure practical reason, that (a) the motive of the morally worthy agent must be extramaterial (a miracle every time), or that (b) the desirable *purity* of the motive of duty is in its complete separation from the empirical life of the human agent? I think that we can hold with Kant that the application of the moral law (to us or to any rational being) cannot be empirical – that the condition of its claim to be the law of the will of any rational being must be "completely a priori and independent of any sensuous data"[18] – only if we interpret this to be a claim about authority, not efficacy. That is, the moral law applies to us, is legitimately regulative of our willings, without regard to the state of our inclinations. This is the condition that secures universal validity. But our motivating understanding of the moral law, what I would call our effective moral motive, need not be pure.[19] What it must involve in an essential way is the acknowledgment of the normative order of incentives.[20]

In the main moral texts, Kant is not often concerned with the fact or the way morally developed or rationalized desire becomes part of the practical provisions of the mature moral agent. But even here we should be wary of exaggeration. Kant has a lot to say about moral education, and when he does attend to practical matters, he shows far greater moral sensitivity than the usual quoted remarks suggest.[21] Probably the most important argument to mark on this issue is, somewhat paradoxically, the discussion of moral incentives in the *Critique of Practical Reason*.[22] Here is Kant in his most puritanical voice, describing the way the moral law thwarts inclination, strikes down the pretensions of self-love (described as "self-conceit"). The moral law brings about a humbling of the material self through the emergence of feelings of respect for the law, in acknowledgment of its supreme authority. Underneath the high rhetoric, however, is a view of the desires, and of the claims made on behalf of the faculty of desire, as responsive to, in a certain sense resonant with, the moral law. There is no a priori necessity that the effect of striking down desire in this way should be an elevated feeling – one that draws us to morality – rather than pain and resistance. But we do not seem to be organized the latter way. What we desire, what we understand ourselves to be desiring, is affected by the evaluative situation in which we find ourselves. This is a fact about the system of desires itself: it can be humbled.[23]

Both theoretical and practical reason provide form for material that is given from external sources (external to reason). So far as we accept the authority of the rules of logic as the correct form of thought regardless of our feelings, we thereby acknowledge our capacity to accept a logical conclusion that we have no interest in, or even, have every interest in denying. Modus ponens is, free association is not, an authoritative form for discursive thought. The moral law offers a comparable compelling form to our practical maxims of action.[24] Why we are responsive to either formal constraint is not a simple matter: in both cases the answer involves some kind of appeal to conditions for our inhabiting an ordered world.[25]

III

The framework for adding an account of moral development to Kant's ethics must take as fundamental the idea of the moral law as the principle of autonomy of the will. The effect of the moral law as a principle of autonomy is to preclude all inclinations from having a *direct* determining influence on the will.[26] This is what has seemed to force desire to the side where moral action is concerned. But if we are no longer restricted to a rigid oppositional model – if the system of desires is itself reason-responsive – the content of desires need not remain unaffected by our developing moral and rational capacities.

This moves the discussion beyond the old issue of the overdetermination of motives. I am not now concerned to argue that the presence of desire is benign, as long as the incentive that is the agent's motive is respect for the moral law. Rather, I want to explore the idea that the strict separation of desire from the reason-connected motive of duty may not be appropriate, given the possibility of connection, in human beings, between reason and the developing system of desire. Just how desire can change and what role it may play in action consistent with the autonomy of the will are the questions that need to be taken up next.

In thinking about the role of desire, given developmental changes in the system of desire, what is to be rejected – really superseded – is the simple version of the desire–belief model of action. I am thirsty; I see that there is fresh water in that glass; putting the desire and belief together, I drink the water. It is not that this cannot happen. It can. The problem arises when such examples are used to represent the building blocks of complex, rational action. I believe that if we are to understand the way rationality exhibits itself in action and judgment, we must begin from the other end: from the complex practical judgments of the mature agent. It will be from getting it right about them that we can intelligibly ask, for example, how an inclination such as thirst can both move someone to act and not influence her will directly when she drinks. When we start with the inclination as the primitive element, the most reasonable account of mature action is unavailable.

"Thirst" seems a likely candidate for a possible primitive feature of the system of desires. It certainly has the role of being last in an explanatory chain of reasons: we do not need to appeal to anything else for a complete explanation of drinking. But that fact, and it is a fact, is misleading. That something can be last in an explanatory chain does not show that it is a primitive element in the system of desires. Consider: In what sense can a neonate have thirst or, stranger still, desire for drink? Certainly there is the physiological condition of fluid deficit, and no doubt a mechanism to trigger suckling (the source of that interesting original confusion of nourishment and intimacy). But this state – hardly distinct in its original form from hunger – is not the thirst that plays a role in explaining purposive drinking action. It lies in its origins; it is part of the natural history of thirst. This is because the physiological condition is not yet an intentional state of the organism: it has no object. There is a condition of agitation; there are mechanical responses. In the natural environment for neonates, nursing or feeding reduces the agitation and gives pleasure. Thirst – a desire for *drink* – can only emerge much later.[27]

Rather than suppose a picture of a set of primal or primitive desires whose objects are in some sense present from the outset and then refined as knowledge and experience are acquired, it seems truer both to our beginning and to the outcome in the normal agent to work with a model that begins with what we might call 'original orectic states' that are developmentally open to the kind of cognitive and volitional capacities our kind of agent has. (It will be no accident that "this feeling" comes to be associated with "that object" – drink.) Now the fact that our desires have a history (and to some extent a

45

natural history) does not imply that in explanations of action the most complete explanation must look to the originating orectic state. We would surely lose the sense of a reason for action if we replaced an explanation given in terms of a desire for an orderly workplace with the primal need to forge boundaries between self and other, even if it were true that the latter belonged to the essential history of the former.

Sometimes, of course, the fact that desires have a history does indicate an explanatorily relevant geology of desire. We commonly explain irrational behavior, urges, and cravings by appeal to something primitive or developmentally undigested, as when the source of addictions are attributed to residual infantile needs, or when self-defeating patterns of behavior call for an investigation into the desire behind a desire (as when the desire for order interferes with work that needs to be done).

The fact that desires have a history (and a natural history), combined with the fact that human development is reason-responsive, alters the way we should think about deliberation and judgment. In the mature agent, objects of judgment (puzzles about what to do, questions about what is right) will present themselves already laden with deliberative and evaluative content. We get it wrong about children if we suppose their harmful demands must rest on some error concerning the relative importance of, say, health and pleasure. Manipulative temper tantrums aside, the frenzied intensity of a young child's demands, the sense of life on the line, is better understood as the product of unmediated desire – desire whose importance is still a direct function of its momentary strength. It is for this reason that small children cannot be rational. They may or may not lack knowledge; their wills are certainly not weak. What is missing, or only present to a very limited degree, is the codevelopment of their desires and rational understanding.

By contrast, the accurate representation of judgment and deliberation in the normal rational adult requires a model that exhibits the enmeshed development of the system of desires and the capacity for effective practical rationality. The transformation of orectic states into desires with objects takes place in an environment regulated by a wide range of evaluative concepts. The desire for drink becomes a desire for safe and pleasant (not dangerous or unpleasant) drink, and also a desire for an available (not otherwise possessed) drink. The desire itself becomes socialized.

This point may seem less strange if we consider weightier objects of desire such as children or expensive consumer goods. My desire for a new computer or car does not (because it ought not) range over those already owned by others; a desire to have a child does not include a desire for anyone else's child. Something has gone tragically wrong when it is otherwise. I think it is reasonable to say that what has gone wrong is something about the desire itself – how it has, or has failed to, develop.

There are, of course, other ways of representing the phenomena. One might tell a story of competing desires – one for drink, another for not taking what belongs to someone else – and rational development looking toward the regulative superiority of the second, either through its increased strength or through the emergence of a second-order desire that selects respect for property as the desire whose satisfaction is a condition for satisfying other desires. What seems wrong here is not that this fails to describe something that could happen, but the implicit idea that the desires themselves, in the normal cases, remain unaffected by the regulative space in which they live, or if affected, more beaten down than transformed.[28]

What would a more adequate account be like? It should be able to capture the complexities of desires that emerge at the intersection of distinct paths of orectic development and be sensitive to the ways that primitive orectic residues remain and become part of the urgency for or insistence behind a developed desire. A model in which desires form a system independent of regulative principle, or one in which desires are seen as descending from each other primarily via instrumental pathways, cannot readily cope with what is so often in our experience and our explanations an elaborate architecture of desire. Further, insofar as we are rational beings, we come to have certain kinds of desires and interests because the developmental path from primitive orectic states to complex desires is partly structured by the principles of practical rationality. The fact that we are capable of learning and eventually capable of conscious and principled self-regulation should be represented as part of the environment in which desires emerge.[29]

The deliberative or evaluative location of a desire will therefore not always be external to it. Unlike the desire to go to sleep after one has had a bad night – a desire that plays against the deliberative current of the day, needing to be ignored, resisted, dosed with coffee – other, more derived desires carry their relative value with them. My desire to go to the movies or to drink wine with good food does not need to be constrained when I set to work in the morning. These desires are in some sense present then, for they enter in planning for the rest of the day. But their content is complex and expressive of various regulative norms that I accept: somewhat stodgy norms of using the mornings to get work done, of commitment to the priority of familial and professional obligations, and so on. Because these norms have a certain structural priority in my life, the value (not the object) that my desires express is different than it was when I was an nth-year graduate student or hanging out in Paris. There is no necessity or fixity in this; I can decide to go to an 11 A.M. movie tomorrow. My point is rather that we will likely misdescribe the desire if we insist on an evaluatively neutral "desire to go to the movies," constrained today, released into action tomorrow. Again, it could be that way; it is possible that the pressure to go to the movies is always there – it is what

I would almost always rather do and so I have to keep my desire in check in order to go about my business. That possibility does not generalize, however. Because the neutral description cannot capture the array of ways one may have a desire for an activity, it masks the way derived desires can function in the deliberation and choices of mature rational agents.

The desires of a mature human agent normally contain, in addition to a conception of an object, a conception of the object's value – for itself, as determined by its fit with other things valued, and as its satisfaction, in general as well as in a given case, comports with the principles of practical reason. We might say that desires so conceived have been brought within the scope of reason, or that the desires themselves have been rationalized, or, to the extent that an agent's system of desires has evolved in a reason-responsive way, that she has, at least in these respects, the character of a rational agent. Of course, the normal agent does not, indeed cannot, have a wholly rational character: not all of our desires are reason-responsive (or wholly so), nor does the natural history of human desire, even if reason-responsive, follow a rational plan.[30]

IV

Suppose we accept such a developmental account of desires – that they do develop, and that the system of desires is reason-responsive. In what way is this an advantage to a Kantian system of ethics? It plainly offers a way to mitigate the hostility between reason and desire, something attractive in itself. It is also, and equally plainly, necessary if Kantian ethics is to support any reasonable account of moral virtue, insofar as it invites a rethinking of the relations of reason and desire in the structure of moral motivation.

On the standard Kantian account, the rational agent acts for ends, not directly from desires – neither desires as impulsions or urgings, nor as the necessary independent condition of the attractiveness of ends. The presence of a desire provides an occasion for action, an incentive. There are other incentives. The question for a rational agent is whether acting in response to a given incentive is good (or justified). As she judges that it is, she has a reason, other things equal, to adopt the relevant end (and so have a maxim), and then to act.[31] I would add: an incentive is available for purposes of *deliberation* as and to the extent that acting for its sake is judged to be in some sense good. It is only then, and in that sense, to be regarded as a possible "motive." Thus, the judgment that "acting to satisfy this desire is good" is part of a motive for action, making the connection between motive, end, and action more than a matter of casual adequacy. That is why, for a rational agent, competing incentives need not always present the threat of competing motives.

48

I use the device of a "deliberative field" to represent the space in which an agent's rational deliberation takes place. It is constructed by the principles and commitments that express her conception of value. Desires and other incentives are present for purposes of deliberation only as they can be located in the field. To say that such incentives are then possible motives is to say that part of what being a rational agent involves is having the motivational capacity to take desires *as valued* as reasons for action. More complex structures of value generate complex motives, setting further conditions on the satisfaction of desires.

An incentive is present in the deliberative field in what we might call a normalized or rationalized form – as a possible motive – to the extent that its representation and affective significance have been transformed from that of an impulse or an intentional disposition into a rational value. Some incentives that "present" to the deliberative field can already be, to some extent, "rational" – that is, their development can have been partially shaped by rational principle. Others come as they are, as it were, gaining entry with the condition added that their satisfaction be dependent on the nonviolation of rational principle. Thus, from the moral point of view, many things can happen to an incentive. An incentive can be only partially transformed; an agent can have internalized some but not all of the constraints of the deliberative field – and, even, some of them in the wrong way.

Consider some of the ways motivation to be moral can be awry. The prudent criminal as well as the timidly obedient agent (who adheres to morality out of fear of the consequences of doing otherwise) have motives that are partly responsive to moral constraints, but in the wrong way. For them, moral constraints function as externally imposed or passively encountered limits, rather like the misplaced stop sign in my neighborhood that gives me no reason to stop except for the fact that the local sheriff's deputies like to lurk nearby and give tickets (a cost I am not willing to risk). For other agents, morality may be experienced as a quasi-physical barrier, more like a taboo or a phobia than a reason – something that incentives cannot get past. In none of these cases is the agent's motive directly or correctly responsive to the moral features of her circumstances. This is not a matter of whether moral norms apply; it is the very different question of the evaluative content of the motives responsible for a rational agent's moral action.

Even where there is motivational connection to morality, it may not be an all or nothing thing. Some features of morality may be separated off, as when a person is sensitive and motivationally responsive to actions and situations that introduce risk of physical harm to others, but indifferent to psychological risk and injury, or concerned about immediate injury but not about injustice. The possibility of a moral form of aspect blindness has posed special difficulties for Kantian theory. We cannot account for failure to recognize the

49

fact and salience of injustice as just a mistake about what follows from the categorical imperative, and it has not been clear what other resources Kantian theory has to provide a more satisfactory explanation or response. This is not the sort of issue that interested Kant, but it is one that ought to concern those of us who are interested in refurbishing Kant for contemporary purposes. One of the advantages of making the story about motivation both natural and complex is that it gives room and sense to such possibilities. In particular, it allows for talk of moral defects of character impinging on moral judgment.

Earlier I spoke of the natural history of desire – shaped by, among other things, the principles of rationality to which the system of desire is developmentally responsive. More recently I have been talking about motives: incentives to action that gain standing in the deliberative field as they survive evaluation and/or transformation by the principles of practical reason. Developed desires and motives should not be confused. While an evolved desire can have internalized moral content – for example, where it is part of the concept of the object of desire that its pursuit not involve violation of moral restrictions – it lacks the *deliberative* content of a rational motive. That is, while it may be the case that, because of good upbringing, one's material desires do not range over other people's possessions, one may still be, in acting for such a desire, acting on a maxim of satisfying one's strongest desire. It is only when one's maxim of desire-satisfaction *contains* the full deliberative framework (one will act for this desire only as and because doing so conforms with prudential *and* moral principle) that one has a (fully) rational motive.

The formation of a motive – the way an incentive gains entry to the deliberative field – involves a process of judgment and evaluation. The pair of the incentive and the range of possible objects of action that match it (object or end) are judged to be good and accepted as grounds for possible action because they are good. Since the principles of practical reason describe the domain of evaluation (the Good), the resulting motive draws content both from practical principles and from the original incentive. Such a motive may yield the same action one would have taken based on the original incentive (and, say, a principle of satisfying my strongest desire), but now the action is performed with and from a different and regulative conception of its value. There is a different maxim.

Here is the new claim. When and to the extent that agents have desires that have evolved in a reason-responsive way, the incentives themselves are open to further, more principled, rationalization. There is, on the one hand, a possible conceptual convergence between motives and developed incentives, and on the other, the practical possibility of the transformation of desire. The evolution of desire is in this way the condition for having a moral character that does not necessarily involve the oppression of one's affective life in general by one's commitment to morality.

But what has happened to the Kantian motive of duty? In all this talk of complexity, development, and the transformation of incentives, it seems to have been lost – its work done by other structures and motives. My thought is this. In an agent with a moral character, the motive of duty is *dispersed* in the motives that satisfy the constraints of the deliberative field. It need not be a separate motive that is to be added on to an already complete intention to act.[32] The idea, then, is that when we act "from duty," we act from a conception of our maxim as having a principle that conforms to universal law, but that this conception need not be motivationally separate from the way we conceive of the action and its end as a justified whole.

Neither the idea of a deliberative field nor this way of thinking about rational character belongs in any special way to Kantian ethics. I believe that both are useful devices for representing the structure of our practical lives when one takes the fact that we are rational agents to be part of the developmental history of our desires and interests (however one fills out the norm or norms of rationality). They are especially appropriate devices for working with Kantian ethics because they exhibit the way that principles of rationality can constitute a structure of value in a rational agent's motives. This structure is essential to understanding the connection between the categorical imperative as a principle of practical reason and the motive of duty as a possible motive of an empirically situated rational agent – that is, a person.

There are considerable practical advantages to a motive of duty understood in this way – as dispersed in the rational agent's motives for action. For example. If we think that practical conflict is a matter of an agent unable to satisfy competing incentives (desires or interests), the primary deliberative problem will be establishing terms of commensurability – finding bases of comparison for urgently felt personal needs, the present relevance of longer-term goals, the current demands of greater and lesser moral requirements, and so on. There is no deep mystery about why moral theorists who present the range of sources for practical interests in this way tend toward some kind of utilitarian calculus (whether of consequences, preferences, or even connection to identity-defining ground projects).

The current contra-utilitarian alternative that appeals to situationally specific judgment obscures more than it clarifies. It is no doubt true that I can know that in a particular circumstance it is better for me, more important, to spend time with long absent friends than to keep some trivial promise. And one may want to say that no deeper or more encompassing knowledge is required. From this it is said to follow that there is no principle that dictates when friendship trumps obligations. One comes to have situated knowledge, acquired through experience, of when it is appropriate to do one sort of thing and when another.

I think it is misleading, however, to represent such judgments as relying on no deeper content. For if one is wrong, as one surely may be, about the relative value of the two options, an explanation belongs to the way one learns from mistakes. It is not like correcting for the wind when one tries to hit a target: you sight a bit to the right, and then a bit more if your first judgment was wrong, and then a bit to the left if you overcorrect. But where you have mistaken the relative importance of obligation and interest, the mistake may not be one of location on some balance of trivial-to-important obligations and moral concerns. There is something amiss in the picture one would have: that in these circumstances, one had valued friendship too much and the obligation too little – as if there was a level of value beyond the obligation and friendship, and one's mistake was there.

The idea of the motive of duty as dispersed – as (ideally) a component of the motive in all maxims of action – changes the look of moral conflict. When the connection between incentive and action is mediated by rational motives, deliberation depends neither on a situation-specific "read" nor on importing a standard that is alien to the values already expressed in an agent's maxim. If I cannot attend to a friend because of the demands of some prior obligation, I need not view myself as subordinating friendship to morality, or valuing friendship less, or differently. The way that morality can make demands is part of the structure of mature friendship; it is why we have reason to believe a true friend will understand.

It will be helpful to consider, in this light, what happens to self-interest. The Kantian charge against self-interest is not that it is inherently contrary to morality; it need not be. The problem lies in its tendency to be presumptive. We are inclined to give special weight to our advantage; we implicitly accept a principle of self-interest as one of the determining grounds of our will. On the standard Kantian account, morality constrains self-interest, offering (through the motive of duty) a kind of counterweight in the contest of reasons. However, if the motive of duty is not merely something that enters into a balance of reasons, but is instead part of the structure of the agent's reasons in general, not only will the account of moral reasons look different, so will the account of self-interest. The fully rational *motive* of self-interest does not carry a presumption of independent authority in the agent's deliberative field. It is not that the moral agent ignores her interests or her advantage. Rather, her conception of self-interest has developed, been shaped or altered, in a reason-responsive way. That is why (some) interests of a self can rebut a moral presumption: it may be permissible to break a trivial promise for matters of great personal importance, but only if the agent's concerns have and are conceived of as having moral standing (Kant would say they must express different grounds of obligation). It is in this sense that the agent's self-interest is not what it was or would have been outside the deliberative field.[33]

As it should, character shapes moral judgment. When I don't pocket the funds entrusted to me at a PTA meeting, it is not that I don't know the advantage in having some extra money; I simply do not regard this money *as available*. This is not because honesty involves a habit of overlooking advantage, or because a commitment to morality sets up a barrier such that the voice of advantage cannot be heard. In these circumstances there is no advantage, no appeal to interests that support a reason. This follows from having a moral character – one in which the moral law belongs to the framework within which desires and interests develop and gain access to the deliberative field.

At the outset of this essay I suggested that there could be an account of Kantian moral judgment that brought a conception of character into the picture via inclusion of nonmoral desires. I believe that the developmental account I have sketched – from incentives to rational motives – shows a way to do this that is consistent, on the one hand, with the natural history of desires and, on the other, with the Kantian strictures about moral motivation. On the desire side, I have accepted as basic that a human agent is "moved" to action only by reasons that are connected, in some way, with desires. However, I have tried to complicate the desire story two ways. First, through an appeal to the idea of a natural history or "geology" of desires: what we take to be desires are already highly evolved intentional dispositions, drawing on various original sources for their force and considerable learning for their array of possible objects. Second is the idea that, as rational beings, it is part of our nature that the evolution of our desires will be, to some high degree, reason-responsive. This structural feature of human development is enough to accommodate a Kantian picture of moral action and to provide natural space for the motive of duty.

V

I also claimed at the outset of this essay that there were certain advantages that came with this revised Kantian picture – in particular, that it offered the right kind of room for moral perplexity. In this last section, I will be able to say only a little about the nature of the issue and even less about the reason for the claim of advantage.

The topics that are central to moral philosophy often reflect concerns that are external to normative ethics. Questions about the relation between reason and motives (the domain of internalism) have made the paradigm case of moral action seem to be one where an agent recognizes that some action is morally significant (obligatory, forbidden, desirable) so that what remains problematic is the knowledge–motivation connection. Puzzles about the nature of the necessity that obligation purportedly carries make conflict of duties the canonical example of moral uncertainty.

What gets lost in the strategic maneuvering of theory is the hard work of moral deliberation that is central to a moral life: the engagement with multiple moral considerations present in an agent's current or anticipated circumstances of action. The range of moral perplexity is much greater than theory suggests, and need not typically involve the agent in finding ways of balancing or weighing competing moral considerations. It may be plain, for example, that a helping action is called for, but problematic how one is to help in a way that preserves the recipient's dignity. A concern to honor standards of equal treatment may appear compromised by evidence that girls perform better in sex-segregated school environments. When a group of California parents objected to the inclusion of a passage from an Alice Walker short story on a statewide exam on the grounds that it was "antireligious," an issue was raised whose moral complexity is not adequately captured in terms of a conflict between freedom of speech and discrimination against local religious values.[34] Because we live in complex and intersecting communities that endorse different standards of injury and offense, we require not only a way of determining when, say, toleration is appropriate, but also ways of engaging substantively with distinct local values that threaten or compete with our own. Some local values that can be threatened by public actions should be protected (penalizing students for religious observances imposes an unjustified cost), while others should not (banning religious benedictions at public school graduations protects a more important range of interests).

Of course, not all interesting examples of moral perplexity involve institutions or competing local values in a liberal, pluralistic state. There are hard adjustments of autonomy and legitimate interference (just ask any adolescent); all sorts of problems that follow from the decision to break a promise (how responsible one is for subsequent effects; issues for establishing future reliance and credibility in different social and personal contexts). The chief advantage of focusing on the social cases is the clarity there of the range of moral issues a responsible agent may confront. However well one is brought up, however complete the internalization of a regulative moral motive, what one will have to know, or how one may have to rethink one's own values, cannot be predicted. There is thus reason, internal to the moral phenomena, to prefer a characterization of the moral life that supports a certain degree of flexibility in both judgment and motivation.

This seems to me to be a clear point of concern for a neo- or new-Aristotelian conception of character as the basis for moral judgment and motivation. Much moral work can be done by a sensitivity that is both world-regarding and motivationally set. Agents are able to determine what is to be done through an appreciation or reading of what is morally salient in their circumstances. As the sensitivity is the judgment side of character, it is the product of upbringing, training, practice, and some amount of reflection. There is no separate question of motivation because moral knowledge is not available without the sensitivity, and the sensitivity is a function, an expression, of a motivational state. What seems to me a matter for concern is the apparent absence, in such a conception of character, of a way to criticize the sensitivity itself – for it to take itself as the object of its own critical regard.

The flexibility I find in Kantian theory comes from the distinctness in kind between motives, on the one hand, and interests and desires, on the other. The process of normalization to the deliberative field transforms interests and desires into motives that are internally responsive to the deliberative requirements of rational principle. It is a different conception of what it is to have a moral character. When formal regulative norms become internal to the agent's conception of her ends, an agent's sense of what morality demands can more readily include an acknowledgment that ways of life taken for granted may turn out to depend on unacceptable practices or traditions.

For example, hiring practices at many elite academic institutions are viewed as exemplary in their openness to quality, regardless of gender, race, and so on. But if the world in which they operate is racially stratified, and if persons of color do not in fact have equal access to the resources of quality, a deeper fairness may be required that will be institutionally uncomfortable and even transformative. Suppose we thought that our profession was unacceptably white. And suppose further that we noticed that our graduate admissions process, however procedurally fair, did not turn up many qualified candidates of color. One response might be regret – that having done what one ought, the results were so meager. But if our commitment is open to a deeper fairness, then we might wonder whether first-tier philosophy departments should do something else – say, develop standing relations with their peers at historically black colleges, in order to be in a better position to evaluate students from institutions whose faculty are (in present circumstances) unfamiliar to us, to provide training, to spend resources on visiting scholar and exchange programs, and so on. More than an appreciation of the need for new means may be involved here. As one comes to see the deeper difficulties in devising fair procedures, one's understanding of what the value of fairness amounts to changes. To the extent that one has a moral character of the sort I have in mind, one is to that extent prepared for the fact that accepting this change can alter familiar terrain of action, and even one's sense of the value of what one does.

Ideally, such changed understanding for a person with Kantian moral character will yield effective practical acceptance because the motives that constitute moral character are not independent of deliberative procedures and outcomes. Of course, the ideal is only that. As with any of our complex motives that arise through psychologically complex processes, the motive is not wholly separated from its structurally more primitive bases, nor fully reason-responsive. What we do have, even in the face of affective failure, are terms of moral criticism whose authority of application is secured.

I have no argument to show that an Aristotelian ethics of character cannot develop comparable resources.[35] Indeed, I have a suggestion for the way it might do this. If the notion of character that it deploys explains the way we register morally salient facts, we might think of the problem that an ethics of character needs to address as one of *new* saliences: how to see that the moral facts have changed. Where the moral world is unpredictable, the moral agent needs to be something of a cosmopolitan explorer. Not everything she encounters will be of equal value; not every value she brings with her will survive in its original form. The openness to conceptual change that comes from a commitment to the (now much maligned) Enlightenment value of Reason seems to be the right sort of equipment to bring along.

NOTES

1. Not that it is so obvious how, even given fixed laws, judgment is to proceed.
2. Sometimes this fact is taken to show "noncodifiability" – the thesis that the moral features of circumstances of action cannot be described by rules. But noncodifiability does not follow from context-dependence.
3. The most powerful and challenging version of this sort of account is to be found in the work of John McDowell.
4. For Kant, desires are incentives that are available for a rational agent to act on as motives, just in case she judges that acting to satisfy a particular desire is in some sense good. Desires are not, of course, the only incentives a rational agent has.
5. It is a story that Kant seems to endorse to explain the motivating effect of every source of action *but* the motive of duty. I do not think this is correct. In this essay, however, I am more concerned with getting out a different view than with proving that it is, or could have been, Kant's.
6. It is, not surprisingly, very difficult to disentangle such accounts from a rule-based conception of morality.
7. Samuel Scheffler, *Human Morality* (New York: Oxford University Press, 1992), chap. 5.
8. Of course, the value of such explanation was not limited to the individual and her symptoms. It also figured in accounts of mass hysteria, the rise of charismatic leaders, and other social pathologies.
9. Scheffler's theoretical program would not be disturbed by this. What he is exploring at this point is the possibility of natural moral motivation that is not tied to the promotion of some end (the well-being of others, self-interest), and so not

defeated when morality fails to support the end. He offers other sorts of argument to constrain moral content.

10. One might say, transparency is to morality what publicity is to justice.

11. Christine Korsgaard argues that there is nothing in the internalist requirement as such that argues against a substantive conception of practical reason ("Skepticism about Practical Reason," *Journal of Philosophy* 83 [January 1986]: 5–25). John McDowell adds to this the possibility of something like "conversion" – a kind of "transcendence of the mere facts of individual psychology" – that can bring an agent into position to deliberate correctly. He imagines the possibility of some nondeliberative process that could, say, by exposure, "bring . . . reasons within the person's notice." Significantly, these can be reasons that we will want to say, and that he may want to say, were reasons for him all along, even though there was no deliberative process that brought him to see what he now takes to be vividly relevant. McDowell's example is of coming to appreciate twelve-tone music – something it is not irrational for agents per se not to like on first notice. But for some agents, with some backgrounds in music, exposure or a description or an understanding of the history may move them – change what they hear. Such a process of making something available is not nonrational for being non-deliberative. See John McDowell, "Might There Be External Reasons?" in J. E. J. Althen and Ross Harrison, eds., *World, Mind and Ethics: Essays on the Moral Philosophy of Bernard Williams* (Cambridge University Press, 1995), pp. 68–85.

12. Not everything can be accomplished through a more robust account of practical rationality; and even if "conversion" is a possibility, some nontrivial background conditions need to be in place. Saul was not just taking a walk to Damascus when he became Paul. See John McDowell, "Two Sorts of Naturalism," in R. Hursthouse, G. Lawrence, and W. Quinn, eds., *Virtues and Reasons: Essays in Honour of Philippa Foot* (Oxford University Press, 1995), pp. 149–79, and "Might There Be External Reasons?"

13. Something like this is to be found in John Rawls's idea that the effect of a public culture of a certain sort will be that citizens come to be motivated by a concern for fairness. It is also, I believe, central to Mill's argument in his *Utilitarianism*. There is, Mill argues, a course of education and civilization through which the good of others comes to be for each person "a thing naturally and necessarily attended to, like any of the physical conditions of our existence" (*Utilitarianism*, chap. 3). It is this possibility, built on natural sympathy and developed through the unifying experience of successful cooperative activity, reinforced by education and religion, that is the ground of the possibility of utilitarianism as a moral way of life.

14. Some have argued that desires are evaluative: to desire X is to see it as in some way good or attractive. I think there is something to be said for such accounts, though not in the limited space of this essay. I also do not want to debate the question of whether evaluation can be captured in notions of nth-order desires. That debate belongs to a different set of questions.

15. See Andrews Reath, "Hedonism, Heteronomy, and Kant's Principle of Happiness," *Pacific Philosophical Quarterly* 70 (1989): 42–72.

16. The fact that an inspired guess hits the target that careful calculation misses gives no reason to abandon calculation for guessing, though one of the attractions of this modified rationalist story is that it can account for real inspiration – i.e., that it is not just a matter of lucky guesses.

17. This partly explains why, although rationality is a defining characteristic of individuals, its expression is social.

18. Immanuel Kant, *Critique of Practical Reason*, ed. L. W. Beck (Indianapolis, Ind.: Bobbs-Merrill, 1956), p. 94.

19. In most cases, the context of remarks about the purity of the moral motive is the danger of confusing motive and ground in moral theorizing: the requirement of purity keeps us focused on the nature and scope of moral obligation, avoiding a "lax or even mean way of thinking which seeks its principle among empirical motives and laws" (*Groundwork of the Metaphysics of Morals*, Ak. 426).

20. See *Religion within the Limits of Reason Alone*, ed. T. M. Greene and H. H. Hudson (New York: Harper & Row, 1960), pp. 21–7.

21. His remarks on the need to exercise and train the natural motive of sympathy, by seeking out the environments where our feelings will be aroused and challenged, are a good example (*The Doctrine of Virtue*, Ak. 455).

22. *Critique of Practical Reason*, pp. 74ff.

23. One might think that perhaps we respond this way to systematic thwarting because of a tendency to identify with the "oppressor" (the Patty Hearst syndrome). I'm not sure this would pose a problem. It is not part of my argument that reason-responsiveness is part of the *telos* of desires. But also, one might think that the Patty Hearst syndrome was itself a sign of a failure or incompleteness of development, much in the way we think that certain rigidities about planning can signal a developmental stall on the way to a capacity for delayed gratification.

24. Consider the Kantian argument to mutual aid. The moral law requires that we recognize the needs of others as making claims on our resources. One could think of this as the imposition of a new end, one added by reason (alone) to the ends we already have. But the nature of the argument suggests we instead view the obligatory end as the resultant of a formal constraint on the ends we naturally adopt: according to the moral law it follows from acknowledging my own status as a dependent being with needs that I must recognize the claim-supporting status of the needs of others. The latter view is the key to the structure of character in Kantian ethics.

25. "For how a law in itself can be the direct determining ground of the will (which is the essence of morality) is an insoluble problem for human reason. It is identical with the problem of how a free will is possible. Therefore, we shall not have to show a priori why the moral law supplies an incentive, but rather what it effects (or better, must effect) in the mind, so far as it is an incentive" (*Critique of Practical Reason*, p. 75).

26. Ibid., pp. 73ff.

27. I am not just claiming that development is required for there to be the concept

of drink and so *desire for* drink. It seems unlikely that thirst, as a distinct felt need, is primitive either.

28. The abnormal cases are important. There are tragic cases where despair at child-lessness has led to desperate actions. And it matters whether we characterize these desires as unmediated or unprincipled, or just so intense that they swamp the second-order commitment to moral constraint. The caution I urge is that we not use the explanation that seems to make best sense of moral failure as the model for normal action. The relation may not be so simple: failures of some kinds may indicate that development has not been normal, either in general or with respect to some subset of desires.

29. It is possible to describe much of this in terms of the neural complexities of brain function: the way patterns are laid down in the system of thalamus and cortex. Neurobiology, or a certain strain of it, seems to be the current legatee of tran-scendental idealism.

30. If Kant saw order even here, it was in the potential for the species as a whole.

31. In this account, freedom and the capacity for practical rationality are one.

32. Agents whose motives are fully normalized to the principles of the deliberative field act on maxims with moral content: they express the agents' autonomy. Agents whose maxims contain a principle of deference to desire (or any other incentive), make a mistake of valuation: they take themselves to be justified when they are not.

33. Kantian grounds of obligation are deliberative principles that set normative pre-sumptions about reasons for action. For example, the categorical imperative's rejection of deceitful maxims (in the standard *Groundwork* example, Ak. 422) sets a deliberative presumption against deceit for reasons of personal advantage. Likewise, the rejection of a maxim of nonbeneficence establishes that one cannot reject the claim of "true needs" of others on grounds of lack of concern or interference with one's projects. It does not follow that one may never not help or deceive. But a maxim of deceit or not aiding can rebut a deliberative pre-sumption only if its justificatory basis is something other than self-interest. (A fuller account of this way of interpreting Kantian principles of deliberation can be found in my "Moral Deliberation and the Derivation of Duties," in *The Prac-tice of Moral Judgment* [Cambridge, Mass.: Harvard University Press, 1993], pp. 132–58.)

34. *Los Angeles Times*, February 26, 1994. Students were asked to write their feelings about the following passage from Alice Walker's story "Roselily": "... She cannot always be a bride and a virgin, wearing robes and veil. Even now her body itches to be free of satin and voile. ... She wonders what it will be like. Not to have to go to a job. Not to work in a sewing plant. ... Her place will be in the home, he has said, repeatedly, promising her rest she has prayed for. But now she wonders. When she has rested, what will she do? They will make babies – she thinks practically about her fine brown body, his strong black one. They will be inevitable. Her hands will be full. Full of what? Babies. She is not com-forted."

35. One might, for example, draw on the aesthetic analogy that has been used to

explain part of what is involved in the link between so-called noncognitive dispositions and moral knowledge. If moral character is at all like either aesthetic enjoyment or artistic activity, there are various stories about how standing norms of excellence or beauty change. Kant, for example, thinks art requires norms and standards for enjoyment, but that artistic genius is the capacity to create convincing examples of new standards. Perhaps the true moral exemplar has such a kind of genius.

II
Eudaimonism

3

Kant's Criticisms of Eudaemonism

T. H. IRWIN

I. Happiness and Eudaemonism

Since most[1] Greek moralists take *eudaimonia* to be the ultimate end of rational action, we may discover some of Kant's main objections to Greek ethics if we examine his remarks about eudaemonism.[2] Some of Kant's students certainly believed that he had exposed the moral absurdity of eudaemonism:

> How often he moved us to tears, how often he agitated our hearts, how often he lifted our minds and feelings from the fetters of selfish eudaemonism to the high consciousness of freedom, to unconditional obedience to the law of reason, to the exaltation of unselfish duty![3]

Since most Greek moralists are eudaemonists, Kant seems to suppose that they are open to this objection of presenting a "selfish" point of view.[4]

To see whether this is an accurate impression of Kant's view, I will begin with some of his descriptions of Greek moral theories and then consider the objections that he raises. I will focus primarily on Kant's explicit remarks about Greek theories. According to Jerome Schneewind, this is an unwise procedure:

> [Kant] is simply not interested in giving a full assessment of Stoic theory. For him Stoic views are useful primarily as ways of describing his attitudes and locating his own position. Consequently his explicit comments about Stoicism do not teach us much about its relations to his philosophical ethics.[5]

Editors' note: Though the author's spelling of *eudaemonism* differs from that of the other contributors to this volume (*eudaimonism*), we accept it as a legitimate alternative and hence retain it here.

I believe, contrary to Schneewind, that we can learn quite a bit from Kant's explicit comments about the relations of his own theory to Greek theories. We will find that Kant's attitude to Greek views is in fact rather complicated, and perhaps even inconsistent.

These questions require us to be careful in our choice of terminology and in our initial assumptions. I will take it for granted that most Greek theorists are eudaemonist, in the sense that they are all concerned with eudaimonia, conceived as the ultimate good. I do not take it for granted, however, that eudaimonia is the same as happiness. Nor do I take it for granted that my use of 'eudaemonist' matches Kant's; in particular, I do not mean to assume that he regards all Greek moralists as holding the sort of theory that he associates with eudaemonism. The importance of these points will soon become clear.

I focus mainly on the second *Critique*.[6] I describe the Greek theories only to the extent that seems necessary for evaluating Kant's criticisms of them. I spend more time on a comparison between Kant and Reid. The details of my remarks on Reid are not necessary for the understanding of my main argument about Kant, but I believe the comparison is instructive. On many important points Reid's discussion of eudaemonism is fuller and clearer than Kant's; the similarities and differences between the two discussions seem to me to throw some light on Kant's position and on the difficulties it faces.

II. Kant's View of Greek Systems

Kant distinguishes the Epicurean and the Stoic views in these terms:

> So far as the definition of the concept of the highest good is concerned, they followed one and the same method, since neither held virtue and happiness to be two different elements of the highest good. . . . The Epicurean said: To be conscious of one's maxims as leading to happiness is virtue. The Stoic said: To be conscious of one's virtue is happiness. To the former, prudence amounted to morality; to the latter, who chose a higher term for virtue, morality alone was true wisdom. (*KpV* 111)

He explains the difference between these two views as a difference about the relative priority of virtue and happiness:

> The concept of virtue, according to the Epicureans, lay already in the maxim of furthering one's own happiness; the feeling of happiness, for the Stoic, was, on the contrary, already contained in the consciousness of his virtue. (*KpV* 112)

Though he began by talking about virtue and happiness, Kant passes easily from happiness to the feeling of happiness, apparently seeing no difference between the two.

He now seeks to correct the Greek theorists, since they misunderstand the relation of virtue to happiness:

> Whatever is contained in another concept, however, is the same as one of its parts, but not the same as the whole, and two wholes can, moreover, be specifically different from each other though they consist of the same content if their parts are combined in different ways. The Stoic asserted virtue to be the highest good, and happiness was only the consciousness of this possession as belonging to the state of the subject. The Epicurean stated that happiness was the highest good and that virtue was only the form of the maxim by which it could be procured through the rational use of means to it. (*KpV* 112)

According to Kant, the Stoics' claim that virtue is happiness really means that the feeling of happiness is a result of being virtuous, and so they ought not to claim that the two things are really identical.[7]

In Kant's view, different Greek theorists hold different views about the relation of virtue and happiness to the highest good. They all believe, however, that the highest good is the basis of morality, and therefore (in Kant's view) they are all open to one general and devastating objection. He states this objection when he contrasts his own position with the different positions that result in heteronomy of practical reason. Previous philosophers

> sought an object of the will in order to make it into the material and the foundation of a law (which would then not be the directly determining ground of the will, but only by means of that object referred to the feeling of pleasure or displeasure); instead, they should have looked for a law which directly determined the will a priori and only then sought the object suitable to it. Whether they placed this object of pleasure, which was to deliver the supreme concept of the good, in happiness, or in perfection, or in the moral law,[8] or in the will of God – their fundamental principle was always heteronomy, and they came inevitably to empirical conditions for a moral law. (*KpV* 64)

Kant makes it clear that none of the Greek moralists escapes this criticism:

> The ancients openly revealed this error in that they devoted their ethical investigations entirely to the definition of the concept of the highest good and thereby posited an object which they intended subsequently to make the determining ground of the will in the moral law. (*KpV* 64)[9]

The same error is present in modern moralists, but it is less obvious because they do not posit a highest good; as Kant remarks, the concept seems to have fallen into disuse, or at least become secondary.

The general error that is "openly revealed" in ancient systems and less clear in modern systems is the error of subordinating practical reason to an object that is referred to feelings of pleasure and displeasure. Kant's objection raises two questions for us: (1) Why does he believe this attitude to the good and the moral law is mistaken? (2) Is he correct in believing that ancient theories take this attitude? The answer to the first question takes us into some familiar Kantian doctrines and assumptions; but I will describe them briefly, since they provide the right starting point for a discussion of some more complex issues.

III. Objections to Happiness: Hedonism

In the first chapter of the *Critique of Practical Reason* Kant argues at length against attempts to treat happiness as a basis for moral principles. His objections to happiness rest on his objections to all "practical principles which presuppose an object (material) of the faculty of desire as the determining ground of the will." In his view, no such principle can be the basis of moral principles (*KpV* 21). The "material of the faculty of desire" is an object whose reality is desired. If the desire for the object precedes any practical rule, the principle is empirical:

> . . . the determining ground of choice consists in the conception of an object and its relation to the subject, whereby the faculty of desire is determined to seek its realization. Such a relation to the subject is called pleasure in the reality of an object, and it must be presupposed as the condition of the possibility of the determination of choice. (*KpV* 21)

Kant commits himself to claiming that pleasure must be the basis of any desire that precedes a practical rule by presenting an end for the practical rule to achieve. Since pleasure is the end, the practical rule must be merely empirical, because we cannot know a priori whether or not we will gain pleasure.

In the next section this hedonist conception of desire is connected with happiness. Kant has claimed that material practical principles aim at pleasure; now he claims that they all belong under "the general principle of self-love or one's own happiness" (*KpV* 22). Kant believes this because he identifies pleasure with the "sensation of agreeableness" produced by the achievement of some objects of desire. He claims that "a rational being's consciousness of the agreeableness of life which without interruption accompanies his whole

66

existence is happiness,[10] and to make this the supreme ground for the determination of choice constitutes the principle of self-love" (*KpV* 22).

Kant commits himself to a hedonist account of happiness. He does not simply identify happiness with pleasure, however; for he seems to suggest that happiness involves some conception of durable and uninterrupted pleasure. While we might have a few seconds of pleasure, Kant does not commit himself to saying that we can have a few seconds of happiness.

Some remarks might actually suggest that Kant does not always accept a hedonist conception of happiness at all. He suggests that knowledge of happiness rests on "mere data of experience" (*KpV* 36), and sometimes even suggests that it is difficult to find the elements of happiness (*Gr.* 417–18).[11] This difficulty would not arise if happiness consisted entirely in the pleasure resulting from the satisfaction of desire; for in that case the only constituent element of happiness would be pleasure, and the difficulty would lie not in identifying the elements of happiness, but in finding the means to happiness. Perhaps, however, we should not take Kant to be speaking exactly when he suggests that the elements of happiness itself are difficult to find. He may simply mean that it is difficult to discover what gives us pleasure. At any rate, when he explains why it is difficult to find the elements of happiness, all he mentions is the difficulty in finding the sources of pleasure. He suggests that "where one places his happiness is a question of the particular feeling of pleasure or displeasure in each man, and even of the differences in needs occasioned by changes of feeling in one and the same man" (*KpV* 25).

Kant must apparently rely on this hedonist conception of desire if he is to defend his claim that every other way besides his own of connecting the moral law with the agent's highest good really commits us to subordinating morality to one's own pleasure. In his view:

> If the concept of the good is not derived from a practical law but rather serves as the ground of the latter, it can only be the concept of something whose existence promises pleasure and thus determines the causality of the subject (the faculty of desire) to produce it. (*KpV* 58)

If we allow Kant this account of desires, then his criticism of happiness is straightforward. He believes that if we understand practical rules as prescriptions for achieving happiness, we make them depend simply on the agent's feelings of pleasure. If some agents are not pleased by the results of a particular course of action, then they have no motive to prefer that course of action, and it would not be rational for them to prefer it.

IV. The Priority of Inclination

These arguments work only against opponents who openly claim to make moral motivation depend on an agent's desire for pleasure, or against those who can be shown to be committed to this account of moral motivation. Kant may well believe that everyone who makes some other desire prior to the moral law is open to his criticisms, because he may well hold that psychological hedonism gives a true account of all desires except for the moral motive.

It would be a mistake, however, to assume that Kant has no plausible arguments left if we reject his hedonist assumptions.[12] His objections to theories that make the good prior to morality need not be presented in a hedonist framework. He presents these objections at length in chapter 2 of the Analytic in the second *Critique*.

Kant claims that all accounts of the basis of morality that take some conception of the good to be primary must make moral agency heteronomous, since they treat moral principles as hypothetical imperatives. They imply that whether or not we have sufficient reason to act on a moral principle depends on whether we have a sufficiently strong inclination toward the end that we would promote by acting on that principle.

This objection underlies Kant's remark that German has terms that draw important distinctions concealed by Greek and Latin. He argues that the Latin '*bonum*' and '*malum*' cover both judgments about weal and woe ('*Wohl*' and '*Weh*'), and judgments about the strictly good and evil ('*Gut*' and '*Böse*') (*KpV* 59–60). I fear that English suffers from the imprecision of Greek and Latin on this point. I have spoken of the "strictly good and evil" because I cannot think of a non-question-begging label for the kind of goodness that Kant is referring to here. Indeed, Kant's division between weal and the strictly good may well be taken to cover more than one distinction, and the different distinctions it covers may have different implications.

Kant does not assume from the outset that the strictly good is to be identified with the morally good. He illustrates the difference that concerns him by remarking that "whoever submits to a surgical operation feels it without doubt as an ill (*Übel*), but by reason he and everyone else describe it as a good" (*KpV* 61). This contrast suggests that the strictly good is to be identified with the good recognized by reason, in contrast to the pleasant. But this contrast does not seem to capture Kant's point completely. For though he recognizes the importance of judging our welfare by reason, "not according to transitory sensation" (*KpV* 61), he does not believe we really have a judgment about the strictly good as long as we are considering our happiness. He argues that reason cannot appropriately be regarded simply as a device for finding means to the satisfaction of inclination (*KpV* 61–2; cf. *Gr.* 395). When we consider the value we attach to reason, we do not, according to Kant, find that it is exhausted by its effectiveness in securing the ends pursued by inclination; indeed, we recognize that it is not always terribly effective in this instrumental role.

Apparently, then, the contrast between judgments of weal and judgments of strict goodness is the contrast between good assessed by reference to effectiveness in satisfying inclination (in the short or the long term) and good assessed by reason independently of inclination. In that case it is easy to see why Kant believes that principles prescribing what is to be done to secure our happiness cannot be judgments about strict goodness.

Kant's specific reason for denying that judgments of weal are judgments of strict goodness appeals to his view that happiness is simply pleasure. But this view of happiness is not needed to make Kant's main point. If we suppose that our inclinations need not be ultimately aimed at pleasure, and that happiness consists in the satisfaction of our inclinations (or most of them, or those we care most about, or a consistent set of them), then we can still claim that judgments about what is required for happiness must be judgments about the sort of goodness that depends on inclination; that is to say, they must be about weal rather than about strict goodness.

This sort of argument underlies Kant's conviction that no appeal to happiness as a basis for morality can be accepted once we recognize that the principles of morality are independent of inclination:

> After all these explanations that the principle of duty is derived from pure reason, it is remarkable how hedonism can survive, though now in a form that makes a certain moral happiness, whose causes are not empirical (a self-contradictory concept) the end. It happens in this way. When the reflective man has overcome the incentives to vice and is conscious of having done his often painful duty, he finds himself in a state which could well be called happiness, a state of contentment and peace of soul in which virtue is its own reward. – Now the eudaemonist says: this delight or happiness is really his motive for acting virtuously.[13]

Kant believes that this eudaemonist position is confused, because the special kind of pleasure that it identifies with 'moral happiness' is unavailable to agents who do not recognize some reason to follow moral requirements apart from the expected pleasure:

> In other words, he must find himself under obligation to do his duty before he thinks of the fact that happiness will result from doing it and without thinking of this. The eudaemonist's aetiology involves him in a vicious circle; he can hope to be happy (or inwardly blissful) only if he is conscious of having done his duty, but he can be moved to do his duty only if he foresees that it will make him happy. (*MdS* 377)

In Kant's view, the specific kind of pleasure that the eudaemonist has in mind cannot be prior to the recognition of the rational grounds for doing what is morally right, and so it cannot provide a justifying reason for doing what is morally right.

In any case, even if the appeal to this sort of pleasure did not involve a vicious circle, it would be open to objection:

> But there is also a contradiction in this sophistry. For he ought to do his duty on moral grounds or without first asking what effect this will have on his happiness: yet he can recognize that something is his duty only on pathological grounds, by whether he can count on gaining happiness by doing that thing. And these two are diametrically opposed to each other. (*MdS* 378)

This interpretation of the eudaemonist position explains why Kant believes that it involves "the euthanasia of all morals" (*MdS* 378). The aim of the Greek moralists was to "posit an object which they intended to make the determining ground of the will in the moral law"; according to Kant, this aim makes feelings of pleasure prior to the moral law. He seems, therefore, to regard all Greek moralists as eudaemonists, in the objectionable sense that he specifies.

While Kant clearly regards eudaemonism (in his sense of the term) as a type of hedonism, its crucial unfitness to provide an account of morality results primarily from its appeal to an inclination that is taken to be prior to rational judgments about what ought to be done. Kant assumes that prescriptions about how to achieve happiness give me sufficient reason to act on them only if I care enough about happiness and about this particular element of it. If I care less about my happiness, or take this particular element of it to be less important, then I no longer have a sufficient reason to follow this particular prescription. This is what Kant has in mind when he claims that the predisposition to humanity, involving the self-love that aims at happiness, "is based on practical reason, but a reason thereby subservient to other incentives." Only the predisposition to personality, involving the capacity for respect for the moral law as in itself a sufficient incentive of the will, is really "rooted in reason which is practical of itself, that is, reason which dictates laws unconditionally."

In speaking of "sufficient reason" here I refer to justifying reasons rather than exciting reasons.[14] If we leave aside questions about what it takes to motivate an agent to pursue a particular course of action, we can still ask what considerations constitute a sufficiently good reason for the agent to pursue it. In many cases it would be appropriate, as Kant says, to appeal to inclinations. The fact that I can buy an air ticket to London more cheaply if I book tomorrow than if I book the next day is a reason for me to book tomorrow only if I want to go to London. When the relevant facts about my

desires and inclinations are supplied, we can see why "You ou̟
tomorrow" satisfies Kant's conditions for being a hypothetical iɪ

Kant believes that imperatives based on happiness depend on
having a desire for happiness and, more specifically, a desire for tnis oɪ ɯaʟ
end as an element of happiness; hence, he must believe that we have no
sufficient justifying reason for doing anything to promote our happiness unless we have a sufficiently strong inclination toward our happiness and this
element of it.

Kant endorses this view of happiness when he claims that the adoption of
happiness as an ultimate end is the result of inclination:

> We find now, however, our nature as sensuous beings so characterized that
> the material of the faculty of desire (objects of the inclination, whether of
> hope or fear) first presses upon us; and we find our pathologically deter-
> minable self, although by its maxims it is wholly incapable of giving uni-
> versal law, nonetheless – as though it constituted our whole self – striving
> to make its claims prior, and to make them the first and originally valid
> claims. This propensity to make oneself, in accordance with the subjective
> determining grounds of one's choice (*Willkür*), into the objective deter-
> mining ground of the will (*Wille*) in general one can call self-love (*Selbst-
> liebe*), which, when it makes itself legislative and makes itself into the
> unconditioned practical principle can be called self-conceit (*Eigendünkel*).[16]

Kant describes our tendency to make the maxims of the pathologically determinable self into "the first and originally valid" claims. We mistakenly
suppose that we need no further reason apart from inclination in order to
have a good reason to act on our inclinations. In contrasting this attitude with
self-conceit, Kant suggests that it is possible to "make the subjective determining grounds of one's choice into objective determing grounds of the will"
without taking the further step that self-love takes when "it makes itself
legislative and makes itself into the unconditioned practical principle." The
difference between self-love and self-conceit is perhaps that self-love does
not claim that nothing could reasonably check it, whereas self-conceit claims
supremacy for itself in contrast to any other motive; that is why self-conceit
is also called "self-satisfaction (*Wohlgefallen an sich selbst*) (*arrogantia*)"
(*KpV* 73).

In both self-love and self-satisfaction Kant suggests that the rational will
(*Wille*) is persuaded to accept maxims that aim at the satisfaction of inclination, in the false belief that we have been given an "objective determining
ground." If we had been given an objective determining ground, we would
be right to believe that there is good reason, not dependent simply on the
inclinations that we happen to have, for acting to advance our own happiness.
In denying that happiness can by itself provide any objective determining

ground, Kant denies that it can provide any considerations that constitute good reasons for action, independently of the inclinations of the subject; let us call these 'external reasons'.[17]

V. Pleasure, Happiness, and Eudaimonia

We can now return to Kant's criticism of Greek eudaemonist outlooks. Two questions need to be raised: (1) He claims that they openly reveal the error of subordinating practical reason to pleasure. Is he right about this? (2) If he is wrong on this point, we still face a question: Do the Greek systems reveal the error of subordinating practical reason to inclination? If they reveal this error, they are still open to legitimate Kantian criticism.

The first question can be answered once we consider how far Kant's conception of happiness matches the Greek conception of eudaimonia.[18] To understand different Greek views on eudaimonia, it is useful to distinguish different answers that Aristotle gives to questions about eudaimonia. I will state the questions in terms that Aristotle himself does not use.

1. What is the concept of eudaimonia? Both the many and the wise agree that 'eudaimonia' is the name of the highest good, and agree that being *eudaimōn* is the same as doing well and living well. In agreeing this far, they agree on the concept of eudaimonia, but they still differ about what eudaimonia is (*EN* 1095a17–22).

2. What are the criteria of eudaimonia? It is the highest good because it is complete and self-sufficient (*EN* 1097a15–b21); but even when we recognize that these are the criteria for eudaimonia, we still want to know more clearly what eudaimonia is (*EN* 1097b22–4).

3. What is the content of eudaimonia? It is activity of the soul in accordance with the most complete virtue in a complete life (*EN* 1098a16–18).

Aristotle's second claim does not take us as far as saying what eudaimonia is, but it still tells us more than we learn simply from being told that eudaimonia is the same as the highest good. When he makes his third claim about eudaimonia, Aristotle believes he has said what eudaimonia is; this third claim is the "account" that he shows to be in agreement with common beliefs about eudaimonia (*EN* 1098b9–20). Even the third claim evidently leaves open the task of giving a more detailed description of eudaimonia; when we know more about what is involved in acting "in accordance with complete virtue," we can explain this clause more fully. Once we know, for instance, that to act in accordance with complete virtue is to act for the sake of the fine, we can add this explanation to clarify our account of eudaimonia.

The interpretation of Stoic views about the final good and eudaimonia is complicated by the fact that our sources do not always tell us clearly which of Aristotle's questions the Stoics are trying to answer. The Stoics, however, have firm views about which question is appropriately answered by different claims about eudaimonia. They more or less accept Aristotle's answer to the first question. In their view, the end is "that for the sake of which all things are done appropriately, while it is done for the sake of nothing" (Stobaeus *Ecl.* ii 46). Being eudaimōn is the end because for its sake everything is done, while it is not done for the sake of anything (Stobaeus, *Ecl.* ii 77.16–17). The Stoics clearly accept Aristotle's view that eudaimonia is the ultimate end and the highest good.[19] They identify being eudaimōn with living 'coherently' (*homologoumenōs*), living coherently with nature, having a good flow of life, and living in accordance with virtue (*Ecl.* ii 77.18–21).

It is not always easy to say which of these Stoic descriptions of being eudaimōn are meant to be relevant at which point in the Stoics' arguments. It is reasonable to suppose, however, that the description of it as the ultimate end appears at an early stage in a dialectical argument from common beliefs, that "living coherently" and "living coherently with nature" appear at an intermediate stage, and that "living in accordance with virtue" appears at a later stage. The appeals to rational agreement and to nature come before the claim about virtue, because someone could agree that eudaimonia has something to do with rational agreement and with nature before being convinced that being eudaimōn consists simply in being virtuous.[20]

The Stoics express their conviction about virtue and eudaimonia in different ways. Sometimes they say that virtue is self-sufficient (*autarkēs*) for eudaimonia,[21] sometimes that only the fine is good (Cicero, *Fin* iii 27–9; *TD* v 18; Diogenes Laertius, vii 101; Plutarch, *SR* 1039c). However their view is expressed, it would be wrong to interpret them as claiming that eudaimonia is only a consequence of achieving the good; they identify eudaimonia with the good as Aristotle does, and identify virtue with eudaimonia. It would equally be a mistake to suppose that Aristotle regards eudaimonia simply as a consequence of virtue. Though he disagrees with the Stoics insofar as he claims that virtue is insufficient for eudaimonia, he regards virtue as a component of eudaimonia, not simply as a means to it.

If this sketch of the Aristotelian and the Stoic views is roughly right, these views about the concept, criteria, and content of eudaimonia are quite different from Kant's views on the corresponding questions about happiness. Admittedly, some Greek eudaemonist theorists are also hedonists (Socrates in Plato's *Protagoras*; perhaps Eudoxus;[22] the Epicureans); but this does not mean that their views about eudaimonia are the same as Kant's views about happiness. On the first and second questions about eudaimonia, Epicurus agrees very closely with Aristotle; his hedonism is introduced in his answer to the third question. Kant, by contrast, seems to assume that the identification of happiness with pleasure tells us what the concept of happiness is; and so he does not offer the three-stage argument (corresponding to Aristotle's three questions) that Epicurus needs to offer in order to defend the claim that eudaimonia is pleasure.

Does Kant see this point, or does he carelessly assume that his conception of happiness matches the Greek conception of eudaimonia? His description of happiness makes it quite unsuitable to capture the concept of eudaimonia, and his account of Greek systems is difficult to understand if he simply identifies eudaimonia with happiness.[23] It is much easier to understand if he identifies eudaimonia with the summum bonum, and takes the question in dispute to be about the place of happiness, understood as pleasure, in the summum bonum. He suggests that each theorist tries to say what the summum bonum is, and different theorists disagree on this question. That is the right way to describe disputes about the nature of eudaimonia.

If we suppose that Kant identifies eudaimonia with the summum bonum, not with happiness, it is easier to understand why he says that no one believes that happiness, without any qualification, is the summum bonum:

> The ancients realized that mere happiness could not be the one highest good. For if all men were to obtain this happiness without distinction of just and unjust, the highest good would not be realized, because though happiness would indeed exist, worthiness of it would not. (*LE* 6)

This is why Greek theorists want to give virtue some special place in the summum bonum; their disagreement is about the relative place of virtue in the summum bonum:

> Epicurus' doctrine was that the highest good was happiness and that well-doing was but a means to happiness. . . . Zeno taught that the highest good is to be found only in morality, in merit (and thus in well-doing), and that happiness is a consequence of morality. Whoever conducts himself well is happy. (*LE* 7)

The Stoics, therefore, as Kant understands them, actually deny that the highest good is happiness.[24]

Now that we have seen how Kant interprets Greek eudaemonism, we can see why his own interpretation of it does not evidently justify his objection that it subordinates morality to pleasure, since the Stoics (for instance) do not identify the summum bonum with pleasure. Kant could defend his objection only by appeal to his general claim that all rational action, except for action on the moral motive, rests on a desire for pleasure. And so, if his objections to eudaemonism rest on his general psychological hedonism, they are not convincing.

74

VI. Eudaimonia, Practical Reason, and Inclination

We have noticed, however, that some of Kant's objections to other accounts of the basis of morality are independent of his acceptance of any general psychological hedonist assumptions. Even if he cannot show that his opponents subordinate practical reason to the desire for pleasure, he has a cogent objection if he can show that they subordinate practical reason to nonrational inclination. Let us grant that if morality is subordinate to the agent's happiness, it is thereby subordinate to inclination. Leaving aside any questions about happiness, let us ask whether subordination to eudaimonia constitutes the subordination of practical reason to inclination.

If Kant's objection to eudaemonism is right, then eudaimonia ought to be parallel to happiness (as he conceives it) in its reason-giving force. But is this a correct description of all defensible versions of eudaemonism? Ought we to agree that we have sufficient reason to pursue our own good only if we care enough about it, or that one thing rather than another is part of our good only if we want the first thing and do not want the second? Another way to put this question is to ask whether Kant is entitled to claim that nonmoral imperatives based on one's own good must always be hypothetical. For convenience I will speak of these as prudential imperatives; I will take it for granted that prudence is concerned with what is required for one's own eudaimonia, and I will ask whether prudential imperatives are so exclusively based on prior inclination that they must be hypothetical. If the reasons underlying prudential imperatives are external, then prudential imperatives are not purely hypothetical.

Kant's view is not the only possible view about how one's own good may be a source of imperatives. We may argue that the very fact that something would promote my welfare makes it reasonable for me to do it, whether or not I happen to care about my welfare, and whether or not I happen to regard this as an element of my welfare. At any rate, it seems quite natural to criticize people for acting unreasonably if they act in ways that violate their welfare, whether or not they happen to care about this. On some occasions we might say that we are criticizing them in the light of what they usually care about, or would care about if they stopped to think. But this need not always be so; if we were convinced that someone who has some foolish inclination that is contrary to his welfare would still have it even if he thought more about it, we might well conclude that he was open to more rational criticism rather than less.

Two different questions really arise here: (1) Is the only justifying reason for acting on my conception of my good a purely inclination-based reason? (2) Is my only justifying reason for pursuing this or that component of my good a purely inclination-based reason? To answer no to the first question is to say that there is an external reason to promote my conception of the good. To say this is consistent with agreeing that my good consists of nothing more than the overall satisfaction of my desires. To answer no to the second question is to affirm that our inclinations are not authoritative about the content of our good, and that there are external reasons for pursuing components of our good that are neither desired nor means to the fulfillment of our desires.

It would be consistent to answer yes to either one of these questions and no to the other one. Still, a negative answer to one makes a negative answer to the other more plausible. Aristotle and the Stoics answer no to both questions, claiming that we have external reasons both for pursuing our conception of our good and for pursuing one conception of our good rather than another. Kant's arguments against eudaemonism require him to answer yes to both questions. I will compare his position briefly with Butler's, and more fully with Reid's. Butler and Reid usefully articulate some Greek eudaemonist assumptions. Moreover, if we compare Kant's position with the positions of two other eighteenth-century philosophers, we will avoid the wholly misleading impression that the differences I will discuss reflect a division between "ancient" and "modern" views.

VII. Butler and Reid on Prudence

An argument for recognizing external prudential reasons is given by Butler. Butler considers the question whether appetite or "reflection" is to be obeyed in cases where they conflict:

> Cannot this question be answered from the economy and constitution of human nature, without saying which is strongest? . . . Would not the question be intelligibly and fully answered by saying that the principle of reflection or conscience being compared with the various appetites, passions, and affections in men, the former is manifestly superior and chief, without regard to strength?[25]

In calling self-love a superior principle, Butler claims that it relies on authority rather than strength of desires; the reasons it gives do not refer to the strength of my inclinations, but claim to apply to me as the sort of agent that I am, and hence are in accordance with my nature. In Butler's view, then, my reason for pursuing my own happiness justifies my inclination to do it, not the other way round.

I mention Butler in this connection because he states briefly and clearly an assumption that is characteristic of Greek eudaemonism; it is shared by (at least) Plato, Aristotle, and the Stoics. This point is recognized clearly by Reid, who exploits Butler's notion of a superior principle to explain the Greek view of eudaimonia. Reid insists that some principles of action are inherently rational; to explain this he relies on Butler's notion of superiority and authority.[26] More precisely, he mentions two connected characteristics of an authoritative principle. First, we recognize an authoritative principle when we recognize that some consideration apart from the strength of my desire favors one course of action over another.[27] Second, an authoritative principle tends to provoke self-approval (if we follow it) and shame or remorse (if we violate it).[28] The second characteristic is presumably explained by the first. For our special kind of reaction to an authoritative principle results from the considerations characteristic of an authoritative principle. Since we think we have some reason to follow it apart from our desire for the end that it enjoins, we have some basis for reproaching ourselves in ways that go beyond simply noticing that our predominant desire in the past was not the same as our predominant desire now.

So far Reid is following Butler; but he exploits this conception of a superior principle to defend a conception of rational self-love that is not explicitly present in Butler. He sees that when Butler speaks of superior principles and claims that they are in accordance with the agent's nature, he is not simply explaining what he means by 'superior principle' or 'nature'. On the contrary, Butler is making an important substantive claim: acting on principles that consider value as well as psychological strength fits our nature as temporally extended agents.

Reid explains that superior principles reflect our conception of our good on the whole, which results from our conception of ourselves as the temporally extended agents whose good is to be considered. Once we recognize that we are temporally extended agents, we realize that we have interests that cannot be achieved by simply following the stronger current impulse; and so we discover that in our own interest we have to follow principles that rely on authority rather than mere strength.[29] Reid recognizes – indeed he insists – that this account of superior principles and of self-love is not an innovation of his own or of Butler's. He claims, quite correctly, to be expressing the sorts of arguments that lead Greek moralists to recognize an ultimate end that underlies all rational desire.[30]

Greek moralists refer to this ultimate end as 'the good' or 'eudaimonia'. Reid usually calls it 'our good on the whole', but sometimes he is willing to use 'happiness' as equivalent to 'our good on the whole'. Hence, his comments on his conception of one's good on the whole sometimes speak of it as happiness.[31] He uses 'happiness' in the same way in his discussion of morality. First he asks whether morality promotes the agent's own good.[32] Then he pursues the same question (as he evidently supposes) by asking, "How can he be happy, who places his happiness in things which it is not in his power to attain . . ." (p. 211), and clearly means to be asking how we can regard these things as contributing to our good on the whole. We discover that we are "social creatures, whose happiness or misery is very much connected with that of our fellow men" (p. 215). According to Reid, both our pursuit of our own overall good and our regard for morality reflect rational principles; and in referring to this doctrine he says: "What I would now observe . . . is that the leading principle, which is called *reason*, comprehends both a regard to what is right and honourable, and a regard to our happiness on the whole" (p. 228). In speaking of "our happiness on the whole," Reid plainly means nothing different from what he described before as "our good on the whole."

VIII. Prudence and Categorical Imperatives

Kant disagrees with Reid on two points: (1) He conceives happiness differently. Reid takes happiness to be eudaimonia, whereas Kant connects it more closely to the satisfaction of desire. (2) Reid believes that both self-love and morality are rational principles, because he believes that prudential imperatives rest on external reasons. Kant believes that only morality counts as a rational principle – what Butler calls a superior principle – because he believes that the justifying reasons derived from one's good all depend on inclination.

Is Kant right to disagree with Butler and Reid on this point? In their view, the fact that restoration of my health, say, would be good for me is by itself a justifying reason for me to restore my health, whether or not I care about my health (or about anything to which my health might be a means).[33] In coming to desire health I do not make it reasonable for me to care about it, but I come to care about something that was reasonable for me even before I cared about it;[34] similarly, if I cease to care about my health, I do not make it no longer reasonable to care about it, but I simply cease to care about what it is still reasonable for me to do. This belief in external reasons is certainly open to dispute; someone might, indeed, argue that Butler's and Reid's conception of a superior principle is misguided. Perhaps it is a mistake to believe that agents may still be open to criticism for irrationality even if they act in accordance with their preferences. The view that facts about a person's good are the source of justifying reasons independent of an agent's desires may be challenged on the ground that it presupposes a view of justifying reasons that is false or even incoherent.

I will not stop now to consider whether these objections to justifying reasons independent of inclinations are sound or not. I will simply point out that Kant must not endorse these objections without qualification. For when he comes to consider moral imperatives, he must treat these as providing external reasons. He must assume that we find it intelligible, and indeed obviously true, that moral imperatives provide justifying reasons that are independent of inclinations. He clearly assumes that agents are open to criticism for acting against reason, whatever their inclinations may have been, if they violate principles of morality. He must be entitled to assume this if he is entitled to say that the imperative of morality is categorical.

Can he appeal to some difference between prudence and morality that entitles him to treat imperatives of prudence as merely hypothetical and imperatives of morality as categorical? The relevant difference is not easy to find. Kant relies on our intuitive judgment that moral imperatives are categorical; we do not suppose that our moral reasons go away if we lose the inclinations that favor the morally right course of action. But he tries to undermine our intuitive judgment that the same is true in the case of prudential imperatives. If he really succeeded in undermining our intuitive judgments in the case of prudence, it is difficult to see how he could avoid raising serious doubts about whether justifying reasons independent of inclination are ever possible. If he raises these doubts, Kant destroys his own argument about moral imperatives.

I cannot defend this judgment with the sort of detailed argument that it needs. I will simply give an example of what I mean. When Kant wants us to understand how the moral law can reveal freedom to us, he appeals to our experience of our capacity to act on moral principles contrary to our purely self-regarding interest; in experiencing this capacity, we recognize that we can do something because we know we ought to do it, and thereby recognize that we are free (*KpV* 30). Reid makes it clear that we have a very similar experience of our capacity to act on rational appreciation of our own good contrary to inclinations. If we are persuaded that one sort of experience is misleading, as Kant's view of prudence implies, it is difficult to see why we should agree with Kant that the other sort of experience is veridical. The experienced difference that Kant appeals to for his distinction between moral reason and nonmoral inclination is very similar to the experienced difference that Butler and Reid mark between power and authority. Butler relies on this difference in order to explain his conception of a superior principle in general. When Kant disagrees with Butler and Reid, he seems to undermine his own position too.

One of Kant's comments on the Stoics unwittingly points out to us the similarity between his claims about morality and Butler's and Reid's claims about superior principles in general. He mentions Poseidonius, suffering from the gout, who said that however annoying (*molestum*) the pain might be, he would never agree that it was bad (*malum*; Cicero, *TD* ii 61). As Kant understands this, Poseidonius says that pain is an ill (*Übel*) but not strictly bad (*Böse*; *KpV* 60). Kant explains:

79

> For the pain did not in the least diminish the worth of his person, but only the worth of his condition. A single lie of which he was conscious would have struck down his pride, but pain served only as an occasion for raising it when he was conscious that he had not made himself liable to it by an unrighteous action and thus culpable. (*KpV* 60)

Since Kant agrees with Poseidonius, he understands 'bad' (*malum*) to mean "morally bad."

Kant endorses Poseidonius' reaction only because he misunderstands it. In denying that pain is bad, Poseidonius cannot have meant simply that it is not morally evil. For he was discussing the Stoic claim that only the fine is good (nihil esse bonum nisi quod esset honestum); he maintained consistency with this claim by denying that pain is evil, and therefore denying by implication that freedom from pain is good. When the Stoics claim that only the fine is good, they do not mean that only the fine is morally good; that would be nearly tautologous, or at any rate quite uncontroversial, whereas their claim is controversial, and indeed paradoxical. They claim that only the fine is good for the agent, so that an agent's eudaimonia is wholly constituted by the fine; hence, their claim that only the fine is good is equivalent to their claim that virtue is self-sufficient for happiness (*hoti autarkēs hē aretē pros eudaimonian*). Though Kant's claims about worth, pride, and culpability certainly capture some of the grounds on which Poseidonius claimed that pain is not bad, they do not capture what Poseidonius meant by the claim; if Kant had understood Poseidonius' claim, he could not consistently have accepted it.

Contrary to Kant, then, Poseidonius' claim about pain uses 'good' and 'bad' in the prudential sense. This means that Kant cannot fairly use Poseidonius to support his claim that judgments of strict goodness are to be identified with judgments about moral rightness and wrongness, and the connected claim that motivation by judgments of strict goodness is to be identified with motivation by moral principles.

If we are willing to take seriously the view that there are external prudential reasons that constitute good reasons independent of the inclinations of a particular agent, we will not be impressed by Kant's assumption that eudaemonism must make practical reason subordinate to inclination. For the eudaemonist is entitled to claim that I have a reason to pursue my eudaimonia not because I desire eudaimonia, but because it is my ultimate good, and my good depends on the sort of being that I am, not on what I happen to desire.

When Kant distinguishes judgments about what is strictly good from judgments about weal, he explains that in judgments about strict goodness "a principle of reason is thought of as already the determining ground of the will without reference to possible objects of the faculty of the desire" (*KpV*

62). Eudaemonists have no reason to disagree; they need only insist that principles derived from one's own good meet this condition. If Kant's objections to eudaemonism apply only to versions of it that make prudential imperatives dependent on inclination, he has given no reason for rejecting those versions of it that treat prudential imperatives as categorical, insofar as they rest on external reasons that are independent of inclination.

IX. Eudaemonism and Morality

If Kant is wrong to claim that prudential imperatives must be hypothetical because they must depend on inclination,[35] then he is wrong to claim that eudaemonism necessarily subordinates practical reason to inclination. If he is wrong about this, he raises an objection to his views about eudaemonism and morality.

For the moment, we may assume that eudaemonism implies some sort of subordination of morality to the summum bonum. It does not follow, however, that eudaemonism implies heteronomy. For heteronomy implies the subordination of the moral law to inclination; it implies that we have a sufficient reason to follow the principles of morality only if we have some prior nonrational inclination to pursue some end to which morality secures the means. Eudaemonism does not imply this subordination of morality to inclination. For if morality is subordinate to the summum bonum, and the summum bonum provides external reasons independent of inclination, then the subordination of morality need not be subordination to inclination.

Once we recognize this possibility, we can see that Kant's arguments against eudaemonism are too simple. In arguing that the summum bonum cannot be prior to the moral law, he argues:

> For one sees from the Analytic that when we assume any object, under the name of good, as the determining ground of the will prior to the moral law, and then derive the supreme practical principle from it, this always produces heteronomy and rules out the moral principle. (*KpV* 109)

We ought to protest, however, that this is not precisely what one sees from the Analytic; what one sees is that if we subordinate the moral law to inclination, the result is heteronomy. If the highest good is not simply an object of inclination, then the result of subordinating morality to it is not heteronomy.

In objecting to an account of morality that treats the highest good "as the determining ground of the will prior to the moral law," Kant assumes that the highest good is an object of inclination if it is taken to be prior to the moral law. He has given no sufficient reason to accept his assumption. On the contrary, we have found that Butler and Reid give us good reasons for challenging the assumptions that underlie Kant's conception of prudential imperatives. If we recognize prudential categorical imperatives, then moral principles could be subordinate to one's own good without becoming merely hypothetical imperatives; for since the pursuit of one's own good would be, as Reid argues, a pursuit determined by reason rather than inclination, morality would not be subordinated to inclination.

X. A Conflict in Kant's Position

So far I have tried to examine Kant's argument against "the ancients" in general. We have seen that, despite the differences he notices between the Stoic and the Epicurean positions, he believes that both eudaemonist schools commit the errors that require the subordination of practical reason and morality to inclination. Hence, he takes all the ancients to commit the errors that he ascribes to (what he calls) eudaemonism.

Kant does not always attribute these errors to all the ancient schools. Up to now I have neglected some remarks that seem to exempt the Stoics from his general objections. In considering the failure of the Greek schools to solve the problem of the practical possibility of the highest good, he contrasts the Epicureans with the Stoics:

> The Epicureans had indeed raised a wholly false principle of morality, i.e., that of happiness, into the supreme one, and for law had substituted a maxim of arbitrary choice of each according to his inclination. But they proceeded consistently enough, in that they degraded their highest good in proportion to the baseness of their principle and expected no greater happiness than that which could be attained through human prudence. (*KpV* 126)

This criticism of the subordination of morality to happiness is familiar. But Kant believes that the Stoics are not subject to it:

> The Stoics ... had chosen their supreme practical principle, virtue, quite correctly as the condition of the highest good. ... they refused to accept the second component of the highest good, i.e., happiness, as a special object of human desire. Rather, they made their sage like a god in the consciousness of the excellence of his person, wholly independent of nature (as regards his own contentment). ... Thus they really left out of the highest good the second element (personal happiness), since they placed the highest good only in acting and in contentment with one's own personal worth, including it in the consciousness of moral character. (*KpV* 126–7)

In saying that the Stoics, in contrast to the Epicureans, make virtue their supreme practical principle, Kant implies that they do not subordinate it to any higher principle. He criticizes them only for believing that happiness could be reduced to the feeling of contentment that, in his view, is the consequence of awareness of one's acting virtuously.[36]

If this is the correct account of the Stoic position, then the mere fact that the Stoics begin their argument from the summum bonum and from eudaimonia does not show that they will give the wrong account of morality. The Stoics, like other Greek moralists, "devoted their ethical investigations entirely to the definition of the concept of the highest good" (*KpV* 64); if this method of investigation does not prevent them from making virtue the supreme practical principle, then it cannot imply the objectionable subordination of morality to inclination. To put it briefly: in acknowledging that the Stoics recognize the supremacy of morality, Kant acknowledges that the primacy of the highest good does not imply the objectionable subordination of morality.

Kant's concession to the Stoics requires a similar concession to Aristotle, if Aristotle is interpreted correctly. For the claim that virtue is the supreme practical principle does not require the Stoic claim that virtue and eudaimonia are identical; it is also implied by Aristotle's view that the requirements of virtue are to be chosen over every possible combination of other components of eudaimonia. This is the view that Plato defends in the main argument of the *Republic;* neither he nor Aristotle believes that virtue is the sole component of eudaimonia. Neither Plato nor Aristotle is evidently open to Kant's objection to the Stoics, that they fail to recognize the nonmoral components of the highest good. I do not believe that Kant's criticism of the Stoics does complete justice to their position, since it fails to recognize the importance of preferred indifferents in the Stoic theory. But if it were a justified criticism of the Stoics, then we could apparently point to Plato and Aristotle as eudaemonists who recognize the supremacy of morality without denying that the highest good has nonmoral components.

We must now compare these remarks of Kant's about Greek ethics with the passage I discussed earlier on the common error of the ancient schools:

> The ancients openly revealed this error in that they devoted their ethical investigations entirely to the definition of the concept of the highest good and thereby posited an object which they intended subsequently to make the determining ground of the will in the moral law. (*KpV* 64)

Here Kant implies that the ancients' method of investigation by itself involves an error about the status of the moral law. On this view, if the Stoics devote themselves to the definition of the concept of the highest good, they must make practical reason and virtue subordinate to an object that is referred to feelings of pleasure; in that case, they cannot really make virtue prior to happiness. Nonetheless, Kant claims that the Stoics avoid the objectionable subordination of virtue, and that therefore they make virtue prior to happiness. These different claims are not consistent. Kant's inconsistency results from his failure to decide whether the method of investigation used by the ancients, starting from eudaimonia or the summum bonum, necessarily implies an objectionable subordination of virtue to happiness.

Kant, then, does not seem to take a consistent attitude to Greek accounts of morality and the supreme good. The apparent conflict in his attitude comes out in his remarks on the Stoics. Though this conflict is surprising, it is not inexplicable. Kant sees that the concept of the summum bonum does not fit his account of the concept of happiness; and since the Stoic account of the content of the summum bonum makes it clear that they do not identify the summum bonum with happiness (as Kant conceives happiness), he sees that the Stoic appeal to the summum bonum cannot be open to the objections that undermine attempts to subordinate morality to happiness. Nonetheless, he sees that the appeal to the summum bonum implies that in some way a conception of the non–morally good is prior to a conception of the moral law. Kant wants to reject this eudaemonist claim, but he offers no argument against it except his objection about the subordination of morality to inclination; this objection is undermined by Kant's own claims about the Stoics. If Kant had freed himself of his conviction that all nonmoral justifying reasons depend on inclination, he might have seen that his different claims about the Stoics cannot all be correct.

XI. Reid on Eudaemonism

Kant's arguments against eudaemonism as the basis of an account of morality rest on his assumptions about nonmoral practical reason. It is instructive to see what sorts of objections to this aspect of eudaemonism are available to us if we reject Kant's assumptions, and agree that prudence is a source of external reasons. While Reid takes this view of prudence, he still believes that eudaemonism gives the wrong account of morality. The reasons he gives for this belief are not conclusive; indeed, Reid falls into an inconsistency very similar to Kant's about the interpretation of the Stoic position.

Reid sees that the Stoics' conception of happiness as our good on the whole, and their arguments about the role of practical reason in reducing irrational dependence on external goods, underlie their defense of the virtues of character. He attributes the same view, free of Stoic exaggerations, to Socrates and Plato as well (p. 212). He agrees that the eudaemonist argument "leads directly to the virtues of prudence, temperance, and courage" (p. 215).

Reid also agrees that eudaemonist arguments go some way toward justifying the other-regarding virtues. He believes that if other-regarding affections are part of our nature, then, for the reasons Butler gives, the satisfaction of them is part of our good:

> And when we consider ourselves as social creatures, whose happiness or misery is very much connected with that of our fellow men; when we consider, that there are many benevolent affections planted in our constitution, whose exertions make a capital part of our good and enjoyment; from these considerations, this [eudaemonist] principle leads us also, though more indirectly, to the practice of justice, humanity, and all the social virtues. . . .
>
> It is true, that a regard to our own good cannot, of itself, produce any benevolent affection. But, if such affections be a part of our constitution, and if the exercise of them make a capital part of our happiness, a regard to our own good ought to lead us to cultivate and exercise them, as every benevolent affection makes the good of others to be our own. (p. 215)

This defense of eudaemonism is reasonable as far as it goes; but it does not recognize a further argument for eudaemonism. Eudaemonists are entitled to ask whether we are better off with or without other-regarding affections, and to argue that, given our nature and needs as a whole, we are better off if we try to develop and to expand them and worse off if we try to eliminate or restrict them.

This is the sort of argument that eudaemonists offer for the value of friendship and the other-regarding virtues; and Reid seems to allude to such arguments when he refers to the fact that we are social creatures. The relevant fact, however, is not simply the fact that we have other-regarding affections; it is also relevant to recognize that we are rational agents who want to express our rational agency in relation to other rational agents. At this point, then, Reid seems not to appreciate the strength of the eudaemonist argument.

Once he has agreed that eudaemonism can give a good reason for cultivation of the virtues, Reid proceeds to point out what he takes to be the defects of the eudaemonist principle when it is applied to morality. It would be easy to expose the inadequacy of eudaemonism if we accepted a hedonist conception of happiness. This is not Reid's conception; and so he cannot rely on Butler's or Price's arguments for the independence or superiority of conscience. We must consider whether his further comments on eudaemonism reflect a full understanding of the conception of happiness that he has attributed to eudaemonist moralists. I believe we will see that Reid takes over some assumptions about eudaemonism that need to be challenged in the light of what he has told us himself about happiness.

Reid argues that "disinterested regard to duty" must be recognized as an independent principle that is not subordinated to self-love (p. 216), and so he argues that eudaemonism, taking self-love to be superior to every other principle, gives the wrong account of conscience. He offers three arguments:

1. The eudaemonist reasoning that justifies the moral virtues is too complicated for everyone to follow and will not necessarily move everyone as sharply as a sense of duty moves us: "There is reason to believe, that a present sense of duty has, in many cases a stronger influence than the apprehension of distant good would have of itself" (p. 217).

2. Eudaemonism provides the wrong motive for cultivating the virtues:

> Yet, after all, this wise man, whose thoughts and cares are centred ultimately in himself, who indulges even his social affections only with a view to his own good, is not the man whom we cordially love and esteem. . . . Even when he does good to others, he means only to serve himself; and therefore has no just claim to their gratitude or affection. Our cordial love and esteem is due only to the man whose soul is not contracted within itself, but embraces a more extensive object: who loves virtue, not for her dowry only, but for her own sake: whose benevolence is not selfish, but generous and disinterested: who, forgetful of himself, has the common good at heart, not as the means only, but as the end . . . (p. 218)

This demand for the appropriate motive in the virtuous person cannot be satisfied with the eudaemonist outlook.

3. The eudaemonist attitude is self-defeating; for if we do not take happiness as our only ultimate end, we will in fact achieve more happiness than if we are eudaemonists. Reid considers a hypothetical case:

> We may here compare, in point of present happiness, two imaginary characters; the first, of the man who has no other ultimate end of his deliberate actions but his own good; and who has no regard to virtue or duty, but as the means to that end. The second character is that of the man who is not indifferent with regard to his own good, but has another ultimate end perfectly consistent with it, to wit, a disinterested love of virtue, for its own sake, or a regard to duty as an end. (p. 219)

The person who takes the disinterested attitude described in Reid's second argument turns out to achieve greater happiness than the mere eudaemonist achieves.

These arguments are worth considering, since they show how Reid understands the eudaemonist principle, and therefore invite us to ask whether he has understood it correctly. His first argument does not seem to say anything that a eudaemonist needs to reject. Eudaemonists need not commit themselves to the implausible claim that we need no secondary principles to guide us; and moral principles should surely be included among these secondary principles. Reid's objections would damage a version of eudaemonism that requires us to deliberate on every occasion about what promotes happiness, or regards it as an open question whether specific moral virtues belong to the kind of life that achieves happiness. But if eudaemonists argue for such virtues as bravery, temperance, and justice, they require us to restrict deliberation about happiness on particular occasions; for just people would not be acting justly if they did not exclude certain kinds of considerations from their deliberation.

Reid does not raise a difficulty, then, for eudaemonism when he contrasts "a cold computation of the good and the ill" with a brave soldier's "noble and elevated sense of military duty" (p. 217); he says nothing that a eudaemonist need reject. Eudaemonists can argue that if bravery is a virtue that belongs in the best life, the appropriate "computation" will result in the appropriate "noble and elevated" attitude to brave action. Once we understand their position, we see that they need not suppose that brave people must be performing some "cold computation" about happiness whenever brave action is called for.

In the second argument Reid implicitly rejects this defense of eudaemonism, by arguing that even if eudaemonists recognize virtue as a source of secondary principles, they must take a mistakenly "mercenary" attitude to these principles. On this point, however, he misrepresents the options open to eudaemonism. Eudaemonists are free to argue that virtuous action is worth choosing for its own sake, and that is why it is a part of happiness; the mere demand that we should value virtue for its own sake does not seem to rule out eudaemonism. Perhaps the disinterested attitude that Reid has in mind is the attitude of people who would choose to be virtuous for its own sake even if they believed that some other course of action would promote their happiness better. But why is this strongly disinterested attitude necessary for virtue?

Reid suggests that "our cordial love and esteem" are directed toward the strongly disinterested attitude to virtue that he has in mind. He suggests that if we discover that people we esteem or admire are really seeking to benefit others for their own good, we will withdraw our esteem or admiration. Is he right about this? We might certainly agree with him if we suppose, for instance, that a politician stands up for a just and unpopular cause because she cares about justice, but then discover that she is doing it to curry favor with other interest groups. But this is not the sort of example that Reid ought to be considering. He needs to show that if someone cares about justice for its own sake, and believes that this is part of her good, we ought to infer that she is not really a just person at all. He cannot appeal to the normal attitudes of moral esteem and admiration in support of this strongly anti-eudaemonist attitude.

The third argument seeks to present a paradox of eudaemonism parallel to the paradox of hedonism, claiming that we realize the hedonist or eudaemonist goal best if we do not take it as our goal. This sort of argument undermines a hedonist view that says we should always be thinking about the yield of pleasure in whatever we are doing. For, contrary to this particular hedonist view, we will enjoy ourselves more if we allow ourselves to get absorbed in some activities without thinking of their hedonic consequences. If this is the paradox, it does not constitute a genuine objection to hedonism as a theory of the good; for while hedonists may need to advocate an indirect strategy for pursuing pleasure, they need not abandon their claim that the only thing worth pursuing as an end is pleasure.

The paradox is more damaging if it turns out that we gain more pleasure from x if we value x for its own sake than if we value x only for the sake of the resultant pleasure. If we agree with this, and also believe that pleasure is the only thing worth pursuing as an end, we do not exactly show that hedonism is false, but we make it difficult for ourselves to be hedonists. For in order to maximize our pleasure we must cultivate in ourselves a belief that we know (if our hedonist theory is true) to be false. If we were not ourselves agents, then this conflict would not raise any difficulties; we would just be offering a hedonist theory of value applying to agents who do not themselves accept the theory. In fact, however, we are agents; and so the conflict that results from accepting hedonism while agreeing that we maximize our pleasure by believing something incompatible with it is a serious objection to hedonism as a theory of value.

Reid's paradox, then, does not affect eudaemonism if it is taken in the first way. Does it work if it is taken in the second way? This question requires us to consider the differences between hedonism and eudaemonism. For eudaemonism does not require us to claim that happiness is the only thing worth choosing for its own sake. In fact, some eudaemonists argue that happiness is the ultimate end because it is composed of ends that are worth choosing for their own sakes. Hence, we introduce no conflict in our beliefs if we believe both that something other than happiness is worth choosing for its own sake and that happiness is the only ultimate end. Reid would raise a genuine difficulty for a eudaemonist if the belief that maximizes happiness is the belief that some particular nonultimate end would still be preferable to anything else if something else promoted my happiness better. But he has not shown that someone maximizes happiness by holding this belief.

Reid's third objection turns out to rest on the sort of misunderstanding that also underlies his second objection. He seems to be wrong about the implications of the eudaemonist claim that happiness is the ultimate end. He supposes that this claim implies a purely instrumental status for other goods; but the eudaemonist has no reason to admit this implication.

Is Reid's understanding of eudaemonism even consistent? He agreed that a eudaemonist has sufficient reason to cultivate the virtues, including even the social virtues. But in his objections to eudaemonism he presents the eudaemonist as having a mercenary and instrumental attitude to the virtues. It is strange if he admits that we can be genuinely just people if we do not care at all about doing the just thing for its own sake, but take a purely instrumental attitude to it. Reid himself recognizes that the right intention is necessary if we are to judge that the agent is good, and not simply that the action was good (p. 396);[37] and if his account of the eudaemonist's motive were correct, he surely ought not to concede that such a motive could make a person virtuous.

In fact, he shows some sign of doubt on this point. Later he reconsiders the eudaemonist argument for virtue; first he says it argues for "the practice of every virtue," but then he also says it leads to the virtues themselves (p. 363). He makes himself a bit clearer:

> And though to act from this motive solely, may be called *prudence* rather than *virtue*, yet this prudence deserves some regard upon its own account, and much more as it is the friend and ally of virtue, and the enemy of all vice; and as it gives a favourable testimony of virtue to those who are deaf to every other recommendation. If a man can be induced to do his duty even from a regard to his own happiness, he will soon find reason to love virtue for her own sake, and to act from motives less mercenary. (p. 363)

In this passage Reid explicitly considers the eudaemonist's motive, and concludes that it is not really the motive of the virtuous person. Perhaps, then, we should attribute this to him as his considered view, and interpret his previous defense of eudaemonist arguments for the virtues in the light of this restriction.

XII. Eudaemonism and the Moral Motive

These objections to Reid's criticisms of eudaemonism should make it clear that several issues turn on whether a eudaemonist must treat virtues as purely instrumental to happiness in some objectionable sense. Reid's arguments clearly damage an account of the relation between virtue and happiness of the sort that is offered by Epicurus. Should we perhaps suppose that Reid is not thinking of the versions of eudaemonism that recognize a closer connection between virtue and happiness?

At this point we encounter the oddest feature of Reid's criticism of eudaemonism. For he clearly does not intend his description of eudaemonism to be restricted to Epicureanism. In attributing eudaemonism to "the best moralists among the ancients," he is thinking above all of the Stoics.[38] He must therefore include them in his objection that eudaemonism results in a mercenary attitude to virtue. But it is difficult to see how he can consistently do this, if we consider some of his other remarks on Stoicism.

Having argued for the insufficiency of the eudaemonist principle, Reid explains the principle of duty and maintains that "the notion of duty cannot be resolved into that of interest, or what is most for our happiness" (p. 223). He argues that this principle is recognized by ordinary people and philosophers of all times and nearly all schools. In his support he appeals to the Greek concept of the *kalon*, rendered in Latin by '*honestum*'.[39] Reid sees nothing anachronistic in attributing to the ancient moralists a belief in moral obligation distinct from self-interest; he avoids a facile and mistaken contrast between Greek and modern moralists that has appeared in some more recent writers on this issue.[40]

Reid believes it is a mark of the morally virtuous person to recognize that conscience and the sense of duty is an independent and sufficient rational principle, and to act on it. He claims that the Stoics clearly acknowledge that the moral motive has this status:

> The authority of conscience over the other active principles of the mind, I do not consider as a point that requires proof by argument, but as self-evident. For it implies no more than this, that in all cases a man ought to do his duty. He only who does in all cases what he ought to do, is the perfect man. Of this perfection in the human nature, the Stoics formed the idea, and held it forth in their writings as the goal to which the race[41] of life ought to be directed. Their *wise man* was one in whom a regard for the *honestum* swallowed up every other principle of action. (p. 255)

The Stoics, then, are described as shining examples of the sort of devotion to duty and the moral motive that Reid takes to be characteristic of the morally good person.

How are we to reconcile this evaluation of the Stoics, however, with the view that they are eudaemonists? While Reid clearly recognizes that they are eudaemonists, he never mentions this fact in the contexts where he emphasizes their devotion to the *honestum*. But given his own objections to eudaemonism, which he clearly takes to apply to the Stoics, surely he owes us some explanation. For his claims seem to convict either the Stoics or himself of inconsistency. If the Stoics are really eudaemonists, then they take the mercenary attitude to virtue that is inconsistent with their devotion to the *honestum*. If, on the other hand, the Stoic position is consistent, then Reid's criticism of eudaemonism must be wrong.

Why does Reid not see this question that arises for someone who thinks about what he says in two adjacent chapters? Perhaps Reid's sources help to explain his oversight. The Stoics' eudaemonism is especially prominent in

Cicero's *De Finibus*, where it is especially clear that they are offering their own answer to the old debate in Greek ethics about the nature of the final good, and are trying to justify the virtues in relation to their conception of the good. On the other hand, the clear and sharp distinction between the morally right and the merely useful is prominent in Cicero's *De Officiis*, where (quite reasonably) less attention is paid to the eudaemonist foundations of Stoic moral theory.

It should not be too difficult to see the connection between Cicero's two discussions; Reid himself quotes a passage from the *De Officiis* on the rational principle of prudence (p. 206). Cicero remarks that the supreme good is relevant to a general theoretical inquiry into duties; it is still relevant, but less obviously relevant to a discussion of the specific questions about duties that arise in everyday life (*Off.* i 7). Still, we can perhaps see why Reid, thinking about Stoic eudaemonism and about the Stoic theory of duties in two different contexts, derived from two different sources, might fail to consider the relation between these two aspects of Stoic ethics. If he had considered the *De Finibus*, it ought to have been more difficult to overlook this question.[42]

However Reid's oversight is to be explained, it is unfortunate. For if he had seen the question that he raises for himself, he might at least have considered how the Stoics seek to reconcile their devotion to moral goodness with their eudaemonism. This question is quite important for Reid's argument. For he introduces the Stoic conception of the *honestum* in order to support Butler's belief in the distinctness and independence of conscience from self-love; but the Stoics themselves clearly do not suppose that their recognition of the *honestum* introduces any principle that is independent of eudaemonism. Where have they gone wrong? Reid ought to explain.

Ought we to object to Reid's claim that the Stoics' conception of the morally right (*kalon, honestum*) indicates their recognition of the moral motive as a distinct principle of action? We need not disagree with him here. He might reasonably argue that the Stoics recognize that the belief that an action is morally right is a different belief from the belief that it contributes to my happiness. They also agree that belief in moral rightness provides a motive that is distinct from the desire for my happiness. They need not, however, infer that moral rightness gives me a justifying reason that is independent of its contribution to happiness.

Reid perhaps overlooks this distinction between the moral motive and the justifying reason provided by the moral motive. He is quite entitled to appeal to the Stoics for evidence of a belief in the distinctness of moral and self-interested motives. But he goes too far in claiming that the Stoic sage was someone "in whom a regard to the *honestum* swallowed up every other principle of action" (p. 254). The claim that the moral motive "swallows up" other principles of action is obscure on the crucial point. The Stoics might agree with Reid's description of them, if it means only that no other principle of action is allowed to conflict with the moral motive. But they cannot accept the suggestion that nothing else matters to sages besides the moral motive; sages also insist that action on the moral motive is the only element in their happiness, and the crucial element in the way of life that they aim at.[43]

If Reid were pressed on the question, he would perhaps answer that the division between the moral motive and the eudaemonic justifying reason does not restore consistency to the Stoic position. For he might argue that acceptance of a eudaemonic justifying reason implies a mercenary attitude to virtue, and that this attitude conflicts with the properly moral attitude to moral obligation. But if this is his answer, it relies heavily on the very dubious arguments that were meant to show that eudaemonism is necessarily mercenary. Perhaps there is some deeper objection to eudaemonism as the basis of an account of moral obligation; but Reid's argument does not identify this objection.

If, then, we consider Reid's various remarks about the Stoics, we discover that they suggest an argument against his own objections to eudaemonism. For he sees both that the Stoics are nonhedonistic eudaemonists and that they attribute the appropriate sort of importance and distinctness to the moral motive. The soundness of his arguments on these points should lead us to question the arguments that seek to prove that the right attitude to the moral motive conflicts with eudaemonism. If these arguments were cogent, there would be a glaring conflict in Stoicism; Reid's complete failure even to suggest that Stoicism displays this conflict betrays the weakness of his arguments against eudaemonism.

Both Kant and Reid, then, fail to give a consistent description of the Stoic position. The explanations for their failure are in some ways different; Reid, for instance, is not prejudiced by Kant's assumption that any justifying reason appealing to some nonmoral good must depend on inclination. But it is useful to compare their attitudes, since they have something in common. Both Kant and Reid acknowledge that the Stoics recognize morality and give it the appropriate status in the concerns of the rational agent. But they share the conviction that we cannot give the right status to morality if we derive moral principles from an appeal to some nonmoral good. Though their view about the Stoics is inconsistent with their general conviction about morality and nonmoral goods, they do not resolve the inconsistency. If they had tried to clarify their description and criticism of the Stoic position, they would also have clarified an obscure area in their own moral theories.

XIII. The Subordination of Morality

Reid's arguments about eudaemonism and morality show that it is not easy to find a decisive objection to eudaemonist views of morality if we forgo Kant's objection about subordination to inclination. Has Kant anything better to offer?

In some places he objects that non-Kantian accounts of moral principles imply heteronomy of choice "because the will does not give itself the law but only directions for a reasonable obedience to pathological laws" (*KpV* 33). Elsewhere, however, he argues that the moral law cannot be based on practical reason that is "subservient to other incentives"; he argues that the predisposition to personality involves the capacity for respect for the moral law as in itself a sufficient incentive of the will (*Rel.* 23). He takes himself to be making the same point in other terms when he sums up the argument in the second *Critique* on the good and the moral law:

> In the preceding chapter we have seen that anything which presents itself as an object of the will prior to the moral law is excluded from the determining grounds of the will, under the name of the unconditioned good, by this moral law itself as the supreme condition of practical reason.[44]

Kant claims to have shown that nothing prior to the moral law can present itself as the unconditioned good, and therefore nothing prior to it ought to be treated as a sufficient determining ground of the will.

In these passages we might try to distinguish two types of subordination of morality: (1) subordination to "pathological laws," resulting in hypothetical imperatives; (2) subordination to nonmoral principles. If our previous argument has been correct, the second type of subordination does not imply the first; for if prudential principles are not derived from inclination, moral principles derived from prudential principles are not derived from inclination either.

Since Kant does not accept this point about prudential principles, he does not allow any nonmoral categorical imperatives, and so he does not distinguish the two types of subordination. But if he distinguished them, and claimed that both types are objectionable, he would have a reason for objecting to theories that set out from the summum bonum and in some way derive the principles of morality from that.

If Kant went in this direction, he would have to articulate his objections to the subordination of morality so that they could be cut loose from his claims about categorical imperatives and autonomy. He would have to admit that moral principles are not the only ones that are categorical imperatives, and are not the only ones that express the autonomy of the will, and he would have to admit that subordination to the highest good does not by itself

threaten their categorical and autonomous status. If he made these conces-
sions, the implications for his views about the connection between morality,
freedom, and the fact of reason would be far-reaching. But might he still be
entitled to object to subordination in its own right?

To answer this question, we would evidently have to consider what kind
of subordination is objectionable, what kind is implied by eudaemonist theories, and whether the two kinds are identical or closely connected. We might
well sympathize with the claim that moral principles are misunderstood if
they are taken to prescribe actions that are valued purely for their causal
consequences in achieving ends that we can reasonably value even if we have
no prior concern with morality. Kant might reasonably seem to be appealing
to an important feature of morality – the fact that it affects our view about
the sorts of things that are to be valued for their own sakes.

If this is the kind of subordination we reject, then we have no reason to
reject eudaemonist theories, since they do not imply this sort of subordination. This point casts serious doubt, as we have seen, on Reid's objections
to a eudaemonist account of morality, since these objections seem to assume
a kind of subordination that need not be attributed to Plato, or Aristotle, or
the Stoics, among others.

We may still claim, however, that these eudaemonist theories are committed to some form of the subordination of the moral to the nonmoral. One
way to express this form of subordination is to say that eudaemonist theories
try to justify morality by reference to some end that is partly distinct from
it; in order to show that a rational agent is justified in accepting the ends
prescribed by morality, we have to show that these ends have something else
to be said for them besides the fact that they are prescribed by morality. This
demand has been expressed by Bradley:

> Is morality an end in itself; and, if so, how and in what way is it an end?
> Is morality the same as the end for man, so that the two are convertible;
> or is morality one side, or aspect, or element of some end which is larger
> than itself? Is it the whole end from all points of view, or is it one view
> of the whole?[45]

If we accept the legitimacy of these questions, then we recognize that an
appeal to an ultimate good for the agent is prior in one important way to
morality. If this appeal to the ultimate good is appropriate, then a justification
of morality requires some connection between the ends achieved by morality
and ends that are recognized as worth pursuing independently of morality.

I will not try to defend or even to clarify these eudaemonist demands any
further. I will not even pursue some rather complicated questions about how
far Kant actually accepts them. I simply want to suggest that if we want to

reject the subordination of morality to the highest good, and we realize that we cannot reject it by appeal to the categorical character of moral imperatives or to the connection between morality and autonomy, these are the demands that we have to consider. Kant cannot fairly take it for granted that the subordination of morality to the highest good is to be rejected without qualification, once we understand what it involves. If he had seen that he must give up the arguments relying on categorical imperatives and on autonomy, he would have had to revise his argument quite significantly.

Consideration of Kant's views on eudaemonism suggests that he ought to have accepted one element of a "dualism of practical reason," insofar as he ought to have admitted prudence as a source of categorical imperatives.[46] Whether he is thereby committed to another element of a dualism of practical reason – the recognition of independent and potentially conflicting rational principles – is a further question that I will not pursue. I have not tried to argue that the weaknesses in Kant's criticisms of eudaemonism are signs of a fatal error in Kant's moral theory. If we accept the objections I have raised, then we must admit that there are more categorical imperatives than Kant admits, and that the will acts autonomously in more circumstances than Kant admits. In admitting these things, we deny the exceptional status of morality among human aims. This denial clearly makes some Kantian arguments more difficult to defend. But it is not an unqualified disadvantage for Kant. If we agree that morality expresses the sort of autonomy that we can see to be desirable and possible even apart from morality, we can already see how we might satisfy the demand to be shown how morality is connected with aims that we can see to deserve our attention even apart from morality. I have tried to show that Kant's criticisms of Greek eudaemonism are mistaken, and that the mistakes he makes reflect deeper difficulties in his position. The correction of these mistakes ought to result not in the collapse of Kantian moral theory, but in a salutary reconstruction.[47]

NOTES

1. I say 'most' rather than 'all' in order to accommodate the Cyrenaics, who are not eudaemonists. See Diogenes Laertius ii 87–8. (Kant mentions the Cyrenaics in the versions of his lectures in Kants Gesammelte Schriften [KGS], vol. 27 [Berlin: De Gruyter, 1974–5], but I have not noticed any place where he remarks that they are not eudaemonists.) The eudaemonist formula I have given here fits the Stoics only if 'end' is taken in their technical sense (for the telos as distinct from the prokeimenon; Cicero, De Finibus [Fin.] iii 22); for they believe it is quite rational to act in order to obtain an external objective (prokeimenon) that is neither included in nor a means to happiness.

2. For this purpose the only Greek theories that he takes to deserve extended consideration are those of the Stoics and Epicureans. On Aristotle and Plato he has only a brief remark at *Critique of Practical Reason* [*KpV*], trans. L. W. Beck (3rd ed., New York: Macmillan, 1993), p. 127n (last sentence).
3. From the recollections of R. B. Jachmann, in *Immanuel Kant: Ein Lebensbild*, ed. A. Hoffman (Halle: Hugo Peter, 1902), p. 23. Quoted in *Kant: Lectures on Ethics* [*LE*], tr. L. Infield (New York: Harper & Row, 1963), p. ix.
4. Kant speaks of 'eudaemonism' in similarly severe terms in *Anthropology from a Pragmatic Point of View* (trans. Dowdell [Carbondale: Southern Illinois University Press, 1978]), Ak. p. 130: "... the moral egoist limits all purposes to himself; as a eudaemonist, he concentrates the highest motives of his will merely on profit and his own happiness, but not on the concept of duty. Because every other person has a different concept of what he counts as happiness, it is exactly egoism which causes him to have no touchstone of a genuine concept of duty which truly must be a universally valid principle. All eudaemonists are consequently practical egoists."
5. See Chapter 10, this volume.
6. I follow Beck's translation of the *Grundlegung* [*Gr.*] (New York: Bobbs-Merrill, 1959) and *KpV* (with Akademie page references), and Greene and Hudson's translation of *Religion within the Limits of Reason Alone* [*Rel.*] (New York: Harper & Row, 1960), except where deviations are mentioned.
7. How might Kant have formed this view of the Stoics? It is natural to suppose that Kant uses 'happiness' to indicate Stoic views about eudaimonia. If so, then he might find some support in some Stoic sources for his claims about happiness. In some places Stoics speak of eudaimonia as a "good flow" (*eurhoia*) of life (Stobaeus, *Eclogae* [*Ecl.*] ii 77.21 W), and sometimes seem to identify this "good flow" with a subjective condition of the agent. If one focuses on these passages to the exclusion of other remarks about eudaimonia and virtue, one might come out with something like Kant's view. (See Irwin, in M. Schofield and G. Striker, eds., *The Norms of Nature* [Cambridge University Press, 1986], p. 225; G. Striker, "Ataraxia: Happiness as Tranquillity," *Monist* 73 [1989]: 99, 107.) If one turned from these passages to the sources in which the Stoics are said to identify the summum bonum with virtue, and one noticed the difference between virtue and a consequence of virtue, one might reasonably come to the conclusion that the Stoics regard eudaimonia as a consequence of the summum bonum rather than as the summum bonum itself.
8. Editors follow Hartenstein in emending to "moral feeling." I am not sure that this is necessary.
9. Beck's translation slightly modified.
10. *KpV* 124 gives a similar account of happiness.
11. In the correction added in the first introduction to the *Critique of Judgment* (printed by Beck as a footnote to *Gr.* 415) Kant actually says that imperatives based on happiness depend on "a definition of what constitutes the end itself (happiness)."
12. See Beck, *Commentary*, pp. 101–2. A. Reath, "Hedonism, Heteronomy, and

Kant's Principle of Happiness," *Pacific Philosophical Quarterly* 70 (1989): 42–72, goes further and actually denies that Kant holds the hedonist views that I have attributed to him. See also H. E. Allison, *Kant's Theory of Freedom* (Cambridge University Press, 1990), p. 103. I don't believe that Reath's arguments are entirely convincing, but I won't discuss them here, since the views about happiness and heteronomy that he is willing to ascribe to Kant (pp. 57–62) still raise the questions that I discuss in the following few sections.

13. *Metaphysics of Morals [MdS]*, in *Kant: Doctrine of Virtue*, trans. M. J. Gregor (New York: Harper & Row, 1964), Ak. p. 377.

14. I use Hutcheson's terms, without following precisely his explanation of the distinction. See *British Moralists*, ed. D. D. Raphael (Oxford University Press, 1969), §361.

15. It is the sort of hypothetical imperative that he calls a counsel rather than a command (*Gr.*, 418).

16. *KpV* 74. Beck's translation slightly modified (partly following S. Engstrom's corrections, in "The Concept of the Highest Good in Kant's Moral Theory," *Philosophy and Phenomenological Research* 52 [1992]: 758). The most recent revision of Beck unfortunately translates '*bestimmbares*' first as "determinable," then as "determined." I have benefited from Engstrom's discussion of the whole passage.

17. In speaking of "external" reasons I am alluding to (though not necessarily following in detail) Bernard Williams, "Internal and external reasons," in *Moral Luck* (Cambridge University Press, 1981).

18. In Latin sources (Cicero's *De Finibus [Fin.]*, *Tusculan Disputations [TD]*, *De Officiis [Off.]*, Seneca's *De Beata Vita*) the question about eudaimonia is usually presented as a question about the nature of the '*beata vita*'. I don't know what Latin sources Kant might have been expected to have known at first hand. K. Reich, "Kant and Greek Ethics," *Mind* 48 (1939): 338–54 and 446–63, mentions (p. 447) that Kant possessed Garve's translation with notes of the *De Officiis*, and that in 1784 (according to a letter of Hamann to Herder) he was working on the reply to Garve that eventually appeared as *Theory and Practice*. Reich says, "Kant read Garve's translation and commentary – or, if we like to put it that way, studied Cicero's *De Officiis* – *immediately* before the composition of the *Grundlegung*." This claim seems to me to assume rather a lot about how Kant might have prepared himself to answer Garve. But the *De Officiis* cannot be the source of, for instance, Kant's comparisons between Stoics and Epicureans. These comparisons might be derived – not necessarily at first hand – from the *De Finibus* or from Seneca's *De Vita Beata*.

19. They modify Aristotle in distinguishing eudaimonia from being eudaimōn (*eudaimonein*), following their distinction between the *telos* and the *skopos*. See Stobaeus, *Ecl.* ii 77.1–5, 21–7.

20. On the Stoics' use of dialectical argument, see the intriguing paper of Jacques Brunschwig, "On a Book-title by Chrysippus," *Oxford Studies in Ancient Philosophy*, supplementary volume (1991): 81–95, at 91–5.

21. Diogenes Laertius vii 127. See also Plutarch, *De Stoicorum Repugnantiis* (*SR*) 1046e.
22. We do not know enough about him to be completely sure that he is a eudaemonist.
23. R. J. Sullivan, *Immanuel Kant's Moral Theory* (Cambridge University Press, 1989), 364n12, suggests that Kant criticizes the Stoics for claiming that to be conscious of one's virtue is happiness or eudaimonia. I cannot see a sufficient basis for supposing that Kant regards this remark about happiness as a remark about eudaimonia.
24. The ancients are also discussed in the versions of Kant's lectures printed in *KGS* xxvii. See p. 101 (the primacy of the question about the nature of the summum bonum); p. 104 (the Stoics on happiness); and pp. 248–50 (the Stoics on the priority of virtue to happiness). Kant's views are similar to those in *LE*.
25. Sermon ii 13, in *Joseph Butler: Fifteen Sermons*, ed. T. A. Roberts (London: SPCK, 1970).
26. "We conceive brute animals to have no superior principle to control their appetites and passions. On this account, their actions are not subject to law. Men are in a like state in infancy, in madness, and in the delirium of a fever. They have appetites and passions, but they want that which makes them moral agents, accountable for their conduct, and objects of moral approbation or of blame" (T. Reid, *Essays on the Active Powers*, ed. B. A. Brody [Cambridge, Mass.: MIT Press, 1969], p. 67). "Thus we see, that, in many, even of our voluntary actions, we may act from the impulse of appetite, affection, or passion, without any exercise of judgment, and much in the same manner as brute animals seem to act" (p. 67). Acting on rational principles involves some sort of judgment. But evidently not every sort of judgment will do. Purely instrumental reasoning about ways to satisfy a particular appetite do not count as action on a rational principle. To isolate the relevant distinction, Reid appeals to Butler's notion of authority: "There is an irrational part, common to us with brute animals, consisting of appetites, affections, and passions; and there is a cool and rational part. The first, in many cases, gives a strong impulse, but without judgment, and without authority. The second is always accompanied with authority" (p. 73).
27. Sometimes one appetite may be restrained by a stronger contrary appetite, as in a hungry dog that leaves its food alone from fear of punishment; but this is not a case of acting on a superior principle. "Do we attribute any virtue to the dog on this account? I think not. Nor should we ascribe any virtue to a man in like case. The animal is carried by the strongest moving force. This requires no exertion, no self-government, but passively to yield to the strongest impulse" (p. 125). "One principle crosses another. Without self-government, that which is strongest at the time will prevail. And that which is weakest at one time may, from passion, from a change of disposition or of fortune, become strongest at another time" (p. 197).
28. "We may resist the impulses of appetite and passion, not only without regret, but with self-applause and triumph; but the calls of reason and duty can never be resisted, without remorse and self-condemnation" (p. 73).

29. "We learn to observe the connections of things, and the consequences of our actions; and, taking an extended view of our existence, past, present, and future, we correct our first notions of good and ill, and form the conception of what is good or ill upon the whole; which must be estimated, not from the present feeling, or from the present animal desire or aversion, but from a due consideration of its consequences, certain or probable during the whole of our existence. That which, taken with all its discoverable connections and consequences, brings more good than ill, I call good upon the whole. That brute animals have any conception of this good, I see no reason to believe. And it is evident, that man cannot have the conception of it, till reason be so far advanced, that he can seriously reflect upon the past, and take a prospect of the future part of his existence. It appears therefore, that the very conception of what is good or ill for us upon the whole, is the offspring of reason, and can be only in beings endowed with reason" (p. 205).

30. "I pretend not in this to say any thing that is new, but what reason suggested to those who first turned their attention to the philosophy of morals" (p. 206). He cites Cicero as his authority: "The most important difference between human beings and beasts is this: Beasts, in so far as they are moved by sense, conciliate themselves only to what is at hand and present, since they are aware of very little of the past and future. A human being, on the other hand, shares in reason, through which he traces consequences, sees the causes of things, notices the mutual relations of effects and causes, compares similarities, and combines and connects future with present things; and so he easily sees the course of his whole life, and prepares the things necessary for living that life" (Cicero, *Off.* i 11; quoted by Reid, p. 206).

31. "We see, indeed, that the same station or condition of life, which makes one man happy, makes another miserable, and to a third is perfectly indifferent" (p. 209). "The evils of life, which every man must feel, have a very different effect upon different men. What sinks one into despair and absolute misery, rouses the virtue and magnanimity of another. . . . He rises superior to adversity, and is made wiser and better by it, and consequently happier" (p. 209).

32. "It has been the opinion of the wisest men, in all ages, that this principle, of a regard to our good upon the whole, in a man duly enlightened, leads to the practice of every virtue. This was acknowledged, even by Epicurus; and the best moralists among the ancients derived all the virtues from this principle [of a regard to our good upon the whole]. For, among them, the whole of morals was reduced to this question, What is the greatest good? Or, what course of conduct is best for us upon the whole?" (p. 211).

33. This parenthesis is to be understood in the following remarks about caring about health.

34. I am deliberately using 'rational' and 'reasonable' without distinction, following Butler's and Reid's usage. Arguments for drawing (or stipulating) a difference of sense rest on controversial assumptions that are connected to our present concerns. See John Rawls, "Themes in Kant's Moral Philosophy," in E. Förster, ed., *Kant's Transcendental Deductions* (Stanford: Stanford Univer-

sity Press, 1989), pp. 87–8; S. Engstrom, "The Concept of the Highest Good," p. 753n10.

35. I am simply trying to assess this reason that Kant offers for denying that prudential imperatives can be categorical. He has other reasons too – for instance, those that appeal to the fact that prudential rules have exceptions. It is a rather complicated matter to decide whether prudential rules differ in this respect from moral principles that are at the same level of generality, and I will not go into these questions.

36. Kant expresses the same view of the Stoics in the places where he expresses approval of their moral ideal as "the most correct pure ideal of ethics," though he criticizes it as false to human nature. See *KGS* vol. 19, p. 106, no. 6607 (cited by K. Düsing, "Das Problem des höchsten Gutes in Kants praktischen Philosophie," *Kant Studien* 62 [1971]: 10). He raises a similar objection when he says in his lectures that Zeno "setzte die Glückseligkeit in den Werth und gab der Tugend keine Triebfeder," xxvii 250 (cf. *LE* p. 9).

37. See also Reid's remarks on the influence of the moral faculty: "No action can be called morally good, in which a regard for what is right has not some influence" (p. 255). The context is also relevant.

38. "These oracles of reason led the Stoics so far as to maintain . . . that virtue is the only good" (p. 212). "This noble and elevated conception of human wisdom and duty was taught by Socrates, free of the extravagancies which the Stoics afterward joined with it" (p. 212).

39. "What we call *right* and *honourable* in human conduct, was, by the ancients, called *honestum, to kalon*; of which Tully says, 'Quod vere dicimus, etiamsi a nullo laudetur, natura esse laudabile' [Cicero, *Off.* i 14]. All the ancient sects, except the Epicureans, distinguished the *honestum* from the *utile*, as we distinguish what is a man's duty from what is his interest. The word *officium, kathēkon*, extended both to the *honestum* and the *utile*: so that every reasonable action, proceeding either from a sense of duty or a sense of interest, was called *officium*" (pp. 226–7). Stewart follows Reid: "This distinction [sc. between duty and interest] was expressed, among the Roman moralists, by the words *honestum* and *utile*. Of the former Cicero says, 'quod vere dicimus, etiamsi a nullo laudetur, natura esse laudabile.' *To kalon* among the Greeks corresponds, when applied to the conduct, to the *honestum* of the Romans" (Dugald Stewart, *Philosophy of the Active and Moral Powers*, in *Works*, vol. 6 [Edinburgh: T. Constable, 1855], ii 2, p. 220). Here Stewart cites Reid in his support, and continues with Reid's comments on different aspects of the *kathēkon*. The passage from Cicero is also quoted (for a different, though related, purpose) by R. Price, *A Review of the Principal Questions in Morals*, ed. D. D. Raphael (Oxford University Press, 1948), p. 62.

40. A good example of the mistake that Reid avoids is provided by Bernard Williams, *Ethics and the Limits of Philosophy* (Cambridge, Mass.: Harvard University Press, 1985), p. 16: "This term [sc. 'deontological'] is sometimes said to come from the ancient Greek word for duty. There is no ancient Greek word for duty: it comes from the Greek for what one *must* do." Reid's comment on the *kalon*

shows where Williams's remark is superficially correct (in saying that there is no one Greek word whose sense exactly corresponds to that of 'duty'), and where it is basically mistaken (in saying that there is no Greek word that can be used to express the concept of duty).

41. Perhaps Reid is thinking of the comparison with games in Cicero, *Off.* iii 42.

42. The *De Finibus* is the apparent source (ii 80–1, 101) of Reid's reference to Cicero on Epicurus at p. 131.

43. This is the *prokeimenon* (the external objective that is aimed at). It is the "life in accordance with nature," which includes the preferred indifferents as well as happiness.

44. *KpV* 73–4. Beck's translation modified.

45. F. H. Bradley, *Ethical Studies*, 2nd ed. (Oxford University Press, 1927), p. 64.

46. This contrast comes from Sidgwick's description of Kant's influence on Whewell, in contrast to Reid: "Whewell's general moral view differs from that of his Scotch predecessors chiefly in a point where we may trace the influence of Kant – viz., in his rejection of self-love as an independent rational and governing principle, and his consequent refusal to admit happiness, apart from duty, as a reasonable end for the individual" (*Outlines of the History of Ethics*, 3rd ed. [London: Macmillan, 1892], p. 233).

47. This attitude to Kant is derived from Green, whom I have discussed in "Morality and personality," in *Self and Nature in Kant's Philosophy*, ed. A. Wood (Ithaca, N.Y.: Cornell University Press, 1984). G. Thomas's comprehensive study of Green (*The Moral Philosophy of T. H. Green* [Oxford University Press, 1987]), pp. 43, 208, discusses relevant aspects of Green's relation to Kant.

4

Happiness and the Highest Good in Aristotle and Kant

STEPHEN ENGSTROM

Kant's ethics has often been thought to differ sharply from ancient ethics, and from the ethics of Aristotle in particular, in its attitude toward happiness. Whereas the starting point for Aristotle's ethical reflections is his identification of happiness, or *eudaimonia,* as the end for the sake of which we do all that we do, Kant seems insistent that we can never determine whether an action is right or good by considering its bearing on happiness. When viewed in the light of this comparison, Aristotle's ethics seems to involve an attractive feature that is not obviously present in Kant's. For by taking happiness as his starting point, Aristotle ensures that the ethical doctrine he articulates is grounded in a conception that gives unity to practical life and whose content has some claim to be our natural end. Kant, on the other hand, while acknowledging that happiness is an end we have by nature, sharply opposes the pursuit of this end to the practice of duty and virtue. Thus, whereas Kant seems to insist that duty and virtue are at odds with our natural end, Aristotle maintains a firm grip on the appealing idea of a complete practical life centered around virtuous action and unified under the conception of our natural end of happiness.

Yet if the apparent disagreement between Kant and Aristotle is as great as this familiar comparison would suggest, then one might well wonder, as I shall (in Section I), whether they have a common conception of happiness in view and hence whether they are, after all, in genuine disagreement. Beyond this, I shall consider whether there is any conception within Kant's ethics that plays the unifying role the conception of eudaimonia plays for Aristotle, and my suggestion will be that for Kant this role is played by his

I am very grateful to Jennifer Whiting for many useful comments and suggestions and also for the leading role she played in organizing the conference at which this essay was presented. I also thank Hannah Ginsborg, Andrews Reath, and Michael Thompson for helpful discussion.

conception of the highest good. Since Kant explicitly criticizes the ancients for taking the highest good as the starting point for their ethical reflection, assessing this suggestion will require an examination of that criticism (Sections II and III). It will also be necessary to consider whether there is any significant agreement to be found between Kant's substantive conception of the highest good and Aristotle's substantive conception of eudaimonia (Sections IV and V). Kant's conception provides a distinctive kind of unity for practical life by furnishing a systematic ordering of goods and by specifying an internal (causal) connection between them; whether such unity is also provided by Aristotle's conception of eudaimonia is less readily apparent.

I. Happiness and the Highest Good[1]

1. On the surface, at least, Aristotle and Kant seem to hold sharply contrasting views about the relation of happiness to morality and virtue. Aristotle takes for granted that we all recognize from the start that happiness is our highest practical good, and he proceeds to argue that to achieve this end we must cultivate and exercise virtue. Kant, on the other hand, maintains that our natural end of happiness cannot be the ground of moral motivation; to suppose that the goodness of a virtuous disposition is contingent upon its contribution to happiness would be to adopt a heteronomous conception of morality.

But if there is a difference here, it is not as great as that between Kant and Epicurus. In opposing heteronomous conceptions of morality, Kant is especially concerned to reject the Epicurean idea that the motive for living virtuously lies in the instrumental value of such living for securing happiness. It is this idea that Kant has in mind when he criticizes eudaimonism:

> When a thoughtful man has overcome the incentives to vice and is aware of having done his often bitter duty, he finds himself in a state of peace of soul and contentment, a state that could well be called happiness, in which virtue is its own reward. – Now the eudaimonist says: this delight, this happiness is the true motive for his virtuous action. The concept of duty does not determine his will *immediately*; rather he is moved to do his duty only *by means of* the prospect of happiness. (*MS* 377)[1]

In supposing that the motive for virtuous action lies in the prospect that happiness will follow as its effect, the eudaimonist follows the path of the Epicureans, who "assumed as the supreme principle of morality a wholly false one, namely, that of happiness, and passed off for a law a maxim of arbitrary choice of each according to his inclination" (*KpV* 126; cf. *Anth.* 130). But even a casual consideration of Aristotle's conception of happiness

103

reveals that for him the virtuous action necessary to achieve the end of happiness is itself part of that end.

2. In fact, the initial appearance of conflict between Aristotle and Kant stems largely from a misleading choice of terms. So far, the word 'happiness' has been used to convey both the conception Aristotle expresses by the term *eudaimonia* (or by *makaria*) and also the conception Kant expresses by the term *Glückseligkeit*. But it is easy to see that these conceptions are by no means the same.

In his preliminary discussion of the question "what is the highest of all practical goods?" – the fundamental question with which his ethics is concerned – Aristotle observes that, as far as the name goes, people generally agree in their answer: they call this good eudaimonia, even though "with regard to what eudaimonia is they differ" (*EN* 1095a14–21; cf. 1097b22–3).[2] Presumably, then, the idea of the highest of all practical goods is part of the meaning of *eudaimonia*. Aristotle goes on to confirm that the highest of all practical goods and eudaimonia are the same, thus positioning himself to answer his fundamental question by working out a substantive conception of eudaimonia, the outlines of which he presents in his well-known "account" (*EN* 1.7). It is clear from the basic clause of that account – "activity of soul in accordance with virtue" (1098a16–17) – that eudaimonia as Aristotle conceives of it includes the exercise of virtue. It is also clear that it involves or requires other goods as well. Aristotle says it involves other goods of the soul – notably wisdom and virtue, as the dispositions exercised in virtuous activity of soul, and pleasure, as the activity's natural attendant (1098b22–99a21). And he says eudaimonia requires in addition favorable external conditions provided by goods external to the soul, such as friends, wealth, power, good birth, good children, and beauty (1099a31–b7). But there is no doubt that he takes eudaimonia to consist, chiefly at least, in activities involving the exercise of virtue: "activities in accordance with virtue are the chief determinants of eudaimonia" (1100b9–10).

3. In order properly to compare Kant's conception of Glückseligkeit with Aristotle's conception of eudaimonia, we need first to sort out two different ways in which Kant articulates it. Sometimes Glückseligkeit is characterized by reference to inclination or its immediate object, the agreeable. Thus it is said to consist in the satisfaction of all one's inclinations (*KrV* A806/B834, *KpV* 73, *G* 399) and is described as a kind of agreeableness of life (*KpV* 22, *KU* 208). So conceived, Glückseligkeit is "not an ideal of reason but of the imagination, resting merely on empirical grounds" (*G* 418): by combining representations of the agreeable objects of inclination, which derive entirely from experience, the imagination frames an ideal in which "all inclinations are united into a sum" (*G* 399).[3] Yet for this ideal to be viewed as agreeable is not yet for it to be regarded as good or as an end of action, much less as

"the highest of all practical goods." Kant denies that the agreeableness of an object entails that it is an end or something good (*KU* 208, *KpV* 58–60).

But Kant does not always characterize Glückseligkeit by reference to the inclinations and the imagination. Sometimes he relates it to the will. He says at one point, for example, that Glückseligkeit is "the condition of a rational being in the world, for whom throughout the whole of its existence *everything goes according to wish and will [nach Wunsch und Willen]*" (*KpV* 124; see also *G* 418, *MS* 387, 480). Kant identifies the will with practical reason,[4] the faculty of acting according to principles (*G* 412); and since (for reasons to be considered later) he takes a principle to be an act that determines an end, he also calls the will the faculty of ends (*KpV* 58–9, *MS* 395; cf. *MS* 385, *G* 433). Hence, on the "wish and will" characterization Glückseligkeit is regarded, not merely as the imagination's maximally agreeable ideal, but as an end of action (cf. *MS* 386, 387, *G* 415); and in being regarded as an end it is regarded as good, as in conformity with reason (*KpV* 57ff.): "The agreeable . . . must first be brought under principles of reason by the concept of an end in order to call it, as an object of the will, good" (*KU* 208).

As this remark about the relation between the agreeable and the good reveals, the difference just indicated between Kant's two characterizations of Glückseligkeit does not amount to a tension in his view. Kant's thought appears to run along the following lines: Everyone agrees that Glückseligkeit consists in everything's going according to wish and will. Though we have great difficulty arriving at a concrete specification of the abstract concept of Glückseligkeit, though we are not able to say determinately and consistently what we really wish and will (*G* 418, *KU* 430), we all know, simply from grasping this concept, that Glückseligkeit is the will of everyone. But our representation of everything's going according to wish and will is not always adequate to the concept. Often it comes to nothing more than the imagined satisfaction of all one's inclinations. Though this representation rightly reflects the fact that the imagination and the desires we have as animal beings are necessarily involved in the specification of the content of the concept (*G* 418, *KU* 430), it is nevertheless inadequate because it fails to keep in view that, since the will is practical reason, the concept's content – everything's going according to wish and will – is an object of practical reason and therefore regarded as good. Now Kant holds that one's consciousness of the moral law reveals that the virtuous activity of a good will – its wishing and willing in accordance with the moral law – is the sole unconditioned good; every other good depends for its goodness on its being the object (or possible object) of a good will (*G* 393–4). Consequently, everything's going according to wish and will turns out to be truly good only insofar as one's wish and will depend on the moral law as their fundamental principle: "Glückseligkeit is always something that, though indeed agreeable to one who possesses it, is not for itself alone absolutely and in all respects good, but always presupposes moral, lawful conduct as its condition" (*KpV* 111). Hence, the conception of everything's going according to wish and will, insofar as it involves regarding this content as good, presupposes that the wishing and willing are virtuous, and it therefore depends on the conception of virtue, even though it does not include virtue as part of its content. When united in this relation of dependence, these two conceptions make up precisely the idea of the highest good (cf. *KpV* 129–30). Since the goodness of Glückseligkeit is conditioned by virtue in the manner just described, Glückseligkeit can have a place as a component within the highest good only insofar as the other component, virtue, is present.[5] Thus, when adequately conceived Glückseligkeit is seen to be, not indeed identical to the highest good, but nevertheless internally related to it: Glückseligkeit can be rationally conceived only *through* the idea of virtue.[6]

4. Glückseligkeit, then, insofar as it is conceived as something good, is to be understood, not merely as the satisfaction of all one's inclinations, nor as including virtuous action as a component, but rather as the complement of such action in the highest good. Therefore, if we assume that Kant and Aristotle share a common conception of virtue at least to the extent that they agree that virtue consists in or essentially involves some kind of excellence or perfection of wish and will (including choice),[7] we can conclude that, since Aristotle takes eudaimonia to include the exercise of virtue as its chief constituent, whereas Kant takes Glückseligkeit to be precisely the part of the highest good that is other than the exercise of virtue, eudaimonia and Glückseligkeit are distinct.

It is worth stressing that the difference here is a difference in concept. Aristotle and other ancients see no conceptual difficulty in regarding the exercise of virtue as internal to eudaimonia. Indeed, as will be emphasized later (Section III.1), Aristotle regards the exercise of virtue as essential, and he also says there is general agreement that at least some degree of virtue is requisite: "no one would maintain that he is blessed [*makarion*] who has not in him a particle of courage or temperance or justice or practical wisdom" (1323a27–9). For Kant, on the other hand, the very concepts of Glückseligkeit, as the complete conditioned good, and virtue, as the unconditioned good, exclude the possibility that virtue could be internal to Glückseligkeit, and this is enough, he thinks, to show that Glückseligkeit is not the highest good (*KpV* 110–11; cf. *KU* 208–9, *KrV* A813/B841). And in the *Lectures on Ethics* Kant suggests that this point was appreciated by the ancients: "The ancients well understood that Glückseligkeit alone could not be the single highest good, for if all men were to hit upon this Glückseligkeit without distinction of just and unjust, then there would indeed be Glückseligkeit, but no worthiness of it and hence no highest good" (*VE* 16 [p. 6]). Moreover, whereas

Glückseligkeit according to its very idea is the sort of *Seligkeit* (blessedness) that depends on *Glück*, or fortune, and as such is the ultimate good among the *Glücksgaben*, or gifts of fortune (*G* 393; cf. *KpV* 25), no notion of dependence on fortune is involved in Aristotle's conception of eudaimonia. For although Aristotle acknowledges that for the human being eudaimonia requires in addition external goods, which depend on good fortune, he also holds that it is the gods that participate in eudaimonia most fully (1178b8–9, 21–2; cf. 1323b23–9); for Kant it would be incoherent to suggest that the Seligkeit of independent, self-sufficient divine activity is a kind of *Glück*seligkeit (*KpV* 25, 123n).

II. The Moral Law and the Highest Good

1. The preceding considerations strongly suggest that the prospect of locating a conception in Kant that answers to Aristotle's conception of eudaimonia will be greatly improved if we turn our attention to Kant's conception of the highest good. Indeed, the concept of the highest good seems a suitable point from which to compare Kant and Aristotle not only on account of its central role within Kant's ethics,[8] but also because it appears to be the very concept Aristotle is attempting to articulate through his conception of eudaimonia. For Aristotle says that the good of which he seeks to give an account – "the highest of all practical goods" – is the "end of all things done" (1097a22–3), the end that stands to all our action as health stands to the entire medical art; and Kant introduces the highest good as "the unconditioned totality of the *object* of pure practical reason" (*KpV* 108), that is, the single end pure practical reason lays down as "the ultimate object of all conduct" (*KpV* 129).[9]

But before we compare their accounts of the highest good, we must examine what appears to be a significant obstacle to any attempt to correlate Kant's conception of the highest good with Aristotle's conception of eudaimonia – namely, Kant's criticism of the ancients for taking the highest good as their starting point in ethics. We have already encountered a special case of this criticism in Kant's criticism of Epicurus for supposing that the motive for virtuous action lies in the prospect of Glückseligkeit. For Glückseligkeit, according to Kant, is what Epicurus takes the highest good to be (*KpV* 112). But Kant's criticism of the ancients for starting with the highest good is in turn a special case of his general criticism of all philosophers who seek to derive moral rules of conduct from an antecedent conception of a good to be achieved. To best ensure an adequate grasp of the point of his criticism, we should consider it in its full generality.

The general criticism receives its clearest statement in the *Critique of Practical Reason*. After commenting on the "paradox" in his method, according to which "the concept of good and evil must be determined, not prior to the moral law (for which it seemingly must even serve as the basis), but only ... after it and through it" (*KpV* 62–3), Kant says that the errors of previous philosophers concerning the highest principle of morality stemmed from the fact that

> they sought an object of the will, in order to make it into the material and the ground of a law (which was then to be the determining ground of the will not immediately, but rather by means of that object brought to the feeling of pleasure or displeasure); instead, they should have first searched for a law that a priori and immediately determines the will and only then in accordance with this determines the object. (*KpV* 64)

Instead of following the paradoxical but true method of first specifying the law that immediately and a priori determines the will and subsequently specifying the object this law determines for the will, previous philosophers first sought out an object for the will – the highest good in the case of the ancients – and subsequently derived a rule for the will, a rule by following which it might attain that object.

2. To bring the point behind this criticism more clearly into view, we need to consider Kant's notions of an object and a law of the will. Since the will is practical reason, and since "a concept [of an object] of practical reason" is "the representation of an object as a possible effect through freedom" (*KpV* 57), an object of the will is what is conceived as a possible effect of the will's exercise. Now Kant defines an end (*Zweck*) as "the object of a concept, so far as the latter is regarded as the cause of the former (the real ground of its possibility)" (*KU* 220), and he defines the will as "the faculty of desire, insofar as it can be determined to act only through concepts, that is, in accordance with the representation of an end" (*KU* 220) – in short, as "the faculty of ends" (*KpV* 58–9). An object of the will is therefore an end: it is the object of a concept that represents it as a possible effect of the will's exercise and in accordance with which the exercise of the will is determined. Since it is through the concept of the end that the will is determined in its exercise, and since it is through that exercise that the object is realized, the object's realization is the effect of that concept.

What, then, is a law of the will? The will, Kant says, is "a kind of causality of living beings, so far as they are rational" (*G* 446), so "in the concept of a will the concept of causality is already contained" (*KpV* 55). But since "the concept of a causality carries with it that of laws" (*G* 446), the concept of law is internal to the concept of the will. In the following passage Kant specifies how a law of the will is related to the will:

> Every thing in nature works according to laws. Only a rational being has the capacity to act *according to the representation* of laws – that is, ac-

cording to principles – or a *will*. Since *reason* is required to derive actions from laws, the will is nothing other than practical reason. (*G* 412)

For a rational being to act according to a law, then, is for it to act according to the representation or conception of that law, and to do this is just to act according to a principle. Kant here defines the will as the capacity to act according to such conceptions, or principles, so the concept of the will involves not only the concept of a law in general but also the specific concept of a law of the will, namely, that of a law such that acting according to it consists in acting according to the representation of it. This internal relation between the concept of the will and that of the law of the will is also implied by the characterization of the will as practical reason (which Kant here infers from his definition of the will). For if the will is *practical* reason, it is a causal power and hence has a law governing its exercise; and if the will is practical *reason*, it is the power of a rational being, and hence its exercise is governed through the conception of that law.

Before proceeding further, we should pause briefly to consider how Kant's definition of the will as the capacity to act according to principles fits with the definition noted earlier, according to which the will is the faculty of desire insofar as it can be determined to act only in accordance with the conception of an end. Viewed from the standpoint of the familiar assumptions that acting on principle involves a certain disregarding of consequences, and that ends can often be pursued in unprincipled ways, these two definitions may seem unrelated or even in tension.

The connection between the definitions lies in Kant's view that one cannot have an end without oneself making the object of one's free choice (through that choice itself) into one's end, that consequently "it is an act of *freedom* ... to have an end of action at all," and that "this act that determines an end is a practical principle" (*MS* 385; cf. *KpV* 58–9). Kant's claim that we freely choose our ends is well known and does not call for comment here. But his claim that the act determining an end is a practical principle has received less attention and may well seem more puzzling. Indeed, it will seem questionable at best to anyone who assumes that in principle a person might make into an end any (attainable) outcome or state of affairs.[10] And it is in any case obvious that whereas a practical principle involves, as Kant himself points out, "a general determination of the will" (*KpV* 19),[11] much of practical life is devoted to the pursuit of aims or objectives we would ordinarily not hesitate to describe as ends even though the commitment to them does not amount to any such general determination (e.g., to advance to a certain social position, or to pay off a debt). But we can make sense of Kant's claim if we suppose that for him, as for Aristotle (1139b2–3, cf. 1153a23–5), true ends are always activities (*Tätigkeiten; energeiai*).[12] For if we bear in mind the feature of intrinsic completeness by which Aristotle distinguishes an activity from a movement or process (1174a13–b5) – the completeness in virtue of possessing which the ϕ-ing in which an activity consists involves having already ϕ-ed, so that the breaking off of an activity (its termination in time) can never leave it incomplete, or unfinished – it is clear not only that engagement in an activity never brings one to a point at which one can say, "Now finally the activity is complete, or finished," but also that the same must be true of action that has an activity as its object. For such action must itself be an activity, regardless of whether the object is or essentially involves the action itself (as in the case of virtuous action), or lies beyond the action (in which case the action consists in the securing and sustaining of the conditions that make it possible to engage in the further activity). But action that by its nature can never pass from being unfinished to being finished is just action according to a *general* determination of the will, or principle, as is reflected in the fact that following a principle never brings one to a point at which one can say, "Now finally I have finished following this principle." Thus, given that true ends are activities, the act that determines an end is a practical principle, and hence Kant's two characterizations of the will are equivalent.

Let us return to the idea of a law of the will. Kant holds that this idea involves "the concept of an *unconditioned* and indeed objective and therefore universally valid *necessity*" (*G* 416). The necessity here is of course that of exercising the will in a certain way, and since it is unconditioned it must stem, not from any specific facts concerning one's will that might distinguish it from the will of another, but merely from the fact that what is being exercised is the will, or practical reason. For Kant says that "for [reason's] legislation it is required that it need presuppose only *itself*, since the rule is objective and universally valid only when it is valid without contingent subjective conditions that distinguish one rational being from the others" (*KpV* 20–1). Thus a law of the will "must in all cases and for all rational beings contain *the very same determining ground* of the will" (*KpV* 25), and laws of the will "must sufficiently determine the will as will, before I ask whether I have the capacity needed for a desired effect or what I have to do in order to bring it about, and must therefore be categorical, otherwise they are not laws" (*KpV* 20). If a law of the will sufficiently determines the will *just as will*, then the necessity of the way of willing represented in the idea of that law is not contingent upon any antecedent act whereby the will has adopted some object as an end. Just as no private citizen is above the law of the land, so no act of volition is above the law of the will; one act of the will can no more than one private citizen be the source of a law for another.

3. The foregoing explications of the notions of a law and an object of the will help clarify what Kant is asserting in his criticism of philosophers who

attempt to derive moral rules of conduct from an antecedent conception of some good to be achieved, but they do not reveal the basis on which that criticism rests. To find Kant's reason for denying that we can have knowledge of some good to be achieved that is conceivable independently of any conception of a law for the will, knowledge that would enable us to establish as a (moral) law for our will that we are to promote this good to the extent that we can, we must briefly examine his exposition of the concept of morality.

Kant's claim that morality has its basis in a law of the will and his complementary criticism of the attempt to derive moral rules from an antecedent conception of some good to be achieved rest together on the idea, elaborated in his analysis of common moral knowledge in chapter 1 of the *Groundwork of the Metaphysics of Morals*, that morality consists in a specific kind of goodness, which is peculiar to the good will and manifested in action from duty. What is distinctive about this goodness, or "moral worth," as Kant also calls it, is that it is "inner unconditioned worth" (*G* 393–4; see also 397–8, 400): "The good will is good not through what it effects or accomplishes, not through its fitness for attaining some proposed end: it is good through its willing alone – that is, good in itself" (*G* 394; cf. 399–400). It is particularly to be noted here that Kant is denying, not merely that the goodness of the good will stems *solely* from the good effects the good will produces, but that its goodness stems from such effects at all. The good will, he says, is "good through its willing alone"; hence it is not any better for being efficacious. Thus he is denying that the good will is aptly characterized as something we "value for its own sake as well as for the good it produces" (as we might value sport or play both for the enjoyment it affords and because it provides exercise needed for good health). To say of the good will that one values it (to whatever extent) for the good it produces would be *ungereimt* – it would be a kind of absurdity, a practical analogue of appealing to experiment to confirm a proposition of pure mathematics, and it would provide grounds for suspicion that it was in fact another concept that one expressed by the phrase 'the good will'.

We can better understand Kant's claim that the good will is good unconditionally or in itself if we bear in mind that he identifies the good in general with the practically necessary, so that his distinction between conditioned and unconditioned goods is one between conditioned and unconditioned practical necessity (the distinction underlying that between hypothetical and categorical imperatives) (*G* 412–14; see also *KpV* 58). Thus, an action is good conditionally insofar as there is something else (the condition) that, being practically necessary itself (hence something good, an object of the will) yet dependent on the action for its realization, makes the action practically necessary. The unconditioned, inner goodness of good willing, on the other hand, lies in the fact that there are no conditions on which the practical necessity

111

of such willing is contingent. Being unconditioned, this necessity cannot depend on any object or act of the will. It must therefore derive from what is the same throughout all possible exercise of the will – from the form of willing, in other words, which is what Kant takes the a priori principle or law of the will to be (*G* 400). So a good will is a will exercised in accordance with its constituting form, or law.

On the basis of the preceding considerations, then, Kant criticizes philosophers who attempt to derive moral rules by showing that the realization of some object antecedently deemed good depends on our acting according to those rules. Since the practical necessity of such action would not be an inner necessity, a necessity deriving from the will itself, any such attempted derivation will fail to account for the moral worth of action from duty, the inner goodness of the good will. To understand the practical necessity of good willing as an inner necessity, we must suppose that morality has its basis in a law of the will.

If we return now to the special case of the highest good, we can see that the fundamental consideration underlying Kant's general criticism has implications bearing on the relation between the highest good and morality. If good willing is good in itself, then its relation to the highest good cannot be such that the goodness of the good will and of the virtuous action expressing it depends on their contributing, whether instrumentally or as constituents, to the highest good. It follows further that arriving at a specification of what good willing and virtue consist in cannot be a matter of finding a specific way of willing or acting that contributes, or best contributes, to the highest good; on the contrary, since nothing can be good that conflicts with what is good in itself, the specification of what the highest good consists in must be in agreement with the exercise of the good will. In short, Kant criticizes the ancients for thinking that the specification of virtue depends on the specification of the highest good. The order of dependence, he maintains, is precisely the reverse: we do not learn about virtue by studying the highest good; we learn about the highest good by studying virtue.

III. Eudaimonia

1. Does this criticism apply to Aristotle? Aristotle identifies life in accordance with ethical virtue as eudaimonia, and he holds that a life of this sort is a life of action, and indeed of good action, since it is in accordance with virtue. But he distinguishes action (*praxis*), or doing, from the exercise of art and in general from all making (*poiēsis*), or producing, on the ground that making has an end other than itself, whereas action does not, since its end is just acting well (*EN* VI.4–5; see also 1105a26–b5), so his recognition that ethical virtue pertains to action rather than to making suggests that, for him,

in life in accordance with such virtue the "end of all things done" does not lie beyond the doing of them. These considerations suggest that insofar as Aristotle identifies eudaimonia with life in accordance with ethical virtue, he is not to be counted as one of the philosophers who take as their starting point in ethics an object of the will.

It is true, of course, that Aristotle begins his enquiry by asking about the highest good. But it can be seen from the way his exposition unfolds in the *Nicomachean Ethics* that he does not follow the approach Kant criticizes. After identifying the highest good with eudaimonia, Aristotle proceeds, on the basis of his consideration of the human function, to characterize this good as activity of soul in accordance with virtue. This characterization determines the direction of the ensuing enquiry by indicating that the task is one of studying the highest good by studying virtue (not the reverse): "Since eudaimonia is an activity of soul in accordance with complete virtue, we must examine virtue; for perhaps we shall thus better see eudaimonia" (1102a5–7). In the life of action this activity of soul is shown to involve wish for the end (i.e., for eudaimonia), deliberation concerning the means whereby the end may be achieved, and choice of action specified through such deliberation. To the extent that they are exercised in accordance with virtue, wish and deliberation issue in the choice of noble action, action chosen for its own sake and not for the sake of some end beyond itself (1120a23–4, 1176b6–9; see also 1325b5–7). The wished-for end, eudaimonia, must therefore be an end in which noble action is *essentially* contained. Hence the conception of that end includes the idea of the noble as something to be chosen "before all else" (1169a32), and thus not only functions as a practical principle, "a general determination of the will," (since eudaimonia is an activity) but also involves an objective principle, a representation of a law; and the activities of wish, deliberation, and choice together constitute the exercise of the capacity "to derive actions from laws" (*G* 412), which Kant identifies with practical reason, or the will.[13] If Aristotle takes noble, virtuous action to be *essentially* contained in the end, then he must suppose, not that the goodness of virtuous action (its nobility) depends on such action's contribution to the highest good, but rather that the achievement of an adequate conception of the highest good depends on the recognition that virtuous action is included within that end. As we have seen, this is just the way Kant thinks virtue and the highest good are related. Therefore, although Kant's characterization of the ancients as "devoting their investigation entirely to the determination of the concept of the *highest good*" (*KpV* 64) applies reasonably well to Aristotle, the conclusion that Kant draws from it, namely, that the ancients "thus posited an object which they intended subsequently to make the determining ground of the will in the moral law," does not.[14]

Aristotle does not, of course, offer anything resembling the "formulas"

113

of the moral law that are presented in Kant's *Groundwork*. But Kant does not think that achieving the abstract representation that a formula provides is necessary in order to understand how virtuous action and the highest good are related; as we have seen, he supposes that the proper understanding of the relation derives directly from the recognition, implicit in common moral knowledge, that action from duty is unconditionally good (*KpV* 8n, *G* 403–4).

2. Yet the foregoing considerations ignore a number of remarks by Aristotle that make it look as though Kant's criticism does after all apply. As we have noted, Aristotle takes as his starting point "the highest of all practical goods," the "end of all things done," and maintains that this end stands to all our action as health stands to the entire medical art (1097a15–24). Since health is an end that lies beyond, or apart from, the exercise of the medical art (1219a8–15), Aristotle's use of this analogy might seem implicitly to suggest that he regards the highest of all practical goods as an end apart from the action undertaken for its sake. The suggestion becomes explicit in Book VI when Aristotle fills out the analogy by likening practical wisdom (*phronēsis*), the virtue of practical deliberation, to medicine, and philosophical wisdom (*sophia*), the excellence of soul exercised in philosophical contemplation, to health. Just as medicine sees how to bring into being health, so practical wisdom sees how to bring into being philosophical wisdom: phronēsis, he says, issues orders for the sake of sophia (1145a6–11). This subordination of phronēsis to sophia seems to be confirmed in Book X, when Aristotle, claiming that noble actions in war and political life aim at some eudaimonia beyond themselves, argues that only the contemplative activity of reason (*nous*) – the activity in which the philosopher engages – is "complete eudaimonia," whereas life in accordance with ethical virtue is eudaimonia only "in a secondary way" (X.7–8). The subordination seems also to be confirmed at the conclusion of the *Eudemian Ethics*, where Aristotle, again drawing an analogy with medicine, suggests both that practical wisdom issues commands for the sake of contemplation of the god, and also that this relation to contemplation provides the "right rule" by which practical wisdom determines the mean in which ethical virtue consists (1249a21–b25; cf. 1198b9–20). To the extent that Aristotle identifies the highest of all practical goods, the ultimate end for the sake of which practical wisdom directs us in action, with philosophical wisdom, or with its exercise in contemplation, and to the extent that contemplation is something apart from action, it would appear that he must be included among the philosophers whom Kant criticizes for taking as their starting point in ethics an object rather than a law of the will.

3. There are further considerations, however, that bear on this question. Aristotle takes philosophical contemplation to be concerned with what is best and most honorable in nature (*EN* VI.7), with the first causes and principles

of things (*Metaphysics* 981b27–82a3), and he regards the element within the human soul that grasps first principles in contemplation – nous, or reason – as the most divine part of the human being and as our true self (1177b30–78a4; cf. 1168b28–69a3). Since Kant similarly regards reason, "the faculty of principles" (*KrV* A299/B356, *MS* 214), as the most divine part of the human being and as our true self (*G* 457–58, 461, *KpV* 86–7; cf. *MS* 439–40), there is reason to consider whether contemplation as Aristotle understands it might involve what Kant thinks of as reason's awareness of its own self-legislated first principles, its "representation of laws," and hence the awareness of the moral law itself and the thought of noumenal reality (in the ideas of freedom, immortality, and God) that this awareness at least implicitly involves. Such rational awareness is a kind of self-consciousness in that there is no distinction between the awareness and its object: as the concept of self-legislation, or autonomy, implies, in a rational being the law in accordance with which its (rational) capacities are exercised and the representation of that law are the same (*G* 412, 431–3).

Although Aristotle does not explicitly say in the *Ethics* that the exercise of nous in contemplation involves the sort of self-consciousness just mentioned, he does seem to think that what is contemplated by nous is not distinct from the contemplation itself. Insofar as contemplation is not only concerned with what is best in nature, but is also itself the best activity, it would seem that perfect, or divine, contemplation must be contemplation of itself; and indeed Aristotle draws on such considerations in arguing that "it must be itself that [divine] thought thinks" (*Metaphysics* 1074b15–75a5; see also 1072b18–30). In the human case a similar conclusion seems to follow. Nous is said to take thought of things noble and divine and also to be the most divine part of the human being (1177a13–15, b30–78a4; cf. 1168b28–69a3); its objects are "supreme among knowable objects," but it is itself "supreme among things in us" (1177a19–21). If divine activity is self-contemplation, if the exercise of nous, the most divine part of the human soul, is of all human activities the most like divine activity, and if it is through nous itself that we know these things (as evidently it must be), then the exercise of nous in the human being should involve self-contemplation as well – the self-contemplation of the first principle in the human being.[15] For Kant, such activity can only be reason's spontaneous, self-conscious exercise, its contemplation of its own constituting principles and ideas, and this activity must include the consciousness of the moral law insofar as it is only in this awareness that there is in us the consciousness of pure reason itself as a first *cause* – that is, the consciousness of pure *practical* reason – which is precisely the consciousness of freedom, "the inner principle of the world" (*KpV* 29–30, 42–3, 4n, *G* 446–7, 453–5, *VE* 269 [p. 252]; cf. *KpV* 132). This contemplation is nothing other than metaphysics insofar as it is related to practice –

insofar, that is, as it consists in the system of pure rational concepts and principles lying at the basis of philosophy understood as the science of the highest good (see *MS* 375–6, *KpV* 108).

Since Kant thus takes morality to be just the practical exercise of pure reason, there is an inner connection for him between metaphysics and morality: the principle of morality "is actually nothing other than obscurely thought *metaphysics*, which is inherent in the predisposition of reason in every human being" (*MS* 376), and consequently the contemplation of the objects of metaphysics cannot fail to issue in good action. Indeed, Kant says that the contemplation – "Betrachtung (*contemplatione*)" – of the moral law elevates the moral incentive (*MS* 397; cf. *KpV* 151–61), and that the systematic comprehension of the principles and ideas of pure reason enlivens and gives durability to our interest in the moral law (*G* 405, 436–7, 462–3; cf. *KpV* 108–9).

It might seem that for Aristotle the possibility of such a connection is precluded by the fact that the activity of contemplation (*theōria*) is theoretical rather than practical. His intimation that the heavenly bodies may belong among the objects of contemplation (*EN* VI.7) and his inclusion of physics and mathematics as well as theology among the contemplative sciences (*Metaphysics* VI.1) indicate that philosophical contemplation as he understands it cannot be simply identified with Kant's practical metaphysics. It is equally true, however, that such contemplation does not reduce to bare theoretical knowledge in Kant's sense. For whereas the latter does not concern itself with the good, or the honorable, or with ends of any sort, philosophical contemplation is above all of what is best, most honorable, and the highest end, and so could prove to be something to which practical wisdom is somehow related (1141a18–b8, 1249b9ff., *Metaphysics* XII.7).

Kant's claim that there is a connection between metaphysics and morality might still seem to be a point of difference with Aristotle, who in criticizing Plato questions the suggestion that knowledge of the Idea of the good, even if this Idea is not itself realizable by us, might yet serve as a pattern that would enable us to know and to attain the things that are good for us (1096b35–97a13), and who mentions Anaxagoras and Thales as examples of men noted for having philosophical but not practical wisdom. But Aristotle also says of the man who contemplates that "insofar as he is a human being and lives together with a number of people, he chooses to act in accordance with virtue" (1178b5–6; cf. 1179a24–30, 35–b4). And in any case Aristotle's idea that it is the business of practical wisdom to issue orders for the sake of contemplative wisdom would be difficult to comprehend were there not some affinity between them – an affinity that is perhaps suggested by his assertion that philosophical and practical wisdom are the excellences belonging to the part of the soul that has reason (*logos*) and whose exercise is truth (1139b12–13, 1143b14–17).[16]

We need to consider, then, whether there is an affinity between practical and philosophical wisdom. If such a relation can be found, contemplation might turn out to be, not a product apart from action, but an activity that is already in a sense presupposed and potentially present in virtuous action itself. In that case, Aristotle would not be susceptible to Kant's criticism.

4. Fundamental to Aristotle's understanding of eudaimonia is the idea of divine life. Aristotle says that eudaimonia is attributed to the gods and to the most godlike of men (1101b23–5), and that as the end for the sake of which we do all that we do, it is a first principle and therefore something godlike (1102a2–4; cf. 1099b16). Indeed, this idea underlies virtually everything Aristotle says about eudaimonia. It can be discerned, for example, in his remark that "the good we divine to be something that belongs to us and is not easily taken away" (1095b25–6) and in his related claim that eudaimonia is "permanent and by no means easily changed" (1100b2–3), for he regards the good as more godlike if our possession of it owes to our own doing, to our own learning and diligence, rather than to fortune (see 1215a12–19, 1099b18–25; cf. 1323b21–9). The idea of divine life is also expressed in the two criteria of the highest practical good – completeness and self-sufficiency – that he presents at the beginning of his investigation (in *EN* I.7); and he has made it obvious by the end of his discussion of contemplation that it is divine contemplation that most perfectly satisfies these criteria (*EN* X.7–8). Aristotle indicates the character of the relation that eudaimonia bears to divine life more explicitly when he excludes the beasts from any share in eudaimonia and claims, "The whole life of the gods is blessed, and that of humans too insofar as it has some likeness of such [namely, divine, contemplative] activity" (1178b25–7). Since divine contemplative life is just the activity of nous (*Metaphysics* 1072b26–7), only beings sharing in nous can share in eudaimonia; hence, eudaimonia extends to human life but not to the life of a beast: "Eudaimonia extends just as far as contemplation does, and those to whom contemplation more fully belongs more fully enjoy eudaimonia, not accidentally, but in virtue of the contemplation; for this is in itself honorable" (1178b28–31).

At first glance, Aristotle's claim that human life shares in eudaimonia or blessedness to the extent that it bears a likeness to the rational, self-sufficient activity of divine self-contemplation might seem to imply that the life he contrasts with the contemplative – the life of action[17] in accordance with ethical virtue – does not strictly speaking count as eudaimonia. But a brief consideration of Aristotle's account of the life of ethical virtue reveals that this life does bear a significant resemblance to divine activity, in particular that it shares in the rational, self-sufficient character of divine life as fully as possible given that it is a life of action, and hence that it is fairly describable as eudaimonia "in a secondary way." First, this life is, of all lives of action, the most permanent (1100b12–17; cf. 1101a8–11, 1105a32–3, 1140b29–30), for it is the most in agreement with itself and hence most closely resembles the simple and unchanging character of divine activity (1166a10–29, b5–29, 1154b20–31). Second, it uniquely involves practical wisdom, which as we have noted is an excellence that belongs to the rational part of the soul and issues directives for the sake of philosophical wisdom and contemplation; and because this life, unlike the life of someone who is merely continent, or incontinent, or vicious, is one in which the nonrational part of the soul is in agreement with this excellence, it is, of all lives of action, the most like divine contemplation in that it satisfies "the best standard of the soul – to perceive the nonrational part of the soul, as such, as little as possible" (1249b22–3; cf. 1102b13–28) – and thus is free of disturbances within the soul that would interfere with contemplation. Third, ethical life essentially involves noble action chosen for its own sake, and hence, like contemplation, it fundamentally includes thought of itself and recognition of its own inner goodness. Consequently, this life is itself, of lives of action, the most suitable for contemplation (being the best) and even one in which a kind of self-contemplation is actually involved: Aristotle says specifically of the good man that his mind is well stored with subjects of contemplation (1166a26–7), and he claims that the man who is *eudaimōn* chooses not only to act virtuously, but also to contemplate his virtuous actions (1100b19–20, 1170a2–3). (Such self-contemplation is difficult for humans, however, and for this reason, among others, Aristotle holds that one who is virtuous needs friends: because friends are other selves, contemplating them is a way of contemplating oneself [1169b30–70a4, 1213a10–26, 1244b1–45b19].)[18]

Finally, ethical life reaches its highest form through its recognition, from its contemplation of itself, of its own godlike character. This self-recognition is the basis of the virtue of magnanimity, which consists in the recognition that one deserves the greatest things and therefore the only external good great enough to be rendered to the gods, namely, honor (*EN* IV.3), which, being at bottom the contemplation of what is divine or godlike (see *EN* I.12; cf. 1183b21–4), amounts here to the contemplation by others of one's godlike life. And since ethical life is made more godlike still by its recognition of its godlike character, magnanimity is "a sort of crowning ornament of the virtues" (1124a1–2). The virtuous self-recognition lying at the basis of magnanimity seems also to be fundamental to what Aristotle calls the truest self-love – the love that assigns to oneself "the things that are noblest and best" (1168b29–30). For since Aristotle argues that the truest lover of self is the man who "chooses the noble before all else" and is therefore "rightly thought to be good'' (1169a31–2), it is such a man who, by recognizing his own goodness, has a basis for the magnanimous recognition that he deserves the highest honor.[19] Now Aristotle identifies the self that the truest lover of self loves, and hence gratifies and obeys, with the most authoritative part within, namely, nous, or reason (1168b28–69a3). Since the exercise of nous is thus itself internal to the life of virtuous self-love and authoritative for it, this life contains within itself its ultimate good. Its ultimate object of concern is what is authoritative within it, the exercise of reason – though since the life in question is a life of action, the exercise of reason is always in action chosen for its own sake according to the direction of practical wisdom.

It seems, then, that life in accordance with ethical virtue does share, so far as is possible in the circumstances of action, in the rational, self-sufficient character of complete eudaimonia.

5. The preceding reflections help point us toward an answer to our question about the relation between philosophical and practical wisdom. Aristotle's distinction between these virtues is tied to a division of the part of the soul with reason into a scientific part, by which we contemplate beings whose principles do not admit of being otherwise, and a calculative part, by which we contemplate variable things (*EN* VI.1). Philosophical wisdom is concerned with the best and most honorable things, and since these are unchanging, it is a scientific virtue; practical wisdom is concerned with actions, which belong among the variable things (1140a1–2), so it is a virtue of calculation. Yet since both virtues belong to the part of the soul with reason, and since, as we have just seen, ethical life in accordance with practical wisdom shares, so far as is possible in the circumstances of action, in the rational, self-sufficient character of complete eudaimonia, philosophical and practical wisdom seem to be related in such a way that the self-thinking of nous involved in the exercise of the former is the contemplation of the unchanging rational principle that practical wisdom, the virtue of deliberation, expresses in the particular, variable circumstances of action through its choice of "the noble before all else." What philosophical wisdom thinks abstractly as a principle, in the idea of complete and self-sufficient rational life, practical wisdom realizes so far as is possible in action. (Practical wisdom might thus itself be described as philosophical wisdom "in a secondary way.") Insofar as the contemplation of this rational principle is a more complete and self-sufficient activity than is the principle's realization in human action through the exercise of practical wisdom, it is a more complete eudaimonia. But since this contemplation is just the actualization in theoretical activity of the same principle or form that is actualized practically in the exercise of ethical virtue, it is not some object to be achieved apart from action, but rather the self-awareness of the very principle in the soul that is expressed in ethically virtuous action itself.

We can now see how Aristotle's analogy between practical wisdom and the art of medicine does not conflict with his claim that practical wisdom is not an art (1140b1–4). Since for Aristotle the physician is able to further and to help sustain the realization of health in the body only by having the medical art, and since to have this art is just to have the form of health in the soul (1032a32–b14), the analogy between medicine and practical wisdom suggests that one who is practically wise is able to further and to help sustain the realization of philosophical wisdom in the soul only by having the form of such wisdom in the soul.[20] But since practical wisdom thus furthers and sustains the realization of the very form or principle in the soul that underlies its own exercise, it works, not to make or to produce something apart from its exercise, as medicine does, but rather to achieve in the most complete, or perfect, form possible the rational activity in which its own exercise consists. If it is true that the end of practical wisdom is acting well, it is also true that the most perfect action is not action of the external, variable sort that issues from choice, but contemplation itself (see 1325b16–23). So despite the resemblance it bears to medicine, practical wisdom is not itself an art; its ultimate end lies in its own exercise and the activity of its first principle in the soul rather than in anything external to itself. Aristotle's identification of contemplation as the complete eudaimonia for the sake of which practical wisdom issues its orders does not, therefore, prevent him from finding inner goodness in virtuous action as well as in contemplation.

The active life in accordance with virtue is thus the life of action in which the divine form is most present, and we might even say that this life is just what the life of contemplation comes to insofar as it is situated in the circumstances of action. Aristotle does seem to imply, or strongly to suggest, that it is one and the same thing that is both exercised in contemplation and also authoritative for us in action when he says this "best thing" in us – nous – "is thought to be the natural ruler and leader and to take thought of what is noble and divine" (1177a14–15). The characterization of nous as ruler and leader and as taking thought of what is noble suggests that Aristotle thinks the very thing exercised in contemplation also gives the standard for action.[21] Aristotle can be understood quite precisely, then, when he says eudaimonia extends just as far as contemplation does (to humans but not to other animals) and even *is* "a sort of contemplation" (1178b24–32). A life of action is a life of eudaimonia just to the extent that it bears the form of, or some likeness to, the life of contemplation, and the life of action that bears this form most completely is the life of virtue: "The whole life of the gods is blessed, and that of humans too insofar as it has some likeness of such [namely, divine, contemplative] activity" (1178b25–7).

120

IV. The Highest Good and Eudaimonia

1. It appears, then, that Kant's criticism of the ancients for taking the highest good as their starting point in ethics does not apply to Aristotle and hence does not threaten the suggestion, broached earlier, that we have a prospect of locating a conception in Kant that answers to Aristotle's conception of eudaimonia if we examine his conception of the highest good. But before we compare Aristotle's and Kant's substantive accounts of what the highest good consists in – eudaimonia as activity of soul in accordance with virtue, according to Aristotle,[22] and virtue accompanied by Glückseligkeit as its consequence, according to Kant – we should briefly consider their formal characterizations of the highest good to determine more conclusively whether both philosophers are indeed working with the same fundamental conception.

To confirm the commonplace that the highest good is eudaimonia, Aristotle lays down two criteria a good must satisfy to be the highest good and argues that each is satisfied only by eudaimonia. According to these criteria, the highest good is (absolutely) complete (*teleion*), that is, "choiceworthy always in itself [*kath' hauto*] and never on account of something else" (1097a33–4), and self-sufficient (*autarkes*), "what by itself makes life choiceworthy and lacking in nothing" (1097b14–15). Presumably it is only through lacking something that life could fail to be choiceworthy, so the self-sufficient good can be characterized more succinctly as what by itself makes life lacking in nothing. Aristotle's understanding of what it is for life to be lacking in nothing seems to be conveyed by his remark that if (contrary to what is in fact the case) eudaimonia were "counted as one good thing among others, it would clearly be made more choiceworthy by the addition of even the least of goods; for that which is added becomes an excess of goods, and of goods the greater is always more choiceworthy" (1097b17–20; cf. 1172b23–34). It appears, then, that for life to be lacking in nothing is for it not to lack anything good, or choiceworthy. As he later says, the man who is blessedly happy "must have what is choiceworthy for him, or he will be lacking in this respect" (1170b17–18). Thus we can say that a good is self-sufficient if there is no good that could be added to it to yield a greater good.

Aristotle says that "the complete good is thought to be self-sufficient" (1097b7–8). This claim is not explained, but he may well have the following in mind: if the complete good were not self-sufficient, then there would be some further good that would need to be added to it (lest life be lacking in a certain respect), in which case there would be a greater good on account of which the complete good would be choiceworthy. This, however, is impossible, since the complete good is choiceworthy always in itself and never on account of something else.[23] It seems equally clear that, conversely, the self-sufficient good is complete (as Aristotle later suggests: 1176b3–6); for there is no good beyond it that could be added to it and hence nothing else on account of which it could be choiceworthy. The notions of the complete good and the self-sufficient good thus seem to be at bottom the same: when explicated, each can be seen to imply the other.

After introducing the highest good as the unconditioned totality of the object of pure practical reason, Kant points out an ambiguity in the phrase 'the highest' (i.e., in *das Höchste* understood as the vernacular rendering of *summa*). It can mean either the supreme (or original), "the condition that is itself unconditioned, i.e., subordinated to no other," or the consummate (or perfect), "the whole that is not a part of a yet greater whole of the same kind" (*KpV* 110).[24] Kant brings out the difference between these two meanings by claiming that virtue is a good that is highest in the former sense, but not in the latter. Virtue is the supreme good, since its goodness lies wholly within it and hence is not in any way contingent on virtue's contribution to any other good. But it is not the consummate good, for the addition of Glückseligkeit yields a greater whole of the same kind, that is, a greater good. Since Kant has identified the highest good with the unconditioned *totality* of the object of pure practical reason, his patent intention is to use the phrase 'highest good' to signify the consummate good.

The good that is not a part of a yet greater good is just the good to which there is no good that could be added to yield a greater good. So the consummate good is the self-sufficient good, and thus Aristotle's and Kant's formal characterizations of the highest good are fundamentally the same.[25]

2. According to Kant's substantive account of it, the highest good is a whole that comprises two interrelated components, virtue[26] and Glückseligkeit. What is particularly noteworthy about this account is the specific way it relates these parts to provide unity for practical life. But before we examine this relation and investigate whether Aristotle's substantive account acknowledges anything comparable to it, we need to consider whether eudaimonia as Aristotle conceives it can be regarded as comprising virtue and Glückseligkeit as components. If we view virtue and Glückseligkeit in abstraction from the specific relation Kant says they bear to one another in the highest good, the fundamental difference between them can be expressed as follows: virtue is the part of the highest good that depends solely on us (on our exercise of will or choice), and Glückseligkeit is the part that depends on other causes and hence belongs among the gifts of fortune (*G* 393, 401, 8:283n, *KU* 431, *MS* 387). So our first question is whether Aristotle recognizes such a distinction within eudaimonia.

As was noted earlier, Aristotle holds that because eudaimonia is the highest good and hence something godlike, it should not be deemed a result of fortune, but should rather be regarded as achievable by a certain learning and diligence (1099b18–25): "the good we divine to be something that belongs to us and is not easily taken away" (1095b25–6). Aristotle's account of eudaimonia as activity of soul in accordance with virtue is plainly tailored to accommodate this idea; for it implies that eudaimonia is "included among goods of the soul, not among external goods" (1098b19–20), which result from good fortune (1099b6–8, 1323b27–8), and further that insofar as "none of the human functions are as secure as activities in accordance with virtue" (1100b12–13), eudaimonia is "something permanent and by no means easily changed" (1100b2–3).

But Aristotle observes that eudaimonia is thought by some to involve favorable external conditions (1098b26) or even to be the same as good fortune itself (1099b7–8), and he notes that this opinion is not likely to be entirely mistaken. Accordingly, he acknowledges that eudaimonia "needs in addition the external goods," which result from good fortune (1099a31–b8); and later he criticizes those who claim that the man who is on the rack or who falls into great misfortunes is eudaimōn if good (1153b19–21), just as Kant criticizes the Stoics for claiming that virtue alone constitutes the highest good (*KpV* 127). It is clear that in acknowledging that eudaimonia needs in addition the external goods, Aristotle is conceding neither that eudaimonia and good fortune are the same (1153b21–3), nor that the external goods are included within eudaimonia itself, for eudaimonia is an activity of soul. His point is rather that these goods, and hence good fortune, are things on which eudaimonia to some extent depends: some of the external goods are necessary as conditions of eudaimonia, and others are naturally cooperative and useful as instruments (1099b27–8).

Aristotle's identification of eudaimonia as a kind of activity makes it reasonable to suppose that at least part of what he has in mind in acknowledging that eudaimonia needs in addition the external goods is that such goods make it possible to engage in this activity fully and without hindrance. This supposition is confirmed when Aristotle remarks, in the course of arguing that eudaimonia is a kind of pleasure insofar as its activities are unimpeded, that "no activity is complete [*teleios*] when impeded, but eudaimonia is something complete; hence one who is eudaimōn needs in addition the goods of the body and the goods that are external and of fortune, in order that he may not be impeded in these ways" (1153b16–19; cf. 1100b28–30, 1178a34–b2). Since completeness is one of the criteria Aristotle uses to confirm that eudaimonia is the highest good, this remark seems clearly to indicate that when he characterizes eudaimonia as an activity, he means, in the first instance at least, unimpeded activity. To the extent that activity is impeded, it falls short of its end and so fails to be "choiceworthy always in itself and never on account of something else." Eudaimonia, then, as the complete good, is unimpeded and hence pleasant activity of soul in accordance with virtue.[27]

But though freedom from external impediment is thus a condition of eudaimonia, Aristotle does not take such freedom to be a condition of virtue: those who claim the man on the rack is eudaimōn if good are mistaken, but not because being on the rack is enough to rob one of virtue (1153b19–21). Nor do external impediments – except perhaps in circumstances that "overstrain human nature" (1110a23–6) – prevent those who are virtuous from exercising their virtue: "none of the human functions are as secure as activities in accordance with virtue" (1100b12–13), and accordingly "the man who is truly good and wise bears all the chances of life becomingly and always makes the best of circumstances" (1100b35–1a3). And if external impediments do not keep us from a virtuous life, neither do external goods enable us to secure it: "mankind does not acquire or preserve the virtues by the help of external goods" (1323a41–b1; cf. 1323b27–9).[28] The exercise of virtue, then, does not seem to depend on external goods and fortune.

It is true, of course, that there can also be hindrances lying within the soul itself, and that Aristotle takes the presence of such hindrances to be incompatible with virtue. Thus it is because the continent man has "strong and bad appetites" that he is not to be counted among the virtuous, even though he chooses and acts correctly (1146a9–16). But since a strong and bad appetite is no less a habit or state of character resulting from our own conduct than is virtue itself (1103b13–22), it depends on us whether we become virtuous or whether strong and bad appetites develop within us (EN III.5). So although there can be internal hindrances whose presence is incompatible with virtue, it remains true for Aristotle that the exercise of virtue does not depend on fortune.

Nor, finally, does the exercise of virtue depend on nature. For though Aristotle points out that there is a sort of virtue – "natural virtue" – that does depend on nature (and in a sense on fortune: see 1179b20–3), the sort of virtue with which he is concerned – "virtue in the strict sense" – does not (EN VI.13, II.1).[29] It appears, then, that Aristotle at least implicitly distinguishes between a part of unimpeded activity of soul in accordance with virtue that depends solely on us – the exercise of virtue (in the strict sense) itself – and a part that depends on other causes.

3. Yet to determine whether such unimpeded activity can be regarded as comprising the two components that Kant distinguishes within the highest good, virtue and Glückseligkeit, it is also necessary to consider whether, as Kant understands them, these components are unimpeded – and hence pleasant – activities of soul in accordance with virtue.[30]

That the exercise of virtue as Kant conceives of it is such activity is readily apparent. Kant characterizes virtue as "the strength of the maxim of a human being in following his duty" (MS 394), which amounts to "a moral strength of the will" (MS 405), that is, a strength in the good will's determination of

124

itself in accordance with the moral law. So the exercise of virtue is an exercise of the will. But *all* exercise of the will is clearly activity of soul, for even though the will always has an object it works to produce (*KpV* 34), the exercise itself, the willing, satisfies the criterion of completeness that Aristotle gives as the mark of activity (1174a13–b5): whenever I am willing anything, I have already willed it. Hence, the exercise of virtue is activity of soul.

That the exercise of virtue is unimpeded follows from the fact that virtue lies in the good will's strength. Kant says that all strength is known only through the hindrances it is able to overcome, and that in the case of virtue the hindrances lie in the inclinations (not in external things) (*MS* 394, 405). Thus insofar as the good will is strong, its exercise is not impeded by inclinations, and accordingly virtue can also be defined as a kind of facility (*Leichtigkeit*) in action: calling such practical facility "readiness" (*Fertigkeit*), Kant defines virtue as "readiness in free lawful action . . . to determine oneself through the representation of the law in action" (*MS* 407). It is noteworthy that Kant's Latin gloss for *Fertigkeit* is *habitus* (*MS* 407): for Kant as for Aristotle, it is because virtue is a well-developed habit (*hexis*) that its exercise is unimpeded (cf. *EN* II.5).

Kant's definition of virtue as a kind of strength might raise the suspicion that virtue as he conceives of it amounts to what Aristotle would regard as mere continence rather than genuine virtue. But this suspicion can be removed by the following considerations. Continence is indeed a kind of strength – as its name, *enkrateia*, implies – but as was noted earlier Aristotle says the continent man has "strong and bad appetites" (1146a9–10), and from this it follows that his will (choice) is to that extent weak, since strength and weakness are relative. The continent man chooses and acts correctly, but not with the *facility* of one who has virtue: continence is stronger than incontinence, but virtue is strongest of all (cf. 1146a5, 1100b12–13, 1107a6–8). So whereas one who is merely continent will still experience the inclinations as hindrances or impediments and overcome them only with difficulty, one who is virtuous will have a mastery of self that entails a life in agreement with "the best standard of the soul – to perceive the nonrational part of the soul, as such, as little as possible" (1249b22–3), the equivalent of what Kant, echoing the Stoics, calls "moral apathy," which consists in the absence of influence on the will by sensible feelings and inclinations that results from the strength of respect for the moral law (*MS* 407–8, cf. *KpV* 79). Moreover, since inclinations as Kant defines them are desires that are *habitual* (*MS* 212), they arise as a result of what we ourselves do (*MS* 394, 405); so if the good will has the strength of virtue, it will not be hindered by "strong and bad appetites," but will instead be assisted by certain "sensefree inclinations" to further its ends: the former will be excluded or extirpated through discipline, and the latter developed through cultivation (cf. *MS* 484–

5, 402, 457, 213, *KpV* 159–60, *VE* 213 [p. 197], *KrV* A709–10/B737–8, *KU* 431–2). Hence, for Kant, as for Aristotle, virtuous action is pleasant (*KpV* 117–18, *MS* 484–5, *R* 23 [pp. 18–19], 1099a7–21).

4. Let us now consider the other component of the highest good. We have already noted that though the rational conception of Glückseligkeit is that of everything's going according to virtuous wish and will, Glückseligkeit can also be characterized by reference to the inclinations (Section I.3). It will prove helpful to begin by focusing on this latter mode of description.

Kant commonly characterizes inclination as "habitual desire" (see, e.g., *MS* 212, *R* 28 [p. 23]), and this broad characterization covers any desire – that is, any representation that, belonging to the faculty of desire, has some tendency to produce its object – regardless of how it arises, provided only that it is habitual. But usually Kant has in mind a narrower conception, according to which inclination belongs under the genus "sensuous desire," that is, desire that results from the subject's being affected through the senses (*MS* 212, *R* 28–9n [p. 24], *Anth.* 251, 265, *G* 413n, *KU* 206). Sensuous desire arises from pleasure felt immediately (i.e., without itself depending on the presence of any antecedent desire) in sensation, the immediate representation of some existing object (*MS* 212, *KpV* 22, *KU* 206–7; cf. *G* 413n). Kant calls this pleasure by means of the senses "gratification" (*Vergnügen*), and that which gratifies – the sensation itself – he calls "the agreeable" (*das Angenehme*) (e.g., "the green color of the meadows") (*KU* §3). Sensuous desire, then, has its source in the agreeable as such and thereby also in the pleasure taken in it (*KU* 207, 266, *KpV* 21). But the agreeable is also the *object* of sensuous desire: the object whose realization sensuous desire has as its effect is the very object whose actuality produces the desire by pleasing the subject (*KpV* 21, 22, *KU* 206–7). Because its effect is the same as its cause, sensuous desire is by its nature habitual: it is directed toward reproducing the very object that gives rise to it, and therefore insofar as it succeeds it reinforces its cause and thus itself becomes stronger and more deeply rooted (cf. *KpV* 118). So right from the start sensuous desire is incipiently habitual, and to the extent that it establishes itself through repeated satisfaction, it reaches the stage of full-fledged inclination (see *R* 28–9n [p. 24]).

From the preceding it is clear that the object of inclination, and hence also Glückseligkeit, includes only the agreeable, or what pleases by means of the senses. But since Kant defines being pleased (or pleasure) in general as the consciousness of the causality of a present representation or state of mind whereby it tends to sustain itself (*KU* 220, 20:230–1; cf. *Anth.* 231, 254), and since a self-sustaining state of mind satisfies Aristotle's criterion of completeness and hence is an activity, the agreeable can be generally characterized as activity of mind conscious of itself through feeling by means of the senses. Kant regards such consciousness by way of feeling as just the inward manifestation of life itself (*Anth.* 286), for he takes the mind to be "for itself alone entirely life (the life-principle itself)" (*KU* 278).[31] Aristotle of course identifies the principle of life with the soul (*De Anima* 402a6–7), so Glückseligkeit consists in pleasant activities of soul.[32]

Since Kant regards pleasure in the agreeable as the consciousness of a life-activity's tendency to sustain itself, it is not surprising that he also holds that the level of pleasure or pain in the activity is a matter of that tendency's degree of strength and freedom from hindrance – a matter, that is, of the heightening or impeding of the activity, of "the furtherance or restriction of the life-powers" (*KU* 278; cf. *Anth.* 231). Nor is it surprising that he holds further that whereas a hindrance to an activity weakens its capacity to sustain itself – the consciousness of such weakening being a feeling of pain (*KpV* 72–3) – the removal of the hindrance heightens the activity's self-sustaining tendency and thereby also the pleasure constituting the consciousness, the inward manifestation, of this tendency: "every diminution of the hindrances to an activity is the furtherance of this activity itself" (*KpV* 79). Thus, the agreeable activities of soul in which Glückseligkeit consists are unimpeded. (Moreover, since the inclinations result from the subject's being affected through the senses, the pleasant activities that are their causes and objects depend on circumstances external to the subject; hence the activities in which Glückseligkeit consists need the external goods in addition in order not to be impeded.)

It was noted earlier that an adequate conception of Glückseligkeit involves the recognition that Glückseligkeit is a component of the highest good and as such consists in the realization of the objects of a wishing and willing that depends on the moral law (Section I.3). It remains true that Glückseligkeit consists in the realization of the objects of all one's inclinations, that is, in agreeable activities; but insofar as Glückseligkeit is a component of the highest good, these objects are also objects of virtuous wish and will, that is, objects that reason can include within its end by bringing them under the concept of the good in accordance with the principles by which it determines that concept's correct application, the most fundamental of which being the moral law itself (*KU* 208; cf. *KpV* 57ff.). Therefore, Glückseligkeit consists in activities in accordance with virtue.

The foregoing comparison reveals that Aristotle's and Kant's substantive conceptions of the highest good agree in the following respects. Both Aristotle and Kant regard the highest good as consisting in unimpeded and hence pleasant activity of soul in accordance with virtue, and both draw a distinction between a part of this good that depends solely on us, which both identify with the exercise of virtue, and a part that depends on other causes, which

127

Kant calls Glückseligkeit, and to which Aristotle refers in effect when he acknowledges that eudaimonia depends on external goods and fortune. We have now to examine how these two components are related.

V. The Unity of the Highest Good

1. Kant's substantive conception of the highest good provides a distinctive kind of unity for practical life through the specific way it represents the relation between virtue and Glückseligkeit. On this conception, as we have seen (Section I.3), the highest good is not a mere aggregate of goods, but a whole whose parts stand in an internal relation according to which Glückseligkeit is good – a part of the highest good – just on the condition that virtue, the unconditioned, or supreme, good, is present (*KpV* 110–11, *KrV* A813–14/B841–2). This conditionality relation accounts for the two other features that chiefly distinguish Kant's substantive conception of the highest good. First, it is the basis of his occasional use of the language of desert to characterize the relation between virtue and Glückseligkeit. Kant explicates the notion of worthiness by asserting that one is worthy of the possession of something just to the extent that one's possession of it "harmonizes with the highest good" (*KpV* 130), so when he describes virtue as "the worthiness to be glücklich" (*KpV* 110; cf. *KpV* 130, *KrV* A813–14/B841–2), and when, correspondingly, he speaks of Glückseligkeit as the appropriate "reward" for morality (*VE* 61 [p. 53], *R* 161–2 [pp. 149–50]), he is expressing the conditionality relation in other terms. The second feature is that in the highest good virtue and Glückseligkeit are causally related. Since the presence of virtue is a necessary and sufficient condition of the goodness of Glückseligkeit, the conception of Glückseligkeit is present in pure practical reason's conception of the highest good as a *consequence* of the presence in the latter of the conception of virtue and its exercise. Therefore, insofar as pure practical reason is efficacious, insofar as it realizes the highest good in accordance with its conception of it, the real consequence of virtuous activity in that realization will be Glückseligkeit itself.

Does Aristotle think the exercise of virtue stands to the activities within eudaimonia that are subject to external impediment in the way Kant thinks it stands to Glückseligkeit in the highest good? Aristotle does not explicitly assert that the highest good comprises goods ordered according to the conditionality relation just described. But if the two features of Kant's substantive conception just now traced to the conditionality relation are discernible in what Aristotle says about the highest good, then there are grounds for surmise that his conception of the highest good involves, if only implicitly, the idea of conditionality present in Kant's conception and to that extent provides the same sort of unity for practical life. The question, then, is whether Aristotle takes the part of eudaimonia that depends on external goods – call it "external prosperity" – to be something the virtuous deserve and that tends to result from the exercise of virtue.

2. There is ample evidence that for Aristotle we deserve external prosperity to the extent that we are virtuous. Speaking of the descendants of a blessed man, he remarks that "some may be good and get the life they deserve [kat' axian], while of others the opposite may be the case" (1100a25). Presumably, Aristotle is supposing here that the life the good descendants deserve is one blessed with external prosperity. For he describes eudaimonia as "the prize [athlon] and end of virtue" (1099b16–17; cf. 1099a5–7), thereby suggesting that one who lives virtuously merits eudaimonia and hence external prosperity as a prize or reward. To suffer great misfortunes is therefore not a suitable fate for virtue: great misfortunes not only oppress or crush blessedness, but also insult or mistreat it (lumainetai) (1100b28–9).[33] Also relevant is the fact, noted earlier, that for Aristotle magnanimity involves the recognition that on account of one's virtue one deserves the greatest things, hence especially honor, "the greatest of the external goods" (1123b20–1). Indeed, Aristotle is explicit that virtue is what makes us worthy of honor: "honor is the prize of virtue," and therefore a bad man is not worthy of it (1123b35); "in truth the good man alone is to be honored" (1124a25; cf. 1095b26–8). And what holds here for the greatest of the external goods seems to hold for the rest of them as well, for since Aristotle makes clear that 'desert' (axia) pertains to the external goods in general (1123b17), it would appear that he is speaking with reference to all the external goods when he claims that "the better man always deserves more, and the best man most" (1123b28). Further evidence is to be found in the Eudemian Ethics, where "righteous indignation," that is, "pain felt at either success or failure if undeserved, or joy felt at them if deserved," is identified as a praiseworthy quality of character intermediate between the extremes of envy and malice (1233b23–6; cf. 1108a35–b4, Rhetoric II.9). These passages and others clearly indicate that Aristotle supposes, and moreover takes for granted that his audience likewise supposes, that external prosperity is the prize or reward that virtue deserves.

3. Does Aristotle think virtue has external prosperity as its effect? Here again there is considerable evidence. Although Aristotle denies, as we have seen, that external goods help us secure virtue, he does affirm the converse: "mankind does not acquire or preserve the virtues by the help of external goods, but external goods by the help of the virtues" (1323a41–b1; cf. 1177b2–4). Indeed, because eudaimonia is the end of virtue, those who are virtuous will act to secure where possible the external goods that eudaimonia needs in addition in order not to be impeded. And since "virtue makes the goal right, and practical wisdom the means" (1144a7–9), what the virtuous

choose and pursue as external goods will indeed be such (1176a15–18, cf. 1113a22–33).[34]

Yet although these considerations indicate that for Aristotle there is a causal connection between virtue and external prosperity, they also suggest that this connection is weaker than the one intended by Kant. Indeed, since the external goods on which external prosperity depends are, just in being external, dependent on good fortune (Section IV.2), external prosperity is not something the exercise of virtue fully ensures. Kant, on the other hand, holds that in the highest good virtue *guarantees* Glückseligkeit. Closer attention to the way Kant spells out his conception of the highest good, however, reveals that this difference is not as great as might initially appear.

Kant distinguishes between the highest good "in a person" and the highest good "of a possible world," and only in the case of the latter does he assert a strong causal connection between virtue and Glückseligkeit (*KpV* 110–11). Precisely because Glückseligkeit depends on external causes, it cannot be guaranteed by the mere presence of virtue in the individual person. The most that virtue in the individual can guarantee is "self-contentment" – a "negative" pleasure taken in one's virtue – which is different from Glückseligkeit, though analogous to it (*KpV* 117–18, *MS* 377). Hence the highest good in a person is not virtue with Glückseligkeit as its necessary effect, but only "virtue and Glückseligkeit together" (*KpV* 110). There can be a necessary connection only if certain conditions external to the individual are satisfied. Kant distinguishes two such conditions, one social, the other natural. First, virtue must be generally shared. For otherwise there is no common end, in which case the actions undertaken by some may render Glückseligkeit unattainable for others (see *KpV* 28, *VE* 28 [p. 17]). So the strong causal connection between virtue and Glückseligkeit holds, not for the individual considered in isolation, but for the community; it is collective rather than distributive (see *KrV* A809–10/B837–8, A316/B373, *G* 438, and *VE* 63 [p. 55]). But this collective connection depends in turn on the second condition: nature must be constituted so as to allow Glückseligkeit to follow from the general practice of virtue, and this is possible, Kant argues, only if it depends on a moral being (*KpV* 124–5, *R* 97–8 [p. 89]). The highest good is really possible, then, only if virtue is generally achievable, and only if nature is congenial to this ultimate end.

Kant devotes considerable attention to these two conditions, and as a result his account of the highest good has a variety of dimensions – political, cultural, religious, and metaphysical, to mention a few – some of which are at best difficult to discern in Aristotle's. Many of the specific features of Kant's account are bound up with his idea that reason (as freedom, "the inner principle of the world") is a moving force in history – that through the agency of the human species reason works (often in indirect ways) on the human species itself to realize the highest good.[35] Though this idea of a rational historical development of the human species does not seem radically incompatible with Aristotle's way of thinking, it does seem to represent a possibility he was not well positioned to consider, and herein lies an important difference that has much to do with the fact that Kant's view of what the realization of the highest good involves is dramatically more expansive than Aristotle's.

Even so, there are clear indications that Aristotle does not leave unconsidered the two conditions just mentioned. He argues that the best life for a *polis* as well as for an individual is one in accordance with virtue (*Politics* VII.1), and that it is a defining feature of a polis that it care for the virtue of its citizens (1280b5–12). He claims (in *EN* IX.6) that insofar as the citizens of a polis are virtuous, they are unanimous in their opinions about practical matters: they "agree about what is in their interest, and choose the same things, and act on their common resolve" (1167a27–8). They have in mind, not just "the same thing" (even competitors want "the same thing" – to win), but "the same thing for the same person" (1167a32–b2; cf. *KpV* 28). Nor is their agreement merely a mutual acknowledgment among citizens with different interests that their interests differ; they agree about what is in their collective interest, so whatever is in the interest of one is in the interest of the others. Thus the virtuous share a common end: they "wish for what is just and what is advantageous, and these they also pursue in common" (1167b8–9). So while citizens who lack virtue, seeking to get more than their share and to give less, come into conflict, thwarting one another's purposes and thus destroying the common good (1167b9–16), virtuous citizens act in concert for a common end and thereby collectively tend to ensure that virtue is attended with the external goods (see 1169a8–10, 1129b14–19).

Attention to the second condition can also be discerned. A number of Aristotle's remarks indicate that his conception of eudaimonia accommodates the idea, implicit in the meaning of the term, that to be eudaimōn is to be favored by a *daimōn* or a god. Thus he says that of all things eudaimonia is most likely to be a gift of the gods and that even if it is brought about by virtue and learning or training it is still "divine and blessed" (1099b11–18), since it will then be "the prize in store for those who make themselves and their acts of a certain character" (1215a18–19). Aristotle denies that the success of the man who is fortunate without being wise or good can be explained by divine provision, for he thinks it absurd that a god or daimōn should love such a man rather than the best and practically wisest of men (1247a24–9; cf. 1207a15–18). But he thinks it reasonable to suppose that the gods have some concern for a man of the latter sort – that they love what is most akin to themselves, namely, reason and wisdom above all else and hence virtue so far as it involves these, and that what they love they favor and reward (1179a23–32).

131

In sum, the foregoing considerations suggest that Aristotle's conception of eudaimonia involves the idea that virtue tends to bring about the external prosperity it deserves. That there is a connection at all is ensured by the fact that virtue itself has eudaimonia as its end; the connection is strengthened to the extent that virtue has been achieved for the polis, and to the extent that the gods have some concern for human affairs. It appears, therefore, that there is a significant measure of agreement between Aristotle and Kant even on this question whether in the highest good virtue is causally related to external prosperity. So despite the specific differences in their accounts, there seems to be a substantive conception of the highest good that they share, according to which virtue and external prosperity are united in the conditionality relation described earlier (Section V.1).

4. The remarks we find in Aristotle and Kant suggesting a divine reward for virtue may leave many of us with the sense of a difference in outlook separating us from both of these philosophers that is greater than the difference separating them from one another. But it is possible to understand this language, and more generally the attention Aristotle and Kant pay to the two conditions of the highest good previously considered, as the expression of a certain presupposition implicit in the virtuous frame of mind – implicit in the conception of the highest good and hence also in the unified practical life it makes possible. This presupposition is that the world – the social world in the first instance, but ultimately the natural world as well – is not at bottom alien or indifferent to virtue; it is the thought that well-ordered society is possible, in which the general practice of virtue can flourish, with general prosperity as its consequence, and hence that (as Kant might have put it) nature is no mere stepmother to virtue. We can still recognize this presupposition to be implicit in the virtuous frame of mind to the extent that we can join into the agreement that the foregoing comparison of Aristotle and Kant suggests is to be found between them – the agreement, namely, that it is through our understanding of virtue, our recognition of its inner rationality or goodness, that we come to understand what the highest good is (not the reverse) (Sections II–III), and that the highest good, thus properly understood as the end that virtue rationally specifies for itself, consists in virtue and external prosperity together, united as cause and effect (Sections IV–V).

This presupposition is reflected in both philosophers' recognition that the study of ethics must be complemented by the study of politics. It is reflected both in Aristotle's suggestion that it is nous that is authoritative for virtue and in Kant's assertion that the moral principle is obscurely thought metaphysics. And it is to be found in the conviction that Kant expresses in the following remark at the conclusion of the *Lectures on Ethics* – a conviction with which we now have good reason to think Aristotle could agree:

God wills not merely that we should be happy, but rather that we should make ourselves happy, and this is the true morality.

Though this conviction opposes itself to eudaimonism, it bears enough of a resemblance to it to raise the question whether eudaimonism, once properly understood (and once its crudest forms have been set aside), might not itself be recognizable as an expression, even if not a perfect one, of the presupposition this conviction reflects – the presupposition that the world can be a home for virtue.

NOTES

1. Listed below are the abbreviations used in references to Kant's works and the translations on which my own translations are usually based. Except for references to the *Critique of Pure Reason*, which use the page numbering of the first (A) and second (B) editions, and references to the *Lectures on Ethics*, which use the numbering of the edition by Gerd Gerhardt (*Eine Vorlesung über Ethik* [Frankfurt am Main: Fischer Taschenbuch Verlag, 1990]), all references use the numbering of the appropriate volume of *Kants gesammelte Schriften, herausgegeben von der Deutschen* (formerly *Königlich Preußischen*) *Akademie der Wissenschaften*, 29 vols. (Berlin: de Gruyter [and predecessors], 1902–); citations of Kant's minor works are given by the volume and page numbers from this edition. References to the *Religion within the Limits of Reason Alone* and the *Lectures on Ethics* include in square brackets the page location in the translation.

Anth   *Anthropology from a Pragmatic Point of View*, trans. Mary J. Gregor (The Hague: Martinus Nijhoff, 1974).

G   *Groundwork of the Metaphysic of Morals*, trans. H. J. Paton (New York: Harper & Row, 1964), a reprint of *The Moral Law* (London: Hutchinson, 1948).

KpV   *Critique of Practical Reason*, trans. Lewis White Beck (Indianapolis, Ind.: Bobbs-Merrill, 1956).

KrV   *Critique of Pure Reason*, trans. Norman Kemp Smith (London: Macmillan, 1929).

KU   *Critique of Judgment*, trans. Werner S. Pluhar (Indianapolis, Ind.: Hackett, 1987).

MS   *The Metaphysics of Morals*, trans. Mary Gregor (Cambridge University Press, 1991).

R   *Religion within the Limits of Reason Alone*, trans. Theodore M. Greene and Hoyt H. Hudson (LaSalle, Ind.: Open Court, 1934; New York: Harper & Row, 1960).

VE   *Lectures on Ethics*, trans. Louis Infield (London: Methuen, 1930).

2. Quotations from Aristotle's works are usually based on *The Complete Works of Aristotle: The Revised Oxford Translation*, ed. Jonathan Barnes, 2 vols. (Princeton,

N.J.: Princeton University Press, 1984). The following translations have also been consulted: *Nicomachean Ethics* (*EN*): Irwin, Rackham; *Eudemian Ethics*: Rackham.

3. For Kant's distinction between ideals of imagination and of reason, see *KrV* A570–1/B598–9 and *KU* §17.

4. Though wish is not similarly identified with practical reason, there is more to wishing than merely having an inclination (see *MS* 212–13). Kant thinks of both choice (*Willkür*) and wish – which differ in that the former is confined to objects one regards as within one's power, whereas the latter is not – as capable of being "contained under" the will to the extent that they can be exercised in accordance with practical reason (*MS* 213). The idiomatic construction in which *Wille* occurs in the above characterization (*alles nach . . . Willen geht*) suggests that, as understood here, Wille includes within its object the objects of wish and choice. But it also seems clear that Kant does not mean to include the exercise of virtue on the part of the agent among the things that go according to wish and will, since (as will be emphasized later) he claims that the exercise of virtue is a good separate from Glückseligkeit and something to which the latter must be added to yield the highest good. Unlike the exercise of virtue, Glückseligkeit depends on *Glück*, that is, on fortune, and hence is an object of wish as well as of will.

5. I discuss this conditionality in "The Concept of the Highest Good in Kant's Moral Theory," *Philosophy and Phenomenological Research* 52 (1992): 747–80.

6. Kant expresses essentially the same point when he says, "Morality in itself constitutes a system, but Glückseligkeit does not, except insofar as it is distributed in exact proportion to morality" (*KrV* A811/B839). Since to conceive of something rationally is to conceive of it in accordance with the idea of a system, Glückseligkeit cannot be rationally comprehended except insofar as it is conceived through its relation to morality (i.e., to virtue).

7. See *MS* 394, 405; 1106b36. Aristotle's and Kant's conceptions of virtue will be examined more closely later (Section IV.2–3).

8. See in particular chap. 2 of the Dialectic of Pure Practical Reason in the second *Critique*, which focuses on the concept of the highest good and includes some discussion of ancient conceptions (for which latter see also *VE* 16–21 [pp. 6–11]). For discussion of the development of Kant's view of the highest good and its relation to conceptions of the highest good in antiquity, see Klaus Düsing, "Das Problem des höchsten Gutes in Kants praktischer Philosophie," *Kant-Studien* 62 (1971): 5–42.

9. It might be objected that when Kant speaks of the highest good, he has in mind an end everyone *ought* to pursue; whereas when Aristotle speaks of the end of all things done, he has in mind, as John McDowell has suggested, an end everyone pursues as a matter of fact ("The Role of *Eudaimonia* in Aristotle's Ethics," in Amélie Oksenberg Rorty, ed., *Essays on Aristotle's Ethics* [Berkeley: University of California Press, 1980], pp. 359–64). But when Kant claims we ought to pursue the highest good, he is speaking of the highest good as specified in the substantive conception of it he articulates in the second *Critique*. If Aristotle holds that everyone in fact pursues eudaimonia, the highest good, it is clear that in holding this

he does not have in mind eudaimonia as specified in the substantive conception of it he develops in the *Ethics*. One may pursue eudaimonia, yet be ignorant of what it consists in (*EN* 1.4–5). Just as Aristotle holds that many have an inadequate conception of eudaimonia – thinking it to be "some plain and obvious thing, like pleasure, wealth, or honor" (1095a22–3) – so Kant holds that anyone (e.g., an Epicurean) who takes our natural and proper end to consist in Glückseligkeit alone has misunderstood that end (see *G* 394–6; cf. *KU* 208–9, 429–31).

10. And also, obviously, to anyone who assumes that a practical principle cannot itself be an act. But Kant's rejection of this assumption is a topic that shall here be left to the side.

11. This is a generic characterization that embraces subjective principles, or maxims, as well as objective principles; only an objective principle is a conception of a *law* of the will (*KpV* 19–20).

12. This supposition will be confirmed later (Section IV.3–4). Activity in the sense intended here is not restricted to the spontaneous activity of intellect (not all Tätigkeit is *Selbst*tätigkeit); the passive workings of the sensible, or receptive, capacities of the mind also count as activities.

13. The suggestion that virtuous action is action according to a *general* determination of the will (i.e., that it is an activity) might seem to conflict with Aristotle's insistence that "action is concerned with particulars" (1141b16; cf. Sarah Broadie, *Ethics with Aristotle* [Oxford University Press, 1991], pp. 425–7). But action can be concerned with particulars while also containing the universal: the derivation of actions suited to particular circumstances from a general conception of the end is made possible by deliberation – or as Kant would say, by judgment, which "finds out the particular for the universal" (see *Anth.* 199–201; cf. *KrV* A304/B360–1, A646/B674). And though it may be denied that a particular action, paying a debt, say, is an activity (since it is finally complete when the debt is paid), that same action, insofar as it is an expression of virtue, is done because it is what the activity of acting justly and nobly comes to in the circumstances.

14. Thus I agree with T. H. Irwin's conclusion in Chapter 3, this volume, that Kant's criticism of ancient ethics does not apply to Aristotle, though the account of Kant's criticism given in Section II differs in some important respects from his.

15. In *De Anima* Aristotle is explicit: "contemplative knowledge and its object are the same" (430a4–5). And in the *Ethics* we learn both that nous grasps first principles (1141a7–8) and that nous is itself a first principle insofar as philosophical wisdom, whose exercise depends on the exercise of nous, is a first or governing principle in the sense in which health (as opposed to medicine) is a first principle (1145a6–11, 1249b7–16; see also 1150a5).

16. For a helpful comparison of the role of contemplation in Aristotle's ethics and the role of the good will in Kant's that contrasts contemplation and good willing more sharply than does the interpretation outlined here, see Christine M. Korsgaard, "Aristotle and Kant on the Source of Value," *Ethics* 96 (1986): 486–505.

17. The life of action is a life whose chief activities consist in the exercise of the rational part of the soul in conjunction with desire rather than in independence

135

of it (cf. *EN* VI.2); it is thus a life in the circumstances of desire (and hence of need) – "human life" (see 1177b26–31, 1178a9–21). The life of contemplation, in contrast, centers on rational activities not subject to such conditions; as Aristotle notes, leisure is a condition of contemplation (1177b4–26).

18. See John M. Cooper, "Aristotle on Friendship," pp. 301–40, and Amélie O. Rorty, "The Place of Contemplation in Aristotle's *Nicomachean Ethics*," pp. 377–94, both in *Essays on Aristotle's Ethics*.

19. For further discussion of Aristotle's conception of self-love and some comparisons with Kant, see the contributions of Jennifer Whiting and Allen Wood, Chapters 6 and 5, respectively, this volume.

20. Thus contemplation is, in a sense, the form as well as the end of virtuous action, just as health is the form as well as the end of the medical art. For if, as Aristotle says, there is a sense in which through the practice of the medical art "health comes from health" (1032b11), then similarly there is a sense in which through the exercise of practical wisdom sophia comes from sophia – that is, the form that is actualized in the exercise of sophia (and in particular in the self-contemplation of nous) is the very thing on which practical wisdom depends as it works to further and to help sustain the realization of sophia. Hence there are two senses in which sophia produces sophia, just as there are two senses in which health produces health (see 1144a3–5): the form of sophia not only actualizes itself directly in self-contemplation but also works indirectly through the exercise of practical wisdom to further and to help sustain that same realization.

21. Similar language is to be found at 1168b28–69a18 (see also 1325b17–23), where Aristotle is clearly discussing nous in the context of action rather than contemplation.

22. To simplify the comparison we may henceforth focus on eudaimonia in the life of action.

23. From the conclusion drawn earlier (Section III.1) that the goodness (nobility) of virtuous action does not depend on the action's contribution to the highest good, it might seem to follow that a life of virtuous action would satisfy the criterion of completeness even if, hampered by some misfortune, it were lacking in some other respect and hence were not self-sufficient. But as will become apparent later (Section IV.2), such a life falls short of the complete good (see 1153b16–19). Because virtuous action is action, it always involves activities that depend on more than the exercise of virtue (1178b1–2), and if such activities are impeded, they are not complete.

24. Here Kant is of course speaking of possible rather than actual wholes. The highest good, as the unconditioned totality of the object of pure practical reason, is the totality of ends, and hence the highest possible good, not merely the highest good so far achieved.

25. I shall not examine here whether Aristotle shares Kant's view that virtue is the supreme good, though there is evidence suggesting he does (see, e.g., 1169a31–2, 1325b5–7, 1183b38–84a3, 1184a34–9; see also Section V, this chapter).

26. Here Kant clearly means virtue *exercised* in "moral, lawful conduct" (*KpV* 111). He has no quarrel with Aristotle's platitude that mere virtue without exercise

lacks the completeness distinctive of the highest good (1095b32–96a2). In the *Groundwork*, Kant mentions in passing that the good will is of course to be understood, not as a mere wish, but as the "summoning of all the means within our power" (*G* 394).

27. Aristotle does not hold that for activity of soul in accordance with virtue to be unimpeded is for it to be easy and altogether free of the involvement of pain. This can be seen from what he says about courage (*EN* III.9), and it seems also to be reflected in his depiction of the magnanimous man as one who relishes great action and great honor (*EN* IV.3). Aristotle's distinction between virtue and continence – a distinction that is often thought to separate him from Kant, who emphasizes that the practice of duty can be painful even for the virtuous – is liable to be given an exaggerated significance if it is not balanced against his distinction between human and divine activities: because human nature is composite, the exercise of virtue can involve pain even when unimpeded (1154b20–31; cf. *KpV* 81–4).

28. Since Aristotle holds that every virtue and in general every state of character arises and is sustained through action (*EN* II.1, 5), and since he says that "for actions many things [namely, external goods or equipment] are needed" (1178b1–2), he clearly seems to think that unless external conditions are sufficiently favorable, it will not be possible to engage in action nor consequently to have the state of character depending on it. It might thus seem that his remark, just noted, that we "do not acquire or preserve the virtues by the help of external goods" should be discounted. But the acknowledgment that certain external conditions are requisite for action and hence for the state of character depending on it does not prevent Aristotle from also claiming that it is still up to oneself how one chooses to act – well or badly – in such conditions, and hence whether the state of character one comes to have is virtuous (cf. *EN* III.5).

29. A similar distinction can be found in Kant; for further discussion, see the contributions by Christine Korsgaard and Jennifer Whiting, Chapters 7 and 6, respectively, this volume.

30. That they are in any case activities is already suggested by the fact, briefly touched on earlier (Section II.2), that Kant's characterization of the will as both a faculty of principles and a faculty of ends is rendered coherent by the supposition that for him true ends are always activities.

31. As Kant uses the term, 'life' (*Leben*) extends only to beings with perception and desire (see *MS* 211, *KpV* 9n; cf. 1097b33–98a3).

32. When considered in the light of the foregoing characterizations, inclination and the agreeable reveal themselves to be intimately related. The agreeable, as activity of soul, tends to sustain itself, but since it pleases by means of the senses, it essentially involves sensation, that is, a representation produced by some object affecting the subject (this affection may be that of an act of the mind on inner sense, as well as that of an outer object on outer sense). Hence the agreeable is an activity that depends on certain conditions: the presence of such an object and the state of the subject's receptivity to it. When these conditions deteriorate or cease to obtain, so does the activity. But the activity is the beginning of something

that survives in the form of a disposition – an inclination – to return to it. Thus, the agreeable and inclination are ultimately but different modes of a single determination of the mind, which is directed toward its full actualization: when conditions are favorable, it is activity and as such tends to sustain itself; when they are not, it is a disposition to return to that activity. If we take into account the *pre*disposition to acquire an inclination for some object upon experiencing it, which Kant occasionally mentions (see *R* 28 [pp. 23–4]; cf. *Anth.* 265), we have a triad that can be subsumed under three well-known headings from Aristotle's psychology: predisposition is potentiality (*dunamis*), inclination is habit (*hexis*), and the agreeable is activity (*energeia*) (see *De Anima* 417a21–b1).

In addition to suggesting that Kant's view of pleasure is closer to Aristotle's than is often supposed, the foregoing considerations reveal that the common assumption that for Kant all "nonmoral motives" stem from a desire for pleasure misses his distinction between the object of sensuous desire (the agreeable) and the related pleasure (gratification). The fact that Kant views the latter as a kind of consciousness of the existence of the former and hence as internally related to it may facilitate the confusion; it enables him to characterize Glückseligkeit not only as the realization of the objects of sensuous desire, but also as the related pleasure (e.g., as "consciousness . . . of the agreeableness of life" [*KpV* 22]). For some recent discussion of Kant's views on pleasure and motivation, see T. H. Irwin, "Morality and Personality: Kant and Green," in *Self and Nature in Kant's Philosophy*, ed. Allen W. Wood (Ithaca, N.Y.: Cornell University Press, 1984), and Andrews Reath, "Hedonism, Heteronomy and Kant's Principle of Happiness," *Pacific Philosophical Quarterly* 70 (1989): 42–72.

33. Compare also Aristotle's remark that the deprivation of certain external goods "sullies" (*hrupainousi*) blessedness (1099b2).

34. It is also worth noting that both Aristotle and Kant suppose that the belief that virtue tends to produce external goods is one people generally share. Aristotle supposes this in his observation that "men seem to pursue honor in order to assure themselves that they are good" (1095b26–8), and both philosophers do in their accounts of how good fortune and external goods can contribute to arrogance (1124a20–b6, *G* 393, *MS* 460).

35. This aspect of Kant's ethics is emphasized by Allen W. Wood; see Chapter 5, this volume, and "Unsociable Sociability: The Anthropological Basis of Kantian Ethics," *Philosophical Topics* 19 (1991): 325–51.

III
Self-Love and Self-Worth

5

Self-Love, Self-Benevolence, and Self-Conceit

ALLEN W. WOOD

Comparing Aristotelian and Kantian ethical theory is, by the nature of the case, less an exercise in the historiography of philosophy than a contribution to ongoing debates in ethical theory itself. Kant's knowledge of Aristotle's ethical writings may have been largely indirect and was in any case not deep. To him Aristotle was, apart from being the proponent of the false doctrine that virtue was a mean between two vices, one of the many eudaimonists of antiquity whose views were to be rejected (*MS* 6:404–5, 432).[1] On the other side, opponents of Kant (such as Sidgwick in the preceding century and MacIntyre in our own time) have often turned to the Aristotelian tradition as a way of distancing themselves from Kant and of finding what they regarded as a healthier and more realistic way of thinking about ethics.

Both Kantians and Aristotelians, then, have often proceeded on the assumption that the fundamental relation between Kant and Aristotle must be one of opposition. But this way of comparing the two philosophers has quite often rested on an unsubtle (not to say invidious) interpretation of one or the other of them. We will do a useful service to ethical theory, though perhaps a largely negative one, if we further a comparison between Aristotle and Kant founded on an accurate interpretation of their theories and a sympathetic view of what each was about.

Once we do th's, we find that it is harder than it seems to say precisely where Aristotle and Kant disagree. The common picture is that Aristotle's is an ethics of virtue or character, while Kant's is an ethics of action on moral

In preparing this essay I greatly benefited from several discussions with Jennifer Whiting. In revising it for publication I also tried to benefit from the acute comments of a number of people with whom I discussed the version presented at the conference in Pittsburgh. I am especially grateful for the comments of Annette Baier, Christine Korsgaard, Amélie Rorty, Jerome B. Schneewind, Nancy Sherman, and Gisela Striker.

rules or principles. It is also taken as self-evident that the rejection of eudaimonism is fundamental to Kant's ethical thought, while Aristotle is regarded as one of the chief representatives of eudaimonism. But the first of these differences begins to look problematic as soon as one realizes the crucial role of "right reason" in Aristotle's theory of virtue, or starts to appreciate the importance of character and virtue in Kant's theory of ethical duties. The second difference also begins to look superficial, perhaps more verbal than real, as soon as we realize that the exercise of moral virtue for the sake of what is fine is the dominant component of *eudaimonia* as Aristotle understands it, while *Glückseligkeit* in the Kantian signification is meant to include only the maximal satisfaction of empirical desires. Admittedly, it still doesn't seem right to say that Aristotle and Kant *agree* on the issues at stake. But the problem may lie not so much in saying what either philosopher thinks as in defining the issues themselves in a way that is theoretically adequate to the task of comparing their views without prejudice to one philosopher or the other. This task may be difficult, and the difficulty is more a matter of ethical theory than historical scholarship.

I

But perhaps some headway can be made even without taking on any of the harder theoretical tasks, if we choose a theme related to but still distinct from the main issues that have usually been thought to separate Kant from Aristotle. It is an important tenet of Aristotle's theory of friendship that each person is her own best friend, or at least that the good person is (*EN* 9:4 1166a–b). Against common opinion, Aristotle maintains that we ought to love ourselves (at least if we are good), and that virtuous actions are performed from self-love (*EN* 9:8 1168b28–69b2). Kant, on the contrary, asserts that when the principle of self-love or "one's own happiness is made the determining ground of the will, the result is the direct opposite of the principle of morality" (*KpV* 5:35).

The difference seems stark enough at first glance, but perhaps like the quarrel over eudaimonism the disagreement here too may be more verbal than real. For Aristotle readily acknowledges that there is an ordinary meaning of 'self-love' in which it is bad; he is arguing only that self-love is good when the term is meant in a different sense (though he thinks this new sense of 'self-love' is more proper). Aristotle agrees that self-love is blamable when it refers to people's tendency to satisfy their own appetites for external goods, such as money, honor, and bodily pleasure, and to award the biggest share of these to themselves (*EN* 9:8 1168b17–20). He thinks I am more truly a self-lover, however, when I love my true self, which is the rational or controlling part of me. If I act on this truer self-love, then I will seek to award

142

to the rational part of my soul the best things, namely, virtuous actions, which are great and fine (*EN* 9:8 1168b22–69a35).

There would be no real disagreement between Kant and Aristotle, then, if the kind of self-love Kant takes to be opposed to the moral law is only what Aristotle considers to be the ordinary or bad kind of self-love. And initially this may seem to be the case. For by 'self-love' Kant means the pursuit of happiness in the sense of pleasure and the satisfaction of natural inclinations, such as those for power, honor, and wealth (*KpV* 5:22; cf. *G* 4:393). Moreover, Kant insists that what is truly good – indeed, the only thing good without qualification – is the good will, since it alone is deserving of esteem (*G* 4:393–4), and what is deserving of esteem seems to be roughly what Aristotle means by 'the fine'. Both philosophers seem to agree that it is good to seek the best sort of good for oneself (namely, what is fine or worthy of esteem) and bad to love oneself in the sense of seeking the greatest possible share of honor, power, wealth, and sensuous satisfaction.

Yet this easy reconciliation breaks down if we look closer still. First consider that Aristotle regards self-love in the ordinary sense as something that is always bad, while Kant does not think that following the principle of self-love is always bad, only that this principle clearly diverges from the principle of morality, so that our prosecution of this principle must be limited by the constraint of the moral law. Further, the reason that Aristotle thinks ordinary self-love is bad is that it seeks to award to ourselves the biggest share of external goods, and he thinks this is bad *for us* because external goods remain genuine goods only to the extent that they support a life of virtuous activity and are chosen both in proportion to the needs of, and for the sake of, such a life (*EE* 7:15 1248b26–35, *P* 7:1 1323b7, *EN* 5:1 1129b2–5, 7:14 1154a10–20, 10:9 1179a1–18). In other words, for Aristotle bad self-love is bad in the sense that it seeks a greater share of external goods than is *good for the agent*. In Kant's view, however, successfully following the principle of self-love, though it might involve doing what is *morally* bad, could never result in what is *bad for me* (since more of my happiness would always be better *for me*). In short, Aristotle's bad kind of self-love is not the same as Kant's principle of self-love. Further, Aristotle's reasons for thinking that the bad kind of self-love is bad are quite different from Kant's reasons for thinking that the principle of self-love is opposed to the principle of morality.

Still deeper differences between the two philosophers become evident if we look at their respective conceptions of self-love. For Aristotle, good or genuine self-love is defined in terms of the various benevolent and participatory attitudes that are constitutive of love (*philia*) in general (*EN* 9:4 1166a1–10). Self-love simply amounts to taking these attitudes toward *oneself*: being in harmony with oneself and wishing what is best for oneself. Kant's conception of self-love, however – and especially his *psychology* of self-love – is more complex and displays a side of human nature that is darker and more questionable, perhaps more distinctively Christian (or post-Christian), than anything we find in Aristotle. The main difference between Kant and Aristotle on self-love, I will contend, is a difference in *moral psychology* – a difference, if you will, in their empirical conceptions of human nature. Both philosophers view self-love as a morally important topic, and both think that what is important about it has to do with alternative conceptions of the self and with people's tendency to employ the wrong conception. But whereas Aristotle thinks that the error can be corrected, yielding a rationally satisfactory conception of self-love, Kant holds that self-love is in itself not only morally problematic but also fundamentally irrational, riddled with psychic conflict and self-alienation, hence that *love* is not an attitude that clear-sighted and rational people could ever take toward themselves. My main purpose in what follows will be to explain and document this last claim.

II

According to Kant, our "predisposition to animality" contains a "mechanical self-love"; it provides us instinctively with certain desires whose natural purpose is our self-preservation, health, and enjoyment of life (*Rel.* 6:26–7, *MS* 6:419–20). This might be thought after all to provide us a parallel with Aristotle, for whom bad self-love is a tendency to gratify natural appetites, while good self-love is the tendency to award to our rational part what is truly good and fine. The opposition between good and bad self-love might thus be seen as parallel to the Kantian struggle of moral reason against the mechanical self-love of natural inclinations. We will begin to see the complexity of Kant's conception of self-love when we realize why this suggestion is fundamentally mistaken.

Kant explicitly denies that our predisposition to animality, or natural inclinations as such, are the enemy of morality, and sharply criticizes the Stoics for taking this view (*Rel.* 6:26–8, 57–8). Kant insists that natural inclinations, considered in themselves, are always good; they become evil only when misused or corrupted through a special propensity of the human will, which Kant regards as closely associated with our *rational* faculty, not as a propensity to the inordinate satisfaction of natural appetites, but as a propensity to take pleasure in ourselves. The enemy of morality, in other words, is located not in natural appetite but in reason, and it consists in a certain tendency to value the rational part of ourselves excessively, in the wrong way, or according to the wrong standards. The enemy of morality, therefore, is not natural appetite, and, since it involves a valuation of ourselves as rational beings, in some respects it bears a closer resemblance to Aristotle's good kind of self-love than to his bad kind.

Kant regularly points out that the word 'love' is ambiguous, referr two quite distinct things: 'benevolence' (*Wohlwollen* or *benevolentia*) a 'well-pleasedness' (*Wohlgefallen* or *complacientia*) (*MS* 6:401–2, *VE* 27:417/ 196). Benevolence is an inclination or wish to benefit someone; well-pleasedness is a pleasure taken in the person, chiefly in the person's perfections. The two sorts of love are distinct, but they appear to be determinately related. The love of well-pleasedness is the basis for the love of benevolence (*MS* 6:402, *VE* 27:417–18/196–7).[2] To love someone, in other words, is to be pleased by them, or by their perfections, and on this basis to have an inclination toward their good. This is why Kant insists that there can be no command or obligation to love: for we cannot constrain ourselves to feel pleased. It is also why "practical love," that is, benevolent conduct from rational grounds (which is the only sort of love that can be the object of an obligation) is not love in the proper sense of the word (*MS* 6:402, *VE* 27: 417–18/196–7; cf. *KpV* 5:83, *G* 4:399).

Since both sorts of love, love as pleasure and benevolent love, apply to oneself, 'self-love' is also an ambiguous term, denoting a similarly complex phenomenon (*Rel.* 6:45–6n). Benevolence toward oneself Kant calls 'love of oneself' (*Eigenliebe* or *philautia*), while well-pleasedness in oneself is called 'self-conceit' (*Eigendünkel* or *arrogantia*) (*KpV* 5:73). Kant describes both forms of self-love, taken together, as "selfishness" (*Selbstsucht*) or (practical) "solipsism." This he identifies in turn with the pursuit of all inclinations taken together, and formed by reason into the idea of a tolerable system, which is what Kant means by the word 'happiness' (*KpV* 5:73, *VA* 7:130).

Kant often seems to treat our desire for happiness as something simply given as part of our finite nature as beings of need; it is a desire as natural and basic as the most animal of the inclinations that go to make it up (*G* 4: 415, *KpV* 5:25). But he does not always do this, and his theory of self-love shows why he should not. For the pursuit of happiness could not possibly arise from mechanical self-love, or from natural inclinations by themselves. Happiness is an *idea* we make for ourselves through imagination and reason. Put otherwise, the desire for it is a second-order desire for the satisfaction of a certain rationally selected set of first-order inclinations. It is far from being the case that every finite being of needs would be able to form such an idea; nor, even if it did form the idea, would every such being have a reason to desire its object. The desire for happiness is a function of a predisposition of our nature that Kant *contrasts* with animality: namely, our predisposition to *humanity*, which provides us with the capacity to set ends according to reason.

The will of a brute beast, in Kant's view, wholly lacks the capacity to set ends. The brute's will in every case operates directly through an impulse or drive (*Trieb*), the representation of an object, accompanied by a feeling of

re. When a dog, for example, is in a physiological state
ives a dish of food, mechanisms of association cause it
ig the food, and this representation is accompanied by a
This state constitutes an impulse, which operates imme-
necessitating it to perform those bodily motions that result
od. The motions are not brought about through choice; the
orm them in response to the impulse to eat is hard-wired
into the ꭐꭒ﹥ stinct (*VE* 27:267/28). By contrast, when a rational being
acts on an impulse or inclination, it does so by taking the impulse or desire
as a *reason* for *choosing* to set an end, to which it then deliberatively selects
(or even creatively devises) the means. 'Humanity' is Kant's technical term
for the capacity just described; it distinguishes any rational or free will (*ar-bitrium liberum*) from a brute will (*arbitrium brutum*).

The pursuit of happiness requires a free or rational will, Kant emphasizes,
because it involves the capacity to *compare* and this capacity belongs only
to reason (*Rel.* 6:27). When Kant says this, we naturally suppose he means
that the objects of different desires must be compared with one another if we
are to decide which of them to take as a reason for setting an end (cf. *MA*
8:111), and that this process of comparison must take place on a larger,
totalizing scale if we are to frame a concept of happiness, that is, of the
satisfaction of an entire system of inclinations. That supposition would be
correct, but Kant thinks that as "humanity" (in this technical sense) is found
in the members of *our* rational species (the human species, in a nontechnical
sense), it also essentially involves comparisons of a different kind. In us,
Kant says, the predisposition to humanity calls for "a physical but *compar-ative* self-love (for which reason is required): namely, judging ourselves
happy or unhappy only in comparison with others" (*Rel.* 6:27/22).

Our pursuit of happiness thus also always involves comparing *ourselves*
with *other people*; further, the original point of considering ourselves to be
happy is that we want to think of ourselves as *better than others*; conversely,
Kant says, we think of ourselves as unhappy or badly off only to the extent
that we think of our condition as one that might cause others to despise us
(*Rel.* 6:94/85). The natural function of our original propensity to seek hap-piness, Kant holds, is to rouse human beings to develop their species' ca-pacities (including understanding and moral reason itself) through the mutual
jealousy and rivalry between people that characterize human civilization in
general (*Rel.* 6:27/22). As a natural phenomenon, then, human reason arises
in close association with what Kant elsewhere calls the "unsociable socia-bility" of the human species – the mutual dependency of human beings
through their restless competition for status in their own and one another's
eyes (*IAG* 8:21–2).[3] This explains why Kant relates the pursuit of happiness,
and the self-benevolence involved in it, to self-love in the form of self-

conceit, and why taking pleasure in oneself is even the original basis of all self-benevolence.

When viewed in terms of its natural purpose, the idea of happiness has another noteworthy feature. There is a tension between Kant's conception of what happiness *consists in* (when, or if, we get it) – namely, pleasure, desire-satisfaction, or contentment – and what *counts as* happiness considered *as an object of pursuit* – an idea whose content depends on our comparison of our condition with that of others. This tension opens up the possibility that even if we achieved what is represented in the idea, we would still not be happy (because we would still be displeased, unsatisfied, or discontented – i.e., disappointed with what we had sought once we actually got it). Kant calls our attention to this feature of the pursuit of happiness when he points out that there can be no imperatives (but only counsels) of prudence, because we can form no consistent and determinate idea of happiness (*G* 4:417–19). For the natural purpose of unsociable sociability is to give people an incentive to develop the faculties of their species through competition. It is essential to this purpose that human beings should be prodded out of their natural laziness by being placed in a condition of *discontent* (*IAG* 8:21/45). This is why Kant says that happiness is "the idea of a state to which we try to make our state adequate under empirical conditions (which is impossible) . . . for it is not his nature to stop possessing and enjoying at some point and be satisfied" (*KU* 5:430). The desire for happiness, far from aiding us in reaching a condition of lasting contentment, involves the formulation of an idea to which our state can never in fact correspond, and it is part of the natural function of this idea that this should be so. To put it bluntly, for Kant our desire for happiness serves its natural purpose by making us *unhappy*. This is the real point of his argument (often misunderstood by his readers, and consequently greeted with puzzlement or incredulity) that reason cannot have been given us in order to make us happy, since it is not well adapted to doing so (*G* 4:394–5).

III

Neither love of oneself nor self-conceit is merely an animal impulse; both are functions of our reason, and hence make claims to objective validity. This has a consequence that has been brought to our attention by Andrews Reath and emphasized more recently by Stephen Engstrom:[4] Love of oneself is not merely an animal impulse directed toward certain results. Rather, happiness is an end I set for myself, taking it to be *objectively good*; accordingly, self-conceit not only is a desire to be worth more than others, but also makes an *objective* claim to *superior self-worth*. Kant puts this point as follows: "The propensity to make the subjective determining grounds of one's choice into

147

an objective determining ground of will in general can be called 'love of oneself'; when it makes itself legislative and an unconditional practical principle, it can be called 'self-conceit' '' (*KpV* 5:74). Kant thus sees the relation within love between benevolence and well-pleasedness, where the former is grounded on the latter, as the expression of a rational connection. Claims on benevolence in general are to be grounded on claims of self-worth.

Here Kant may be seen as agreeing with Aristotle, at least as Jennifer Whiting has interpreted him. For according to Whiting, Aristotle holds that self-love is fundamentally a desire for self-worth, and benevolence to yourself is similar to benevolence to others in that both are grounded on the conviction that the object of the benevolence has the corresponding degree of excellence.[5] Thus, if (as Kant thinks) our desire for happiness is naturally a desire to be happier than others, and this desire takes the form of a conviction that our happiness is objectively good, then it must be founded on the conviction that we are worth more than others.

But is one person ever really worth more than another? Aristotle clearly thinks so. This is the basis of his account of distributive justice (*EN* 5:3 1131a8–b24), as well as his account of the (unequal) proportions of love and benefit that are appropriate to friendships between unequals (*EN* 8:7 1158b12–59a12). Aristotle regards those who make claims on great things in proportion to their worth as having the virtue of magnanimity, while those who have greater worth than others but make no greater claims are said to have the opposed vice of pusillanimity or smallness of soul (*EN* 4:3–4 1123a33–25a35).

Kant might appear to agree with this when he characterizes the good will as the worthiness to be happy (*G* 4:393) and considers the highest good in the world to include the apportioning of happiness in accordance with this worthiness (*KpV* 5:110). Yet the term *Eigendünkel*, like the English term 'self-conceit', connotes a pretense to self-worth that is false, perhaps even offensively self-deceiving. And Kant indicates that the effect of awareness of the moral law on us is always to "strike down" our self-conceit (*KpV* 5: 74). This seems to imply that no person could ever have valid pretensions to a self-worth greater than that of any other.

I think this *is* Kant's position. The basis of Kantian ethics, as presented in the formula of humanity, is that every rational being ought to be treated as an end in itself (*G* 4:429). The conception of an end in itself is closely associated with the *dignity* of rational nature, that is, the thesis that rational nature in each *person* possesses an absolute worth that can never be compared with or traded off against any other value (as the worth of all *things* may be) (*G* 4:434). Perhaps Kant makes his most vivid statement of the point in the essay "Conjectural Beginning of Human History," when he describes the change that Adam and Eve wrought in their status when they acquired knowl-

148

edge of good and evil, that is, when they broke away from natural instinct and began to set ends according to reason: "The human being thus stepped into a position of *equality with all rational beings of whatever rank* (Gen. 3: 22), namely, in respect of his claim to be himself an end, to be valued as such by every other rational being and not to be used by any as a mere means to other ends" (*MA* 8:114). The biblical reference (to God's remark that Adam has "become one of us, knowing good and evil") underlines the unqualified claim that Kant intends to be making: every rational being, simply as such, is equal to all others, even to God.

Kant argues for the dignity of rational nature in various ways. Their common basis is the idea that the very possibility of a categorical imperative depends on there being an objective end or end in itself, something whose existence has absolute worth independently of our choices or inclinations, and could therefore serve as the objective ground of a categorical imperative or practical law (*G* 4:427–8). Kant tries to show that if there is such a thing, it could only be rational nature.[6] Christine Korsgaard has brought out one line of argument for this, which she calls a "regress on conditions." Here Kant argues that because the capacity to set ends according to reason has a value-conferring status with respect to those ends, it conditions the possibility of goodness in general, and hence serves as the unconditioned condition of all goodness, which makes it absolutely good.[7] At other times, however, Kant seems to be saying that dignity belongs to rational beings not in virtue of their end-setting capacity, but in virtue of their capacity to be moral agents and actualize the good will: "Thus morality, and humanity, so far as it is capable of morality, alone have dignity" (*G* 4:435). The end in itself, he says, "can never be other than the subject of all possible ends themselves, because this is at the same time the subject of a possible will which is absolutely good" (*G* 4:437). These passages suggest that it is not so much *humanity* (the capacity to set ends) that has dignity as *personality* (the capacity to act from pure reason alone and have – or be – a good will). Here I intend as far as possible to bypass both the interpretation and the evaluation of Kant's arguments for the claim that rational beings have dignity. Instead, I will try to understand how the claim itself bears on the nature of self-worth and hence on the pretensions of human self-love.

IV

People are endowed unequally by both nature and fortune, allotted different degrees of strength, beauty, intelligence, talents of all kinds, varying temperaments, different shares of happiness (*G* 4:393–4). In Kant's view, however, none of this has anything to do with their true self-worth, which is always equal. Yet the worth of different rational beings is not merely equal re were some privileged respect in which we could compare their find it present in equal measure. Rather, the dignity of rational ...ure implies that every rational being's worth is *absolute*, beyond the reach of any possible comparative measure. Kant's view is that all the normal comparative measures of self-worth that people use – honor, wealth, power, social status in all its forms (success, prestige, attractiveness, charm, charisma, even success in relationships with others) – are expressions of an utterly false sense of values.

It seems to be a more difficult question whether for Kant there could be differences in the self-worth of people based on *moral* virtue or character. He identifies the human being's dignity with the capacity to act according to reason. But a capacity seems valuable only insofar as it is exercised (this is why Aristotle regards the human good as the exercise, not merely the possession, of virtue, *EN* 1:8 1099al), and for Kant the capacity to set ends rationally confers objective value only on ends actually set according to reason (thus not on ends contrary to morality). This points in the direction of saying that rational beings have self-worth only insofar as they act virtuously. And this seems to imply that those who act virtuously have more self-worth than those who do not.

Yet the arguments on the other side seem stronger, and even conclusive. For Kant holds that rational beings confer objective value on all their permissible ends, not only those adopted virtuously or from duty. Besides, Kant thinks we can never be certain, even in a given case, that anyone has acted virtuously or purely from duty (*G* 4:407). In any case, the moral law's command is supposed to be valid independently of whether it has ever actually been followed (*G* 4:407–8). If only virtuous wills have the status of dignity or absolute worth as ends in themselves, then it will be uncertain, or at any rate purely contingent, whether there really is an end in itself. In that case, the moral law will never be able to have the apodictic grounding it needs to command categorically. Finally, the self-worth of a rational being is supposed to be *absolute*. There is no room for degrees of membership in the realm of ends. Any being that is included, however imperfect it may be, has the same absolute worth as those perfect beings (if there are any) that exercise their rational capacities successfully on every occasion.

I conclude, then, that the only conception of self-worth that is consistent with Kant's overall position is that all rational beings have absolute worth, hence that their self-worth is incomparable and therefore entirely independent of their respective degrees of virtue. It is also his consistent position. Kant never denies (and often affirms) that even the worst human being has dignity, hence absolute worth (*G* 4:428, 431, 436, *MS* 6:329–30, 402–3, 434–5, 441, 462–3); though he sometimes relates dignity to the *capacity* for moral conduct, he never makes it contingent on acting morally.

Kantian ethics does require us to make one kind of comparative moral judgment: we are to compare ourselves with the moral law and the idea of virtue. In terms of this comparison we do gain in self-worth as we acquire virtue and meet the law's demands. Performance of duty gives us "self-contentment," while violations of duty are occasions for "self-contempt and inner abhorrence" (*KpV* 5:117, *MS* 6:387, *G* 4:426, *Rel.* 6:45n; cf. *KpV* 5: 37, *MS* 6:429).[8] Kant also thinks of virtuous conduct as an object of esteem and sometimes concludes from this that a virtuous person should have more self-esteem than a morally bad person (*G* 4:398, *KpV* 5:38, 73, 77, 81, *MS* 6:391, 405–6). But it is noteworthy that he seldom if ever expresses the esteem due to virtue and the self-contempt appropriate to moral failure in terms of comparisons between people. His most characteristic stance is to allow that one's moral achievements (over and above one's rational capacities) can be a basis for self-worth, but to block (usually on epistemic or pragmatic grounds) any attempt to use this as a basis for moral judgments involving comparisons between people. He repeatedly insists that moral judgments should involve a comparison of the agent only with the moral law or the idea of moral perfection, never with other moral agents: "Moral self-esteem, which is grounded on the dignity of humanity, should rest on a comparison not with others but with the moral law" (*VE* 27:349; cf. *MS* 6: 480).

The pragmatic argument Kant gives for this is that human nature being what it is, it has a morally bad effect on us to make moral comparisons. Our self-conceit selects comparisons that will make ourselves look good and causes us to take a self-deceptively begrudging attitude toward the virtues of others (*VE* 27:436/215). Thus, when people are encouraged to make moral comparisons between themselves and those who appear to be better than they are, the result – human nature being what it is – is not an accurate self-assessment, but only jealous hatred of those who make them look bad (*MS* 6:480, *VE* 27:437/216). On the other hand, Kant also warns against moral comparisons between people on epistemic grounds. He holds that we can never be in a position to make accurate moral comparisons, because our true moral merit is always hidden from us (*G* 4:407, *MS* 6:392–3, *VE* 27:418).

Kant's pragmatic and epistemic arguments are consistent with the position that people do regularly differ in self-worth on moral grounds, only we cannot know which comparative judgments of this kind are true, and moreover that our groundless conjectures about this tend to make worse people of us. But I have been arguing that Kant's overall position is (and for consistency must be) even more extreme: namely, that since the self-worth of every rational being is absolute, no judgments according one person more self-worth than another, even on moral grounds, could possibly be true. In practice Kant does remain strikingly faithful to this more radical position, especially in just those

151

passages where he explicitly discusses the respect we feel for the merits of others. For what Kant does is to reinterpret the comparative moral judgments we are accustomed to make in such a way that their import turns out to be wholly noncomparative. Consider the following passage:

> Before a lowly, common man, in whom I perceive an uprightness of character in greater measure that I am conscious of in myself, *my mind bows* whether I choose or not, however high I carry my head that he may not forget my superiority. Why? His example holds before me a law which strikes down my self-conceit when I compare my own conduct with it. (*KpV* 5:77)

As Kant describes it, the result of comparing myself with the humble but upright man is *not* that I admire the humble plain man for his superior virtue or merit. Instead, the effect described is twofold: first, I become aware that my own pretensions to *greater* self-worth based on my nonmoral advantages (such as my social superiority, wealth, or greater learning) are entirely hollow; second, this realization leads me to compare my conduct not with the upright man's but with my own self-given moral law. The point of my reflections on the humble man's virtue is not that I come to think of this man as better than myself, but only that I come to think of myself as less worthy in relation to the moral law than I would have been if I had done a better job of following it.

Equally striking is that later in the same passage Kant reinterprets respect for the *nonmoral* merits of others in exactly the same way:

> The respect we have for a person (really for the law, which his example holds before us) is, therefore, not mere admiration. This is confirmed by the way the common herd of amateurs give up their respect for a man when they think they have found out the badness of his character (as in the case of Voltaire); but the true scholar still feels respect at least for his talents, since he is himself involved in a business and vocation which makes imitation of him to some extent a law. (*KpV* 5:78)

The true scholar is in a position to have genuine respect for Voltaire's talents, because they serve to remind him of his duty. The judgment of the amateurs does not count as a genuine case of respect for Voltaire's talents, because Voltaire provides them with no occasion to reflect on their duty. In the case of both moral and nonmoral merit, Kant radically reinterprets respect for another in such a way that comparison between persons drops out completely. This illustrates the general truth that philosophers tend to be at greatest pains to save ordinary ways of talking precisely where they are most at odds with ordinary ways of thinking.

Kant knows that he is fighting a long ethical tradition at this point. He realizes that the illusion that self-worth can be comparative is deeply involved in the judgments of customary propriety out of which he takes rational morality to have evolved (*MA* 8:113/224, *VE* 27:300–1). As human culture began to develop, Kant thinks, people found that to maintain their sense of self-worth, they needed to behave in ways that inspire the approval of others or at least avoid inciting their contempt. Kant chides classical ethical theory because it merely supports the customary morality arising in association with this social sense of self-worth. Because the "ethical theories of the ancients" permit moral comparisons between ourselves and others, Kant says, they are all fundamentally "impure and not in keeping with the moral law"; they are not grounded in "moral humility, regarded as the curbing of our self-conceit in the face of the law" (*VE* 27:349–50/127–8; cf. *MS* 6:435–6).

V

The claims of self-conceit, therefore, are "struck down" by the moral law because they are always false a priori. Our propensity to self-conceit is thus a tendency to adopt a false set of values and a tendency to self-deception about our own worth. As Kant often emphasizes, this tendency disposes the human race both to mendacity and to self-opacity, as we try to present ourselves both to others and to ourselves as worth more than we are in comparison to them (*VA* 7:121, 132–4, 136, 332).[9] Self-conceit, as Kant depicts it, also involves a desire that is irrational in its insatiability. It is as if we were trying to vindicate our sense of the absolute (but noncomparative) self-worth that we possess as rational beings by claiming absolute comparative superiority over all our fellow rational beings. For Kant this insatiable delusion regarding our self-worth in relation to others is the basis of the *passions*, which are rationally uncontrollable desires, always directed in some way at other human beings – desires for honor, power, and wealth, for the sexual subordination of others' bodies to our pleasure, and for lawless freedom from all restraints imposed on us by their existence (*VA* 7:265–74). Since in self-conceit it is the craving to be superior to others that produces the belief that we are superior to them, self-conceit also causes us to soften the perceived demands of morality so that we may more easily persuade ourselves of our merits (*G* 4:404–5, *KpV* 5:82–7, *VA* 7:275–6, *VE* 27:357–60).

We have seen that self-conceit is a propensity to regard our own inclinations as legislative, thereby placing our comparative self-worth above the absolute worth other rational beings have according to the moral law (*KpV* 5:74). This very same propensity to invert the rational order of incentives, to place the incentives of our inclination ahead of those of the moral law, is what Kant identifies in the *Religion* as the innate propensity to radical evil

153

in human nature, which we have as rational-social beings who compare ourselves with others and seek superiority over them (*Rel.* 6:27, 93–4). 'Self-conceit' and 'radical evil' are therefore two names for one and the same propensity.

Kant's thesis of radical evil is usually regarded as a version of the Christian doctrine of original sin. (This is why it shocked and disappointed Goethe and Schiller.) Since Kant himself presents the thesis in this light, it would be pointless to quarrel with this characterization. But by emphasizing some of its non-Christian (or post-Christian) features, we may be able to avoid succumbing to the spirit of condescension in which the thesis is often discussed. The thesis of radical evil is anthropological, not theological, both in its ground and its content: its basis is not religious authority but a naturalistic anthropology and theory of history that owes more to Rousseau's *Discourse on the Origin of Inequality* than to anything we might find in the New Testament. If radical evil is rebellion, it is a rebellion not against the deity or divine law but against ourselves and the legislation of our own reason. If it is prideful self-assertion, this self-will is directed not against God's majesty, but against the dignity of our fellow human beings. Thus, we deceive ourselves if we dismiss the thesis of radical evil as some sort of superstitious or premodern misanthropy; on the contrary, it is based on a shrewd analysis of the psychology of people as they have made themselves in society – especially, in modern bourgeois society.

The thesis of radical evil represents human nature as doomed to a basic internal conflict between two equally necessary, but utterly irreconcilable standpoints regarding our own self-worth. It is nature's plan that our reason should develop through antagonism, that we should measure our worth by comparing ourselves with others and seeking superiority over them. But as reason does develop, it makes us aware that our true self-worth is of an entirely different nature, absolute and incomparable, and moreover that this very same incomparable worth belongs to all those fellow beings our natural-social self-love causes us to see as rivals and obstacles to our self-worth. Our historical destiny as rational beings is to strive to live up to the dignity of our rational nature as displayed in this new, rational standard of self-worth, by turning it against the older, natural-social standard. Our most clear-sighted experience of this conflict is to be found in the uncanny combination of abasement and exaltation that Kant calls 'respect' (*Achtung* or *reverentia*) before the moral law or the dignity of humanity. Respect combines the pain of our humiliated self-conceit with our awe and wonderment at the dignity and sublime vocation we have as rational beings (*KpV* 5:73, 161–2, *KU* 5: 245, *Rel.* 6:49).

But if the claims of self-conceit are always struck down by the law, the claims of love of oneself are merely limited by it. Love of oneself claims that my happiness is something objectively good, and in Kant's view, this may often be true. All rational beings are ends in themselves; the ends set by such beings according to reason are objectively good, and one end that all human beings have is their own happiness. Since I too am a rational being, it follows that my ends that are set according to reason, including my happiness, are objectively good.

From one point of view, my happiness is objectively good whenever it, and the actions necessary to achieve it, are morally permissible. This is the criterion of objective goodness that Kant thinks we should apply to the happiness of others, and he evidently intends the same account to apply to ourselves as well, since he thinks we have a natural (and entirely permissible) disposition to seek our own happiness whenever this does not conflict with duty (*MS* 6:388). Kant gives the name 'reasonable self-love' (*vernünftige Selbstliebe*) (or 'moral self-love') to this permissible degree of self-seeking (*KpV* 5:73, *Rel.* 6:45n). But there seems to be a difference (at least in concept) between the happiness we may enjoy without any violation of duty and the happiness of which we have made ourselves worthy by our conduct. The former is merely happiness I may permissibly seek and receive; the latter is happiness regarded as a confirmation of the self-worth I have achieved as a moral agent.

From this latter standpoint, we can view the condition that makes a rational being's happiness objectively good as its being an end set in accordance with a disposition that contrary to our propensity to self-conceit, restricts the claims of self-love by those of the moral law. Looked at in this way, what makes my happiness objectively good is that my willing of it is part of such a virtuous disposition. In that sense, the good will is what makes me worthy of happiness (*G* 4:393).[10]

It is important to recognize that the standpoint from which we see our happiness in this way is not one that is concerned with the project of making ourselves happy but rather with measuring our self-worth. Judgments about worthiness to be happy should not be seen as playing any role in deciding when we human beings are to pursue happiness (either our own or – especially – that of another). Kant never suggests, for example, that we should deprive ourselves of (otherwise permissible) happiness just because we are conscious of moral failings or lack of good will in ourselves. On the contrary, he condemns the "penance of the repentant sinner" as a form of religious hypocrisy (*Rel.* 6:12n). Still less does he suggest that we should deprive others of happiness because we judge that they don't deserve it. (This is *not* the rationale Kant gives for punishment under penal laws, which is instead that coercive force must be used to protect the right to external freedom [*MS* 6:231, 235, 331–7]. Kant has no other conception of humanly administered punishment; unlike Mill, for instance, he does not regard ordinary moral blame or feelings of bad conscience as informal punishments inflicted on people by public opinion or a system of moral education.)[11]

Notice also that when I consider my worthiness to be happy, I compare my disposition only with the moral law; I do not compare my worthiness or deserved happiness with that of someone else. This is Kant's characteristic way of considering the virtue-plus-proportionate-happiness that constitutes the highest good: he nearly always talks about each person's happiness (or even "my" happiness) and seldom about a cosmic justice that distributes happiness differentially to an entire world, rewarding some and punishing others (*KpV* 5:110–11, *Rel.* 6:5–6, *MS* 6:482, *VpR* 28:1011/41). Careful attention to the texts will show that Kant presents divine justice as comparative in this way mainly when he comments on more traditional religious conceptions (such as that of a last judgment), and tries to assimilate his own view to them (*Rel.* 6:145–6n, *ED* 8:329–30). Some of Kant's readers (e.g., Schopenhauer) have interpreted this predilection as a sign that in defiance of his own anti-eudaimonism, Kant means our interest in divine justice to be selfish.[12] My alternative interpretation of this "egocentrism" in thinking about worthiness and happiness is that Kant prefers not to think of divine justice as involving comparisons between different people's deserts because he thinks that *in comparison to one another*, people are always equal in self-worth, and therefore someone's worthiness to be happy cannot be perspicuously represented in terms of a comparison with others, but only in terms of a comparison of the person's actions or disposition with the moral law.

VI

Aristotle holds that the proper attitude of good people toward themselves is one of self-love. I believe we are now in a position to see why Kant does not agree. For Kant, self-love is a combination of well-pleasedness with oneself and benevolence toward oneself, where the former feeling serves as the basis of the latter practical disposition. Kant thinks the good person will show a limited degree of self-benevolence (love of oneself, in the form of reasonable self-love), but not on the basis of any pleasure in oneself (*MS* 6:403, *VE* 27:358/136). For a person's self-worth is not founded on what is pleasant, or useful, or honorable, or any of the other things that could lead us to be pleased with ourselves.[13] When we are conscious of having done our duty, we experience what Kant calls "self-contentment"; but this is a merely "negative satisfaction" (*KpV* 5:117). Kant rejects the traditional term 'moral happiness' as a description of self-contentment precisely because self-contentment should involve no feeling of pleasure taken in oneself. Such a pleasure would be mere self-conceit, incompatible with "moral humility" (*KpV* 5:117, *MS* 6:387–8). Moral humility, however, is by no means a consciousness of a *lack* of worth in ourselves; on the contrary, it is based on a sense of our self-worth for which a term like 'self-love' would be far too weak. One's experience of oneself as a rational nature, and especially of one's moral predisposition, is rather an experience of wonderment and awe, "exaltation and the highest self-esteem, the feeling of his inner worth (*valor*), in terms of which he is above any price (*pretium*) and possesses an inalienable dignity (*dignitas interna*) which instills in him respect for himself (*reverentia*)" (*MS* 6:436).

Aristotle (*EN* 9:4 1166a1–10) lists a series of loving or friendly attitudes that (he argues) good people will take toward themselves while bad people will not (*EN* 9:4 1166a10b–25). Kant is in partial agreement with Aristotle's contentions here, but it will be more instructive to consider where the two philosophers differ. Kant entirely agrees with Aristotle that good people will wish themselves to be and live for their own sakes. For the good person is a rational being, an end in itself, something whose life and existence are absolutely and incomparably good. But Kant is only in qualified agreement when Aristotle says that good people will wish goods (or apparent goods) to themselves, since Kant holds that people of virtuous disposition will limit their claims on happiness to those of reasonable self-love.

Aristotle holds that good people will wish to spend time with themselves, in the sense that they will find it pleasant to contemplate their state of soul and their past and future actions (*EN* 9:4 1166a23–7). Kant, however, regards self-familiarity or self-examination not as a pleasure but as a duty (*MS* 6: 441). Its performance will not be pleasant even for a good person, since the best any person can hope for is the negative satisfaction of self-contentment, and the more one examines oneself the more one will inevitably become aware in oneself of the corrupt human propensity to self-conceit or innate evil. Kant even thinks self-examination can be carried too far (as it was, in his view, by Pascal and Haller); the zeal for self-knowledge becomes counterproductive when we begin to find in ourselves only what we have put there, and lose ourselves (as religious people often do) in anguishing or terrifying fantasies; beyond this point he thinks that straining ourselves to achieve greater self-honesty will lead not to truth but only to madness (*VA* 7:133–4).

Aristotle holds that good people will agree with their own choices and share their own distress and enjoyment, while the bad person will have conflicting desires, feeling both pleasure and pain at the same things (*EN* 9:4 1166b20–5). Kant agrees with this only to the extent that the good person will strive to cultivate those inclinations that are likely to harmonize with morality (*MS* 6:402, *VE* 27:456–7/236–7). But Kant insists that no inclination will ever *reliably* produce good actions; only the motive of duty can do that (*G* 4:390). This is because in his view the human will is irredeemably in conflict. The pretense that we might someday be able to do good spontaneously, without the self-constraint of the law, is nothing but sentimental "moral enthusiasm" and a dangerous form of self-conceit (*KpV* 5:82–6, 155). If I am the best sort of person it is possible for me to be, I will resolve to combat my innate propensity to evil. Hence not only will I be in conflict with myself, but I will *deliberately create* a state of antagonism with myself regarding my fundamental maxim (*Rel.* 6:47–8). Even the pure feeling of respect itself is deeply conflictual, involving as it does a mixture of humiliation and exaltation. Thus, good people as well as wicked ones are bound to be self-alienated and antagonistic to themselves. They will be, to put it in Aristotle's terms, torn apart by different desires and distressed at having one set of desires restrained while another set are satisfied (cf. *EN* 9:4 1166b20–5).

VII

Kant and Aristotle are in fundamental agreement on many points about the human self, self-worth, and self-benevolence. They identify the self with rational nature, which has in it something capable of inspiring reverence and awe – in that sense something akin to the divine (*EN* 10:8 1177b28). They agree too that rational self-benevolence follows upon rational self-esteem and that true self-worth, which derives from virtuous action, is to be judged only from the standpoint of reason. From these points Aristotle infers (quite straightforwardly) that good people will take pleasure in themselves, seek their own good, and live with themselves in psychic harmony. For Kant, however, good people will value themselves and seek their own good wherever self-benevolence violates no duty, but they will not be friends to themselves in most of the ways Aristotle had in mind.

Kant's reasons for taking this position are partly ethical – based on the idea that the self-worth of every rational agent is absolute, hence equal to that of every other. But they are also, and to an even greater extent, psychological or anthropological, based on Kant's theory of the empirical constitution of human nature and the powerful role that the irrational propensity to self-conceit plays in our psychological economy. It should not surprise us, of course, that beings who are deeply irrational are not destined to be their own best friends. But we understand Kant's ethical theory better if we appreciate that its fundamental commitment to the sovereignty of reason takes the form it does only because human nature is understood to be so profoundly resistant to reason.

NOTES

1. In citing works of Aristotle and Kant, the following abbreviations will be used:

Works of Aristotle

Aristotle's works will be cited by book, chapter, and Bekker number.

EE   *Eudemian Ethics*
EN   *Nicomachean Ethics*
MM   *Magna Moralia*
P   *Politics*

Works of Kant

Kant's works will be cited by volume and page number in the edition of the Berlin Akademie (1910–) (sometimes page citations to a standard English translation will also be provided).

ED   *Das Ende aller Dinge* (1794).
        "The End of All Things," in L. W. Beck, ed., *Kant on History* (Indianapolis, Ind.: Bobbs-Merrill, 1963).
G   *Grundlegung zur Metaphysik der Sitten* (1785).
        Foundations of the Metaphysics of Morals, trans. Lewis White Beck, 2nd edition (New York: Macmillan, 1990).
IAG   *Idee zu einer allgemeinen Geschichte in weltbürgerlicher Absicht* (1784).
        "Idea for a Universal History with a Cosmopolitan Purpose," in Hans Reiss, ed., *Kant: Political Writings*, 2nd edition (Cambridge University Press, 1991).
KpV   *Kritik der praktischen Vernunft* (1788).
        Critique of Practical Reason, trans. Lewis White Beck (Indianapolis, Ind.: Bobbs-Merrill, 1956).
KU   *Kritik der Urtheilskraft* (1790).
        Critique of Judgment, trans. Werner Pluhar (Indianapolis, Ind.: Hackett, 1987).
MA   *Muthmasslicher Anfang der Menschengeschichte* (1786).
        "Conjectures on the Beginning of Human History," in *Kant: Political Writings*.
MS   *Metaphysik der Sitten* (1797).
        Metaphysics of Morals, trans. M. Gregor (Cambridge University Press, 1991).
Rel.   *Religion innerhalb der Grenzen der blossen Vernunft* (1793–4).
        Religion within the Limits of Reason Alone, trans. Theodore M. Greene and Hoyt H. Hudson (New York: Harper & Row, 1960).
VA   *Anthropologie in pragmatischer Hinsicht* (1798).
        Anthropology from a Pragmatic Standpoint, trans. Mary J. Gregor (Dordrecht: Nijhoff, 1974).

159

VE   *Moralphilosophie Collins.*
        Lectures on Ethics, trans. Louis Infield (New York: Harper, 1963).
VpR   *Religionslehre Pölitz.*
        Lectures on Philosophical Theology, trans. Allen W. Wood and Gertrude
        M. Clark (Ithaca, N.Y.: Cornell University Press, 1978).

2. It is true, as Christine Korsgaard has pointed out to me, that Kant never says this
directly in so many words. But I think it is clear nevertheless that this is what he
thinks. Kant's interpretation of the biblical injunction "Love your neighbor" is
"Do good to your fellow human being and your benevolence will produce love
of human beings in you (as an aptitude of the inclination to benevolence in general). Hence, only love that is well-pleasedness [in another's perfection] (*amor
complacientiae*) is direct" (*MS* 6:402). When Kant calls *amor complacientiae* (love
as pleasure) the only "direct" love, he implies that *amor benevolentiae* (benevolent love) is indirect, and that we get benevolent love indirectly through love as
pleasure. What, after all, is it that Kant thinks will be produced in you by benevolent conduct? Surely it is an inclination to such conduct. But then what this
passage seems to be saying is that benevolent love as inclination to benevolent
conduct isn't produced directly by benevolent love as a moral disposition, but
instead this is produced indirectly, that is, via a different sort of love; and in the
very next sentence he says that the only "direct" love is love as pleasure. In the
lectures (*VE* 27:417–18/196–7) Kant distinguishes between love as pleasure and
benevolent love, and between sensuous and intellectual forms of the latter; then
he asks, "Which well-pleasedness of the intellect is it that generates inclination
[to benevolent love]?" This question seems to presuppose that well-pleasedness
(love as pleasure) generates inclinations to benevolence. But there is no reason to
think that this connection between love as pleasure and benevolent love is thought
to exist *only* when the love as pleasure is produced by a morally benevolent disposition; on the contrary, the benevolent disposition is merely one way of bringing
about pathological love in general, which is a pairing of love as pleasure and
benevolent love, with the former producing the latter.

3. This is the meaning of Kant's words in the opening paragraph of the *Foundations*
(which we read right over without understanding them): "Power, riches, honor,
even health, general well-being, and the contentment with one's condition called
happiness, make for pride and even arrogance if there is not a good will to correct
their influence on the mind" (*G* 4:393). Arrogance is not merely one possible side-
effect of thinking oneself happy; rather, Kant thinks that arrogance is the whole
rationale for wanting to be happy in the first place. We form the idea of a comprehensive whole of satisfaction in order to compare ourselves with others, always
with the hope that the comparison will make us look good.

4. Andrews Reath, "Kant's Theory of Moral Sensibility: Respect for the Law and
the Influence of Inclination," *Kant-Studien* 80 (1989): 284–302; Stephen Engstrom, "The Concept of the Highest Good in Kant's Moral Theory," *Philosophy
and Phenomenological Research* 52 (1992): 747–80.

5. Jennifer Whiting, "Impersonal Friends," *Monist* 74 (1991): 3–29.

6. He apparently thinks the argument is fully complete only in sect. 3 of the *Foun-*

dations, after it has been shown that we must attribute freedom to the will of all rational beings, because rational volition is truly such only if the will is free (*G* 4:429; cf. *G* 4:447).

7. Christine Korsgaard, "Kant's Formula of Humanity," *Kant-Studien* 77 (1986): 196–7.

8. This is the Kantian way of understanding such moral attitudes as shame, guilt, and penitence – to the extent that such attitudes can be endorsed by reason at all in their customary religious form; Kant thinks these attitudes are often nothing but emotional self-indulgence and an easy substitute for improving one's conduct (*Rel.* 6:51/47, 76/71, 172/160).

9. This is also his basis for characterizing inclination as "the deceiver within ourselves" (*VA* 7:151).

10. The argument behind this claim is worked out in detail by Engstrom, "Concept of the Highest Good," esp. pp. 762–7.

11. John Stuart Mill, *Utilitarianism*, ed. George Sher (Indianapolis, Ind.: Hackett, 1979), pp. 27–8.

12. Arthur Schopenhauer, *The World as Will and Representation*, trans. E. F. J. Payne (New York: Dover, 1958), vol.1, p. 524.

13. Aristotle seems to express agreement with this thought at least once, since he says of the man who awards himself the fine that he is not a *philautos*, but rather a *philagathos* (*MM* 2:14 1212b17).

6

Self-Love and Authoritative Virtue: Prolegomenon to a Kantian Reading of *Eudemian Ethics* viii 3

JENNIFER WHITING

My primary text is the last chapter of the *Eudemian Ethics*, where Aristotle introduces the distinction between the merely *agathos* (or good) man and the *kaloskagathos* (or fine-and-good) man.[1] Since the concerns of this text may seem somewhat far removed from the topic of self-love and self-worth, I should explain how I came to focus on it.

Allen Wood and I were originally paired (at the conference on which this book is based) because he had been relying in his interpretation of Kant on a view I had attributed to Aristotle: the view that there is an important sense in which self-love is, or should be, based on self-worth.[2] Kant's idea, according to Wood, is that the capacity to set ends is what gives rational nature an absolute or unconditional worth, making it an end in itself. Moreover, the exercise of this capacity is the condition for the goodness of all other ends. On this view, "the goodness of any [other] end consists in the fact that it is an object of rational choice." Rational choice thus becomes what Korsgaard calls a "value-conferring property," and practical reasoning is grounded in the self-worth of rational beings in the following way: it makes sense for an agent to value the ends she sets only to the extent that she esteems herself as a being who sets ends according to reason.[3]

Since Wood was suggesting similarities between Kant's view and the view I had attributed to Aristotle, I set about contemplating the extent to which my Aristotle could agree with Wood's Kant. What troubled me most was the

I would like to thank the Andrew W. Mellon Foundation for supporting my fellowship at the Center for Advanced Study in the Behavioral Sciences, during which I completed this essay. I would also like to thank Allen Wood, David Gauthier, Brad Inwood, Phillip Mitsis, and Gisela Striker – as well as those attending the Aristotle–Kant seminar I gave with Steve Engstrom – for helpful comments at various points along the way. I am especially indebted to Steve for much profitable discussion and many helpful comments on the penultimate draft. But my greatest debt is to Terry Irwin, for all that I've learned from him about Aristotle's ethics.

idea of attributing to Aristotle the view that rationality is (in the relevant sense) a value-*conferring* property. What stuck in my head was Aristotle's claim – in a passage where he is explicitly concerned with *rational* desire – that we do not think things *kalon* (or fine) because we desire them; rather, we desire them because we think them fine (*Metaphysics* 1072a28–9). And though we might take this simply as a psychological claim that has no bearing on the issue of what *makes* things fine, I've always taken it to suggest that Aristotle takes the independent value of the objects of choice to be what justifies the choice of these objects. If this is right, then Aristotle – insofar as he takes the value of the *object* to determine the value of the *choice* – seems to deny that rational choice is what confers value on its objects.

There is, however, one place where Aristotle seems to suggest that a certain sort of rational choice confers a certain sort of value on an object. So I turned to that text thinking that there, if anywhere in the Aristotelian corpus, I could find something at least *structurally* similar to taking rational choice as a value-conferring property. What I found was a text whose Kantian themes far surpassed my expectations. Not only does Aristotle allow something structurally similar to taking rational choice as a value-conferring property. He seems also to share Kant's concern with the problem of constitutive luck, expresses doubts about the extent to which someone like Kant's man of sympathetic temperament deserves to be praised for acting from his sympathetic inclinations, and introduces something like Kant's distinction between acting in *conformity* with duty and acting from the *motive* of duty. Moreover, he concludes with the recommendation that rational agents choose among natural or external goods (such as wealth, honor, and power) with the least possible interference from the irrational part of the soul – that is, with the least possible interference from their inclinations.[4]

The text is *EE* viii 3, where Aristotle suggests that the kaloskagathos – in choosing natural goods for the sake of something fine – confers a certain sort of value on those goods: *because* he chooses them for the sake of something fine, they *become* fine for him.[5] In this respect, the kaloskagathos differs from the merely agathos, for whom the natural goods, not being chosen for the sake of something fine, are good but not also fine. The merely agathos in turn differs from the non-agathos for whom these things are not even good.

Aristotle's account of the distinction between the agathos (whether *kalos* or not) and the non-agathos appears to rest on the Socratic view (expressed in Plato's *Euthydemus*) that the so-called natural goods are in themselves neither good nor bad for an agent because these things, when misused (as they tend to be) by an ignorant or vicious agent, are more harmful to the agent than their opposites. For Aristotle says, in introducing this distinction:

163

A good man, then, is one for whom the natural goods [*ta phusei agatha*] are goods. For the goods which are contested [*ta perimachēta*] and seem greatest – honor, wealth, bodily excellence, good fortune and power – are natural goods, but may be harmful to some [men] on account of their dispositions [*dia tas hexeis*]. For neither the foolish nor the unjust nor the intemperate would gain any benefit from using them, just as one who is sick does not [benefit from] using the food of the healthy man and one who is weak and maimed does not [benefit from using] the accessories of one who is healthy and whole. (*EE* 1248b26–30)

On Socrates' view, wisdom – which he elsewhere identifies with virtue – is the only thing that is good in itself or, as Kant might say, the only thing that is unconditionally good: the goodness of all other things is conditional on their being used correctly by wisdom or virtue.[6]

This Socratic "conditionality thesis" should call to mind the opening of the *Grundlegung*, where Kant claims that a good will is the only thing that is good without qualification, and then argues that qualities of temperament, as well as goods of fortune and even happiness itself, though obviously good and desirable in many respects, can also be extremely bad and harmful when the will that uses them is not good.[7] It is worth noting that Kant includes among the things whose goodness is conditional on their use by a good will even things like "moderation in the affections and passions, self-control, and sober reflection" (*Gr.* 393–4). For Aristotle, too, suggests something like this when he says that the natural virtues, which do not involve practical wisdom (*phronēsis*), are harmful to those who possess them in the absence of understanding (*nous*) (*EN* 1144b4–14).[8] It thus appears that Aristotle and Kant agree not only in accepting something like the conditionality thesis, but also in applying this thesis even to qualities of temperament or to what Aristotle calls "natural" virtues: these things – in the absence of phronēsis or a good will – may harm their possessors.

Before laying the ground for my "Kantian" reading of *EE* viii 3, I should note that it is important to me that there be Socratic sources for the "Kantian" views I ascribe to Aristotle. This is important lest the alleged Kantianism of Aristotle be thought due to an anachronistic tendency on my part to read Aristotle through Stoic lenses. If, as I suspect, my "Socratic" Aristotle was an important influence on the Stoics, it may also have been (via the Stoics) an important influence on Kant.[9]

I. *EE* viii 3: Two Puzzles

We can better interpret our text, and appreciate its Socratic background, if we examine it in context. For Aristotle clearly has Socrates in mind throughout *EE* viii, even if it is not always clear whether (and to what extent) he agrees or disagrees with Socrates. *EE* viii (or what remains of it) proceeds roughly as follows. Chapter 1 explicitly rejects Socrates' identification of virtue with knowledge (*epistēmē*) as Socrates conceives it, but hints at the possibility of identifying virtue with Aristotelian phronēsis, which, unlike epistēmē, cannot be misused. Chapter 2 then rejects the Socratic attempt (in Plato's *Euthydemus*) to assimilate (or reduce) good fortune to wisdom (*sophia*), which might easily be identified with Aristotelian phronēsis. In chapter 3, then, Aristotle proceeds to clarify the relationship of phronēsis, first to the goods of fortune, and then to theoretical wisdom (references to which are conspicuously absent from statements of the Socratic view). It is thus possible – pace Woods and other commentators – to read *EE* viii as a coherent (if fragmentary) whole in which Aristotle aims to clarify his somewhat complicated relationship to Socrates.[10]

Let's turn, then, to chapter 3, which falls reasonably neatly into two parts. In the first part, Aristotle explains the distinction between the merely agathos and the kaloskagathos. Since the difference between them lies primarily in their mode of choosing among natural goods, Aristotle goes on in the second part to specify the *horos*, or standard, with reference to which one ought to choose among natural goods. The idea is presumably that the kaloskagathos chooses with reference to this standard in a way in which the merely agathos does not. The standard is as explicit – and as explicitly contemplative – as anything we find in the entire corpus.[11] After claiming that phronēsis rules by issuing commands for the sake of the theoretical faculty – just as medical science issues commands for the sake of health – Aristotle concludes by saying:

> Then whatever choice and acquisition of natural goods will produce above all the contemplation of the divine – whether of bodily [goods] or money or friends or the other goods – this [choice] is best, and this standard [*horos*] is most fine [*kallistos*]. And whatever [choice] either on account of deficiency or on account of excess hinders serving and contemplating the divine, this is base [*phaulos*]. Thus it is with the soul, and this is the best standard for the soul – whenever it perceives as little as possible the irrational [*alogou*] part of the soul, insofar as it is such [*hē(i) toiouton*]. (*EE* 1249b16–23)

Let's focus now on the first part of the chapter. The announced topic is *kalokagathia*, or fine-and-goodness, which Aristotle describes as a whole composed of each of the particular virtues. Aristotle then introduces a distinction among ends, or things such-as-to-be-chosen for their own sakes.[12] Some are such-as-to-be-praised (*epaineta*), and these are fine (*kala*). They include the various virtues, like justice and temperance, and actions stemming from these virtues. Others are not such-as-to-be-praised, and these are good but not also fine. They include things like health and strength, and their effects. Aristotle's explanation of this distinction as one between ends that are and ends that are not suitable objects of praise suggests that he has in mind a distinction between ends that are somehow "up to the agent" and ends that are not "up to the agent," but rather mere "goods of fortune." And his examples bear this out.

Aristotle relies on this distinction among ends in explaining the distinction between the merely agathos and the kaloskagathos. While natural goods are good but not fine for the merely agathos, such goods are both good and fine for the kaloskagathos because he – unlike the merely agathos – chooses them for the sake of something fine. As Aristotle puts it:

> Things are fine whenever that for the sake of which men do and choose them is fine. Wherefore the natural goods are fine for the kaloskagathos. (EE 1249a5–7)

Now this may give us pause. It's easy enough to understand how the virtues and virtuous actions, being up to the agent, are suitable objects of praise (where this is a condition of their being fine). But what should we make of Aristotle's claim that the natural goods are fine for the kaloskagathos, if this is supposed to involve their being suitable objects of praise? For Aristotle generally views the natural goods as goods of fortune the possession of which is not within the agent's control. So how can these goods – or even their possession – be suitable objects of praise? This is the first of two puzzles that I aim eventually to resolve.

The second puzzle arises from the fact that Aristotle illustrates the character of the merely agathos by appeal to the "civic disposition" (hexis politikē) characteristic of the Spartans. These men believe correctly that they ought to possess virtue, but they believe incorrectly that they ought to possess it for the sake of natural goods. Because of this mistaken belief, the Spartans do fine things only coincidentally (kata sumbebēkos). Kant might say that they act only in conformity with duty and not from duty. Aristotle thus claims that the Spartans are merely agathoi. For kalokagathia requires choosing fine things for their own sakes, and not for the sake of natural or external goods.

But Aristotle's distinction between performing virtuous actions and being virtuous raises a puzzle about the sense in which he takes the Spartans to be good. For on his view, it is not sufficient for being virtuous that one reliably perform virtuous actions. There are three further conditions: first, one must know what one is doing; second, one must decide on doing these things and decide on them for themselves; and third, one must act being firmly and unalterably disposed to do so (EN 1105a30–4). And it seems clear that the Spartans fail the second condition: they do not decide on virtuous actions for *themselves.* That's why Aristotle says that they do fine things only coincidentally. Aristotle says nevertheless that they are good, and applies some version of the conditionality thesis to them, distinguishing them from the non-agathoi who – on account of ignorance and vice – misuse the natural goods so that these things are not even good for them. In what sense, then, are the Spartans supposed to be good, given their failure to choose virtuous actions for themselves?

Sarah Broadie proposes to resolve this puzzle by distinguishing the first-order attitudes of agents engaged in practice from the second-order attitudes of agents reflecting on their first-order practices. On her view, we cannot explain Aristotle's claim that the Spartan is good unless we allow that his first-order practice (like that of the kaloskagathos) involves choosing virtuous actions for themselves.[13] The difference lies in what the merely agathos will *say* when he reflects on the ultimate rationale for his first-order practices (including their concomitant attitudes). As Broadie puts it:

> The merely good man certainly cares about virtue: he seeks to inculcate it in his children; he deplores its absence in others; in each situation he wants to know what it is right to do so as to act upon it; and he may put even his life on the line in doing what he sees himself called upon to do. He behaves as if good conduct matters most, and his behavior is itself a judgement to this effect. But when asked why virtue matters most, the answer he gives, *if he makes anything at all of the question,* is that it is for the sake of the natural goods. We should note that for a person to count as good and as living a life of virtue, it is not necessary that he have a general view about why virtue is important. Nor is it necessary that he think about his own virtues or about his actions as exercises of virtue. He may simply make and stand by good decisions, each as it comes along.[14]

Broadie thus represents the merely agathos as a nonreflective, but nevertheless genuinely virtuous agent. Though she allows that false reflection can undermine good practice, she denies that true reflection is necessary for good practice. So the kaloskagathos, though superior in reflective understanding, is not necessarily superior in practice. Broadie takes Aristotle to be making the anti-Socratic point that virtuous practice does not require articulate knowledge of the good.

I'm less confident than Broadie in the practical congruence of the kaloskagathos and the merely agathos. It is clear from *Politics* ii 9 (and elsewhere) that Aristotle thinks that the reflective view that virtue is to be pursued for the sake of natural goods renders the Spartans practically deficient in a variety of ways.[15] They emphasize one part of virtue (namely, bravery) at the expense of others (particularly justice and temperance). And though the demands of war provide temporary incentives to just and temperate behavior, these in-

167

centives do not survive in times of peace. Moreover the Spartans, though knowing how to *acquire* natural goods, do not know how to *use* these goods correctly: they know nothing about how to spend or enjoy the leisure for the sake of which war is waged. This last point reinforces the second puzzle: for insofar as the Spartans fail to use natural goods correctly, they seem to resemble the non-agathoi. In what sense, then, does Aristotle think them good?

The last point serves also to indicate the connection between the first and second parts of *EE* viii 3. Aristotle's point seems to be that knowing the contemplative standard with reference to which natural goods are to be chosen is what distinguishes the kaloskagathos from the merely agathos, and saves him from the fate of the Spartans. We needn't take this to require that the kaloskagathos himself live the contemplative life. He may be a legislator who arranges the state so that those capable of contemplation are able (unlike their Spartan counterparts) to achieve it, at least during times of peace. I want to leave that question open for now. I also want to suspend judgment on the extent to which Aristotle is making an anti-Socratic point.

My dissatisfaction with Broadie's account of the distinction between the merely agathos and the kaloskagathos leads me to seek an alternative – one that explains, moreover, how natural goods can be fine (and so objects of praise) for the kaloskagathos, thus resolving the first as well as the second puzzle.

II. *Megalopsuchia* as *Kalokagathia?*

Let us begin by turning to the *EN*, to see whether it sheds any light on the Eudemian distinction between the merely agathos and the kaloskagathos. Though it is often claimed that this distinction is without parallel in the *EN*, this is not obviously so. For the *EN* introduces two distinctions, each similar in important ways to the distinction between mere goodness and kalokagathia. One is the distinction (discussed in Section VII, this chapter) between "natural" and "authoritative" virtue. The other is the distinction (discussed here) between *megalopsuchia* and its unnamed counterpart.

Megalopsuchia (magnanimity) resembles kalokagathia in two ways. First, each consists in having all the particular virtues. Second, each involves having the right attitude to natural (or external) goods. This raises the possibility of taking the distinction between megalopsuchia and its modest counterpart as a Nicomachean version of the distinction between kalokagathia and mere goodness. This may seem implausible given that that *EE* iii 5 also contains an explicit discussion of megalopsuchia, parallel to the discussion in *EN* iv 3. But I think this possibility worth exploring briefly, if only on account of what we learn in rejecting it.

The *megalopsuchos* (or magnanimous man) is one who rightly thinks himself worthy of great things. Aristotle presents him as lying in a mean between the conceited man, who wrongly thinks himself worthy of great things, and the pusillanimous man, who is worthy of great things but thinks falsely that he is not. Aristotle also recognizes another character who resembles the megalopsuchos in having a true conception of his own worth but who differs from the megalopsuchos insofar as he is worthy only of modest (and not of great) things. His virtue is unnamed, but he lies in a mean between the honor lover (*philotimos*) and his contrary (*aphilotimos*), who is indifferent to honor.

Aristotle says that this unnamed virtue stands to megalopsuchia as ordinary generosity stands to magnificence, thus suggesting that the difference between megalopsuchia and its unnamed counterpart is primarily one of scale, where this may involve some distinction between public and private deeds. This suggestion is confirmed by the fact that the Eudemian account says explicitly that the man with the unnamed virtue is "the same in nature as the megalopsuchos," and the sort of man who might become megalopsuchos (*EE* 1233a22–5). This suggests that their common nature lies in the sort of self-knowledge we might call "appreciating one's own virtue," however grand or modest it may be. So we might treat megalopsuchia and its unnamed counterpart as two forms of *appreciating one's own virtue*.

Talk of appreciation is especially apt insofar as it connotes valuing, and so has practical implications. Agents who correctly appreciate their own virtue will not make the Spartan mistake of choosing virtue for the sake of what are in fact lesser goods. Nor will they be tempted to sacrifice their virtue in exchange for lesser goods. In this respect, agents who appreciate their own virtue seem to resemble the kaloskagathos. But there is no obvious difference in this respect between the megalopsuchos and his unnamed counterpart. Each has the right attitude toward honor, valuing it correctly in relation both to virtue and to other goods. So neither seems likely to make the Spartan mistake of choosing virtue for the sake of what are in fact lesser goods. The difference between them seems to lie in the magnitude and not in the nature of their respective virtues.

The distinction between the megalopsuchos and his unnamed counterpart thus seems to be quantitative in a way in which that between the kaloskagathos and the merely agathos is not. For the latter distinction turns on a difference in kind of motive: the kaloskagathos chooses virtuous actions for themselves, while the merely agathos chooses virtuous actions for the sake of external goods. It seems, then, that we must reject the suggestion that kalokagathia is to be identified with megalopsuchia. This conclusion seems required, moreover, by Aristotle's claim (at 1124a3–4) that megalopsuchia is "not possible without kalokagathia." But this claim, in suggesting that kalokagathia is a necessary condition for megalopsuchia, suggests another possibility – namely, that megalopsuchia is something like large-scale (or heroic)

169

kalokagathia. On this account, megalopsuchia would stand to kalokagathia as magnificence stands to generosity.

Some might object to this hypothesis on the ground that the megalopsuchos, in choosing virtue for the sake of honor, makes the Spartan mistake, and so cannot be kaloskagathos. This objection, if correct, would of course conflict with Aristotle's claim that kalokagathia is necessary for megalopsuchia. But the objection rests on the misguided view that the megalopsuchos is excessively concerned with honor and indeed motivated by consideration of it. It will prove worthwhile to consider precisely what is wrong with this objection.

III. The Megalopsuchos as *Philotimos?*

Commentators who represent the megalopsuchos as thus concerned with honor may be misled by the fact that Aristotle describes these virtues, along with their respective vices, as being "about honors and dishonors" (*peri timas kai atimias*; 1123b21–2). But this does not mean that winning honor (or avoiding dishonor) is the primary object of concern or end for the sake of which the megalopsuchos and his unnamed counterpart act. The point is simply that these men have the right attitude toward honor, valuing it neither too much nor too little in relation to other goods. This should be clear from a quick look at what Aristotle says some of the other virtues are "about."

Bravery is "about fear and confidence" (*peri phobous kai tharrē*; 1115a5–6). It is, roughly, a state lying in a mean between excessive or inappropriate fear and excessive or inappropriate confidence. But having appropriate fear and confidence is not itself the object of the brave man's concern or the end for the sake of which he acts: his object or end is to secure the safety of his *polis* or of his friends and loved ones. Appropriate fear and confidence are part of what enable him to secure these objects.

Generosity is "about wealth" (*peri chrēmata*; 1119b23). More specifically, it is about the correct *use* of wealth. So it is concerned more with giving and spending than with taking and keeping, which are forms of possession (*ktēsis*) rather than use (*chrēsis*; 1120a8–9). Because the generous man does not honor wealth, and regards acquisition "not as fine but as necessary in order that he be able to give," he does not take from the wrong sources (1120a31–b2). Giving, however, he regards as fine, and does for the sake of the fine (1120a23–4). It is, in fact, characteristic of the generous man to exceed in giving, so as to leave less for himself. This makes it clear that Aristotle's claim that generosity is "about wealth" is not meant to suggest that wealth is the object of the generous man's concern or the end for the sake of which he acts. The generous man does not honor wealth for itself. He values it primarily for the sake of the generous actions it enables him to

170

perform. These actions (along with their intended results) are the proper objects of his concern, and the ends for the sake of which he acts. Wealth, Aristotle might say, is something he values "coincidentally."

Here, however, someone might object that the practical necessity of wealth for the exercise of generosity makes it easy to explain the sense in which generosity is "about wealth" in a way that it is not so easy to explain the sense in which megalopsuchia and its counterpart are "about honor." The instrumental status of wealth allows us to take wealth as a coincidental object of the generous man's concern, the proper object being that to which wealth contributes (where this includes not only generous action but also, and more importantly, its intended effects). But there is nothing so obvious for which honor is practically necessary or to which honor contributes in quite the same way: though the desire for honor may serve as an inducement to virtue, it isn't necessary for virtuous action in the way that wealth is necessary for generous action. So it is more tempting to assume that honor is the proper and not the coincidental concern of the megalopsuchos and his counterpart.

But even if honor isn't necessary for virtuous action in quite the way that wealth is necessary for generous action, it might be necessary in some other way. It may, for example, be part of the concept of virtue that it is the sort of thing for which one *deserves* to be honored. The institution of virtue might be such that it could not exist apart from agents' tendencies to honor and dishonor one another. In this case, honor and dishonor would be necessary for virtue, not in the sense that one could not perform a virtuous action without being honored (or without aiming to be honored) for it, but in the sense that we couldn't attribute virtue to someone without thereby thinking of him as deserving honor. In this case, the pursuit of virtue would coincide with the "pursuit" of worthiness-to-be-honored, even where the agent himself is relatively indifferent to considerations of honor. So the megalopsuchos can value honor coincidentally, though in a way somewhat different from that in which the generous person values wealth coincidentally. And the same goes for his unnamed counterpart. Each can value honor insofar as he values virtue and views honor as the proper reward (though not the object) of virtue.

The emphasis on honor is unfortunate because it obscures a point that comes out most clearly in Aristotle's discussion of the pusillanimous man – the man who is worthy of great things but fails to claim them because he thinks falsely that he does not deserve them. Aristotle says that such men "hold back from fine actions and practices, and similarly also from external goods, on the ground that they are unworthy" (1125a25–7). The point here seems to be that having a proper sense of one's own worth plays an important role in the production of virtuous action: the agent who underestimates his own worth will attempt (and therefore accomplish) less in the way of fine action than he would if he had a proper appreciation of his own worth. He may, for example, decline political office (which can constitute a kind of honor) because he thinks falsely that others are more capable (and hence more deserving) than he is. This shows how honor can play an important role in the production of virtuous action without itself serving as an incentive or motive to such action: the practice of honoring agents in proportion to their virtue contributes to the sort of self-knowledge necessary for virtuous action by teaching agents what exactly they are and are not capable of achieving. So honor may after all play an instrumental role in the production of virtuous action much like that played by wealth in the production of generous action. This of course assumes proper practices of honor: honor bestowed by those who know and appreciate one another's virtues for what they are.

The foregoing examples should suffice to show that Aristotle's claim that megalopsuchia and its unnamed counterpart are "about honors and dishonors" should not be taken to imply that honor is the object of the megalopsuchos's concern or the end for the sake of which he and his counterpart act. It is no more reasonable to represent the megalopsuchos or his counterpart as preoccupied with honor than to represent the generous man as preoccupied with wealth. The point is not that the megalopsuchos cares very much about honor, but only that he cares more about honor than about any other external good, though less about honor than he cares about internal goods (like virtue and contemplation). In this respect, the megalopsuchos differs from the Spartans, about whom Aristotle says in the *Politics*: "They are right in thinking that the contested goods are acquired by virtue rather than vice, but wrong in thinking these things superior to virtue" (1271b7–10). So the megalopsuchos's attitude toward honor is no obstacle to identifying megalopsuchia with large-scale kalokagathia.

This account of the megalopsuchos's attitude to honor receives further support from the unequivocal location of honor among contested goods in Aristotle's account in *EN* ix 8 of the distinction between proper and improper self-love. For Aristotle draws a clear distinction there between the proper self-lover's pursuit of the *kalon* and the improper self-lover's pursuit of honor and other contested goods. And he firmly locates the megalopsuchos among proper self-lovers – that is, among those who pursue the kalon and not among those who pursue honor and other contested goods. Let's turn then to this chapter, which has often been interpreted as recommending a kind of "moral competition" in which virtuous agents – especially the megalopsuchoi – seek to outdo one another in performing virtuous action.

IV. Competitive Self-Love?

The announced topic of *EN* ix 8 is whether one ought to love oneself or someone else most of all. Aristotle goes on to distinguish two ways in which we speak of self-love, one "loose and popular," the other "strict and philosophical."[16] He then argues that the self-lover in the "loose and popular sense" should not love himself in that sense at all (let alone above all others), while the self-lover in the "strict and philosophical sense" should love himself in this sense (apparently above all others).[17]

The first sort of self-lover identifies his "self" with his appetites and the nonrational part of his soul. His self-love consists in lavishing upon *that* self contested goods like money, honors, and bodily pleasures. This is the sort of self-love Aristotle regards as improper. It is crucial to note that Aristotle locates honor – the object of the naturally competitive spirit, or *thumos* – here among contested goods.

The second sort of self-lover identifies his "self" with his *nous* – that is, with his reason or understanding, which Aristotle says is his best and most authoritative (*kuriōtatō(i)*) element.[18] His self-love consists in gratifying and obeying *that* in everything he does, and Aristotle makes it clear in the remainder of the chapter that this sort of self-love may even require one to give up one's life for the sake of one's friends and polis. There is little doubt that Aristotle here intends to refer to the megalopsuchos, whom he described at 1124b8–9 as "unsparing of his life since he does not think life at all costs worthwhile" (Irwin's translation).

In order to reconcile what appears to be such extreme sacrifice with what Aristotle explicitly describes as the best sort of self-love, commentators often read the remainder of the chapter as touting what they call "moral competition" or "moral rivalry," as if Aristotle identified proper self-love with aiming to outdo all others (except perhaps one's other selves) in virtuous action.[19] Some even introduce the notion of competition explicitly in their translations, as Irwin did in early printings of his translation at 1169a8–11:

> And when everyone competes [*hamillōmenōn*] to achieve what is fine and strains to do the finest actions, everything that is right will be done for the common good, and each person individually will receive the greatest of goods, since that is the character of virtue.[20]

Such "competitive" readings help to explain Wood's view that Aristotle's proper self-love corresponds to that essentially comparative satisfaction with oneself that Kant condemns – that is, "self-conceit" (*arrogantia* or *Eigendünkel*).[21] But *EN* ix 8 needn't be read competitively, and there is a strong case for saying it shouldn't be read this way. Proper self-love may yet prove more Kantian than it appears at first glance.

Let me begin by explaining how I propose to use the "competitive" label. I propose to take the absence of any need for interpersonal comparison as sufficient for a reading's being "noncompetitive." I recognize of course that we often speak of "competing against oneself" or "against the clock," and

173

that one might thus interpret self-contained striving to achieve an absolute standard as involving a kind of competition. But this metaphorical extension threatens to obscure the important difference between these cases and those in which interpersonal comparisons are required. The need for interpersonal comparison is thus a minimal condition for a reading's being "competitive." But something further seems required as well – something like a process that aims to yield a winner (even if we sometimes end up with a tie) or a zero-sum condition (in which one person's gain is another's loss).[22] We needn't, however, worry too much for present purposes about how exactly to formulate this further condition. I've said enough, I think, to allow for reasonably clear and uncontroversial classification of the relevant interpretations. Let's turn then to my argument that there is a strong case for preferring a "noncompetitive" (or "noncomparative") reading of *EN* ix 8.

First, consider the passage quoted earlier. Although the verb *hamillaomai* is most often used in a competitive sense, where interpersonal comparisons are essentially involved in an attempt to identify winners, it can also be used in a noncompetitive sense, where no interpersonal comparisons need be involved. See, for example, *Republic* 490a, where Plato speaks of the philosopher "striving after" being or truth. In this case, no interpersonal comparison seems to be involved: the philosopher strives after truth, and may attain truth, regardless of how and what others do. This may be the sort of striving Aristotle has in mind when he suggests that everyone can achieve the greatest good if everyone strives to do what is fine, the idea being that each can seek and attain the good regardless of how and what others do.

This noncomparative or noncompetitive reading is plausible given the role played in Aristotle's argument by the distinction between contested goods (*ta perimachēta*), like honor and power, and goods that are not so contested, like virtue and contemplation. The point is presumably that it is at least logically possible for everyone equally to achieve virtue or contemplation in a way in which it is not logically possible for everyone equally to achieve essentially comparative goods like honor and power.[23] Moreover, and more importantly, it is in principle possible for each to achieve his goal, and to know that he has achieved it, without knowing how he stands in relation to the achievements of others.

Next, consider the following passage, which is often taken to support the competitive interpretation:

> The decent person does the things he ought to do. For every *nous* chooses the best for itself, and the decent person obeys *nous*. And it is true of the excellent person that he does many things for the sake of his friends and fatherland, and will even die for them if he must. He will yield[24] money, honors and contested goods generally, in achieving the *kalon* for himself.

174

For he would choose to be intensely pleased for a short time rather than moderately pleased for a long time, to live finely [kalōs] for one year rather than in any old way for many years, and [to perform] one fine and great action rather than many small ones. This is presumably true of those who die for others. For they choose something great and *kalon* for themselves. They will yield money, if their friends gain more. The friend gets money, while he gets the *kalon*. So he awards himself the greater good. It is the same way, with honors and offices; he will yield all these to his friend, for this is *kalon* for him and such-as-to-be-praised. So he is reasonably thought to be excellent, choosing the *kalon* above all things. And it is even possible that he will yield [virtuous] actions to his friend, it being finer to be the cause of his friend's doing them than to do them himself. (*EN* 1169a16–34)

This passage, which clearly refers to the megalopsuchos, sharply distinguishes the pursuit of the kalon from the pursuit of honor: the agent, in pursuing the kalon, yields honors (along with wealth and power) to his friends. This fits the picture of the megalopsuchos sketched earlier: he may care more about honor than about any other external goods, but this doesn't mean that he cares very much about honor.

Now giving up things that one doesn't value much to begin with isn't all so heroic, and one might even object that such "sacrifice" is ultimately selfish insofar as the agent thereby secures for himself the kalon, which is explicitly said to be a greater good than these other things. And this, according to some commentators, is exactly the point if such "sacrifice" is to be viewed as a form of *self*-love. But there are two things to notice here.

First, it is important, though rarely remarked, that the kalon – insofar as it consists in virtue and virtuous action – is not generally the sort of thing one *can* secure for one's friends. Aristotle notes, as if to forestall the foregoing objection, that one may provide one's friends with *opportunities* to secure the kalon by providing them with opportunities for virtuous action: but virtuous action is – and this is a logical point – something one can secure only for oneself.[25] The kalon isn't like money or political office: it's not the sort of thing you can choose either to give to another or to keep for yourself. You can provide others with opportunities to achieve it, but the achievement itself is largely up to them. That's why the kalon is not among the goods of fortune.

Second, commentators tend to speak as if Aristotle's claim that the agent awards himself the greater good must be read as involving a choice between awarding the greater of two goods to himself and awarding the greater of two goods to someone else. But we've just seen reasons for doubting that this *could* be the relevant choice. Moreover, assuming that the relevant goods here are the kalon (which is the greater good) and some external good (which is the lesser good), and assuming that one can achieve the kalon only for oneself, it's perfectly reasonable to view the agent's choice as one between awarding himself the greater good and awarding himself the lesser good. Aristotle may be claiming only that the agent, in choosing the kalon, awards himself the greater of two goods than he would have awarded himself had he chosen the external good instead. In this case, the relevant comparison is not with what the agent *actually* awards to *someone else*, but rather with the goods he might *hypothetically* have awarded *himself* instead of the greater good.[26]

The main obstacle to this reading is at 1169a8–10, where the contrast, signaled by the '*men . . . de . . .*' construction, is clearly between what the friend gets (i.e., external goods) and what the agent gets (i.e., the kalon). But even in this situation, the agent gets a greater good than he would have got had he acted differently. So this passage does not show that Aristotle does not also have in mind the contrast I suggest. Moreover, I think my reading is supported by the fact that Aristotle goes on almost immediately to speak of situations in which the agent may secure something more kalon for himself by yielding actions (or opportunities to secure the kalon) to his friend. For it's not at all obvious in this case, where both may secure the kalon, that the agent secures a greater good than his friend secures. Here the comparative clearly needn't be taken as claiming that the agent secures for himself something more kalon than what his friend secures: the point may be simply that he secures for himself something more kalon than he would have secured had he not provided his friend an opportunity to secure the kalon too. The fact that Aristotle chooses to end on this note renders it plausible to read the chapter as "deconstructing" or rejecting the terms of the comparative question with which it began. For it seems to me significant that he concludes by saying not that one ought in the "strict and philosophical sense" to love oneself "most of all," but only that one ought to love oneself in this sense period.[27]

But even if one declines to read Aristotle as deconstructing his initial *aporia* in this way, one can still make sense of his claim that the good person ought to love himself most of all without introducing moral competition. Since loving someone (whether oneself or another) consists at least partly in awarding goods to the beloved, and since the best sort of goods – internal goods like virtue and contemplation – are the sorts of things that one can strictly award only to oneself, there is an important sense in which the good person cannot help but love himself most of all: if he is going to award the greatest goods to anyone at all, he must award them to himself. This may sometimes involve asking whether it would be more kalon to provide someone else an opportunity for virtuous action than to do the action oneself.

176

But even in this case, the agent cannot (logically) award the kalon directly to someone else. Moreover, in providing someone else with an opportunity to achieve the kalon, the agent does not then award the kalon to someone else instead of himself. For in providing another with the opportunity to achieve the kalon, the agent thereby achieves the kalon for himself. That's why the kalon is not among the contested goods.

One might of course object that taking the "self-sacrifice" passage as referring to the megalopsuchos undermines my attempt to read it noncompetitively, given the competitive terms in which Aristotle describes the megalopsuchos elsewhere. I'm thinking primarily of the passage in *EN* iv 3, where he says that the megalopsuchos prefers benefiting others to receiving benefits from others, because benefiting others is a sign of superiority and receiving benefits from others a sign of inferiority. Aristotle goes on to say that the megalopsuchos seeks to display his greatness only in the company of those who are worthy, where it is difficult and impressive to achieve superiority, and not in the company of average men, where superiority is easy to achieve but vulgar to pursue.

There is of course no denying the presence of competition here. But it's worth noting an important limitation in its scope: the megalopsuchos no more bothers competing with average men than world-class athletes bother competing with local amateurs. This may suggest that it is not superiority per se that he seeks, but rather the sort of accomplishment to which competition with formidable opponents is often – though not always – the best means. I say "not always" because truly exceptional individuals who are not sufficiently challenged by the available competition often do better to aim at an absolute or impersonal standard instead. Such cases suggest that interpersonal comparison is not essential – and so that competition is not essential – to the life of the megalopsuchos.[28]

This clears the way for a noncompetitive reading of *EN* ix 8, which suggests the possibility of reading Aristotle in something like the way in which Wood reads Kant – that is, as recommending that our assessments of self-worth be based not on any comparison of ourselves with others, but rather on a comparison of ourselves with something like Kant's moral law. This is suggested by one moral that Aristotle draws (in a somewhat different context) from the identification of a man with his *nous* – namely, that he ought to strive as far as possible to live the life of a god. For there is no suggestion in Aristotle's text that the agent will be satisfied with outdoing actual competitors, who may or may not be worthy competitors: the agent is supposed to do the best of which he is capable, whatever others do. Moreover, this is perfectly compatible with his seeking to help his friends – especially his character friends but perhaps also citizen friends – to do the best of which they are capable, even in cases where they threaten to outstrip him. The point

177

is simply that the virtuous person will aim at this standard whatever others, however much better or worse than him, happen to do.

There is thus ground for a Kantian reading of Aristotle's identification of a man with his nous. But before developing this reading, we must pause briefly (after summarizing the argument thus far) to examine the connection Aristotle sees between justice and proper self-love. For Aristotle's meritocratic conception of justice seems far removed from the radical egalitarianism that Wood ascribes to Kant.

V. Self-love, Justice, and Kalokagathia

We began searching in Section II for Nicomachean parallels to the Eudemian distinction between kalokagathia and mere goodness. And while rejecting the hypothesis that megalopsuchia is to be identified with kalokagathia, we retained the hypothesis that megalopsuchia is large-scale kalokagathia (the idea being that the unnamed counterpart of the megalopsuchos also possesses kalokagathia, but on a smaller scale). But this hypothesis is tenable only given the plausibility (demonstrated in Section III, this chapter) of rejecting the common picture of the megalopsuchos as concerned primarily with honor. For Aristotle clearly distinguishes the kaloskagathos, who chooses virtuous actions for themselves, from the merely agathos, like the Spartan, who chooses virtuous actions for the sake of external goods (including honor).

Section IV, this chapter, was meant to reinforce the argument for rejecting the common picture of the megalopsuchos by appealing to *EN* ix 8, where Aristotle assigns the megalopsuchos to the class of proper self-lovers (who pursue the kalon) as opposed to the class of improper self-lovers (who pursue contested goods like honor), thus preserving the tenability of the hypothesis that megalopsuchia is large-scale kalokagathia. Given Aristotle's claim that the megalopsuchos and his unnamed counterpart share the same nature, it seems plausible to view both as proper self-lovers, and to draw some distinction within proper self-love (parallel to that drawn within kalokagathia) between larger- and smaller-scale instantiations. This allows us to hypothesize that kalokagathia is to be identified with proper self-love, without abandoning our hypothesis that megalopsuchia is large-scale kalokagathia. For we can easily take megalopsuchia as proper self-love writ large, while taking its unnamed counterpart as proper self-love writ small. And this distinction makes good intuitive sense: an agent of modest ability does himself no good – and may actually harm himself – by laying claim to goods (like political office) that he is not equipped to handle.

Here, however, there might seem to be a problem, given Aristotle's claim that kalokagathia is complete virtue in the sense that it is a whole composed of each of the particular virtues (*EE* 1248b8–16). For Aristotle says in his account of justice that justice is "complete virtue" (*teleia aretē*; 1129b30) and "not a part but the whole of virtue" (*ou meros aretēs all' holē aretē*; 1130a9). And this might seem to suggest that kalokagathia is more plausibly identified with justice than with self-love, which seems at most only a part of virtue.

Before addressing this problem, it is necessary to say a few words about Aristotle's conception of justice. The first thing to note is that Aristotle regards a distribution as just if it involves what he calls 'proportional' as distinct from 'numerical' equality, where this means that external goods (like wealth, honor, and political office) are to be distributed to agents according (or in proportion) to their merit or worth (*kat' axian*).[29] Since Aristotle identifies an agent's worth largely if not exclusively with the extent to which he succeeds in actualizing virtue, Aristotelian justice consists roughly in distributing external goods in proportion to actualized virtue. This has both a retrospective (or meritocratic) and a prospective (or quasi-utilitarian) rationale. The virtuous person makes the best (or most beneficial) use of the external goods he receives because he benefits others not equally but in proportion to their virtue. Speaking roughly, he benefits others in proportion to *their* tendency to benefit others. Note, however, that the just man must also distribute external goods to himself according to this principle. This helps to explain the claim (at *MM* 1212a37–40) that the virtuous agent will yield goods like wealth and political office to those who are able to make better use of these goods than he will. For this is required not only by justice, but also (as we've just seen) by proper self-love: a man may harm himself by laying claim to goods that others can put to more beneficial use.

The next thing to note is that Aristotle seems to think that (at least in well-ordered societies) actions in accordance with each of the particular virtues tend to promote just distributions, while actions that violate any of the particular virtues tend to upset just distributions. (Intemperance, for example, leads men to help themselves to other men's women, while temperance restrains them from doing so.)[30] Aristotle is thus inclined to regard all genuinely virtuous actions as just (insofar as they promote just distributions) and all vicious actions as unjust (insofar as they upset just distributions), with the result that he views each of the particular virtues as parts of what he calls 'general justice', which he identifies roughly with obeying the laws enjoining virtuous actions and prohibiting vicious ones.

But Aristotle recognizes an important distinction between agents who commit acts of general injustice out of greed or the desire to have more than their fair share of various goods as such and agents who commit acts of general injustice from other motives, like the desire for pleasure (which might lead a man to seduce his neighbor's wife) or fear (which might lead a man to shirk his military duty). Agents motivated by greed – or a desire for *more than their fair share as such* – commit what Aristotle calls 'special' injustice. Agents who commit only general injustice perform actions that tend as a matter of fact to promote unjust distributions, though this is not the end for the sake of which they act. But unjust distributions are precisely the ends for the sake of which those who commit special injustice act. These men want more than their fair share of contested goods like money, honor, and political power.[31]

Note, however, that in both cases – the special and the general – it follows from the conditionality thesis that any so-called goods that an agent secures for himself in excess of his fair share will *not* be good for him, and may actually harm him. So injustice, both general and special, is incompatible with self-love conceived as a form of what Kant calls 'self-benevolence'.[32] This suggests that general justice (including special justice) coincides with proper self-love, which might explain why Aristotle qualifies his claim that justice is complete virtue by saying that it is complete virtue "not absolutely but in relation to another" (1129b25–7). For the qualification may be intended to reflect the fact that proper self-love is the flip side of justice, something Aristotle might call "complete virtue in relation to *oneself*."[33] If so, then justice and proper self-love are plausibly viewed as two aspects of a single virtue that consists in distributing external goods – to oneself and to others – in proportion to virtue.

The coincidence of justice with proper self-love thus solves the foregoing problem. For given this coincidence, Aristotle's reference to general justice as 'complete virtue' does not require us to identify kalokagathia with justice rather than proper self-love. We can instead view kalokagathia as a single virtue that can be viewed either under the aspect of justice or under the aspect of self-love.

It is important to the coincidence of justice with proper self-love that the principle of distribution in proportion to virtue be impartial in the following sense: the agent is to distribute goods – to himself and to others – in proportion to their virtue and without regard to any relationships (including that of identity) in which they stand to himself. That this is a matter not simply of justice but of proper self-love is suggested by a passage from the *Magna Moralia* parallel to the account in *EN* ix 8 of proper self-love:

> In one sense, [the good man] loves his friend more than himself; in another sense, he loves himself most of all. For [he loves] his friend more in matters of profit [*kata to sumpheron*], but [he loves] himself most of all in matters of the fine and good [*kata to kalon kai agathon*]. For he gains these things, which are most fine, for himself. He is, then, a lover-of-good [*philagathos*], not a lover-of-self [*philautos*]. For he loves himself only, if at all, because he is good. (*MM* 1212b15–20)[34]

180

This suggests that the proper self-lover values his virtue primarily qua virtue and not qua his. And it follows from this that he values virtue impartially: he will value it, and want to reward it, whenever and wherever it appears. So he is no more (and no less) inclined to value virtue in himself than to value virtue in others.

This talk of "valuing virtue" should call to mind the account in Section III of megalopsuchia and its unnamed counterpart as sharing a common nature insofar as each consists in a sort of self-knowledge aptly described as "appreciating one's own virtue" (however grand or modest it proves to be). But it is now tempting (in light of the *Magna Moralia* passage) to drop the reference to self, and to speak simply of "appreciating virtue" (whether one's own or another's). And such appreciation is plausibly identified with kalokagathia. For this identification serves to explain why the kaloskagathos makes neither the Spartan mistake (of choosing virtue for the sake of lesser goods) nor the vulgar mistake (of sacrificing virtue in exchange for lesser goods).[35] Moreover, this identification is consistent with our hypothesis that megalopsuchia is large-scale kalokagathia. For megalopsuchia, like its unnamed counterpart, is a form of appreciating virtue.

VI. Nous and the Moral Law

There are no doubt important differences between the Kantian view (according to Wood) that all rational beings have absolute (and therefore equal) worth and Aristotle's conception of justice as a kind of proportional (as opposed to numerical) equality. But the commitment to impartiality implicit in Aristotle's conception of justice is arguably a step in the Kantian direction. For even if Aristotle's demand that external goods be distributed to agents in proportion to their merits requires Aristotelian citizens to make the sort of comparative judgments that Kant eschews, this needn't be taken to involve any *intrinsically* inegalitarian motives on their part or even on Aristotle's. Moreover, Aristotle seems to allow that it is in principle possible – and perhaps ideally the case – that all men (anyhow) should be equally virtuous, in which case they should take turns ruling and being ruled.[36]

Aristotle discusses this point in *Politics* iii 16, where his commitment to some sort of impartiality is evident. After saying that equals should take turns ruling and being ruled, he suggests that the rule of law (*nomos*) is in principle preferable to the rule of men, and that men should rule primarily as servants and guardians of the law. He seems to think that rule by men is a matter of practical necessity because the law cannot determine and legislate in advance what should be done in all possible or even actual circumstances. For this reason, men who administer the law are explicitly allowed to correct the law in cases where experience proves something superior to the established law.

But Aristotle contrasts such rule by men, even as servants and guardians of the law, with rule by law alone:

> The one, then, who commands that the law should rule seems to command that the God and intelligence alone [*ton theon kai ton noun monous*] should rule, while the one who commands that man [should rule] adds also a beast. For appetite [*epithumia*] is such, and *thumos* corrupts even the best of men who rule. Wherefore, the law is *nous* without desire [*aneu orexeōs nous*].[37]

It is clear from what follows that Aristotle prefers rule by law to rule by men because he takes rule by law to be impartial in a way in which rule by men is not. For he proceeds to contrast human administration of law with human administration of medicine by saying that doctors do nothing contrary to principle (*para ton logon*; presumably medical principle) from motives of friendship, but simply cure for a fee, while those who administer the law are accustomed to do many things with a view to profit or favor (*pros epēreian kai charin*). The idea is apparently that desire (for goods like pleasure) and *thumos* (for goods like honor) leads men who administer the law to act against principle (including the principle of distribution according to worth) for the sake of personal or filial gain.

Such behavior is no doubt an expression of improper self-love, and incompatible with proper self-love. For given the conditionality thesis, any so-called goods that a ruler secures by violating the principle of distribution according to worth will not in fact be good for him and may actually harm him. This explains why the identification with one's nous, associated in *EN* ix 8 with proper self-love, is so valuable a trait in a ruler. For one who identifies with his nous will not be led by desire or thumos to administer the law in ways that are contrary to the principle of distribution according to worth. Moreover, it follows from Aristotle's identification of (anorectic) nous with law that the agent who identifies with his nous identifies ipso facto with this law. He will thus serve himself by serving this law.

Furthermore, Aristotle's association of nous with the divine provides some license for taking the identification of self with nous as positing an absolute standard, within the self, analogous to Kant's moral law. And this renders my noncompetitive reading more plausible. For this makes it easier to read Aristotle as recommending that our assessments of self-worth be based on a comparison of ourselves not with other men, but with an absolute standard analogous to Kant's moral law – that is, with the God.

VII. Nous Identification and Constitutive Luck

My Kantian reading derives further support from the plausibility of taking Aristotle to share something like Kant's concern with autonomy. This is best seen if we read *EE* viii 3 in the context provided by viii 2, where Aristotle is concerned with something like the problem known among contemporary Kantians as that of constitutive luck.[38] It's clear from viii 2 that Aristotle takes some men to be consistently fortunate in the sense that they "do the right thing" in spite of the fact that they lack the sort of knowledge or understanding that ordinarily explains such success (including, most importantly, "ethical" success). Aristotle is tempted to attribute such success to the fact that nature has endowed such men with good impulses in much the same way that nature endows some men with the musical talent that enables them to sing in spite of the fact that they lack musical knowledge.

But there is a disanalogy here, insofar as Aristotle's teleology requires the relevant impulses to be relatively widespread in a way in which natural operatic talent is not: these are the impulses from which virtue develops, and the capacity for virtue (though occasionally lacking) belongs by nature to those to whom it belongs (i.e., to most men). Assuming, then, that the majority of men are neither wise nor consistently fortunate, there will be many men who have good impulses but consistently fail (on account of their ignorance) to do the right thing. So good natural impulses cannot be the whole story.

Aristotle suggests, not surprisingly, that something divine makes the difference, though he has just expressed worries about this on the ground that it would be strange for a god or a *daimōn* to favor the ignorant (and thus undeserving) rather than the wise (and thus deserving). But the issue here is the agent's initial endowment, not what he deserves or merits as a result of what he does with this endowment. And though Aristotle is ultimately ambivalent about whether to describe the source of initial endowment as natural or divine, he remains confident that there is such a thing. And he thinks that there is an important difference between what nature or divine causes make of one, and what one makes of oneself.

This is clear from *EN* x 9, where Aristotle – in discussing whether men come to be good by nature, habit, or instruction – says:

> It is plain that the [contribution] of nature is not up to us [*ouk eph᾽ hēmin*], but belongs on account of some divine causes [*dia tinas theias aitias*] to those who are truly fortunate [*tois hōs alēthōs eutuchesin*]. (1179b20–3)

Aristotle makes essentially the same point in *EE* i 3, though the divine appears there in a slightly different role:

> If, on the one hand, living finely [*kalōs*] lies in the things that come to be as a result of fortune or in the [things that come to be] as a result of nature, then it would be a hopeless prospect for the many. (For the possession [of it] is not [in this case] the result of practice, nor up to them or their con-

duct.) But if, on the other hand, [living finely] lies in one's self, as well as one's actions, being of a certain character [tō(i) auton poion tina einai kai tas kat' auton praxeis], then the good would be both more common and more divine – more common because it is possible for more to partake of it, and more divine because *eudaimonia* belongs to those who make themselves and their actions to be of a certain sort [tois autous paraskeu-azousi poious tinas kai tas praxeis]. (*EE* 1215a13–19)

The shifting role of the divine can be explained in the following way.

What we are like depends initially on external sources, whether natural or divine. (Habituation, for which our elders are typically responsible, eventually comes to play a similar role.) But with the development of nous, which Aristotle describes as "the divine in us," the role played by external sources in determining what we are like diminishes, and that played by internal sources, particularly nous, increases – presumably because nous allows us to reflect critically on what nature and habit have made of us, and to change ourselves if nous doesn't like what it sees. So to the extent that we come to *identify* with nous, and nous is responsible for what we are like, we ourselves become responsible for what we are like.[39] In coming to determine our characters, we come to do for ourselves what we initially relied on nature or the divine to do for us, as a result of which we gradually become more self-determined and more like God.[40]

Note that God serves here as the standard against which we compare ourselves. Here, however, God serves as our standard, not qua contemplator, but qua self-determined. That Aristotle takes God to serve as a standard in this sense is clear from the *Politics*, where he explicitly connects the issue of responsibility for character with the relationship between virtue and natural goods. This passage provides the clearest evidence for my interpretation of *EE* viii 3 as concerned with autonomy. After saying that no one will dispute that there are three kinds of goods or that the *eudaimōn* agent must have all three, Aristotle says – as in *EE* viii 3 – that men do differ about the relative superiority of these goods. The passage concludes as follows:

> The external [goods] have a limit, like any instrument, and all are useful for something; and an excess of these must either harm or be of no benefit to those who possess it. But with goods of the soul, each is, by however much it exceeds, that much more useful (if it is even appropriate to apply not only [the term] *kalon* but also [the term] 'useful' to them). . . .
>
> Further, it is for the sake of the soul that these [external and bodily goods] are naturally such as to-be-chosen, and that all those who are wise ought to choose [them], and not the soul for the sake of them. Let us agree then that each person has as much *eudaimonia* as he has virtue and *phronēsis*, and acting in accordance with these, taking the God as our witness.

He is *eudaimōn* and blessed, not on account of any external goods, but on account of himself [*di' hauton*], and being of a certain sort with respect to his nature [*tōi poios tis einai tēn phusin*], since good fortune [*eutuchia*] must differ from *eudaimonia* on account of these things: of goods external to the soul, the cause is the automatic and fortune [*hē tuchē*], but no one is just or temperate as a result of fortune or on account of it. (*Pol.* 1323b7–29)

The context provided by *EE* viii 2 – in conjunction with this passage from the *Politics* and the foregoing passage from *EE* i 3 – supports taking *EE* viii 3 to suggest that the kaloskagathos is self-determined in a way in which the merely agathos is not.

This raises the possibility of taking the distinction between mere goodness and kalokagathia to coincide with the other possible Nicomachean parallel mentioned at the outset – that is, the distinction between natural virtue and what Aristotle calls *kuria* (authoritative) virtue. For he takes the authoritatively virtuous agent to be the *author* of his actions – and presumably also of his self – in a way in which the naturally virtuous agent is not.

VIII. Kalokagathia as Authoritative Virtue?

The plausibility of taking the distinction between mere goodness and kalokagathia to coincide with that between natural and authoritative virtue receives support not only from the fact that kalokagathia and authoritative virtue resemble one another (and differ from mere goodness and natural virtue) in being identified with the whole of virtue, but also from the similarities between the passages in which each of these distinctions is introduced. Aristotle introduces the distinction between natural and authoritative virtue in *EN* vi 13, where he is concerned, as in *EE* viii, with the Socratic identification of virtue and knowledge. Both passages speak of men becoming simultaneously wise and good. And both refer to *deinotēs* (cleverness), rarely mentioned by Aristotle. Moreover, there is the striking similarity between the end of *EN* vi 13 and the end of *EE* viii 3, each of which invokes the analogy between *phronēsis* and medical science in the service of what appears to be the same point.[41]

Aristotle introduces the distinction between natural and authoritative virtue by comparing it to that between mere cleverness (*deinotēs*) and genuine phronēsis. One point of this comparison is to suggest that authoritative virtue develops from natural virtue in much the same way that phronēsis develops from cleverness. The developmental picture is clear from *EN* 1144b2–14:

As *phronēsis* is to cleverness – not the same but similar – so natural virtue is related to authoritative [*kuria*] [virtue]. For each type of character seems

185

to belong to all [those who possess it] in some way by nature. For we are just and temperate and brave and have the other [states] immediately from birth. Nevertheless, we seek something different, the authoritatively good [*to kuriōs agathos*] and [suppose] such things belong in a different way. For the natural states belong even to children and beasts, but without intelligence [*aneu nou*] they are evidently harmful . . . just at it happens to a strong body moving about without sight to take a strong fall, so too it happens here. But if one gets hold of *nous*, he excels in action. His state, being similar [to natural virtue], will then be virtue in the authoritative way.

The plausibility of viewing the process of acquiring nous as one in which we shed the effects of constitutive luck is suggested by a memorable slogan, taken from a passage in the *Magna Moralia* bearing a striking resemblance to *EE* viii 2: "Where there is most *nous* and *logos*, there is least fortune [*tuchē*]; and where there is most fortune, there is least *nous*" (*MM* 1207a4–6). The most obvious way to take this is as making the point made in the *Euthydemus*, that you're better off being caught in a storm with a knowledgable than with an ignorant pilot. But the context here suggests another way to take it, compatible with the first: we can take it as saying that in identifying your self with nous, you insulate your self as far as possible from the effects of fortune in the sense that you become responsible for who you are and what you do. The significance of this will be clear when we return to viii 3.

First, we must examine the case for taking the distinction between natural and authoritative virtue to coincide with that between mere goodness and kalokagathia. One superficially plausible argument for accepting this coincidence runs as follows. Aristotle says explicitly (in *EE* viii 3) that kalokagathia is a whole composed of each of the particular virtues, thus associating kalokagathia with the sort of unity (or reciprocity) of virtue that he takes to characterize authoritative (as distinct from natural) virtue. And Aristotle says explicitly (in the *Politics*) that the Spartans cultivate one part of virtue at the expense of others, thus associating the mere goodness of the Spartans with the lack of unity characteristic of natural as distinct from authoritative virtues. So it's tempting to conclude that Aristotle takes the distinction between natural and authoritative virtue to coincide with that between mere goodness and kalokagathia.

Note, however, that *EE* viii 3 does not mention the lopsidedness of Spartan virtue, but focuses instead on the fact that the Spartans rank virtue behind natural goods. So we shouldn't rashly assume that it is the lopsidedness of their virtue that leads Aristotle to take the Spartans as exemplars of the merely agathoi. But even so, it doesn't follow that we're on the wrong track in taking kalokagathia to coincide with authoritative virtue. For the *Politics* passage (quoted at the end of Section VII) shows that Aristotle links the Spartans' other flaw – that of ranking virtue behind natural goods – with a failure of self-determination. So even if Aristotle does not identify mere goodness with natural virtue, he may still object to mere goodness on the ground that it (like natural virtue) lacks the self-determination characteristic of authoritative virtue, thus confirming my suggestion that we identify kalokagathia with authoritative virtue. The point is simply that we'll have to recognize other states, besides natural virtue, that fall short of authoritative virtue.

This strategy receives support from *EN* iii 8, where Aristotle describes five states that resemble authoritative bravery, and are often called by the same name. One is the so-called bravery of those who endure dangers on account of spirit or thumos. Aristotle says that this sort of bravery is "most natural" and becomes genuine bravery once the agent acquires *prohairesis* and the right goal, clearly referring to the transition from natural to authoritative virtue (1116b24–17a6). Another such state, especially relevant for our purposes, is what Aristotle calls 'civic (*politikē*) bravery', as a result of which citizens endure dangers both to avoid penalties and disgrace, and to win honors. Aristotle says that this state is most like genuine bravery because it stems from a kind of virtue, being associated with a sense of shame and a desire for what is fine. The fact that Aristotle refers to this state, like that of the Spartans, as 'civic' suggests that this may be the sort of state he has in mind when he speaks of mere goodness in *EE* viii 3.

The connection between thumos and both shame and the desire for honor is clear from some of Plato's more graphic images – the image (at *Republic* 439e) of Leontius, whose thumos renders him ashamed of his necrophilia; and the image (at *Phaedrus* 253d) of the good horse, said to be a lover of honor with temperance and a sense of shame. Aristotle's account of thumos preserves the central features of Plato's account, particularly the idea that thumos is capable of hearing and obeying reason, though it sometimes – especially when corrupted or poorly trained – mishears or disobeys. When Aristotle says in *EN* x 9 that the soul of one who is to become virtuous must be habituated to feel affection for the fine and distaste for the shameful so that it can appreciate reason and argument, his point surely concerns the proper training of the thumos.

Moreover, there are important similarities between Plato's account (in *Republic* viii) of the timocratic constitution and man, and Aristotle's criticisms (in *Pol.* ii 9) of the Spartan constitution: both mention the bad influence of greedy women, as well as the predominant emphasis on military and competitive virtues. There is an important connection between these points: since property, wealth, and political office can all be forms of honor, competition for honor often takes the form of competition for such material goods. Plato connects these points when he claims that the timocratic son grows up hearing his mother complain that her husband is not among the rulers and does not care much about wealth, the idea being that she acquires fewer of the material rewards of honor than she would like. Plato explicitly blames the competitive aspects of the timocratic constitution on the predominance of the *thumoeidēs*, and it's hard to imagine that Aristotle would not agree.

These passages return our attention to the problem of constitutive luck, suggesting how Aristotle's concern with this problem might lead him to classify civic virtue together with natural virtue, and to contrast both states with authoritative virtue.[42] For just as it is bad constitutive luck to be born too sanguine or too hot-blooded, or to grow up with a timocratic father, so too it is bad constitutive luck to grow up in a place like Sparta, especially since critical reflection – one's only hope for the sort of self-determination required for authoritative virtue – is not encouraged in such places.

The fact that constitutive luck seems to be involved not only in the case of natural virtue, but also in the case of civic virtue, supports taking civic virtue (like natural virtue) to be opposed to authoritative virtue. The fact that the Spartans possess civic virtue can then be taken to suggest that the contrast in *EE* viii 3 between mere goodness and kalokagathia is ultimately a contrast between civic and authoritative virtue. This allows us to identify kalokagathia with authoritative virtue, without having to identify the distinction between mere goodness and kalokagathia with the distinction between natural and authoritative virtue: the contrast in *EE* viii 3 is between authoritative and civic virtue.

Moreover, it seems plausible – given Aristotle's claim that civic bravery is most like genuine bravery – to suppose that civic virtue is most like authoritative virtue. The fact that the Spartans possess civic virtue will then help to explain Aristotle's willingness to call the Spartans "good" even though they fall short of kalokagathia, thus helping to resolve our second puzzle about the sense in which the Spartans are good, given that they mistakenly value virtue for the sake of external goods. Here it is important to recall Aristotle's claim (in his discussion of megalopsuchia) that honor is the "greatest of external goods" (1123b20–1). For honor is clearly the external good most valued by the Spartans, who presumably value virtue primarily for the sake of honor. Aristotle clearly thinks that the Spartans, though wrong in valuing virtue for the sake of honor, are on the right track in valuing honor above all other external goods.

This is the key to solving our second puzzle. For those who value honor above the other external goods will be least tempted to sacrifice virtuous action for the sake of the other goods, and best situated to develop a proper appreciation of virtue. Focused as they are on honor, with other goods out of their deliberative way, they are best situated to come to see the true connection between honor and virtue. If they reflect, they may come to see that the phenomena – namely, that men are honored because they are virtuous and not virtuous because they are honored – betray the primacy of virtue over honor, thus suggesting that virtue is to be chosen for itself, and perhaps also (in times of peace) for the sake of contemplation. There is of course no guarantee that the Spartans will come to see this. But they are as close to authoritative virtue as they can get without already being there. What they need now is reflection.

I will return to this puzzle about the sense in which the Spartans are good after suggesting a solution to the first puzzle. But before tackling that, I should note that identifying kalokagathia with authoritative virtue does not require us to abandon any of our preceding claims. We can still take kalokagathia as a single virtue that can be viewed equally under the aspect of justice and under the aspect of self-love. And we can still allow within kalokagathia a distinction between the large and small scale, thus preserving our hypothesis that megalopsuchia is large-scale kalokagathia. We will simply have to allow a similar distinction within authoritative virtue, and to allow that authoritative virtue can be viewed equally under the aspect of justice and under the aspect of self-love. Whatever goes for kalokagathia will also go for authoritative virtue.

IX. Solution to the First Puzzle: Distribution *kat' Axian*

Let us return, then, to our first puzzle. It is clear in *EE* viii 3 and elsewhere that Aristotle thinks that what is fine is such-as-to-be-praised in a way in which what is merely good is not. This leads to our first puzzle, which is concerned with the question of how natural goods, being goods of fortune, can be fine, where this involves their being suitable objects of praise.

The puzzle arises because there is a tension between something's being a suitable object of praise (and so up to the agent) and its being a good of fortune (and so not up to the agent). We can resolve this puzzle by taking Aristotle's claim that the natural goods are kala for the kaloskagathos as claiming that the kaloskagathos's possession of these goods is kalon, where this involves taking his *possession* of these goods to be a suitable object of praise. We can take his possession of these goods as a suitable object of praise not only insofar as he deserves such goods on account of his virtue, but also – and more importantly – insofar as he has whatever such goods he happens to have on account of his deserts and not simply as a result of fortune.[43]

Aristotle's commitment to the conditionality thesis renders this claim true, even if only trivially so: insofar as the goodness of natural goods for an agent is conditional on his virtue, his virtue will be what *makes* whatever natural goods he happens to have *good for him*. However many friends and possessions the nonvirtuous agent has, these things will not be good for him, and they may actually – especially if he is vicious – harm him. This yields a sense in which genuine (as distinct from merely apparent) good fortune is unavailable to the nonvirtuous agent: however many undeserved "externals" he has, these things will not be goods for him, so his having them cannot count as genuine good fortune. Moreover, if an agent is vicious, these things may actually harm him. In his case, what appears to be good fortune is really ill fortune.

There is another sense, less trivial and more vulnerable to external circumstances, in which the virtuous agent may have the goods he has *because* he deserves them. In a well-ordered Aristotelian society, where external goods are distributed according to worth (*kat' axian*), the virtuous agent will to some extent have the external goods he has on account of his virtue. In this case, however, it will not be appropriate to say that his possession of them is due to fortune. Here again, fortune – at least good fortune – seems to recede. The apparent good fortune of the virtuous agent is not fortune but desert, while the apparent good fortune of the nonvirtuous agent is not good.

This suggests that Socrates' assimilation – or better, reduction – of good fortune to wisdom contains a deeper insight than appears at first glance. In a well-ordered society, where justice prevails, there will be an important sense in which it is no longer appropriate to speak of the external goods as 'goods of fortune': if such goods are distributed to agents in proportion to their virtue, each agent will have the external goods he has not as a result of fortune, but because he deserves them. If I am right in suggesting that Aristotle adopts this Socratic view, then Aristotle may anticipate Kant's conception of the summum bonum as *happiness* in proportion to virtue (where happiness is not Aristotelian *eudaimonia*, but rather the sort of happiness Kant associates with fortune – namely, *Glückseligkeit*).[44]

X. Solution to the Second Puzzle: Praise versus Esteem

The connection between praise and the kalon leaves us with a variant of the the second puzzle, concerning the sense in which the Spartans are good. For this connection may seem to imply that the merely agathos differs from the kaloskagathos in not being subject to praise and blame. But this seems implausible, given that Aristotle views the Spartans as exemplars of the merely agathoi. For he clearly regards the Spartans as subjects of praise and blame. It seems more likely that Aristotle views the kaloskagathos as subject to a different (and higher) sort of praise than that to which the merely agathos is subject.

There are thus two ways in which we might interpret *EE* viii 3. First, we

might appeal to the ambiguity in *epainetos*, and take Aristotle to be suggesting that the kaloskagathos is praiseworthy, while the merely agathos,
though not praiseworthy, is *such-as-to-be-praised* (presumably for instrumental or pragmatic reasons).[45] Alternatively, we might take Aristotle to be
suggesting that the merely agathos, though genuinely praiseworthy, merits a
different (and lesser) sort of praise than the kaloskagathos. The second alternative is reminiscent of Kant's claim (at *Gr.* 398) that a beneficent action
done from inclination rather than duty

> stands on the same footing as other inclinations – for example, the incli-
> nation for honour, which if fortunate enough [*glücklicherweise*] to hit on
> something beneficial and right and consequently honourable, deserves
> praise and encouragement [*Lob und Aufmunterung*], but not esteem
> [*Hochschätzung*].[46]

Aristotle may be making a similar point: that the merely agathos deserves
praise and encouragement, but not esteem. And this seems plausible, if praise
and encouragement play a role in establishing and maintaining the natural or
habitual virtues that might, given the right sort of reflection, become authoritative.

Such a reading receives some support from the *Magna Moralia*, which
draws a distinction between *timia* (goods that are honored, including nous
and virtue), and *epaineta* (goods that are praised, including the virtues):

> Of goods, some are to-be-honored [*timia*], and others are such-as-to-be-
> praised [*epaineta*], while others are potential.
>
> By to-be-honored I mean this sort of thing: the divine, the better (for ex-
> ample, soul and *nous*), the more ancient, the [first] principle, and such
> things. For to-be-honored are all the things to which honor applies, and
> honor attends all such things. Virtue [*aretē*], then, is to-be-honored, at least
> in cases where someone has come to be excellent as a result of it. For then
> he has *already attained* the character of virtue.
>
> Such-as-to-be-praised are, for example, virtues [*aretai*], for praise stems
> from actions according to these.
>
> Potential are, for example, office, wealth, strength and beauty. For the
> excellent man is able to use these well, the base man badly.[47]

The shift from the singular *aretē* to the plural *aretai* – where the singular
aretē is to-be-honored and the plural *aretai* are such-as-to-be-praised – may
indicate implicit reliance on the distinction between kalokagathia (complete
and authoritative virtue) and the various particular natural or civic virtues. If
so, then it's plausible to read *EE* viii 3 as allowing that the natural or civic

virtues of the merely agathos are such-as-to-be-praised but not to-be-honored, thus recalling Kant's claim.[48]

Since Aristotle explicitly places the divine among things to-be-honored, the fact that *EE* viii 3 goes on to say that the divine – qua object of contemplation – provides a standard with reference to which the kaloskagathos is to select among natural goods strengthens this suggestion, and appears to add a decidedly non-Kantian but characteristically Aristotelian intellectualist twist. It suggests that Aristotle may take the kaloskagathos to deserve honor (and not simply praise) because he – unlike the merely agathos – is virtuous for the sake of contemplation (and not for the sake of honor and other external goods).

There is, however, another more Kantian way to read this passage, not necessarily incompatible with the first. For we've seen that the divine – qua final cause and object of imitation – may serve as our model in either, and indeed both, of two ways. The god is not only a subject (and object) of contemplation. The god is also maximally – indeed exclusively – self-determined both in the sense that he is governed by an internal standard and in the sense that fortune plays no role in determining his being. Fortune does not endow him with natural impulses that might tempt him to depart from his own internal standard. So praise won't in his case serve its normal practical role. It won't, for example, motivate him to resist temptations posed by unfortunate desires. In this sense, the god is beyond praise: he is to-be-honored.

EE viii 3 can thus be read as suggesting that the kaloskagathos deserves honor (and not simply praise) because he (unlike the merely agathos) is maximally self-determined. For his nous, with which he identifies, serves as an internal standard – a "law within" – regulating his conduct. Nous enables him to determine the relative values of various goods for *himself*, and without reference to externally imposed standards. He sees that contemplation and virtue are to be chosen for themselves and not for the sake of contingent rewards (like wealth and honor). So he is internally and not externally motivated.

In this respect, the kaloskagathos differs from those (like the merely agathoi) who choose virtue for the sake of external goods (like wealth and honor). For their behavior is (as Aristotle clearly recognizes) vulnerable to public opinion about what is and is not to be honored in their society in a way in which the behavior of the kaloskagathos is not.[49] In this sense, the behavior of the merely agathos is "heteronomous." But the kaloskagathos, in identifying with his nous, is maximally self-determined. He has shed as far as possible the effects of constitutive luck and has made the transition from civic virtue, a product of (external) habituation, to authoritative virtue, a product of (internal) reflection. In his case, praise no longer plays its normal

192

practical role, which we can now see is primarily developmental. For praise serves to motivate those – like the merely agathos – who haven't yet come to appreciate virtue for itself. But the kaloskagathos, who has come to appreciate virtue for itself, no longer needs praise and encouragement: he now deserves honor or esteem.

NOTES

1. I follow Franz Susemihl, *Aristotelis Ethica Eudemia* (Leipzig: Teubner, 1884), in referring to this chapter as *EE* viii 3, taking it together with the two preceding chapters to constitute (part of) a book distinct from *EE* vii. So does Michael Woods, *Aristotle: Eudemian Ethics Books I, II and VIII* (Oxford University Press, 1982). Others take these chapters as belonging to *EE* vii, referring to them as *EE* vii 13–15, as in the Revised Oxford Translation, edited by Jonathan Barnes (Princeton, N.J.: Princeton University Press, 1984), and the new Oxford Text, prepared by R. R. Walzer and J. M. Mingay (Oxford University Press, 1991). There is controversy about the proper location of these chapters, which are fragmentary and seem to pick up in the midst of a discussion that does not follow naturally on the discussion of friendship in *EE* vii. See note 41. I will use the following abbreviations to refer to other works by Aristotle (all in the Revised Oxford Translation): *EN, Nicomachean Ethics; MM, Magna Moralia; Pol., Politics*. All translations are my own, except where indicated.
2. Allen Wood, "The Dignity of Rational Nature" (unpublished), relying on my "Impersonal Friends," *Monist* 74 (1991): 3–29.
3. See Christine Korsgaard, "Kant's Formula of Humanity," *Kant-Studien* 77 (1986): 181–202 (esp. 196–7).
4. On natural or external goods, also known as goods of fortune, see John Cooper, "Aristotle and the Goods of Fortune," *Philosophical Review* 94 (1985): 173–96.
5. This needn't conflict with the *Metaphysics'* claim that we desire things because we think them fine, which may refer only to what is fine in itself and not to things that become fine (or fine for the agent) as a result of being chosen for the sake of what is fine in itself.
6. See Plato's *Euthydemus* 279–81, and compare *Meno* 87–8. On these texts, see Gregory Vlastos, *Socrates: Ironist and Moral Philosopher* (Ithaca, N.Y.: Cornell University Press, 1991), pp. 200–32; T. H. Irwin, "Socrates the Epicurean?" *Illinois Classical Studies* 11 (1986): 85–112; and Christopher Bobonich, "Plato's Theory of Goods in the *Laws* and *Philebus*," *Proceedings of the Boston Area Colloquium in Ancient Philosophy* 9 (1995): 101–39
7. See Immanuel Kant, *Groundwork of the Metaphysic of Morals*, trans. by H J. Paton. Compare with *Euthydemus* 280b–1b, where Socrates emphasizes the importance of use (*hē chrēsis*) – and ultimately right use – as opposed to acquisition or possession (*hē ktēsis*).
8. Socrates may agree. He introduces temperance, justice, and bravery (at 279b5) separately from wisdom (*sophia*). And he explicitly considers (at 281c) the possibility of misusing (to one's own detriment) bravery and temperance. For a com-

parison of Kant's views with those expressed by Socrates in the *Euthydemus* and *Meno*, see Stephen Engstrom, "Kant's Conception of Practical Wisdom," *Kant-Studien* 88 (1997): 16–43

9. There is, however, debate about the Stoics' familiarity with Aristotle. See F. H. Sandbach, *Aristotle and the Stoics* (= *Proceedings of the Cambridge Philological Society* 10 [1985]). Moreover, one might object that I read Socrates through Stoic lenses, but that is a matter that I cannot discuss here. On Kant's acquaintance with the ancients, see Klaus Reich, "Kant and Greek Ethics," *Mind* 48 (1939): 339–54, 446–63. See also Julia Annas, "The Hellenistic Version of Aristotle's Ethics," *Monist* 73 (1990): 80–96; and Chapter 8, this volume, which fails (in my view) to do justice to the Socratic antecedents of the Stoic views she contrasts with those of Aristotle. I find it odd that she turns to the Stoics (rather than to Socrates) for evidence that a sharp distinction between moral and nonmoral reasoning was conceptually available to Aristotle.

10. This raises the possibility of reading Aristotle's conception of phronēsis as the result of reflection on the sort of knowledge required if we are to accept the Socratic identification of virtue with knowledge. For discussion of this possibility, see John McDowell, "Virtue and Reason," *Monist* 62 (1979): 331–50.

11. I discuss intellectualist interpretations of *EN* x in "Human Nature and Intellectualism in Aristotle," *Archiv für Geschichte der Philosophie* 68 (1986): 70–95.

12. Since the *-etos* suffix in adjectives like *hairetos* and *epainetos* may indicate either (a) that something is *in fact* the sort of thing that is chosen (or praised) or (b) that something is the sort of thing that *ought* to be chosen (or praised), I render these adjectives 'such-as-to-be-chosen' and 'such-as-to-be-praised', with a view to capturing this ambiguity. For this formulation (unlike 'choiceworthy' and 'praiseworthy') seems to me to allow sense (b) without requiring it: an action may be such-as-to-be-praised in the sense (a) that members of a given society typically praise such actions, even though it is not such-as-to-be-praised in the sense (b) that it is praiseworthy.

13. Think here of Kant's men of sympathetic temperament, who "without any further motive of vanity or self-interest find an inner pleasure in spreading happiness around them" (*Gr.* 398). For more on these men, see C. M. Korsgaard, Chapter 7, this volume.

14. Sarah Broadie, *Ethics with Aristotle* (Oxford University Press, 1991), p. 379, emphasis added. Cf. Anthony Kenny, *Aristotle on the Perfect Life* (Oxford University Press, 1992).

15. For useful general discussion of the Spartans, see Stephen White, *Sovereign Virtue* (Stanford, Calif.: Stanford University Press, 1992), pp. 219–46.

16. These labels are borrowed from Bishop Butler's discussion of personal identity in the first appendix to *The Analogy of Religion* (1736).

17. I add the parenthetical "apparently" because I want to suspend judgment for now on Aristotle's commitment to the comparative claim, which is the focus of my discussion. Although Aristotle begins with an explicitly comparative question – whether one ought to love oneself or someone else most of all – it doesn't follow that his answer will ultimately be comparative. For in prefacing his question by

194

saying "it is puzzled" (*aporeitai*), Aristotle indicates that he seeks here to resolve an *aporia*. And it is characteristic of him to resolve such *aporiai* by rejecting the initial terms in which they are stated.

18. I say "element" here rather than "part of soul" in order to allow for the possibility that nous is (as Menn has argued) the *virtue* of the rational part of soul. See Stephen Menn, "Aristotle and Plato on God as *Nous* and as the Good," *Review of Metaphysics* 45 (1992): 543–73.

19. See Richard Kraut, *Aristotle and the Human Good* (Princeton, N.J.: Princeton University Press, 1989), esp. pp. 115–28; and Julia Annas (with comments by Kraut), "Self-Love in Aristotle," *Southern Journal of Philosophy* 27, supplementary volume (1988): 1–23.

20. Irwin has changed this in recent printings, which now read "when everyone *contends* to achieve what is fine and strains to do the finest actions" (emphasis added). But Irwin still speaks of competition in his commentary, at 1168b26. The change in translation is no doubt motivated by his desire to discourage the tendency to read Aristotle as committed to an objectionable sort of moral competition. But Irwin still wants to say that Aristotle is committed to an unobjectionable sort of moral competition, like that attributed to him by Kraut. See Irwin, "Prudence and Morality in Greek Ethics," *Ethics* 105 (1995): 284–95, commenting on Nicholas White, "Conflicting Parts of Happiness in Aristotle's Ethics," ibid., 258–83. See also note 26, this chapter.

21. See Allen Wood, Chapter 5, this volume.

22. Strictly speaking, a zero-sum condition (in which one person's loss is another's gain because the sum of benefits to be distributed is fixed) is too strong. For competition may increase the sum of benefits to be distributed, and this seems especially likely in the sort of competition Aristotle seems to have in mind. But insofar as competition is essentially comparative in that one person wins (regardless of his absolute "score") only if he has more than his competitors, so that one person's gain (even if only relative) is typically another person's loss (even if only relative), we might represent the competitive dimension itself as having a zero-sum character.

23. A point apparently missed by Kraut, who speaks as if competitions never ended – and indeed couldn't end – in ties. See Annas ("Self-Love in Aristotle") for a reading similar to mine, though she finds it so difficult to admit that Aristotle is not talking about competition that she ends up claiming that he "reinterprets the notion of competition" so that "true competition is not really competition at all." It seems to me less oxymoronic to claim that he's talking about competition (if at all) only in the metaphorical sense mentioned earlier.

24. I prefer the more neutral 'yield' to Irwin's 'sacrifice' for *proēsetai*, which is often used in the sense of 'to abandon freely', as in the case where someone gives something up without asking anything in exchange.

25. Kant makes a similar point in the *Metaphysics of Morals*, where he claims (at 386) that "it is a contradiction for me to make another's *perfection* my end" (Gregor's translation, emphasis added).

26. This suggests that one might also reject Irwin's rendering of 1168b25–9, which

(like the Revised Oxford Translation) represents Aristotle as saying that the proper self-lover aims to do virtuous actions above all other *agents*. It is possible, however, to read Aristotle as claiming that the proper self-lover aims to do virtuous actions above all other *things*, taking *pantōn* as neuter. But even if one insists on taking *pantōn* as referring to persons, one needn't take it as part of the *content* of the virtuous person's aim. We can take Aristotle as claiming (a) that the virtuous person, above all others, aims to do virtuous actions; rather than (b) that the virtuous person aims at outdoing all others in virtuous action. Irwin, however, wants (in his comments on White) to attribute a version of (b) to Aristotle. But as I argue in note 28, it's not obvious that Aristotle views the virtuous agent as seeking to outdo his friends in the pursuit of virtuous action.

27. See note 17.

28. It seems plausible that the competition to which Aristotle refers in *EN* iv 3 is *not* competition between the megalopsuchos and his character friends, but rather competition between the megalopsuchos and less intimate but nevertheless worthy characters. This would be fully compatible with the megalopsuchos doing all he can to bring it about that his character friends achieve the best of which they are capable, even in cases where they are likely to outstrip him. That superiority per se is probably not the issue can be seen by asking oneself whether the megalopsuchos would be more likely to choose for his character friend (a) someone slightly superior to him in virtue or (b) someone slightly inferior to him in virtue. My hunch is that the true megalopsuchos, appreciating the value of virtue as he does, will choose the superior friend. This hunch receives some support from *Laws* 731d–2b, where Plato says (in a passage that anticipates Aristotle's association of megalopsuchia with proper as distinct from improper self-love) that the man who strives to be "great" (*megan*) will not love himself excessively (i.e., improperly) but will pursue one who is better than himself. Plato's use of *diōkein* with the accusative of person suggests a lover's "pursuit" of his beloved, thus suggesting that the megalopsuchos will pursue someone better than himself, not only in order to associate with his superior (presumably for the sake of self-improvement), but also (as suggested here) with a view to awarding goods (like political office) to those (if any) more deserving than himself (cf. *MM* 1212b15–20, quoted in Section V). Plato also says here that improper self-love is the cause of all wrongdoing, thus anticipating the view I attribute to Aristotle (in Section V) that proper self-love is in a sense the whole of virtue. For more on Plato's anticipation of the views I attribute to Aristotle, see note 37.

29. See *EN* 1131a24ff. and *Pol.* 1301b30ff.

30. Distribution of women *kat' axian* may sound silly to us, but one need think only of the quarrel between Achilles and Agamemnon to see how seriously Aristotle might have taken it.

31. For a discussion of this distinction, see Bernard Williams, "Justice as a Virtue," in Amélie Rorty, ed., *Essays on Aristotle's Ethics* (Berkeley: University of California Press, 1980), pp. 189–99; and David K. O'Connor, "Aristotelian Justice as a Personal Virtue," *Midwest Studies in Philosophy* 13 (1988): 417–27.

32. See Wood, Chapter 5, this volume, on Kant's distinction between "self-

benevolence'' (*Eigenliebe*, or *philautia*) and ''self-conceit'' (*Eigendünkel*, or *arrogantia*).

33. The fact that *EN* ix contrasts proper self-love with friendship rather than justice is not a problem for this view. For it is clear in *EN* viii 9 (and elsewhere) that Aristotle takes friendship and justice to be closely related. See, for example, his claim (at 1155a28) that ''the justice that is most just seems to belong to friendship'' (Irwin's translation). Consider also the importance he attaches to ''civic friendship,'' discussed by John Cooper in ''Political Animals and Civic Friendship,'' in G. Patzig, ed., *Aristoteles' ''Politik''* (Göttingen: Vandenhoeck & Ruprecht, 1990), pp. 220–41.

34. For some defense of the authenticity of the *Magna Moralia*, see Franz Dirlmeier, *Aristoteles, Magna Moralia* (Berlin: Academie Verlag, 1963); and John Cooper, ''The *Magna Moralia* and Aristotle's Moral Philosophy,'' *American Journal of Philology* 94 (1973): 327–49. Even if the *Magna Moralia* was not itself written by Aristotle, I take it to provide genuine evidence of his views.

35. We needn't worry here that identifying virtue with appreciating virtue is circular or regressive. For we're talking about the whole of virtue, whose content is provided by the various particular virtues (just as the content of general justice is provided by the particular virtues of which it is said to be the whole). But it is instructive to think here of the problems raised in Plato's *Charmides* concerning the proposed identification of temperance with self-knowledge.

36. See *Politics* vii 14 and the use Kraut makes of it in chap. 2 of *Aristotle on the Human Good.*

37. *Pol.* 1287a28–32; cf. 1296a 16–20 and *EN* 1134a35–b8. The idea of nous as divine and as providing a kind of law within the self did not originate with Aristotle, and is familiar from Platonic texts. See, e.g., *Laws* 714a, where Plato says that we should obey what is immortal in us, assigning the name 'law' to the distribution (presumably of goods and offices) commanded by nous (*tēn tou nou dianomēn*), and *Republic* 591d, where Plato says that it is better for everyone to be governed by what is divine and intelligent (*hupo theiou kai phronimou archesthai*), the best situation being one in which this principle is proper (*oikeion*) and internal to the subject rather than imposed from without. Other sources invoke the idea of a law within the soul, an idea whose time for historical study has come. See, e.g., Democritus B 264, which says that one should have a sense of shame (or awe) most of all in relation to oneself (*heōuton malista aideisthai*), letting this be established as *law in one's soul (touton nomon tēi psuchēi kathestanai)*. For discussion of this and other texts relevant to many of my present concerns, see Douglas L. Cairns, *Aidōs: The Psychology and Ethics of Honor and Shame in Ancient Greek Literature* (Oxford University Press, 1993).

38. On this problem, concerning the role played by factors beyond our control (like upbringing and natural endowment) in determining what sorts of characters we have, see Thomas Nagel, ''Moral Luck,'' in *Mortal Questions* (Cambridge University Press, 1979), pp. 24–38; and Michele Moody-Adams, ''On the Old Saw That Character Is Destiny,'' in O. Flanagan and A. Rorty, eds., *Identity, Character and Morality* (Cambridge, Mass.: MIT Press, 1990), pp. 111–31. I do not

mean to suggest that Aristotle's concerns are precisely the same as those of contemporary Kantians. I think, for example, that my view is compatible with Meyer's view that Aristotle's concern with responsibility for character does not stem from the "modern" assumption that responsibility for character is a necessary condition for holding agents morally responsible (and so praise- and blameworthy). See Susan Sauvé Meyer, *Aristotle on Moral Responsibility* (Oxford: Blackwell, 1993), esp. chap. 5. For I assimilate Aristotle's concern with responsibility for character to his view that we should strive as far as possible to achieve the sort of self-sufficiency characteristic of the gods, whom Aristotle takes to be beyond praise and blame. So even though I disagree with many of the details of Meyer's account, I do not think her basic picture incompatible with mine. But a full discussion of Aristotle's views on responsibility for character and their relation to my basic picture calls for a separate discussion.

39. Here I accept Meyer's account of habituation as proceeding in two stages, an early stage in which parents and educators are responsible for a child's development, and a later stage (in play at *EN* 1179b34–80a4, 1103b14–21, and 1114a3–13) in which a young adult, who now knows that he will become virtuous (or vicious) as a result of repeatedly performing what he has been taught are virtuous (or vicious) actions, thus comes to be responsible, in performing such actions, for the sort of person he is. Meyer argues that this responsibility is only "qualified" and not "full," since the young adult may fail (through no fault of his own) to be properly equipped to embark on the final stage of habituation: he may, for example, have been poorly habituated at the first stage, so that he now has the wrong beliefs about what sorts of action are and are not virtuous. Here, however, I'd like to suggest that Aristotle's attitudes toward responsibility for *character* may be asymmetrical in a way in which his attitudes toward responsibility for *actions* are not. Even if he rejects the Socratic view that agents are responsible for virtuous actions in a way in which they are not responsible for vicious actions, Aristotle may still believe that agents are responsible for having virtuous characters in a way in which they are not responsible for having vicious characters. For he may think that those who are fortunate enough to have a good upbringing develop the nous that enables them to "ratify" their characters, thus achieving fuller responsibility for their characters than their poorly habituated counterparts can achieve. I take it that Aristotle's teleological approach to explanation renders him receptive to asymmetrical accounts of this sort.

40. There is need here for an account of what nous is, and of how exactly this process of identification with one's nous is supposed to work. These are tasks for another essay, which must take as its point of departure the work of Stephen Menn. (See note 18.)

41. Such similarities together with the order of topics in the *MM* – which tends to follow the order of the *EE* – support Dirlmeier's hypothesis (to which I am sympathetic) that *EE* viii was meant to precede the discussion of friendship in *EE* vii. If this is right, then it's plausible to view *EE* viii as an early version of material later replaced by the common books on the intellectual virtues and incontinence. This has the advantage that it allows us to remain agnostic about the

original home of the common books, though it fails as a result to provide an unambiguously Nicomachean parallel to *EE* viii 3. But I'm less concerned with the original home of the distinction between natural and authoritative virtue than with its correspondence to (and ability to shed light on) the distinction between mere goodness and kalokagathia.

42. We might also ask whether the other states falling short of authoritative bravery can be construed as products of something like constitutive luck. This certainly seems plausible in the case of those who appear brave because they tend to be hopeful (*euelpides*) as a result of past victories.

43. This does not require us to take praise to play any role in motivating the kaloskagathos, though it may play a role in motivating others to distribute goods to him according to his worth. Nor does this require us to say that Aristotle regards virtue as an infallible means to securing the natural goods one deserves on account of one's virtue. It requires only that he take virtue to be the cause of an agent's having whatever such goods he happens to have.

44. See Stephen Engstrom, Chapter 4, this volume, and "The Concept of the Highest Good in Kant's Moral Theory," *Philosophy and Phenomenological Research* 52 (1992): 747–80.

45. On this ambiguity, see note 12.

46. Note also that Kant sometimes appears to subscribe to something like the first view: beneficent actions done from inclination are such-as-to-be-praised (by our legislators and fellow citizens who take an external and legal point of view) even if such actions are not praiseworthy (the determination of which requires us to take an internal and moral point of view). Kant would say that our legislators and fellow citizens are no more able than we ourselves are to know how praiseworthy our actions really are.

47. *MM* 1183b20–30; emphasis added. See *EN* i 12, where Aristotle asks whether *eudaimonia*, which is clearly not a potential good, is among the *epaineta* or rather (as he affirms) among the *timia*. Both passages should be compared with *EE* 1219b8–16.

48. It is important to note that the two puzzles concern different objects of praise. Praising the *virtues or virtuous actions* of the merely agathos (as required by our solution to the second puzzle) is not incompatible with refusing (as required by our solution to the first puzzle) to praise his *possession of external goods*.

49. See *EN* 1095b24–6, where Aristotle says, "[Honor] seems to depend more on those honoring than on the one being honored, while we divine that the good is something proper [*oikeion ti*] [to the agent] and not easily taken away."

IV
Practical Reason and Moral Psychology

7

From Duty and for the Sake of the Noble: Kant and Aristotle on Morally Good Action

CHRISTINE M. KORSGAARD

Philosophers have long supposed that Aristotle and Kant disagree about many fundamental issues in moral philosophy. Aristotle tells us that an agent lacks virtue unless he enjoys the performance of virtuous actions, while in the *Groundwork* Kant seems to claim that the person who does her duty in the teeth of contrary inclination displays an especially high degree of moral worth. Aristotle argues for the virtuous life by attempting to prove that, given the human *telos*, some form of the virtuous life is the happiest that we can live. Kant scorns appeals to happiness as irrelevant to morality and bids us remember the special vocation of an autonomous being. Aristotle emphasizes the difficulty of formulating general principles of action, and the important role of judgment and perception in practical deliberation. Kant, on the other hand, provides us with a method for testing proposed maxims to see whether their actions are permissible, forbidden, or required. And finally, Aristotle has lately been categorized as a "virtue theorist" who holds that an action's value consists in its being the expression of a virtue; while Kant is supposedly a deontologist who thinks that the value of an action rests in its conformity to a rule.

Yet behind these contrasts, apparent and real, is one undeniable similarity. Aristotle and Kant both believe that in human beings, reason can be practical. This is a view about what specifically human action is, or about how human action is different from that of the other animals. It is the view that human beings exercise *choice*, in a specific sense that I will explain in this essay, in the determination of our actions. Since moral or ethical value pertains only to human action, it seems natural to think that it is somehow related to, or supervenes on, the specific character of human action. And I think that we do find this idea in both Aristotle and Kant. Both of them believe that the moral value of an action is a function of the way in which it is chosen.

I believe that these claims about the practical employment of reason are

203

deeper, both in fact and in Aristotle and Kant's theories, than philosophers have generally recognized. To say that human beings are rational is not just to say that we are rule-following or logical, but rather to say that we are capable of authentic mental activity, of an engagement with the world that goes beyond mere reaction. In Aristotle's account of theoretical reason, the ultimate expression of our rational nature is our participation in the active intellect that imparts form and intelligibility to the natural world. In Kant's more skeptical account, it is the mind's attempt to construct a systematic, unified, and intelligible world out of the confused mass of phenomena that are presented to it. To say that reason is also *practical* is to say that our actions, the expressions of our wills, can in a similar way be fully active, self-generated, or in Kant's special sense, spontaneous.[1] And if morality is the full expression of practical reason, then this is the distinguishing feature of the moral agent: that her actions are more truly active, more authentically her own, than those of agents who fall short of moral goodness. To have the distinctively moral attitude, then, is to have an active as opposed to a merely reactive relationship to the world around us.[2]

At the same time, both of these philosophers were aware that the human mind (unlike the divine one) is also passive or receptive with respect to the world. A central concern of both Aristotle's *On the Soul* and Kant's first *Critique* is to explain the respective contributions of activity and passivity to our mental lives. And this is a central concern in the ethical writings of both philosophers as well. Aristotle and Kant of course acknowledge that passions, inclinations, and impulses, as well as reflective deliberation and choice, play an important role in the determination of action. And I believe that for both, the concern of a theory of *virtue*, in particular, is to explain how that role may be accommodated in a theory of rationally governed and so authentically self-generated conduct.

These are large claims, and obviously I cannot undertake to defend them in any adequate way here. I offer them as background to the argument I am going to make, which concerns the very first contrast that I mentioned. In the first section of the *Groundwork*, Kant claims that a person who helps others with pleasure from motives of natural sympathy displays no moral worth, while a person who lacks any natural inclination to help others but nevertheless does so, from the motive of duty, does display moral worth (*G* 398).[3] This appears to be in stark contrast with Aristotle's claim that it is the mark of a good person to take pleasure in moral action (*NE* 1.8 1099a 16–21). In this essay I will argue that this apparent contrast does not reflect any ethical disagreement between the two philosophers at all. There is a disagreement at work here, but it is psychological rather than ethical. My argument will take the following course. In Section I, I will look at Kant's view of what gives an action moral worth, as presented in the first section of the

Groundwork, and in the course of that explain why Kant says what he does about the naturally sympathetic person. In Section II, I will argue that Aristotle holds an essentially similar view about what gives an action moral worth. Both philosophers, I will argue, think that what gives an action moral value is the fact that it is chosen for its intrinsic rightness. Finally, in Section III, I will return to the question of the value of acting from natural inclination, and try to explain the real source of Kant and Aristotle's apparent difference on this point.

I. Acting from Duty

Groundwork I opens with a claim that Kant believes his readers will accept, namely, that the only thing in the world that has unconditional value is a good will. The good will is good "through its willing" (*G* 394), which means that it is in actions expressive of a good will, morally good actions, that we will see this unconditional value realized. Now the project of *Groundwork I* is to discover the principle of the good will, for this will be the moral law. Kant's idea is this. Good-willed actions are good because of the way that they are willed, or, as I will put it, chosen. So once we know how they are chosen, we will know what makes them good. Since the moral law tells us to perform good actions, it will tell us to perform actions that have that feature – whatever it is – that makes actions good. Since you and I already know how the investigation turns out, I can perhaps try to say this more clearly. Kant thinks that what makes an action good is that its maxim qualifies to be a universal law. So what he is going to try to show is that the principle of a good will is that of choosing actions whose maxims qualify to be universal laws. That's what good people think about when they choose their actions – whether their maxims qualify to be universal laws.

Now in order to bring this out, Kant says, he is going to look at a particular class of good actions, namely those that are done from duty. Duty is the good will operating under "certain subjective restrictions and hindrances, which far from hiding a good will or rendering it unrecognizable, rather bring it out by contrast and make it shine forth more brightly" (*G* 397). To discover what is distinctive about good-willed actions, what their principle is, Kant proposes to compare actions done from duty with actions done from other kinds of motives, to see what makes them essentially different. He mentions three other kinds of actions. Actions that are recognized as contrary to duty are set aside. It is worth attending to Kant's own words here; he says, "I here omit all actions already recognized as contrary to duty, *even though they may be useful for this or that end*, for in the case of these the question does not arise at all whether they might be done from duty" (*G* 397, emphasis added). I take Kant to be saying that any value these actions may have must come from their utility. Kant also sets aside, and for the same reason, actions that are in accordance with duty but that are not chosen for their own sakes. The prudent merchant who always charges honestly because a good reputation helps his business exemplifies this category. Kant clearly takes it to be obvious, just as Aristotle does, that a morally good action must be chosen for its own sake. But being chosen for its own sake is not sufficient to make an action morally good. This point is brought out by the next three examples, in which people who act from duty are contrasted with people who do the same actions from direct or immediate inclination. It is possible to do an action for its own sake just because it is what you like to do. The naturally sympathetic person's action falls into this category. Kant says:

> ... there are many persons so sympathetically constituted that, without any further motive of vanity or self-interest, they find an inner pleasure in spreading joy around them and can rejoice in the satisfaction of others as their own work. But I maintain that in such a case an action of this kind, however dutiful and amiable it may be, has nevertheless no true moral worth. It is on a level with such actions as arise from other inclinations. (G 398)

Some readers have supposed that what Kant is saying here is that the sympathetic person is really acting for the sake of his own pleasure; that is, that his real purpose is to please himself. According to this view, Kant believes in some sort of psychological hedonism about nonmoral motives, and so supposes that our inclinations are all selfish.[4] Such a reading would be inconsistent with several of the things Kant says, some of them in the passage I just quoted. Kant characterizes the sympathetic person as "amiable" and without any motive of self-interest, for instance. Most importantly, however, it flies in the teeth of the conclusion Kant draws from these examples, which is this: "From what has gone before it is clear that the purposes which we may have in our actions . . . cannot give to actions any unconditional and moral worth" (G 400). What makes this clear is precisely the fact that a person who does a beneficent action from immediate inclination and a person who does one from duty have the *same purpose* – namely, to help someone. Both of these people help others for its own sake. Kant goes on to assert that what gives an action moral value, then, is not the agent's purpose, but rather the "maxim" or "principle of volition" on which it is done.[5]

To understand these claims it is necessary to understand the psychology behind them. According to Kant, our nature presents us with what he calls 'incentives' (*Triebfedern*), which prompt or tempt us to act in certain ways. We might say that the incentives present certain actions along with their ends to us as eligible. We are, at least in part, passive with respect to these, although that is a remark I will qualify later. Among these incentives are our ordinary desires and inclinations. Now the incentives do not operate on us directly as causes of action. Instead, they are considerations that we take into account in deciding what to do. If you decide to act on an incentive, you "make it your maxim" to act in the way suggested by the incentive. How do you decide that? In the *Groundwork* and even more specifically in *Religion within the Limits of Reason Alone* (*Rel.* 36/31), Kant suggests that there are two principles of volition or choice that might govern this decision: morality or self-love.[6] If you are operating under the principle of self-love, your choice is to do what will gratify you, what will satisfy your desires. Kant's point about the naturally sympathetic person is that he is acting under this principle of volition or choice. The trouble with him is not that he wants to help others only because it pleases him to do so. The trouble is that he *chooses* to help others *only* because he *wants* to. His action is chosen as a desirable one, one that he would enjoy doing.[7]

The person who acts from duty, by contrast, chooses the action because she conceives it as one that is required of her. And here we must be careful to draw the lesson from what has gone before. The point is not that her *purpose* is "to do her duty." As I said before, she chooses the action for its own sake: her purpose is to help. The point is that she chooses helping as her purpose *because* that is what she is required to do. Kant takes this to be equivalent to being moved by the thought of the maxim of the action, the principle of doing it, as a kind of law. The dutiful person takes the maxim of helping others to *express* a requirement. Rather subtly, the contrast between doing the right thing from duty and doing the right thing from immediate inclination is also supposed to show that seeing a maxim as a law is attending to something about its form rather than about its matter. The person who acts from immediate inclination and the person who acts from duty in a sense act in accordance with the same material principle, which Kant specifies as "to be beneficent where one can" (*G* 398). But the person who acts from self-love sees such action as desirable, while the person who acts from duty takes that principle to be a law. So the dutiful person's principle of volition is to act on those maxims that have the form of a law. This also makes a difference in the kind of value that these two agents accord to the action. For the person who acts from inclination, the action has an extrinsic value, a value that it inherits from his own desires. But the person who acts from duty sees the value of the action as intrinsic: lawlike form is a property that is internal to the maxim and so is in the action itself.[8]

Later in the *Groundwork* (*G* 421-3), and also in the second *Critique* (*C2* 67-70), we learn more about what this thought involves. To think about whether your maxim has the form of a law is to think about whether you could will to be part of an order of things in which everyone acted in the way specified in the maxim. So it is to think about what sort of world this would be if everyone acted as you propose to act. The dutiful person helps, then, because the vision of a world in which people do not help one another is in a certain way unacceptable to her, and she is moved by that fact. I do not mean, of course, that she is moved by some thought about the consequences of what she actually does – she does not see doing a beneficent action as a way of producing a world in which everyone helps. It is rather that if we could not choose to live in a world in which no one helps, if we find that we *must* will that people should help, then the principle of beneficence must be a law by its very nature, a law in itself. Seen this way, it looks as if the difference between the two characters is that the dutiful person has a further thought about *helping*, or takes a more reflective stance toward it, than the naturally sympathetic person. Helping is not just something that it is nice to do, but something that one must do, because of the sort of action that it is. Since the good person chooses her actions by attending to their lawlike form, that is what the moral law instructs us to do – to choose those maxims that have lawlike form.

There is a hitch in this argument, which I will come back to in a moment. At this point I want to focus attention on two important features of the account. First, Kant gives us what we might call a double-aspect theory of motivation. An agent's motivation to act involves two things – the incentive that presents the action along with its end as eligible, and the principle of volition that governs the agent's choice to act on that incentive. Second, moral value rests specifically in the principle of volition that is exercised in the choice of the action. Moral value supervenes on *choice*.

This has several important implications. One is that on this account the presence or absence of a natural inclination makes no difference to the moral value of the action. It is obviously possible to choose an action because you see it as intrinsically required while also thinking that it will be a pleasant thing to do. Kant chooses to discuss cases of good-willed motivation in which no inclination is present – that is, cases of action from duty – for exactly the reason he says he does, because in such cases the operation of the moral principle is especially perspicuous. Relatedly, as I said before, the problem with the naturally sympathetic person is neither that he has an inclination nor that his inclination is covertly selfish, that his own pleasure is his real purpose. His inclination is disinterested, which is why Kant says he is amiable. The problem is that he chooses to help others only because he *has* this inclination. His principle of volition is the problem – it is the principle of doing what he likes to do.

Now in one way this makes it look as if Kant is, after all, saying that the naturally sympathetic person is covertly selfish. If a person chooses to satisfy his inclinations because it gratifies him, doesn't that after all show that he looks to himself? In sorting this issue out I think it will be useful to make a distinction that Kant doesn't make. Kant thinks that when we choose an action we employ some principle of volition. But obviously he does not mean that we always consciously recite this principle in our minds or even that we are always aware of it as we make the choice. Sometimes, the principle is just implicit in the *way* we make the choice. Now this suggests that we can distinguish between more and less reflective versions of both of the characters we are considering here. The unreflective sympathetic person may simply be thinking "I want to help" or perhaps just "This person needs help" and he is moved by that thought. As Kant imagines him, it is his natural inclination to make others happy that interests him in helping, which is why Kant thinks he is implicitly or tacitly acting under the principle of self-love. The more reflective sympathetic person who *consciously* employs the principle of self-love entertains a further thought, but it is a thought about himself, not a thought about helping: "Doing this sort of thing makes me happy, makes me feel good, so I will." Or we might even imagine that he does a calculation of prudence and works out that of all the activities that he finds attractive, helping others will make him happiest: he enjoys it, it makes people like him, and it lacks some of the untoward side effects that other pleasant pursuits may have.[9] In this case, the pleasure he takes in helping may be disinterested, but the decision to pursue that pleasure is not. Similarly, a person may act from duty in a completely unreflective way, simply thinking of an action as required, without thinking much about why it is so or even without really thinking that there *is* a reason why it is so. We might think here of some ordinary conscientious person who has simply accepted the conventional or religious moral system according to which he was brought up. But of course there are more sinister entries into this category: the Nazi soldier who thinks of "duty" as carrying out the orders of his superiors comes immediately to mind. This, as I have tried to bring out, is not how Kant is thinking of the person who acts from duty. For Kant, to act from duty is not just to be moved by a blank conviction that an action is required, but rather to be moved by a more substantial thought that inherently involves an intelligent view of *why* the action is required.[10]

With this distinction in hand it is possible to make certain points. First of all, if we imagine the *reflective* versions of these two characters as I have just described them, it is not hard to accept the claim that the person who acts from duty exhibits a moral worth that the person who acts from inclination lacks. The agent who consciously employs the principle of self-love in his choice does seem to look to himself; in fact he seems to choose beneficence as one might choose a hobby. Second, I think it is pretty clear that many of the readers who find what Kant says here wildly counterintuitive are in fact comparing the *unreflective* versions of both of these characters. If we compare the person who helps impulsively, thinking nothing but "This person needs help'' and being moved by that thought, with a person for whom duty is just blind obedience to an abstract rule, then the first of these two characters seems much more attractive than the second. The right thing to say to such readers, of course, is that this is simply not the comparison that Kant has placed before us.

But it does raise a question about the comparison that Kant *has* placed before us. I think that the comparison that Kant has placed before us is between the more attractive members of each of these two pairs. Kant means to compare the unreflective sympathetic person, who thinks simply, "This person needs help," with the more reflective person who acts from duty with some comprehension of why helping is required. But it is also clear that Kant thinks that the unreflective sympathetic person is tacitly or implicitly acting on the principle of self-love. At least, this is what I am supposing Kant means when he says that the action is on a level with other actions from inclination (*G* 398). So Kant's view seems to be that if you act unreflectively, the principle of self-love is your principle of volition by default. Why does Kant think this?

One answer that I think we should reject is that your tacit principle of volition is what you would say about your choice if you were invited to reflect on why you made it. According to this view, if we asked the impulsively sympathetic person why he helps, and he started to think about it, all he could say is: "I just like to; it gives me pleasure." Perhaps this is why he helps, but once he starts to reflect on his reasons, it will be natural for him to switch from a merely theoretical self-scrutiny to a more practical form of reflection. The question, Why do you help people? is naturally understood as a request for justification and so transmutes into the question why one should help people. So the claim is not that "it gives me pleasure, I like it" is what the unreflective sympathetic person would say if he started to think about why he helps. If he starts to think about why he helps, something altogether different will happen.[11] In fact Kant's argument relies upon this point, since he thinks that the pursuit of reflection – that is, enlightenment – will lead us to a recognition of the categorical imperative as the law of our own autonomy and so to the good.[12]

So I think that all Kant means is this: as long as you haven't reflected on why you help, you are just following your inclinations where they lead. And as long as you are just following your inclinations where they lead, your choice is implicitly governed by the principle of doing what you are inclined to do, what you like. To say that the naturally sympathetic person acts from self-love is not to assign him an unconscious ulterior motive, or a secret selfish thought. It is, precisely, to record the fact that he hasn't thought, that he is allowing his choices to be governed by his natural inclinations, and so is simply following where nature leads.

Now I want to come back to the hitch I mentioned in the argument. I said earlier that the conclusion is that the good-willed person attends to the lawlike form of her maxim in making her choices, and therefore that that is what the moral law tells us to do: to respect, or attend to, lawlike form. But there are, in fact, two senses in which a maxim may have lawlike form. A maxim may be one that *can* be willed as a universal law – it qualifies to be a law. Action on such a maxim is permissible. Or the maxim may be a law in the sense that it *must* be willed; that is, it expresses a duty. The conclusion that Kant is looking for in *Groundwork I* is that a good action is one whose maxim qualifies to be a law. The principle of a good will is to act on a maxim only if it *can* serve as a universal law. But Kant has chosen to focus on the more specific category of duties, actions whose maxims *must* be willed as laws. So the hitch is this: it is unclear how Kant wants us to make the step from the fact that people who act from duty choose their maxims because they see them as principles that *must* be willed as laws to the conclusion that the principle of a good will is that of acting only on maxims that *can* be willed as laws.

I do not know of a smooth way to rescue the presentation of the argument in *Groundwork I*, but it seems clear enough that these two ideas are related. One connection between them is revealed in the negative way in which the categorical imperative is here formulated – "I should never act except in such a way that I can also will that my maxim should become universal law" (*G* 402). Using this formulation we discover that a maxim must be regarded as a law by discovering that the opposite maxim – that of not doing the action in question – cannot be regarded as a law. That Kant has this connection in mind is clear from the fact that in two of the examples, it is the *same* person who first acts from immediate inclination and later, when he has lost his inclination through sorrow or adversity, acts from duty.

Consider, for instance, the naturally sympathetic person. At the beginning of the story, he is a happy person, full of spontaneous sympathy for others. He sees people living on the street and he feels sorry for them. He gives them food or money, and he likes to see the relief and gratitude in their eyes. He enjoys spreading joy around him as he goes about his own business. He's sympathetic and so their delight gives him direct pleasure. Then bad things happen to him. Maybe his wife gets cancer, or his child runs away, or his work, which once seemed promising, comes to nothing. And there is no pleasure in anything for him any more. He is absorbed in his own sorrows, and he has no sympathy for anyone else. But since he has always given to those in need before, it occurs to him that he might, and now for the first time he *thinks* about it. Or maybe one day he passes by someone whom he has often helped before and the person says: "Aren't you going to help me today? You helped me last week, and I am just as hungry as I was last week."

211

And now our hero says to himself: "After all, it is not just because it gives me pleasure that I should help. These poor people are living on the street, and they don't have enough to eat. Someone must help them! What sort of world would we live in if no one helped people who are in need?" Moved by this thought, he helps. And now for the first time his helping has moral worth.[13]

This is the kind of story Kant has in mind in *Groundwork I*. But what I have just said might lead to a misunderstanding. I do not mean to suggest that the only reason a good-willed person asks whether her maxim can be a law is as a way of ferreting out those maxims that must be laws. The categorical imperative test is not a kind of Geiger counter for discovering whether there are any duties in the neighborhood. I do not know how to fit this point into the argument of *Groundwork I*, but I believe that Kant's thought is that a reflective person asks herself whether the consideration on which she proposes to act may really be treated as a *reason* to act. To ask whether a consideration is a reason is to ask whether it may be taken as *normative*. And that, in turn, is to ask whether the maxim of acting on that consideration can be regarded as a kind of *law*. When we experience some incentive to act – say a desire or inclination – you might say that our nature makes a proposal to reason. The proposal is a maxim and it includes a purpose: do this for the sake of that, or do this for its own sake. Reason steps back and considers the proposal; that is, it considers the action as a whole, including the purpose, and determines whether it is a good thing, a thing to be done, or not. Its decision is an act of volition, performed in accordance with a principle of volition. So to *choose* an action is to be moved by the conception of the impulse to do it as a reason. And its being a reason is an intrinsic property, a property of the maxim's form. Reason says yes to the proposal if it can recognize its own form, the form of normativity or law, in the maxim. In that case, the reason for action and so the action itself, having reason's endorsement, are good.

But actions done from duty are reason's own actions in a special way. To see this, recall once again the person whose natural sympathy is blunted by sorrow, but who still helps from the motive of duty. He tests the maxim of not helping, and he finds he must reject it. He is thereby moved to help. What is the incentive in this case? Kant's answer is that it is the feeling of respect for law. The very thought that shows him his duty – the thought that one *must* help those in need – in this case operates as the incentive.

Kant thinks that we cannot say how it is possible for reason to provide an incentive, since that is identical to the question how reason can be practical. But in the second *Critique* he undertakes to describe what happens in us when we are so moved. Let me just quickly sketch this account. Human beings, according to Kant, have a natural tendency to treat our desires and

212

inclinations as authoritative – that is, to think that the fact that we want to do something is in and of itself a reason for doing it. Kant calls this tendency 'self-regard' or 'self-love', and it is more or less identical with the tendency to operate under the principle of self-love as I have described it. There are two strands to this tendency – the selfishness that makes us long for the satisfaction of our inclinations, and the self-conceit that inclines us to take the bare fact that we want to do something as a justification for doing it. When the moral law commands us not to do an action to which we are inclined, it thwarts the inclination, and it humiliates our self-conceit. These feelings are painful. At the same time, however, we experience an awareness of our freedom, which is revealed by our capacity to set inclination aside. We experience freedom as a sense of independence from the neediness of inclination, a sense that is akin to pleasure in that it resembles the divine bliss. The complex mix of affect that results is the feeling of respect for law. Respect for law is not a desire to obey the moral law, or more generally a feeling that exists independently of the law and interests us in it. It is the law itself, the very thought of a requirement, operating as an incentive.[14]

When we are motivated by respect for law, the rational will provides not only the ground of choice but the incentive to act in accordance with that ground. Since the incentive as well as the volition are reason's own productions, a person who is motivated by duty is to an especial degree active and truly spontaneous. She is not reacting to nature's proposals at all, but actively imposing on her own actions, and through them on the world, a kind of shape or form that is the dictate of her own mind. This is the fullest expression of autonomy, and it is this that gives her actions their special moral worth.

II. Acting for the Sake of the Noble

Aristotle, I will now argue, holds a similar conception of what gives actions moral value. That is, he also holds a double-aspect account of motivation; and he holds that what gives actions value is the way that they are chosen. Three aspects of his theory may be mentioned in support of these claims: first, the possibility of continence; second, his account of the role of choice (*prohairesis*) in human action; and third, his claim that a good action is done for the sake of *to kalon* or the noble.

The bare possibility of continence, of course, shows that Aristotle thinks that human agents have the power to step back from our inclinations and decide whether to act on them or not. We sometimes decide not to act on our inclinations; they do not simply drive us into action, or we could not do that. But one might be tempted to think that according to Aristotle such rational control needs to be exercised only by the continent, since the virtuous person's passions are in order, and can be trusted to direct her automatically to the good. But that cannot be right. At least, the difference between continence and virtue cannot lie in whether the *exercise* of reason is involved in the action. For Aristotle makes it clear that what makes continence and virtue both good states is the fact that both of them involve the right kind of choice.

What Aristotle says about choice is initially one of the more puzzling parts of the *Nicomachean Ethics*. Choice, he tells us, is voluntary, but it is not the same as the voluntary since the latter is a wider category. Children and animals do things that are voluntary, but they do not act from choice, and some adult actions – those done ''on the spur of the moment'' – are not chosen although they are voluntary (*NE* III.2 1111a4–10). For an action to be voluntary it is enough that the moving principle is in the agent (*NE* III.1); for choice, something more is needed. After exploring various possibilities, Aristotle decides that since the object of choice is something in our own power that is desired after deliberation, choice must be the deliberate desire of something in our own power (*NE* III.3 1113a10–12). An action is chosen when we have exercised rational deliberation in determining what we are to do, and we are moved by that deliberation to act.

But of course Aristotle also says, notoriously by now, that "we deliberate not about ends but about what contributes to ends" (*ta pros to telos; NE* III.3 1112b12). If we take this to mean that rational deliberation is always instrumental, we will be led to conclude that choice pertains only to actions undertaken for instrumental reasons, or perhaps some natural extension of that category. Chosen actions, that is, would be those that we have determined are necessary and desirable because they will help us to realize ends other than those actions themselves. It would then be the intellectual ability to engage in such rational calculation – instrumental reasoning and other things that are like it – that distinguishes adult human beings from children and animals, and, as a result, chosen actions from the merely voluntary.

This view, however, sits very uneasily with certain other important claims Aristotle makes about choice. For instance, he tells us that virtue is a state of character concerned with choice (*NE* II.6 1106b36), and that choice is more closely bound up with virtue and discriminates character better than actions do (*NE* III.2 1111b5–6). He even says that the virtues are choices or involve choice (*NE* II.5 1106a3). He also tells us that the continent person acts in accordance with his choice, while the incontinent person does not (*NE* III.2 1111b14–15; see also VII.3 1146b22–4). We can hardly suppose that Aristotle is suggesting that instrumental reasoning or some natural extension of it is the surest sign of a person's character, or that he thinks that incontinent people do not engage in any calculation about how to achieve their goals. What is more, Aristotle says that an action is not virtuous unless it is chosen for its own sake (*NE* II.4 1105a30–2, VI.5 1140b5–10). So whatever he means when he says that deliberation concerns what is toward the end rather

214

than the end itself, he cannot mean that an action is never chosen for its own sake.

The interpretative crux here is of course the much-debated question just what sort of a limitation Aristotle means to be imposing on deliberation and choice when he says that they do not concern ends but only what contributes to ends. Some commentators have focused their attention, usefully, on the idea of what is "toward the end" or contributory to the end, emphasizing that this should not be taken to refer only to instrumental reasoning in the narrow sense. Constitutive reasoning should certainly be included, and perhaps we may also include those more distinctively moral forms of reasoning that tell us, say, that an action falls under a principle, conforms to the *orthos logos* or right reason, is in the mean, exemplifies a virtue, or whatever.

This is part of the answer, but it is also important to look closely at Aristotle's conception of an end. Aristotle tells us that wish (*boulēsis*) relates to the end, and that wish is for the good or the apparent good (*NE* III.4 1113a15). He says that choice is "near to" wish, and that we choose to get or avoid something good or bad (*NE* III.2 1111b20; 1112a4). Wish, however, belongs to the rational part of the soul (*OS* III.9 432b5–6). An end, therefore, is not merely a goal, something with a view to which some agent acts. To be an end, something must be conceived as good, where that conception in turn is an act of the rational part of the soul. And to be chosen, to be an object of deliberate desire, an action must be one that contributes to an end in this sense, one that contributes to what is conceived as good. If we then also take "what contributes to the end" in the widest possible sense, the puzzle about virtuous actions being chosen for their own sake dissolves. The deliberation that shows us that an action contributes to the end may be instrumental, constitutive, or moral (i.e., reasoning about what is in the mean, or in accordance with the *orthos logos*). That doesn't matter. What matters is that the deliberation shows us that the action is in some respect *good*. It is the *fact* that we have engaged in rational deliberation to arrive at the idea that the action is good, and been motivated by that deliberation, not the *form* of the rational deliberation, that is definitive of choice.[15] So what Aristotle means is that distinctively human actions, chosen actions, are ones that on deliberation we conceive to be good and desire to do under that conception. That is why chosen actions are the best indicators of character – because they embody, express, or reflect the agent's conception of the good. The incontinent person, incidentally, does not act from choice even if he does engage in some sort of calculation about how to satisfy his vicious desires, because his calculations are not about what contributes to an *end* at all. Since the goal he is pursuing is not even an apparent good – he knows it is bad – it is not in Aristotle's sense an end.

I take it that Aristotle and Kant, therefore, share a view about the distinctive character of human action, or at least – to add Aristotle's characteristic qualification – *adult* human action. Human action, to put it simply, is action that is governed by reason: that is, it is chosen. To say that an action is chosen is to say that it has the endorsement of the agent's reason, that it is conceived as good, and that it is by that conception that the agent is moved.

Kant, as we saw, moves from this picture of human action to a picture of moral value. A morally good action is one chosen because it is *intrinsically* good, because it has the intrinsic form of a law. Is there anything similar to this in Aristotle? If we do not assume in advance that what these two philosophers are saying must be different, one thing looks immediately similar. Aristotle insists that virtuous action must be in accordance with the *orthos logos*, the right reason or right rule. In fact he says it must not merely be in accordance with it but from it: "For it is not merely the state in accordance with right reason, but the state that implies the presence of right reason, that is virtue" (*NE* VI.13 1144b26–7). This suggests that Aristotle thinks a good action is one whose agent sees it as the embodiment of right reason, just as Kant thinks that a morally worthy action is one whose agent sees it as an embodiment of the very form of law. I will come back to this point.

First, however, I want to consider the important argument that can be drawn from Aristotle's view that morally good actions are done "for the sake of the noble" (see e.g., *NE* III.7 1115b12, III.8 1116b3, III.9 1117b9, 1117b17, III.11 1119b15, IV.1 1120a23, IV.2 1122b6). Aristotle tells us three different kinds of things about why good actions are done by virtuous agents. First of all, in at least some cases the actions are done for some specific purposes. For instance, Aristotle tells us that the courageous person who dies in battle lays down his life for the sake of his country or for his friends (*NE* IX.8 1169a17–30); in the same way, it seems natural to say that the liberal person who makes a donation wants to help somebody out; the magnificent person who puts on a play wants to give the city a treat; and so on. At the same time, Aristotle says that virtuous actions are done for their own sake; indeed, action is distinguished from mere production or "making" (*poiein*) by the fact that "good action itself is its end" (*NE* VI.5 1140b5–10). And finally, virtuous actions are done for the sake of the noble.

If we oversimplify Aristotle's moral psychology these will look like three competing accounts of the purpose or aim of virtuous action. If we take Aristotle to hold a double-aspect theory of motivation, however, there is no problem at all. When we say that the courageous person sacrifices himself in battle for its own sake, we need not be denying that he sacrifices himself for the sake of his country. It is the whole package – the action along with its purpose, sacrificing your life for the sake of your country – that is chosen for its own sake. As for nobility, Aristotle seems to think of it very much as Kant thinks of good will – it is the specific kind of *intrinsic* value that moral

216

actions and those who perform them possess. This thought is supported by the account of nobility in the *Rhetoric*, where Aristotle says that the noble is "that which is both desirable for its own sake and also worthy of praise" (*Rhe*. I.9 1366a33). The *Rhetoric* account also confirms the claim that nobility is a property that attaches to an action along with its purpose, for in it Aristotle assigns nobility particularly to actions done for certain purposes, such as to benefit others. In fact, Aristotle suggests here that he shares Kant's view that moral value is exhibited in a special way in actions from which we are sure the agent gets nothing. He says that nobility is exhibited in actions that benefit others rather than the agent, and actions whose advantages will only appear after the agent's death, since in these cases we can be sure the agent himself gets nothing out of it (*Rhe*. I.9 1366b38–67a5).[16]

Now I can be more specific. The view that I take Kant and Aristotle to share is this: when human beings act, we are not driven or directly caused to act by desire, passion, inclination, or instinct. Some incentive, to use Kant's language, presents a certain course of action to us as eligible – it suggests to us that we might undertake a certain action in order to realize a certain end. But reason gives us the capacity to stand back, form a view of this course of action as a whole, and make a judgment about its goodness. This isn't a judgment about whether doing this action will serve some further purpose, about whether it is useful. It is a judgment about its goodness considered as an *action*, not as a mere production. Both Aristotle and Kant would say that to value an action merely as a form of production, as consequentialists later did, is not yet to value it in its specifically ethical character as an action at all. As Aristotle says, "Making and acting are different ... so that the reasoned state of capacity to act is different from the reasoned state of capacity to make (*NE* VI.4 1140a4–5) ... while making has an end other than itself, action cannot; for good action itself is its end" (*NE* VI.5 1140b5–10). This is why *technē* and *praxis* (art and action), are different things (*NE* VI.4). It is with that same thought that Kant sets aside cases like that of the prudent merchant who is honest because it is useful as being wholly irrelevant to his attempt to analyze the moral value of actions. People who view actions merely as useful are not thinking of them, or valuing them, as actions at all. (On this view, we might say that consequentialism is not an ethical theory because it fails to address the subject, which is the goodness of action as such, not as a form of production.) So the capacity to choose is a capacity to make a reflective judgment about the value of an action as such and to be moved by that judgment to perform or avoid the action. Importantly, this is at the same time a form of self-command, a capacity to give shape to our own characters and identities. When the agent asks whether the action is a good one, she is also asking, "Do I wish to be a person who is so moved, a person who does *that* sort of act for *that* sort of end?" To relinquish this prerogative of self-command for the sake of some mere experience or gratification is in Kant's language *heteronomous* and in Aristotle's *base*. To exercise it, especially under circumstances that make it difficult, is to act from duty and so to display that special form of moral worth that Aristotle calls nobility.

Now I want to raise some questions about how far this comparison can be pushed. To act from duty, as we have seen, is to do an action because you think its maxim has the form of a law, that it is intrinsically right or good. Aristotle, by contrast, does not tell us much about which property of an action it is that "nobility" names. He certainly does not attempt to analyze the motive of nobility to arrive at a formulation of the moral principle, in the way that Kant analyzes the motive of duty to show us what the principle of a good will is. Aristotle is famously skeptical about the possibility of articulating general principles that will guide our moral reasonings in any very exact way (*NE* II.9 1109b13–26).[17] Still it does seem natural to identify an action's nobility with the fact that it is in accordance with the *orthos logos*, the right reason. Its being in accordance with the *orthos logos* is what makes it intrinsically right, and it is to this intrinsic rightness that the virtuous person responds. If this is right, a noble action, like a good-willed action, is one that embodies a principle of reason.

It is even possible to argue that nobility is a *formal* property. Elsewhere I have argued that we can appeal to Aristotle's concept of form to explain what Kant means by the form of a maxim.[18] In Aristotle's metaphysics, a thing is composed of a form and a matter. The matter is the material, the parts, from which it is made. The form of a thing is its functional arrangement. That is, it is the arrangement of the matter or of the parts that enables the thing to serve its purpose, or to do whatever it characteristically does. Now a maxim also may be seen as having parts. Since every human action is done for an end, we may say that a maxim of an action characteristically has two parts, the act and the end.[19] The form of the maxim is the arrangement of its parts. In particular, it is the functional arrangement, the arrangement that enables the maxim to do its job, which is to be a law. A maxim passes the categorical imperative test only if everyone with *that* purpose could do *that* action – that is, if the parts are combined so that the maxim can be universalized and so can serve as a law. Now when Aristotle specifies the *orthos logos*, he always gives us a list of what we might also think of as the parts of the action. The action that is in accordance with the *orthos logos* is done in the right way and at the right time, directed to the right objects, and so on. So we might think that its overall rightness consists in the way its parts are combined, that is, in its form. The parts are combined in a way that enables them to function, taken together, as a reason for action.[20]

Now I want to push the comparison one step further. Kant's analysis of the motive of duty turned on a comparison between two different ways in which we might choose a morally good action for its own sake – from duty or from immediate natural inclination. Does Aristotle similarly think that there is another way to value an action for its own sake, apart from valuing it for its nobility? Is there a character in Aristotle who, like Kant's naturally sympathetic person, simply enjoys doing the actions that are morally good, without quite grasping the reasons why they are morally good?

Of course there is. Aristotle says:

> For all men think that each type of character belongs to its possessors in some sense by nature; for from the very moment of birth we are just or fitted for self-control or brave or have the other moral qualities; but yet we seek something else as that which is good in the strict sense – we seek for the presence of such qualities in another way. For both children and brutes have the natural dispositions to these qualities, but without thought these are evidently hurtful. Only we seem to see this much, that, while one may be led astray by them, as a strong body which moves without sight may stumble badly because of its lack of sight, still, if a man once acquires thought, that makes a difference in action, and his state, while still like what it was, will then be virtue in the strict sense. (*NE* VI.13 1144b3–14)

And here we have an alternative description of the naturally sympathetic person of Kant's example. Humanity, of course, is not an Aristotelian virtue, but that is not what concerns us here, and for the rest of the essay I will ignore that complication. If it were, Aristotle would say that Kant's naturally sympathetic person has a natural virtue.

III. Acting from Natural Inclination

This brings me back to the more specific question with which I began, the question of Kant and Aristotle's attitudes toward somebody like the naturally sympathetic person, and the more general question of the role of natural inclination in the moral life. Now at this point I hope you will see that as far as the case Kant actually discusses in *Groundwork I* is concerned – the case of the *unreflective* or *unreasoning* sympathetic person – there is going to be little disagreement between Aristotle and Kant. Both think that his motivational state is both incomplete and unreliable until he reflects on the reasons why he should be beneficent, until his actions imply the presence of right reason. What he needs in order to become a good person is to *think,* and to act as a result of his thinking.[21]

In connection with this point, it is worth noticing that the inclination to which Kant compares natural sympathy is the inclination to honor:

... an action of this kind [i.e., like the naturally sympathetic person's] however dutiful and amiable it may be, has nevertheless no true moral worth. It is on a level with such actions as arise from other inclinations, e.g., the inclination to honor, which if fortunately directed to what is in fact beneficial and accords with duty and is thus honorable, deserves praise and encouragement, but not esteem; for its maxim lacks the moral content of an action done not from inclination but from duty. (*G* 398)

The choice of honor as the comparison is important because elsewhere Kant calls the love of honor a "semblance" of morality; in the same place he describes those moved by the love of honor as "morally immature" (*IUH* 26/49). In the discussion of punishment in *The Metaphysical Principles of Justice*, Kant suggests that people who commit murder from motives of honor, such as young officers who become involved in duels, should perhaps not be subject to capital punishment. Legislation itself, Kant urges, is responsible for the fact that these people are still morally backward, so that the incentives of honor are not yet attached to the proper principles (*MM* 337). In the *Anthropology* Kant calls the love of honor "the constant companion of virtue" (*A* 257). Honor, as Kant conceives of it, seems to be a natural tendency to live up to certain standards of conduct, not for the sake of any gain from following them but for their own sake, and out of a kind of pride. It is not yet mature virtue, for the laws of honor do not spring from the honorable person's own will, and he is concerned with what others think of him; yet it does make him receptive to the more mature state of autonomy. In a similar way, we might take sympathy to be a natural tendency to respond to the plight of others in ways that are prescribed by the Formula of Humanity. The sympathetic person is a *Menschenfreund*, a friend to humanity. In the *Anthropology*, Kant says that it was wise of nature to give us the predisposition to sympathy, as a "temporary substitute for reason" (*A* 253). All of this suggests that sympathy and honor are Kantian natural virtues, corresponding to the real virtues of humanity and autonomy respectively and making us receptive to the development of those real virtues. If this is right, Kant and Aristotle need have no disagreement about this kind of case at all.

Now I don't think that this is quite right – I think there is still some disagreement – but its nature is best brought out by asking the more interesting question whether they would disagree about the case of actions that do have moral worth, about whether those must be done with pleasure or some other appropriate feelings. So I want to turn to that question.

A preliminary point is that we must not exaggerate the views of either philosopher if we are to get this right. Kant thinks that in order to be receptive to moral reasons we must cultivate the virtues, and cultivating the virtues is a matter of adopting certain obligatory ends, such as one's own perfection and the happiness of others. At this point I come to an issue I mentioned at the beginning of the essay – the fact that our mental lives have a passive or receptive as well as an active dimension. There is an important difference between giving an account of what sorts of reasons for action morality prescribes and giving an account of how we become receptive to those reasons. There are two problems of receptivity. One is how we are motivated by the dictates of reason when those dictates are presented to us, whether by the arguments of others or simply by the workings of our own minds. To some extent this is just the problem of how pure reason can be practical, which Kant takes to be insoluble; to the extent that we can say anything about it, it is the problem that Kant is addressing in his account of how the thought of the law gives rise to the incentive of respect. The second problem is how we come to think about our duties at all, how we come to notice which reasons we have. The negative character of the Formula of Universal Law reveals this problem in an especially acute way. Under the Formula of Universal Law you arrive at the duty of helping when you consider the maxim of not helping, but it is only under extremely unusual circumstances that you would consider the maxim of not helping. The naturally sympathetic person, whose mind becomes clouded by sorrow, is in such circumstances. As I portrayed him, he considers the issue of helping for the simple reason that he used to help, or perhaps because someone reminds him of that fact. But what if the idea of helping simply doesn't occur to you one way or another? As Kant himself says in *The Metaphysics of Morals*, ''In ethics maxims are regarded as being such subjective principles as merely qualify for universal legislation – which is only a negative condition. . . . How then can there further be a law for the maxims of actions?'' (*MM* 389). What he is asking is how there can be a law that says we must *have* certain maxims. This is the problem that Kant addresses in *The Metaphysical Principles of Virtue*. He argues that we have a duty to cultivate moral ends and the feelings that are naturally attendant upon having those ends so that we will notice the occasions of virtue.[22]

Sympathy is naturally associated with having the happiness of others as your end, which is required, and in *The Metaphysical Principles of Virtue*, Kant does not scruple to say that sympathetic feeling is a duty. Being sympathetic helps us to be aware of those cases when our assistance or support will be called for. And if we cultivate moral ends and the feelings that are naturally attendant upon having such ends, then in the normal course of events we will also take pleasure in successful virtuous action. If I have made your happiness my end and I do something that successfully promotes it, I will of course take pleasure in that fact. It doesn't matter whether my original impetus for making your happiness my end was natural inclination or the rational acknowledgment of the value of your humanity; if it really is my

221

end it will normally give me pleasure to promote it. This is an ordinary fact about human motivation: once you have backed a certain horse, for whatever reason, you are going to be thrilled if it wins. Since virtue requires the adoption of ends, it requires, indirectly, the development of a range of feelings, the feelings associated with having those ends. The method, not surprisingly, is habituation:

> Beneficence is a duty. Whoever often exercises this and sees his beneficent purpose succeed comes at last really to love him whom he has benefited. When therefore it is said, "Thou shalt love thy neighbor as thyself," this does not mean that you should directly (at first) love and through this love (subsequently) benefit him; but rather, "Do good to your neighbor," and this beneficence will produce in you the love of mankind (as a readiness of inclination towards beneficence in general). (*MM* 402)

Kant both requires and expects that the virtuous person will in this way at once become receptive to the occasions of virtue and, at the same time, able to take pleasure in virtuous action. He even says:

> And what is done not with pleasure but as mere compulsory service has no inner worth for him who so responds to his duty. Such action is not loved; on the contrary, one thus avoids, as much as possible, the occasions for practicing virtue. (*MM* 484)

On the other hand, even Aristotle must admit that at least in very hard cases, it is only *successful* virtuous action that will necessarily bring us pleasure, and that in only a limited way. I have a specific hard case in mind. In the Book IX account of the relation between virtue and self-love, Aristotle makes the outrageous suggestion that the person who dies in battle gets the greater good because he prefers a short and noble life to years of humdrum existence (IX.8 1169a 22–4). In the Book III account Aristotle is more honest:

> Hence also courage involves pain, and is justly praised, for it is harder to face what is painful than to avoid what is pleasant ... death and wounds will be painful to the brave man and against his will, but he will face them because it is noble to do so or because it is base not to do so. And the more he is possessed of virtue in its entirety and the happier he is, the more he will be pained at the thought of death; for life is best worth living for such a man, and he is knowingly losing the greatest of goods, and this is painful. But he is none the less brave, and perhaps all the more so, because he chooses noble deeds of war at that cost. It is not the case, then, with all the virtues that the exercise of them is pleasant, except insofar as it reaches its end.

222

Aristotle then concludes, rather lamely, "But it is quite possible that the best soldiers may not be men of this sort but those who are less brave but have no other good" (III.9 1171a33–b20). And it is worth remembering that two of the cases of action from duty that Kant discusses in *Groundwork I*, that of a person who wants to commit suicide because of the acuteness of his misery, and that of a person in the grip of some great sorrow, are tragic cases. Aristotle firmly repudiates the Stoic view that virtue is sufficient for happiness even at moments like this, although I suppose he might still want to say that there is some pleasure to be taken in the virtuous action at hand (*NE* I.8 1099b1–8). But then Kant would say *that*, too – acting from respect for law does always have a pleasant dimension, although the pleasure is of a rather rarefied kind.

Aristotle and Kant might still disagree about one case. There are two characters who are beneficent from duty in the *Groundwork* examples: the one whose mind is clouded by sorrow and another, whom I haven't discussed yet, who is temperamentally cold. This person seems to be incapable of enjoying beneficent action. I suppose that Aristotle would characterize him as continent rather than virtuous, and would think that this is a less good state, and maybe, although I am not sure of this, judge that he is a less good person. Kant doesn't make the distinction between continence and virtue. But by now I hope it is clear that if he did, he would not say that continence is a *better* state, or that the cold person is a *better* person, than the virtuous person who also enjoys beneficence. What Kant says about the cold person in the *Groundwork* is only that he has a moral worth that the *unreflective* sympathetic person lacks; he does not compare him either positively or negatively with someone who helps from the motive of duty and also enjoys it. Aristotle does not, as far as I know, ever make the parallel comparison, which would be between merely natural virtue and continence. I assume he would agree with Kant, though, that continence is better than merely natural virtue, since the continent person has the first principle, and this is the important thing.[23] There remains only this difference: Kant would certainly not say that the cold person, provided he somehow managed to do his duty, was any less good, or was in a less morally good state, than the person who does his duty and also enjoys it.

But the reason why this one difference still remains throws light, I think, on the question why Kant doesn't characterize sympathy and honor as natural virtues, even though he comes very close. What is at work here is a difference between Kant's and Aristotle's views of what inclination is which in turn depends on a difference in their views of what pleasure and pain are. The difference is that Aristotle thinks of pleasure and pain as something like perceptions of the reasons for actions, while Kant apparently does not believe that pleasure and pain in general play this role. Respect for law comes closest to doing this, since it is a feeling produced by the activity of reason itself, but the pleasures and pains that are associated with ordinary inclinations do not.

Let me first mention the textual evidence for these claims and then say why I think they make a difference. Aristotle tells us that passions are "feelings that are accompanied by pleasure or pain" (NE II.5 1105b19). The accounts of pleasure in the Nicomachean Ethics itself are mostly concerned with the pleasures we take in activities as we do them; the question of what it means for some state of affairs to seem pleasant or painful to us in the way that is involved in passion is a little different. In On the Soul, Aristotle explains the relationship between pleasure and pain and passion this way:

> To perceive, then, is like bare asserting or thinking; but when the object is pleasant or painful, the soul makes a sort of affirmation or negation, and pursues or avoids the object. To feel pleasure or pain is to act with the sensitive mean towards what is good or bad as such. Both avoidance and appetite when actual are identical with this: the faculty of appetite and avoidance are not different, either from one another or from the faculty of sense perception; but their being is different.
>
> To the thinking soul images serve as if they were contents of perception (and when it asserts or denies them to be good or bad it avoids or pursues them). That is why the soul never thinks without an image. (OS III.7 431a7–16)

To take pleasure in or be pained by something is to perceive it as good or bad, that is, as a reason for pursuit or avoidance. This is why Aristotle insists, throughout the ethics, that it is so essential to get our pleasures right. He says that when we go wrong in our "wishes" – that is, our conceptions of the good – the error is due to pleasure, "for it appears a good when it is not. We therefore choose the pleasant as a good, and avoid pain as an evil" (NE III.4 1113a35–b1). I don't think Aristotle means merely that we are inclined to count pleasant things among the goods. I think he means that when something is pleasant it literally looks good to us. Aristotle's own favorite comparison of virtue to health can be used to illustrate the point. The healthy person's appetites, which are in a mean, are a reliable guide to what is good for her, that is, to what will preserve her in health. The amounts she enjoys eating and exercising are actually the amounts she needs, so that her perception of the good – of what she has reason to do – is correct. Hunger tells her something – that she is in need of nourishment, that she has a reason to eat – and if she is in good condition, hunger is right. Since the appetites and passions all involve pleasure and pain, this means that what it is to be in the grip of a passion is to see a situation as being a reason for pursuit or avoidance of a certain kind.[24] To be angry is to perceive a reason to fight, or, as Aristotle puts it: "Anger, reasoning as it were that anything like this must

224

be fought against, boils up straightaway'' (*NE* VII.6 1149a32–3); to be scared is to perceive a certain situation as a reason to flee; and so on. And since the soul never thinks without an image, as Aristotle says in the passage above, our conceptions of good and evil *must be accompanied* by images of our circumstances as pleasant or painful in certain ways. These images provide the material with which the intellect works in conceiving the good. It is because of the way the mind works that the virtuous person must experience pleasures and pains in the right way in order to think correctly about practical matters: thinking of something as good is inseparable from imagining it, so to speak, as pleasant.

Now the merely continent person's contrary passions make it difficult for her to maintain the required images, which is why, as Aristotle says, it is the same person who is both continent and incontinent (*NE* VII.1 1145b10–11). Mere continence is an unstable state, for the tendency to incontinence, its inevitable partner, can bring about a battle between intellect and passion for control of the agent's perceptual imagination. This is why Aristotle says that it is not knowledge proper but perceptual knowledge that is dragged about by passion in incontinent action (*NE* VII.3 1147b15–17). The virtuous person's reason, by contrast, is in unchallenged control of her perceptual imagination. And this is Aristotle's solution to the problem of receptivity. In the fully virtuous person, the entire appetitive part of the soul serves as a kind of sensorium for reason.[25]

Kant, by contrast, denies that pleasure and pain tell us anything about anything:

> Now the ability to take pleasure or displeasure in a representation is called feeling, because both pleasure and displeasure contain what is merely subjective in our representations and have no relation to an object so as to contribute to the possible cognition of it (not even the cognition of our own state). Usually, sensations, except for their quality, which depends upon the nature of the subject (e.g. the quality of redness, of sweetness, etc.), are related to an object as part of our cognition; but pleasure or displeasure expresses absolutely nothing about the object but simply a relation to the subject. (*MM* 211–12)

Now Kant shares Aristotle's view that inclination involves pleasure: he defines an appetite as a determination of the faculty of desire that is caused by pleasure, and an inclination as a habitual appetite (*MM* 212). But since Kant thinks that pleasure and pain are mere feeling, that they are, to put the point a little bluntly, stupid, he also thinks that inclination is stupid. The fact that you have an inclination for something does not tell you anything about that thing or even anything about your own condition. It only signals the thing's relationship to you.[26]

225

And this makes for an important difference between what Kant says about the naturally sympathetic person and what Aristotle would say about him if humanity were an Aristotelian virtue. We have a reason to help human beings who are in need, and Aristotle's account of inclination allows him to see our natural inclination to help as an inchoate grasp of that reason. It is the kind of perceptual starting point from which, in his methodology, we can work up to a more conceptual grasp of the first principles or reasons involved (*NE* I.2 1095a31ff., and many other places). When Aristotle says that the state of the authentically virtuous person is "not the same as that of the naturally virtuous person but like it," I take him to mean that the authentically virtuous person perceives the reason for action too but perceives it in that special way in which, according to Aristotle, you perceive matters that you also understand.[27]

But Kant cannot see natural sympathy as an inchoate grasp of the fact that there is a reason to help. He thinks that an inclination signals only a certain subjective suitability between the sympathetic person and the promotion of the happiness of others, a fitness of sympathetic action to gratify this particular person. This is the real reason why Kant describes this person as acting implicitly or tacitly under the principle of self-love, rather than as having a natural virtue. For Kant, sympathy is not a protovirtue, but merely a kind of substitute for virtue that nature has given us in the meantime. And this makes it look as if the inclinations and feelings that we are required to develop to solve the problem of receptivity will also have to be regarded as mere tools and helps.

The question which of these conceptions of inclination is correct is an extremely difficult one. The intuitive appeal of Aristotle's conception, at least about certain cases, is obvious. Sympathy for the troubled or the needy, in particular, presents itself to us as a response to the fact that there is a reason to help them. Such sympathy is painful, not pleasant, and if we regarded it merely as a source of feeling we would take an aspirin to make it go away. We don't do that, because of what we think sympathy reveals to us – that we have a reason to relieve someone's distress.[28] Of course, as the accusation of "sentimentality" shows, we also do sometimes dismiss inclinations, pains, and pleasures as *mere* feeling. There are people – I am one – who take our natural sympathy with the other animals, our acute sense of their pain and vulnerability, to be perceptions of the reasons we have to be merciful and protective toward them. And there are other people who dismiss this as mere sentimentality, as just so much personal feeling that doesn't mean a thing. But the very fact that this is offered as a criticism, or as debunking, shows that we do not in general take our pains and pleasures to be meaningless. We take them, as Aristotle thought, to be indications of what is good or bad, and what we have reason to do.[29]

But intuition by itself cannot settle the question in Aristotle's favor. Much more work in the philosophy of mind would be needed to show how Aristotle's view could possibly be true.[30] That we are attracted to a view like Aristotle's, however, does seem to me to explain why we are uncomfortable with what Kant says about the naturally sympathetic person in the *Groundwork*. Aristotle seems to give us a superior account of what is going on in this premoral case, and if he does, he may also be able to give us a superior account of how receptivity works in the case of fully realized virtue as well.

But I do not think that this marks a difference in the basic *ethical* outlooks of Aristotle and Kant. Although there is a difference in the way these two philosophers propose to solve the problem of receptivity, this problem arises for both of them because of the deep similarity in their general conception of what ethics is all about. Human action is not like anything else: as human beings we *choose* our actions, and, because of that, it is possible for us to transcend mere reactivity in our relationship to the world. The most general and substantive question of ethics is what we should do with this power, which actions we should choose. The more specific question of *virtue*, the question to which Aristotle gave most of his attention, is the question how the receptive part of our nature needs to be configured if this kind of transcendent choice and action are to be possible. It is the question, that is, of what we have to be like, in order to choose autonomously, and for the sake of the noble.

NOTES

1. Spontaneity, in Kant's sense, means having an original source in the agent's own mind or will, rather than in some external cause.
2. It is worth noticing the comparison with Nietzsche, who also places a high value on this attitude, although of course with more ambivalence about whether it may be identified with the moral attitude. In Essay One of *The Genealogy of Morals*, Nietzsche proposes that the values "good" and "bad" were born from the spontaneous evaluative acts of the noble or master types, as an expression of the value they set on themselves, while the opposed values "evil" and "good" were the result of *reaction* against the masters on the part of the oppressed and enslaved. (See Walter Kaufmann and R. J. Hollingdale, trans., *On the Genealogy of Morals*, in *On the Genealogy of Morals and Ecce Homo* [New York: Random House, 1967], esp. §§10–11, pp. 36–43.)
3. References to the works of Kant and Aristotle will be inserted into the text, using the following abbreviations for the titles and page numbers:

Kant's Works

A   *Anthropology from a Pragmatic Point of View.* Translated by Mary Gregor (The Hague: Martinus Nijhoff, 1974).

227

C2   *Critique of Practical Reason.* Translated by Lewis White Beck (Indianapolis, Ind.: Macmillan Library of Liberal Arts, 1985).

G   *Groundwork of the Metaphysics of Morals.* Translated by James Ellington in *Kant's Ethical Philosophy* (Indianapolis, Ind.: Hackett, 1983).

IUH   "Idea for a Universal History with a Cosmopolitan Purpose." Translated by H. B. Nisbet, in Hans Reiss, ed., *Kant: Political Writings,* 2nd. ed. (Cambridge University Press, 1991).

MM   *The Metaphysics of Morals.* Translated by James Ellington in *Kant's Ethical Philosophy* (Indianapolis, Ind.: Hackett, 1983).

Rel. *Religion within the Limits of Reason Alone.* Translated by Theodore M. Green and Hoyt H. Hudson (New York: Harper, 1960).

Following standard practice, I have used the page numbers of the Prussian Academy Edition (Berlin: de Gruyter, 1902–), which are found in the margins or inserted into the text of most translations, including *Critique of Practical Reason, Groundwork,* and *The Metaphysics of Morals* listed above. These numbers are not supplied in the translations of the *Religion* or *Kant: Political Writings* so in those cases I have supplied both the Prussian Academy page and, following it, the page of the translation.

Aristotle's Works

NE   *Nicomachean Ethics.* Translated by W. D. Ross and revised by J. O. Urmson, in *The Complete Works of Aristotle,* edited by Jonathan Barnes (Princeton, N.J.: Princeton University Press, 1984).

OS   *On the Soul.* Translated by J. A. Smith in ibid.

Rhe. *Rhetoric.* Translated by W. Rhys Roberts in ibid.

Again following standard practice I supply the book and chapter number of the treatise in question followed by the page, column (a or b), and lines of the Greek as found in the Bekker edition and indicated in the margins of all translations.

4. Terence Irwin, in Chapter 3, this volume, suggests that Kant has a hedonistic conception of desire and therefore of happiness, and that this is one basis for his criticism of his eudaimonist predecessors. It will be evident that I cannot agree with this. Irwin himself acknowledges that Kant's criticism of eudaimonism need not depend on this thesis, however, since its essence is that action governed by considerations of one's own good is essentially heteronomous. Irwin thinks that this criticism is not decisive, since one may argue that eudaimonistic principles do not derive their authority from our inclination to achieve happiness. One may instead suppose, as Butler and Reid did, that the principle of pursuing our own good has an authority of its own, just as the categorical imperative does. I believe that this argument misses the main thrust of Kant's objection to eudaimonism, although I think that Kant himself is partly responsible for the misconception. There are two elements to Kant's notion of heteronomy: (a) the law is not the will's own law, but rather is given to it from outside, and (b) the will therefore can be bound by that law only through an inclination or an interest, which renders the imperative to follow the law hypothetical. As this way of putting the point

makes clear, Kant himself argues and may have thought that these two elements are inseparable, and he therefore sometimes emphasizes the second element, which Irwin takes to be the essence of heteronomy. But I think that the real essence of heteronomy lies in the first element: the problem with the eudaimonistic principle is that it is not the will's *own* law. The possibility of the two elements of heteronomy coming apart is illustrated by a case I discuss later in this essay, the case of someone who is motivated by considerations of honor. One is not bound to considerations of honor by inclination or interest: one is honorable for its own sake, moved by a conception of how one ought to act. Yet this kind of action is still not fully autonomous, because the laws of honor are not the will's own laws. Only the categorical imperative, which *describes* the activity of a free will as such (a free will as such chooses a maxim it regards as a law), is the will's *own* law. (For a fuller account of this point, see my "Morality as Freedom," in Yirmiyahu Yovel, ed., *Kant's Practical Philosophy Reconsidered* [Dordrecht: Kluwer, 1989], p. 30; also chapter 6 in Christine M. Korsgaard, *Creating the Kingdom of Ends* [Cambridge University Press, 1996].)

5. Kant evidently thinks that there are three ways to value, and therefore to choose, an action: as useful (as the prudent merchant values honesty); as good for its own sake, in the sense of being immediately desirable (as the sympathetic person values beneficence); and as morally required (as the dutiful person values beneficence). If the argument of this essay is correct, this coincides with Aristotle's view that there are three objects of choice – namely, the advantageous, the pleasant, and the noble (*NE* II.3 1104b30–1).

6. This is a little oversimplified: in *Religion within the Limits of Reason Alone*, Kant argues that we are in general influenced by both moral incentives and incentives of self-love. Whether one has a good will depends on which of these is made the condition of the other (*Rel.* 36/31). This suggests that the moral principle will be something like "Do your duty, and what you like if that is consistent with your duty," while the principle of self-love will be "Do what you like, and your duty if that is consistent with your happiness." This complicates the picture in ways that I want to leave aside here, however, since these formulations presuppose a certain view of the role of natural inclination in the moral life, the basis of which I will call into question in Section III.

7. For a rich and subtle account of Kant's views on the operation of the principle of self-love, see Allen W. Wood, Chapter 5, this volume.

8. I do not agree with J. S. Schneewind's view that "for Kant nothing possesses the kind of intrinsic value that G. E. Moore thought would belong to a beautiful world even were there no observers of it" (Chapter 10, this volume). Schneewind is right, of course, to insist that in Kant's account value is not independent of rational willing: a maxim is an act of rational willing, and it is the maxim, and the good will expressed in the maxim, that possess this value. For a comparison between Kant's conception of unconditional value and Moore's conception of intrinsic value, see my "Two Distinctions in Goodness," *Philosophical Review* 92 (April 1983): 169–95; also see chapter 9 in Korsgaard, *Creating the Kingdom of Ends*. For a more detailed account of the sense in which maxims have intrinsic

value, see my *Sources of Normativity* (Cambridge University Press, 1996), §§ 3.3.5–6.

9. Joseph Butler, in Sermon XI of his *Fifteen Sermons Preached at the Rolls Chapel* (Sermon IV in Stephen Darwall, ed., *Joseph Butler: "Five Sermons Preached at the Rolls Chapel" and "A Dissertation upon the Nature of Virtue"* [Indianapolis, Ind.: Hackett, 1983], pp. 46–57), and, following him, David Hume, in the conclusion of the *Enquiry Concerning the Principles of Morals* (in *David Hume: Enquiries Concerning Human Understanding and Concerning the Principles of Morals*, ed. L. A. Selby-Bigge and P. H. Nidditch, 3rd ed. [Oxford University Press, 1975], pp. 281–2) make arguments in favor of beneficent action that take this form. To be fair, neither of them thinks that this is the way to establish the *moral* value of beneficence; it is just a way to establish the harmony of beneficence and self-interest. For further discussion see my *Sources of Normativity*, § 2.2.3, and Charlotte Brown, "Hume Against the Selfish Schools and the Monkish Virtues" (forthcoming).

10. Kant has some tendency to exaggerate the active reflectiveness of human beings, and the possibility of an unreflective version of the motive of duty may not even have occurred to him. In the *Critique of Practical Reason*, for example, after explaining how a natural law can serve as a "type" of the moral law, he says: "Everyone does, in fact, decide by this rule whether actions are morally good or bad. Thus people ask: If one belonged to such an order of things that anyone would allow himself to deceive when he thought it to his advantage . . . would he assent of his own will to being a member of such an order of things?" (*C2* 69). Probably the most startling instance of this optimism occurs at *G* 451, where Kant suggests that "even the commonest understanding" draws a rough distinction between the sensible and intelligible worlds. But optimism about human reflectiveness is not the only thing at work here. Perhaps the closest thing to an unreflective version of the motive of duty in Kant's system is the inclination to honor; and I will explain later why Kant didn't see this as an unreflective version of the motive of duty.

11. I thank Arata Hamawaki and Michael Hardimon for pressing me on this point, and for useful discussion of this argument in general.

12. I describe this process of reflection and how it leads one to a recognition of the moral law in more detail in "Morality as Freedom," pp. 27–31.

13. There is an important similarity between this way of characterizing the difference between the naturally sympathetic person and the dutiful person and the way in which, according to Jennifer Whiting, Aristotle characterizes the difference between merely *agathos* (the merely good person) and the *kaloskagathos* (the noble and good person) in the *Eudemian Ethics*. The *kaloskagathos*, as Whiting characterizes him, is superior in his reflective understanding of the reasons for good actions and therefore chooses them for their own sake, rather than for the sake of external or natural goods (see her Chapter 6, this volume). I would not say that the naturally sympathetic person chooses beneficence merely for the sake of the natural goods, but rather that he chooses it merely as a natural good. Whiting (ibid.) compares the *agathos* in the *Eudemian Ethics* to a character in the *Nicom-*

achean Ethics, namely, the person who has merely natural as opposed to "authoritative" virtue; later in this essay I will compare this same character to the naturally sympathetic person.

14. These remarks are based on the discussion in the *Critique of Practical Reason* chapter entitled "The Incentives of Pure Practical Reason" (especially *C2* 71–6), with some supplementation from the discussion of how pleasure and pain are related to moral motivation at *C2* 116–18. For an interesting account of how the experience of respect for law is related to the workings of the principle of self-love, see Allen W. Wood, Chapter 5, this volume.

15. John McDowell (Chapter 1, this volume) suggests that Aristotle sometimes overstates the extent to which actions that reveal virtue "issue from actual courses of thinking." I do not really mean to disagree with that claim here: McDowell and I would agree, I think, that the important point is that the actions be conceived as in some way good, where the good is the object of reason or thought. We might disagree somewhat about how articulate Aristotle expects his agents to be – and how articulate agents ought to be – in explaining why the action is good, and so about the extent to which they must be capable of providing something like a retrospective deliberation if asked to justify their actions. This however is a disagreement about a matter of degree. I am not certain what exactly McDowell has in mind when he criticizes those whom he supposes envisage a "straightforward" or "mechanical" application of principles; or at least I think it must be a misleading way to describe his worry (ibid.). The application of a principle by a thinking or conscious agent is always going to be perceptual rather than mechanical: perhaps there are places where the perceptual and the merely mechanical seem to run together, say for instance in the phototropic responses of plants, but this has nothing to do with the subject. The question, as I expect McDowell would agree, is surely about how much moral content perception must already have before we can begin to articulate, deliberate, and argue about the application of principles. I believe that even on the most algorithmic conception of the categorical imperative procedure, the Kantian answer to that question could not be "none," because an agent who views others as *persons*, and things and actions as possible *means and ends*, has already taken up what is broadly speaking an ethical perspective on the world. But this is not the place to pursue this point.

16. I owe these references and some of what I say here about their implications to Terence Irwin, who discusses them in the notes to his translation of the *Nicomachean Ethics* (Indianapolis, Ind.: Hackett, 1985). See especially the discussion of *to kalon*, or as he renders it, 'the fine', at pp. 401–2. Julia Annas (Chapter 3, this volume) focuses on these same passages to support her claim that Aristotle like Kant draws a distinction between moral and nonmoral reasoning: "for the sake of the noble" is a distinctively moral reason. While I am of course sympathetic to the comparison, I would prefer to phrase the conclusion in what is to some extent an opposite way: that both think there is only one kind of reason, although the considerations we use to identify a reason are complex. This is because I do not think that Aristotle would agree that you could ever really have a reason to do something base or ignoble, any more than Kant would agree that

you could really have a reason to do something immoral. The person who fails to take nobility or obligation into account acts at best for an imperfect or incomplete reason, not for a different kind of reason. This is not merely a verbal fuss, for the question is whether we may avoid the Sidgwickean problems that arise when one acknowledges two distinct sources of normativity.

17. Actually, there are two points to this skepticism. One point is the denial that we can formulate any reliable general rules to guide us morally: moral value belongs intrinsically to *particular* actions, and no set of general rules is sufficiently refined to pick them out. The other is the view that we must (therefore?) pick them out by means of perception. Now Kant has no reason to disagree with the first point. He certainly thinks that moral value belongs to particular actions, indeed that it is an intrinsic property of those actions. They do not inherit their value from any rules that are external to them. (See my "Kant's Analysis of Obligation: The Argument of Foundations I," *Monist* 72 [July 1989]: 311–40, esp. 326–8, and chapter 2 in *Creating the Kingdom of Ends*, for a discussion of this important point.) The categorical imperative test is a test on *particular* maxims, and any circumstance that is really relevant to the moral value of an action may properly be included in its maxim. Kant himself may have had some tendency to exaggerate the extent to which the categorical imperative's findings could be captured in a set of general rules, but nothing in the theory requires this. Now precisely because there is such a thing as the categorical imperative test, Kantians must deny that the failure of general rules leaves us no recourse but perception. But of course perception and judgment must at some level play a role, as anyone must agree (see note 15). So even this disagreement between Kant and Aristotle has been exaggerated. On the essential point, that moral value is an intrinsic property of *particular* actions in all of their rich particularity, Aristotle and Kant are in accord.

18. *The Sources of Normativity*, § 3.3.5.

19. Where the action is done for its own sake, these will not be different.

20. Now that I have made some fairly strong claims about Aristotle and Kant sharing a view of moral value, I want to wave my hands a little over the vexed question of categorizing ethical theories. People used to categorize theories as deontological or teleological; lately, we have started opposing deontology to consequentialism, and what seems to be a new category, "virtue ethics," has come upon the scene, although it is unclear whether it is a rival theory or a rival view about what the direction of our attention should be. Certainly no one seems to have a very clear idea what deontology, consequentialism, and virtue ethics might be three theories *of*, but suppose we try saying that they are theories of what makes an action right. Consequentialism is the theory that what makes an action right is its consequences; deontology is the theory that the action's rightness is intrinsic, or consists in its conformity to a rule; and virtue ethics is the theory that what makes an action right is that it is the sort of action a good person would do. If "the action's rightness is intrinsic" means that the outward performance, the act, has intrinsic rightness, then perhaps only traditional rational intuitionists, like Clarke, Price, Ross, and Prichard, are deontologists, if

anybody is. Kant and Aristotle, like Hume and Hutcheson, think that what makes an action right is that it is the sort of action a good person – for Kant an autonomous person and for Aristotle a person of practical wisdom – would choose. "Virtue ethics," however, would be a rather wild misnomer for this view in their case, since one does not have to have the virtues in order to choose well; even Aristotle admits that a continent person may choose well. On the other hand, suppose we say that deontology is the view that what makes an action right is its conformity to a rule of reason. Then Kant and Aristotle, along with rationalistic consequentialists like Sidgwick, are deontologists, as opposed to Hume and Hutcheson. On this view, in fact, Aristotle and Kant must be categorized as both deontologists and virtue theorists, since they think that the good person acts in accordance with, or even is the source of, a rule or at least a direction of reason. Since this seems unhelpful, suppose we say that the categories do not represent three views about what makes an action right, but three views about what gives an action moral worth. The resulting view about consequentialism – that consequences give an action moral worth – seems insane, and I am sure no one holds it. Consequentialists, if they are going to employ the notion of moral worth at all, will have to hold that it is the *intention* to produce good consequences that constitutes moral worth, and then their view will be a species of so-called "virtue ethics." (Of course, I have already suggested in the text that consequentialists might better be thought of as not employing this notion, or even, in this sense, as doing ethics.) Traditional rational intuitionists will hold that it is the intention to do what is right that gives an action moral worth, so they will be virtue ethicists too. This is no good. Perhaps, then, we should return to the earlier distinction, between deontology and teleology? Deontologists are interested in rightness and rules; teleology thinks that ethics has something to do with value or the good. Fine. If teleology is the view that the moral value of an action consists in its *promoting* the good, then Aristotle is a deontologist, since he thinks moral actions embody the *orthos logos* and so are good in themselves. If teleology is meant to include the view that moral actions are themselves good, then Kant is a teleologist, since he holds this view. Do you find that these efforts to categorize theories fill your mind with darkness rather than light? That of course is the point. Well, then maybe we should drop that, and oppose theories like Aristotle's and Hume's, which are primarily concerned with the virtues of character, with theories like Kant's and Sidgwick's, which are primarily concerned with the rightness of actions? I won't even bother to object to these tendentious descriptions of the "primary concerns" of these philosophers, since it is easier to ask what possible reason we could have for opposing theories if they have different primary concerns. Well, it may be replied, the issue is a methodological one: in subtle and even unconscious ways, our theories are shaped by their primary concerns. Now there is a great deal in this, and it is worth being aware it of when we study another philosopher's theories. But it is not a ground for opposing or categorizing different kinds of theories. Nor can we choose our own methodology by deciding in advance in which subtle and unconscious ways we would like our theories to be shaped. See also Barbara Herman, "Leaving

Deontology Behind'' in *The Practice of Moral Judgment* (Cambridge, Mass.: Harvard University Press, 1993), pp. 208–40.

21. At this point it is worth mentioning one apparent difference between the two philosophers. Earlier I mentioned that Aristotle supposes that adult human actions done ''on the spur of the moment'' are voluntary but not chosen. This raises a question: Would Aristotle say that an act of impulsive sympathy was voluntary but not chosen? If so, he would not only deny Kant's view that it was done under the tacit or implicit principle of self-love, but that it was done under any principle of volition. More generally, the point is that Kant seems to suppose that any adult human action is implicitly or tacitly done under some principle of volition, while Aristotle seems to think that merely voluntary action is still possible for adult human beings. Kant's view seems to be that the capacity for reflective choice, whether exercised or not, makes a difference to every action: adult human actions take place in the light, so to speak, of reflective thought, and can no longer be exactly like the actions of children and animals. Who is right? I believe that this question raises very complex issues about the third-person attribution of mental states and conditions (belief, choice, etc.), and whether those attributions are moral or merely factual. Aristotle's view suggests that a merely voluntary action performed ''on the spur of the moment'' is not a proper subject of moral judgment, since the agent is just following nature, and it is choice, not the merely voluntary, that reveals character. But there is something to be said for Kant's view, for surely if an adult human being performed too many actions on the spur of the moment, and failed to sufficiently *exercise* the power of choice, we would make a negative moral judgment about him (perhaps the judgment that he lacks character). This shows that we do think that once the capacity to exercise choice is present, it makes a difference to every action (or at least to actions in general), just as Kant says. But Kant's decision to attribute a principle of volition to people who perform thoughtless actions is not a guess about their actual volitional states. It is a moral choice, a decision that adult human beings are to be held responsible for thoughtless actions, because they might have thought. (For further discussion see my ''Creating the Kingdom of Ends: Reciprocity and Responsibility in Personal Relations,'' *Philosophical Perspectives.* Vol. 6: *Ethics*, James Tomberlin, ed. [Atascadero, Calif.: Ridgeview, 1992], and chapter 7 in *Creating the Kingdom of Ends.)*

22. I do not mean in this sentence to have said what the argument is; it is actually rather subtle and I am not taking it up here.

23. At least this is why Aristotle says that incontinence is a better state than intemperance (*NE* VII.8 1151a25). Although the merely naturally virtuous person and the continent person each lack an essential element of fully realized virtue, and this might seem to put them on a footing, still, the continent person can perform a noble act for the sake of its nobility, and the merely naturally virtuous person cannot do this essential thing.

24. I think this shows that McDowell is wrong in characterizing the natural virtues as ''mindless behavioral propensities'' that merely ''correspond'' with the virtues (see Chapter 1, this volume). But I think this conclusion is one that he should

welcome as friendly to his reading of Aristotle. McDowell thinks that the result of habituation is a primitive form of practical wisdom (ibid.). As I understand it, there is already a primitive form of practical wisdom built into the passions of the naturally virtuous person; the result of habituation is to refine it, and the result of intellectual training is to render it articulate. I think that this makes it clearer why habituation and intellectual training must proceed together (rather than ha- bituation coming entirely first) and also avoids committing us to the somewhat implausible idea that habituation changes the ontological status of the passions altogether – transforming them from mere mechanical propensions into percep- tions, as McDowell's view, as it stands, seems to imply.

25. This point may be strengthened by the following consideration. What health does is preserve the form of the living body; what virtue does is preserve the form of the soul. The form of the human soul is that it is governed by reason: that is why reason is the human function (*ergon*). Healthy actions – those motivated by healthy appetites – tend to preserve health in the body. Virtuous actions, then, tend to preserve reason's government in the soul. This shouldn't sound wild – I mean, at least as an attribution to Aristotle – since it is the view explicitly ad- vocated by Plato in *Republic* IV, at 443cff. I take it to be the view that Aristotle is also espousing when he says "the intellect always chooses what is best for itself, and the good man obeys his intellect" (*NE* IX.8 1169a16–17). Of course making these claims plausible or even comprehensible is another matter. They are abstract because it seems so difficult to form a conception of how virtuous actions tend to preserve the rational form of the soul. I have discussed Aristotle's view on this question in "Aristotle on Function and Virtue," *History of Philos- ophy Quarterly* 3 (July 1986): 259–79; lately, it has seemed to me that Plato's attempt to explain it in Books VIII and IX of the *Republic* may be more per- spicuous. In any case, if virtue puts reason in a position to choose what is best for itself, then virtue does enable reason to be active rather than merely reactive in its relationship to the world. Choice choosing choice mimics the divine activity, the purest of all activities, thought thinking itself (*Metaphysics* XII.6–9). But I leave these extremely abstract thoughts for another occasion.

26. The infamous passages in the second *Critique* in which Kant sounds so much like Bentham (*C2* 22–4) are actually an expression of this view. The point isn't that all we care about is our own pleasure. The point is that if our carings are just feelings, it doesn't really matter which ones we satisfy – that is, we have no reason, intrinsic to those carings themselves, to satisfy one rather than another.

27. In *Nicomachean Ethics* VI Aristotle seems to struggle to give a correct account of the respective relations of perception, practical wisdom, and *nous* (see, e.g., *NE* VI.7 1141b14–23, VI.8 1142a23–30, VI.11 1143a35–b6). I believe his view is that both practical wisdom and scientific wisdom are like perceptual states, both in the sense that you have a direct grasp of the first principles or reasons of things, and in the sense that that grasp somehow *inhabits* your actual percep- tions of the particulars. To the person of practical wisdom and to the person of scientific wisdom, the world literally looks different than it does to those who perceive but do not yet understand. The person of scientific wisdom *sees* the

235

essences of things unfolding in their activities; the person of practical wisdom *sees* the good, and opportunities to realize the good, in the circumstances in which she finds herself. Providing textual evidence for this view would be an immense undertaking, so for now I will just state that I think that's what he means.

28. I defend the claim that pain is the perception of a reason in *The Sources of Normativity*, § 4.3.4–12. In § 4.3.5, I cite some other philosophers on the pains of pity in particular, and it may be useful to repeat those citations here. Hutcheson says, "If our sole Intention, in Compassion or Pity, was the Removal of our Pain, we should run away, shut our Eyes, divert our Thoughts from the miserable Object, to avoid the Pain of Compassion, which we seldom do: nay, we crowd about such Objects, and voluntarily expose our selves to Pain" (*An Inquiry Concerning Moral Good and Evil*, quoted in Selby-Bigge, *British Moralists* [Oxford University Press, 1897], p. 93). The point is reiterated by Thomas Nagel: "Sympathy is not, in general, just a feeling of discomfort produced by the recognition of distress in others, which in turn motivates one to relieve their distress. Rather, it is the pained awareness of their distress as *something to be relieved*" (*The Possibility of Altruism* [Princeton, N.J.: Princeton University Press, 1970], p. 80n). Wittgenstein says, "How am I filled with pity *for this man*? How does it come out what the object of my pity is? (Pity, one may say, is a form of conviction that someone else is in pain)" (*Philosophical Investigations*, trans. G. E. M. Anscombe [New York: Macmillan, 1968], § 287, p. 98).

29. Some might think that the view suggested – that there is such a thing as perceiving a reason – implies a form of realism about reasons that is inconsistent with Kant's constructivist outlook. In *The Sources of Normativity*, I present a version of Kant's view that may be characterized as constructivist, and in § 4.5.6 I explain the sense in which it can be harmonized with a form of realism. The view of pleasure and pain sketched at § 4.3.1–12 is intended to show how the thesis that pleasure and pains are perceptions of reasons fits into that view.

30. The type of work I have in mind is exactly that Barbara Herman undertakes in Chapter 2, this volume.

8

Aristotle and Kant on Morality and Practical Reasoning

JULIA ANNAS

Until recently, it was common for philosophers to take Aristotle and Kant as paradigms of ancient and modern ethical theories, and to claim that we find striking and systematic differences between them. The contrast, of course, has generally not been made solely to achieve disinterested historical understanding. Often it has been made in the interests of contrasting our modern way of looking at ethical matters with that foreign country, the past, where they do things differently. And this can go either with the view that we have progressed, and may justifiably condescend to more primitive forebears, or with the view that we should be dissatisfied with our outlook and can learn from studying the insights of the past. The search to understand ancient ethics and the search to understand our own position are intertwined. This is not, I think, something to be deplored, nor need it stand in the way of rigorous historical scholarship. Indeed, it underlines the urgency of achieving a proper understanding of the contrasts that we are drawing. In recovering an accurate picture of the relationship between Aristotle's and Kant's ethics, we are positioning ourselves better to understand what is at stake when we set our own moral perspective against that of the ancients.[1]

I shall defend what may at first look like a version of the traditional view: between Kant's theory and Aristotle's there is a large and important difference, at least in the area that this essay deals with – the role of morality in the agent's practical reasoning and the consequences of this for the agent's moral psychology. However, my reasons for defending my claim are different from the traditional ones, and thus this essay is not a defense of the traditional view. I hope that this will contribute to a general tendency, already visible, to question the terms in which the traditional view is formulated, and

I am grateful for helpful discussion from a number of people at the conference on which this book is based, and also for comments from Edvard Petterssen.

to try to develop a more subtle and precise approach both to the comparison of Aristotle with Kant, and to the comparison of ancient with modern moral theories.

One handicap in this endeavor is the tendency to treat Aristotle as paradigmatic of ancient moral philosophy generally. I have argued at length in my recent book[2] that ancient ethical theories have a distinctive common structure, and that Aristotle's particular theory is only one among many ways in which that structure can be filled out; some features of Aristotle's theory should not be taken as typical of ancient moral theories in general. I shall contrast Aristotle's position with that of the Stoics; the point of this is to show that there is a position within ancient moral theory which contrasts with Aristotle's but which is reached within the same general framework as his and was thus conceptually available to him. Proceeding in this way enables us to focus more precisely on the motivation for Aristotle's holding the particular position that he does, rather than regarding it as a shared assumption of all ancient moral thought.

Does Aristotle have a moral theory in the first place? It has often been assumed in contemporary discussions that he does not, because ancient ethical theories are not theories of morality at all, but rather theories of something else (which can perhaps be called ethics), while morality is a modern invention. This view can coexist with either of two opposed positions as to its evaluation: on the one hand, it can be thought that modern, post-Kantian morality is a fundamentally flawed idea, so that Aristotle represents a refreshing alternative;[3] on the other, it can be held that ancient theory is defective just because it does not accommodate a Kantian view of the moral. I have argued elsewhere that ancient ethical theories are indeed theories of morality, and cannot do more here than indicate in general terms what the issues are. Because it is so difficult, in the modern world, to come up with a characterization of morality which is not contested, it is better not to try to show that there is one definite modern notion which the ancients either had or lacked. Rather, I point out that ancient discussions of virtue are naturally taken to express a concern with morality, as that is broadly understood and accepted, and that arguments commonly brought to defeat this presumption do not work. This leaves us with the justifiable assumption that ancient and modern theories differ, where they do, in being concerned with differing conceptions of morality.[4]

This essay focuses on the difference between Aristotle and Kant as far as concerns the place of moral considerations in practical reasoning, and the consequences of this for the agent's conception of herself as a reasoner who is a moral reasoner. This is, I argue, a difference from Kant which is specific to Aristotle; it shows up by contrast with other ancient theories and is thus not a difference between ancient and modern moral theories in general; and it is a difference, not between moral reasoning and something else, but between two conceptions of moral reasoning and its relation to other practical reasoning.

It is obvious enough that Kant draws a sharp distinction between moral and nonmoral reasoning. This is the point of some of his famous distinctions: that between duty as "the necessity of an action done out of respect for the law" and action done from inclination,[5] and that between the categorical and the hypothetical imperative.[6] The former clearly points to a distinct kind of motivation, one that *compels* or necessitates compliance, as opposed to the motivation provided by desires, which do not compel in this way; and such a force belongs only to moral reasons. The latter distinction indicates that the difference between moral and nonmoral reasons is to be characterized not as a difference of content but as a difference of standing with a rational agent: a categorical imperative compels regardless of the agent's own aims or priorities, whereas a hypothetical imperative draws force only from the aims that the agent happens to have. And this marks a difference between moral and nonmoral reasons which is unlike any difference among nonmoral reasons themselves. Recent writers have stressed that it may be a mistake to regard these distinctions, or stress on moral rules and formal features of moral reasoning, as definitive of Kantian ethics, or as forming the starting point from which the other features of Kant's ethics derive. Kant, after all, begins the *Grounding* not by stressing rules or duty, but (in a strikingly Stoic way) by stressing the distinctive goodness of the good will. I agree with writers like Barbara Herman that to see Kant as a 'deontologist' in the traditional way may well be misleading.[7] However, what I am discussing does not depend on the centrality to Kant's ethics of his distinction between moral and nonmoral reasoning. It is enough that Kant does draw this distinction in an uncompromising way.[8]

Aristotle nowhere draws a sharp distinction between two types of reasoning, one of which we would regard as moral and the other not. This is often regarded as completely unsurprising, since Aristotle regards practical reasoning as concerned with achieving the agent's final good, happiness,[9] and it is sometimes thought to follow from this that there will not be a deep split between two kinds of practical reasoning. Of course, as is well known, happiness or *eudaimonia* in ancient theories is not the same as happiness in modern theories; eudaimonia is defined by the formal features of being complete and self-sufficient, and different theories vary widely in their claims about its content. Aristotle, however, regards it as important to give an account of happiness which will not diverge too much from widespread reputable opinions about it, and so his own account, unlike those of the Epicureans and Stoics, stays close to the common view that happiness requires some measure of external goods and worldly success. To achieve hap-

239

piness one must, according to Aristotle, deliberate well about one's life as a whole,[10] about the whole field of one's concerns and projects. Excellence in practical reasoning is shown by the person who has developed the virtues and so aims at the fine, or *kalon*, and who uses his virtuous deliberation to achieve success both in the acquisition of external goods and in the achievement of valued public and private goals.

It is sometimes assumed that a unified conception of practical deliberation and reasoning, unsplit between moral and nonmoral reasoning, is simply part and parcel of a eudaimonist theory: if one is aiming at one's final end, happiness, in one's life as a whole, then it would be strange to think of the practical reasoning which achieves this as containing a sharp division between moral and nonmoral reasoning. We shall come back to this idea, and the source of its plausibility. Meanwhile, however, it is important to notice that the Stoics, who are also eudaimonists, do give us an example of a theory which takes the agent's practical reasoning to be aimed at her happiness overall, but which also takes that reasoning to be sharply divided into two kinds.

It is true that there is an earlier example of a theory of such a kind, namely, that found in some of Plato's writings. In some of the Socratic dialogues, Plato's Socrates draws a sharp distinction between virtue and all other kinds of good; one of these passages is strikingly reminiscent of the Stoic distinction.[11] However, this is never developed into an account of two sorts of reasoning, of the kind we find in the Stoics. Moreover, its status in Plato's work as a whole is puzzling. In the Socratic dialogues this line of thought is not sharply distinguished from a different, more Aristotelian way of looking at the distinction between virtue and other goods; and another dialogue in which the difference is drawn, the *Laws*, is late and un-Socratic.[12] Disentangling these strands in Plato is an important task, but too complex to deal with adequately here. It is preferable to concentrate on the clearer and more consistent way in which the Stoics formulate the distinction.[13]

For the Stoics, nothing but virtue is good; other kinds of thing have a different kind of value and are called indifferents. (This distinction can, again for reasons which cannot be fully rehearsed here, be regarded as equivalent to the distinction between moral value and value of a nonmoral kind.) This claim is, of course, very unintuitive and opens the Stoics to superficial charges of absurdity. In particular, a superficial reaction to the distinction would be to complain that in restricting goodness to virtue, they leave us with no account of why we should go for, or avoid, anything other than virtue; they leave us with no rational basis for choice between health and disease, wealth and poverty. The Stoics are not, however, forced into this absurd position: there are reasons in the nature of things why humans go for health and the like and recoil from disease, and so things like health and wealth, which we generally have reason to go for, are *preferred* indifferents, while their opposites are *dispreferred*.[14]

The corollary of this for practical reasoning is drastic: only virtue is *chosen*, while the preferred indifferents are *selected*. This is an artificial distinction which the Stoics introduce to underline the difference in kind of value between virtue and the preferred indifferents.[15] If I decide to act bravely, for example, then if this is done in the right way, from the right kind of disposition and so on,[16] I choose virtue. When I act to avoid illness, or to earn money, I am selecting the preferred indifferents of health and wealth over the dispreferred indifferents of disease and poverty. For clarity, I shall stick to this usage and use 'deliberation' for practical reasoning that covers both choice and selection. Since choosing is a different kind of thing from selecting, there is no such thing as a coherent form of deliberation simply made up by combining both. There is no single kind of reasoning which compares and weighs up the advantages of profit, for example, against the appeal of bravery. The model of comparison that holds within the nonmoral goods (the preferred indifferents) does not hold between nonmoral and moral goods (the preferred indifferents and virtue). If I choose the virtuous course virtuously (for the right reason), then I choose it for reasons of virtue, not because I find it better than the outcome of the nonmoral course. Virtue is not better than the preferred indifferents, because they are not even good; only virtue is. We also have to be cautious in stating what we mean when we say that deliberation shows the virtuous course to be preferable to the nonvirtuous course. What is chosen is not, strictly, preferred over what is selected, since they manifest different kinds of value; they are not on the same scale for deliberation to be able to prefer one over the other.

The question at once arises as to what sense the Stoics make of our commonsense understanding of overall deliberation that includes moral and nonmoral factors; we shall return to this. For the moment I want merely to establish that the Stoics mark a sharp disjunction within practical reasoning between the moral and the nonmoral, but also regard practical reasoning as having as its task the achievement of the agent's overall final good, happiness.

If we look at Aristotle's account of the agent's practical reasoning, we find one feature that suggests a similarity with the Stoics, but in the end their accounts differ on the central point that we are considering.

Aristotle's virtuous person acts "for the sake of the fine" (kalon). There are several aspects of his characterization of this which might reasonably induce us to think that a distinction is being drawn here between two kinds of reasoning that we might call moral and nonmoral. The kalon is a distinctive aim of action: the good person tends to go right, and the bad person to go wrong, about the three objects of choice and avoidance – the fine, the useful, and the pleasant.[17] Actions done from virtue are fine and are done for the

241

sake of the fine.[18] Thus, the virtuous person acts for a kind of reason that is not shared by the nonvirtuous – she does a fine action and does it because it is fine.[19] The nonvirtuous person might perform a fine action, but would not do so because of its being fine.

Aristotle does not, in the ethical works, give us much positive characterization of the fine. He does say that the virtuous person does the virtuous action for its own sake,[20] and although he does not explicitly bring this into connection with the idea of doing the action for the sake of the fine, it is reasonable to think that the two are connected. Doing the virtuous action for its own sake excludes doing it for some ulterior motive; insofar as the action is a virtuous action, the action is then done for the sake not of what is useful or pleasant, but what is fine.[21]

In the *Rhetoric* we find some indications as to what everyday intuitions about the fine were, but they are of little help as far as concerns Aristotle's theory. We find that "the fine is either the pleasant or what is choiceworthy in itself";[22] "the fine is what is, being choiceworthy in itself, praiseworthy, or whatever, being good, is pleasant because it is good";[23] virtue, whose aim is the fine, is especially associated with producing benefit for others.[24] However, none of these intuitive indications is taken up into Aristotle's own account; we are simply left with the connections that Aristotle draws between virtue, the fine, and doing the virtuous action for its own sake.

Nonetheless, we might still think that what we find here looks, on any reasonable interpretation, like an attempt to distinguish moral from nonmoral reasoning. For the virtuous person does not just perform a certain kind of action; she does it for a distinctive kind of reason – because it is the fine action. And this point is not spelled out in any further substantive manner, despite available intuitive ways in which this might be done; rather, it is presented as a kind of reason that is ultimate, one which excludes ulterior reasons, and is understood rather via the kind of reasoning producing it, namely, the reasoning of the virtuous person.

These points justify, I think, the kind of claim I initially agreed with, namely, that Aristotle has a theory of moral reasoning, not a theory of something else. What I now want to point out are other aspects of Aristotle's account of virtuous reasoning that suggest that this initial distinction of virtuous from nonvirtuous reasoning is not regarded as a sharp distinction in the way that we expect, at least if our account of moral reasoning is influenced by Kantian, or Stoic, expectations.

The first problem is found in the way that Aristotle treats some cases as unproblematic examples of the virtuous person aiming at the kalon, where it can reasonably be doubted that moral reasoning is what was in question. This is noticeable with the 'large-scale' virtues discussed in Book IV of the *Nicomachean Ethics*. The person who is 'magnificent' (*megaloprepēs*), for example, aims at the fine in what he does, and the person who fails to be magnificent does so by failing to aim at the fine, aiming instead, for example, at mere display of wealth.[25] Magnificence, however, is the virtue of proper public spending on a large scale. There are two kinds of reason why we are reluctant to call it a moral virtue. First, it is explicitly limited to the rich. A poor person who tries to be magnificent will not even achieve an analogous result proportionate to his means, but is merely silly; he is in the wrong game.[26] Second, the forms of excess and defect that characterize the analogous vices seem even more clearly not to be moral failings, but lapses of taste; the excess is vulgar show, like dressing the chorus in purple, and the defect is meanness that shows up in spoiling the ship for a ha'p'rth of tar.[27] Magnificence, in short, is not a moral virtue, and the magnificent person who aims at the kalon in exercising this disposition displays appropriate taste and judgment, but hardly moral motivation. A similar case can be developed for others among Aristotle's virtues, but magnificence makes the point vividly.

Several responses are possible here. One that we might be initially tempted toward is saying that Aristotle is really concerned about the virtues that he takes to be basic – courage, temperance, justice, and practical wisdom – as are other ancient ethical theories, and that the restricted virtues, dispositions that a person can only have if he is rich, well situated in society, and so on, are not as important to him and can be dismissed as a kind of appendage. This could not get us out of the present problem, however, since Aristotle explicitly says that the magnificent person spends his money "for the sake of the fine; for this is common to the virtues."[28] Aristotle clearly regards his account of virtue as applying to justice and magnificence alike.

The fact that he does so requires more explanation than it often receives. It is often claimed that Aristotle reads his account of the virtues off the social expectations of prosperous male Athenian citizens of the fourth century, and there is undoubtedly something to this charge; but it is striking that in doing so he is at variance not only with Plato, who regards virtue as being the four 'cardinal virtues' of justice, temperance, courage, and wisdom,[29] but with later theories, which similarly regard a theory of virtue as applying to these cardinal four (which are sometimes subdivided).[30] Aristotle is unusual in regarding such dispositions as magnificence, tact, and social friendliness as virtues comparable with courage and justice.

That he does so demands some explanation in terms of his method. Aristotle is more concerned than are other ancient theorists to answer to the most important of the *endoxa*, or reputable opinions of the many and the wise, on the topic. Here this is the most obvious explanation of what has happened. Commonsensically, virtue is not strictly confined to moral virtue, so that magnificence and tact are virtues, just as are courage and justice. For Plato and the Stoics, this is not a reason for putting them on the same footing.

243

The virtues, in a system of ethics, are taken to be moral virtues, and so are shown only in the basic areas of courage, justice, and so on. Magnificence and tact merely mark out, in conventionally drawn ways, areas of social intercourse within which the virtues can be exercised. One can think of ways, for example, in which public spending requires the agent to be just and temperate. But public spending does not in itself mark out an area for which there is a specific moral virtue, as, for example, the claims and rights of others mark out an area for which justice is the virtue. We can see why: public spending is not an area which demarcates a particular kind of moral concern. It is just like other areas of life in which moral concern might or might not be displayed. Aristotle has made virtues out of what others regard as the material for virtues: dispositions for dealing with conventionally demarcated areas of life. Unsurprisingly, these dispositions themselves include a great deal which is conventional.[31]

Aristotle's account of virtue and its aim, the kalon, then, has a disturbing feature: the account of moral virtue is extended to areas where moral virtue is not what is in question. It seems clear why this is so: Aristotle's conservative methodology gives more weight than it should to commonsense usage, which blurs the distinction between a moral virtue like courage and a conventional 'virtue' or disposition like magnificence. Arguably, Aristotle could have avoided this; he could have given an account which, like earlier and later theories, treated magnificence and tact not as virtues in their own right but rather as conventional dispositions, in the development of which any moral element would be due to virtue. Since he does not do this, his theory takes over from common sense the tendency to blur moral and nonmoral dispositions, to lose sight of the very different ways in which they can be *aretai*, and, to that extent, to blur the line between moral and nonmoral reasoning.

This is not, it should be stressed, a revival of the old notion that Aristotle does not properly have the notion of morality, and that an Aristotelian *aretē* is not a moral virtue, but rather an 'excellence' of an undifferentiated kind.[32] That thesis does not do justice to the texts, and a great deal of its appeal has, I suspect, come from too narrow an interpretation of eudaimonism. If we identify the happiness which is our final end with a narrow conception of pleasure or good feeling, then it may well seem hopelessly implausible that we need moral virtue to achieve that. But Aristotle, along with other ancient ethical theorists, does not identify happiness with any such rigid and narrow conception. Happiness is an initially unspecific notion; not until we are in possession of an ethical theory are we in a position to determine whether moral virtue is an appropriate way of achieving it or not. It is quite wrong, then, to think that eudaimonism raises even a prima facie difficulty for the idea that virtue should be construed as moral virtue and not as an undiffer-

244

entiated excellence. Moreover, we can see from Aristotle's accounts of the four major virtues that he is not telling us that justice and courage are ways of being generically excellent and so achieving a restrictively understood conception of happiness. The just or courageous person has a virtue and aims at the kalon – does the right thing for the right reason. Justice and courage especially give rise to cases where it is very clear that exercising the virtue has nothing to do with excellently achieving happiness restrictively conceived. The demands of the basic Aristotelian virtues are moral demands.

That Aristotle also talks of magnificence and tact as virtues shows not that he lacks the concept of moral virtue, but that he does not draw as sharp a line as we would expect between moral virtue and its aim, on the one hand, and some conventionally demarcated dispositions and their aims, on the other.[33] The courageous agent faces death in battle, because it is kalon. The magnificent person produces a tragedy in a sumptuous but tasteful way, because it is kalon. The contrast here with the Stoics, who do distinguish sharply between what can be (morally) chosen and what can be (nonmorally) selected, is striking. The Stoics are not impressed by common sense into thinking that the area of public spending demarcates a virtue; it merely marks off an area of indifferents within which the virtuous agent can display, or not display, her virtuous deliberation in the selection of the right indifferents.[34]

The second problem that we find with Aristotle's account of the fine concerns the importance of actual success in action for the virtuous agent.[35] Aristotle's virtuous agent displays good practical reasoning, which is of course part of what it is to have a virtue: the virtuous person gets it right. As a result, she is successful; her actions are sometimes described in terms of success, the word that the Stoics were to take over as their term for a virtuous action done as a virtuous person would do it, for the right reason.[36] But once again we can see by contrast with the Stoics that Aristotle understands this kind of success in terms which tend to blur the line between moral and nonmoral reasoning.

The Stoics insist that the virtuous person is successful, because in being virtuous he exercises skill, and the skillful person gets it right. But the skillful person achieves the end appropriate to his skill, and this is done in acting virtuously, doing the right thing for the right reason. Although a virtuous action normally involves making a correct selection among indifferents, the agent who acts virtuously can be successful even if the indifferents in question are not in fact forthcoming. The Stoics' sharp distinction between virtue and indifferents, and their insistence that only virtue is good, and so beneficial, commits them to finding the results of a virtuous action, in terms of indifferents, to be not themselves good, and so not contributory to happiness.[37] Hence, two of their positions which in isolation sound especially odd.

One is the thesis that all virtuous (and vicious) actions are 'equal', differing in their consequences but not insofar as they are virtuous (or vicious).[38] The other is that virtue is a skill, but a skill of a special kind; it is valued entirely for the way it is exercised and not at all for its products. This severs the notion of skill involved in virtue from everyday notions of skill. It has the interesting consequence of 'internalizing' the successful exercise of virtue. What the successfully virtuous person has done may amount to no more, in everyday terms of success, than going through virtuous reasoning and coming to the right conclusion. Nevertheless, it is an exercise of skill, and a successful one.[39] The Stoics are committed to this view by their sharp separation of the value of virtue and the value of other things, but it fits well with other aspects of Stoic ethics: the result, for example, that virtue, unlike other things, is up to us. At this point the Stoics can be said to approach the Kantian idea of virtue as located in the good will, rather than in what one succeeds in achieving.

When we look at Aristotle, we find that he does not have the means to make such a sharp separation between the external way of looking at the action, in terms of actual success in the result, and the internal way of looking at the action, in terms of the agent's aiming at the kalon. When he talks of success, or of the agent achieving the mean rather than the extremes, or exercising correct deliberation, what does he have in mind? Does he mean that the just person actually manages to make the correct allocation, or merely that she does everything that is in her power to make the correct allocation? It is easy to imagine cases where the just person goes through all the right reasoning, but through no fault of hers, the goods to allocate, for example, are not available when needed. Aristotle could say that in the second case the just person has acted justly anyway – after all, we tend to praise her and give her credit even though the intended result did not come about. Or he could say that in the second case the just person has tried, but failed, to act justly. This leaves it open for praise, credit, and so forth to be given to the attempt, not to the action itself.

It may seem that Aristotle takes the second way, since he says that choice (*prohairesis*) seems to be most appropriate to virtue and to distinguish character better than actions do.[40] This, however, is put forward not as his own argued view but as what seems to be the case intuitively. It would, though, seem difficult for Aristotle to take the first option. It is very counterintuitive to say that the virtuous person has actually done a generous or just action if the gift or allocation was not forthcoming. Whereas the Stoics are unafraid of individual counterintuitive theses, and anyway can cope with this particular issue,[41] Aristotle has no obvious way of understanding the claim that a person deserves praise for doing a just act if the distributable good did not, in fact, for reasons beyond the agent's control, get distributed. Aristotle does not actually address the issue, surprising as this is.

Because he does not address it, an important ambiguity is left in the notion of aiming at the kalon. What exactly is the virtuous person aiming at? In one sense this is obvious: he is aiming to act justly, generously, and so on. But the problem is precisely the uncertainty over what this is. Does he require the appropriate external result to have acted justly or generously? Or will he have done so if he has done what he could, but in a way that leaves him blameless, the external result fails to come about? Aristotle leaves this point indeterminate in a way that the Stoics do not.

I have contrasted Aristotle with the Stoics, but it is also a point at which we are bound to think of Kant; indeed the Stoic position on this issue is easily seen as a Kantian one. For Kant, the success of a moral performance cannot depend on the external result; famously, the good will shines with its own light even when stepmotherly nature makes niggardly provision. For Aristotle's position to be uncertain and indeterminate on this point is for it to be decisively different from a theory that gives an account of moral reasoning in anything like a Kantian way.

Can we come to understand why Aristotle is left in this position? We have to come up with our own diagnoses here, since the problem does not become obvious until the Stoics make distinctions, such as that between choosing and selecting, which force us to question their absence in Aristotle, and which also make clearer to us the kind of difference we find between Aristotelian and post-Kantian theories of ethics, which on this point stand closer to the Stoics than they do to Aristotle.

I would like to suggest two considerations of a general kind which seem to me to have weighed with Aristotle, though they are not made explicit in his works, and which go some way both to explain the features of Aristotle's account which I have focused on, and to stress the kind of difference that we are bound to find between Aristotle on the one hand and the Stoics and Kant on the other. (I do not, of course, claim that these are the only considerations that we need to bear in mind.)

First, Aristotle is, I think, committed to the unity of practical reasoning – not just in the weak sense demanded by any eudaimonist theory that takes practical reasoning to be aimed at a single overall goal, happiness, but in a stronger sense that brings together all kinds of factors in a single kind of unified deliberation. Second, Aristotle takes morality to be a part of the world that is not essentially problematic in its relation to the rest of the world. He holds a view of the world in which there are no deep problems of principle as to how morality fits into the world and is explained as part of that world. These are very general claims, and I shall try to explicate both of them by

247

reference to something which we do find in the texts, and which is helpful in two ways. Aristotle regards it as part of common sense, so we can see his use of it as being part of an attempt to stay close to common sense. And it also figures in his successors who are responding to the Stoic alternative in ethics, so we can see that it came to be regarded as an important point in Aristotelian ethics.

What I am referring to is the claim that there are three kinds of good – goods of the soul, goods of the body, and external goods – and that happiness requires the agent to have all three. This idea appears in late Plato in virtually the same form,[42] but Aristotle treats it as part of common sense and generally accepted ideas, presenting his own theory as doing justice to it. In the *Nicomachean Ethics* it appears as the very first of the commonly held ideas to which Aristotle refers in his account of happiness.[43] It is an ancient view, he says, and also agreed on by philosophers, presumably with Plato in mind. In the *Politics* the idea appears as uncontroversial: "nobody would dispute" that there are three divisions of goods – external, bodily, and those of the soul – and that all of them are required for happiness. Aristotle goes on to stress the utter absurdity of a conception of happiness which excludes any of them, and adds that although all would agree on this, this leaves room for controversy as to the amount of each required and their relative importance.[44] Similarly in the *Magna Moralia* the division appears as "another division"; it certainly is not Aristotle's own invention.[45]

Thus money, health, and justice are all goods – goods of different types, but nevertheless comparable, since they are all good. We have a strong contrast with the Stoic insistence that only virtue is good, other things being indifferent, as well as with Kant's insistence on the difference between conditional value and the unconditional value of the good will. We should be careful, though, not to overdraw the contrast by assimilating it too readily to modern ones. The thesis that money, health, and justice are all good does not amount to the thesis that quantities of each sort can be measured against quantities of the others in such a way that a calculation of the amounts of money, health, and justice involved in an action will result in a single computation of which is greatest in amount and so best. For virtue is not just a good to be measured against the other goods: the other kinds of good can be put to virtuous or vicious use, and so there is a limit beyond which they do not contribute to happiness in their own right, only as rightly used, while there is no such limit to virtue.[46] It is thus not the case that loads of money or a lot of health but no justice make an outcome better than one with justice but little or no money and health.

Nonetheless, the thesis that virtue, health, and money are all good is still distinctively different from the Stoic thesis that only virtue is good, while other things are indifferent. For unlike the Stoics, Aristotle does not claim

248

that there is a difference of kind between deliberating between money and health on the one hand, and between money and virtue on the other, only that virtue always has more weight in deliberations than money or health do. We can see for ourselves that Aristotle could find the resources to draw a distinction between reasoning about virtue and reasoning about bodily and external goods; for it is, obviously, the fact that virtue deliberates as to how best to put the other goods to use, which is the source of the thought that there is a limit to the usefulness of these other goods in the life of the virtuous person, and no such limit in the case of virtue. However, Aristotle himself never develops such thoughts and seems not to see the need to do so in the context of living the virtuous life. Once the Stoics did so, however, the issue was seen as a crucial one, as we can see from the continuing Stoic–Peripatetic debates about our final end. There are two points which emerge as particularly salient.

The first is the unity of deliberation. As already mentioned, it appears that a position like the Stoics', which sharply distinguishes between choosing and selecting, has a problem accounting for the apparent unity of our overall deliberation. Are they not committed to splitting the person into a self that reasons morally and a self that reasons nonmorally? In fact they are not, because of their firm subordination of nonmoral to moral reasoning within the overall pursuit of happiness. Nonmoral reasoning is uncontroversially employed in selecting indifferents in the early stages of moral development; when the agent has developed to a stage where he can recognize the moral point of view, he reasons in a way which continues the tasks of nonmoral reasoning, but in a way subjected to the constraints of the moral point of view. The agent who realizes that the value of virtue is different in kind from that of other things continues to be interested in the other things, but in a way that does not allow the pursuit of them to interfere with the pursuit of virtue.[47] But the person is not divided into two sources of reasoning, standing in a problematic relation to one another. Rather, we all reason nonmorally; those who develop in the right way come to reason in a way which takes up the previous tasks of nonmoral reasoning but carries them out in a way subordinated to the achievement of the moral point of view.

Kant, by contrast, does notoriously have a problem here. Categorical imperatives are possible, he says, "because the idea of freedom makes me a member of an intelligible world;"[48] the presupposition of morality is a kind of freedom that we cannot fully make sense of in the kinds of 'empirical' terms of the explanations that we apply to the natural world around us. Insofar as we take the idea of morality seriously, we are forced to regard ourselves as subject to a kind of division in the self between the empirical self and the moral self, the latter being the locus of our ability to reason morally. The moral self stands in an inherently problematic relation to the empirical self

249

by virtue of the character of moral reasoning. It is true that this division in the Kantian moral reasoner can be exaggerated and overplayed, and it may be misleading to take this division to be fundamental to Kantian ethics as a whole. But it is undoubtedly important to Kant that the nature of morality and moral reasoning does compel us to recognize a crucial discontinuity within practical reasoning.

It has sometimes been thought to be an obvious virtue of Aristotle's position that he does not face this problem. Aristotle's virtuous person uses *phronēsis* to make the correct decisions between nonmoral goods, and also to make the correct decisions where moral goods are concerned. Of course, the kind of reasoning is not just the same in both cases, for nonmoral goods can, at least some of the time, be straightforwardly weighed up against one another, whereas virtue cannot be outweighed by money and health. Yet the idea that virtue, health, and money are all *goods* makes it hard to see what the difference is supposed to be, other than that virtue, for some reason which is never explicated, always matters a great deal more than the other things.

Indeed, an Aristotelian kind of theory which sticks to the 'three kinds of good' thesis is bound to have difficulty explaining why virtue matters more than the other kinds of good, given that they are all good. How can it be the same kind of deliberation that we bring to bear when deciding among non-moral goods, and when we decide between them and virtue? For virtue may always demand that we sacrifice the goods which it was the business of our original deliberation to obtain. This is not so difficult to understand if moral reasoning is in some way distinctively different, if it puts us in touch with a value of a new kind, one which overrides or outshines or in some way brushes aside the claims of nonmoral goods.[49] But if virtue is still one kind of good among others, the new force of moral claims comes to seem highly mysterious. We can see this problem from the hand waving that goes on at this point in Antiochus's theory, for he is aware of the Stoic alternative and determined to avoid it, yet can do no better than stipulate that virtue always matters more than the other kinds of good. If we put all other goods in one scale of a balance, Antiochus claims, and virtue in the other, it will still always weigh them down. Here we see the counterintuitive nature of the claim: for what is it about virtue that makes it a good which will always mysteriously outweigh the other kinds of good? Moreover, the image of the balance seems exactly wrong here: to think of moral and nonmoral goods as being weighed up against one another makes it especially mysterious how virtue could have the essential extra density.[50]

There is, then, a cost to preserving the intuitive unity of deliberation, at least for theories which hold that virtue is necessary for happiness. Virtue is a good among other goods, yet it has a mysterious primacy which has to be taken for granted in the theory. But because Aristotle thinks it important to sustain the intuition that virtue is a good among other, nonmoral goods, he cannot mark this primacy by saying that our reasoning about it is different in kind from our reasoning about other kinds of valued thing. The kind of deliberation that we employ to decide on courses of action involving non-moral goals is, it seems, the same kind of deliberation that we use when moral factors come into play – except that virtue comes with a built-in special weight.

As in other areas, Aristotle's theory is intuitive at one point, at the cost of raising difficulties at another. Aristotle's agent deliberates in a way that is held together by the overall search to achieve happiness and is assumed to be unproblematically unified. But he does not want to reduce virtue to the role simply of one good among others in a way that could leave it outweighed by sufficient money, say. In insisting that virtue have primacy among other goods, but refusing to account for its special force in something like the way that the Stoics do, he is left with a position that is awkward and undermotivated. We have seen that Aristotle's agent aims at the kalon in acting morally, but also in some contexts that are not moral ones, and that he has no way of drawing a clear line between them.

The second issue raised, which I have here the scope merely to mention, is a metaphysical one: the place of virtue in one's account of the world more generally. Here again Aristotle's insistence on staying with common sense concerning the 'three kinds of good' leads to a position which is distinctively different from those of the Stoics and Kant; and once again Aristotle's reliance on intuitions at one point commits him to taking on a certain cost in his theory as a whole. For Aristotle there is nothing essentially problematic about the place of virtue, and the kind of value that it has, in the world as a whole. It puts no strain on explanation; it is, after all, good, and lots of other things are good also.

Kant by contrast thinks that the role and place of morality in the empirical world is problematic in the extreme; humans are members of two 'worlds', as we have seen. Even if we take care not to exaggerate the nature of the difference that Kant is talking about, it is clear that there are two points of view, which stand in no easy relation: the viewpoint of our empirical nature, with the kind of explanation appropriate to that, and the viewpoint of morality, from which we cannot understand ourselves as long as we stay within the bounds of the first point of view. The contrast here between Aristotle and Kant cannot just be due to Kant's rejection of a eudaimonist framework (since the Stoics, working within such a framework, have a position more like Kant's on this issue than like Aristotle's) but must lie instead in differing views as to the nature of morality.[51]

Here we cannot, of course, adjudicate the matter simply, since the question at issue between Aristotle and Kant, the place of morality in the world, is a deeply disputed one. Some think that an Aristotelian approach is basically right; morality is simply a part of the everyday world, and we can account for it and its force without expanding or going beyond the types of explanation that we apply to nonmoral matters. The appeal, for the agent, of virtue is not of its own nature more mysterious than the appeal of health or money; virtue may have primacy, but it does not introduce an incalculable or strange element. Others disagree: morality *is*, they hold, quite mysterious, and to explain how we get from the appeal of money or health to the kind of hold on the agent that virtue has, especially when it demands the sacrifice of money or health, we need to realize that something quite different has entered in. For the Stoics this is value of a distinctively different kind. For Kant it is a factor which demands a shift of metaphysical perspective. Those who are persuaded that morality and its hold on us are pretty hard to explain will find Aristotle's approach lacking: he does not adequately account for morality. Those who think that it is not at bottom ineliminably difficult to explain will find Kant's view (and the Stoics', though less so) extravagant.

This difference will carry on to a different account of what is at issue between the competing Aristotelian and Stoic/Kantian models of overall practical reasoning. Those who hold that morality requires a special kind of motivational authority that cannot be derived from our given attitudes and sentiments will claim that Aristotle is missing something important in the nature of things, and that his theory is simply inadequate to explain the phenomenon of morality. But supporters of an Aristotelian kind of theory will counterclaim that Aristotle's theory explains all that there is to explain, since there is no such thing to explain as the supposed extra motivational force that morality is supposed to exert, different in kind from the motivations that we recognize in nonmoral cases. Since the two sides do not agree on the data to be explained, but disagree about explanandum and explanans together, the issues are tangled and the depth of the dispute is unsurprising. But one point can perhaps be made in a way which does not presuppose prior commitment. If Aristotle's theory is adequate, and there is no such item as the missing extraordinary force of morality, then we seem to need an "error theory" of some kind to explain why the Stoic/Kantian kind of theory finds something missing. This is not an objection that we can press on Aristotle himself, who did not write in a context where there was an established competitor of the Stoic/Kantian form to meet, but it is a point that can fairly be pressed on any modern defender of an Aristotelian kind of theory.

It is not for nothing that the later Stoic–Peripatetic debate revolved so much around the issue of 'three kinds of good'; the issue, which may sound to us scholastic and unexciting, encapsulates views of morality and its place in reasoning which are the source of deep disagreement. Aristotle's apparent unwillingness to distinguish as we would expect between moral and nonmoral reasoning rests on a desire to preserve certain appearances or established reputable views. One is that an agent's practical reasoning is unified in that bringing morality into her deliberations does not introduce a fundamentally new kind of consideration, one whose relation to previous considerations is well-marked and problematic.[52] Another is that morality occupies a place in the world, and hence in our reasonings, that is not fundamentally problematic either and can be accounted for without introducing any radical divisions or dualisms into our explanations. I am not suggesting that this tendency on Aristotle's part to want to save these appearances is the whole story as concerns his account of morality in practical reasoning. But we can recognize that there is a profound division here about the nature of morality, one which is bound to show up in differences about practical reasoning and one which illuminates the respects in which Aristotle and Kant are bound to disagree.

NOTES

1. In this essay I shall not challenge the assumption that Kant's ethics articulates a conception of morality which has been found central to modern theories. To the extent that this can be queried, the essay can be read as dealing simply with the relationship between Aristotle and Kant, rather than between Aristotle and modern post-Kantian ethical thought.
2. *The Morality of Happiness* (Oxford University Press, 1993).
3. Again, this view can be divided between those who see in it a possible model for our own moral theory making (cf. the work of John McDowell) and those like Bernard Williams, who regard it as attractive in principle but nowadays conceptually unavailable to us.
4. See *The Morality of Happiness*, chap. 2, sec. 7, and my "Ancient Ethics and Modern Morality," *Philosophical Perspectives* 6 (1993): 119–36. It has been claimed that ancient ethical theories lack some or all of the following marks of concern with the moral: a sharp distinction between moral and nonmoral reasons; a concern with right moral action and correct moral decision making; a fundamental, underivative concern for the interests of others; a concern for morality distinct from a concern with happiness. When examined, all these alleged contrasts turn out not in fact to pick out genuinely deep divergences.
5. *Grounding for the Metaphysics of Morals*, trans. J. Ellington (Indianapolis, Ind.: Hackett, 1983), Akademie (Ak.) ed., p. 400.
6. Ibid., p. 416.
7. See Barbara Herman's collected Kantian papers, *The Practice of Moral Judgment* (Cambridge, Mass.: Harvard University Press, 1993), esp. "Leaving Deontology Behind," pp. 208–40, as well as Chapter 2, this volume. The same kind of stress on Kant's conception of value, as well as his concern with the form of moral reasoning, is to be found in the writings of Thomas Hill and Christine Korsgaard.
8. It is also of interest in that he thinks that this feature of his theory is intuitively easy to recognize and accept. See Ak. ed., p. 411n.

9. Practical reasoning is also, of course, concerned with producing conditions enabling others to achieve their happiness; indeed Aristotle sometimes regards this as a higher task than "merely" achieving one's own happiness. But in his ethical works Aristotle makes the same assumption that other theorists do in their ethical works: the task of practical reasoning is to achieve the agent's final good, i.e., happiness.

10. *Nicomachean Ethics* (*NE*) 1140 a 25–8.

11. *Euthydemus* 278e–82e. See Jennifer Whiting, Chapter 6, this volume. On the relation of the *Euthydemus* passage, together with the passage at 288d–92e, to the Stoic distinction between the value of virtue and other kinds of value, see my article "Virtue as the Use of Other Goods," in *Virtue, Love and Form: Essays in Memory of Gregory Vlastos*, ed. T. Irwin and M. C. Nussbaum (Edmonton: Academic Printing and Publishing, 1994), pp. 53–66 (*Apeiron* 24, 3–4). In the article I show that although Plato has Socrates draw a sharp (and Stoic-looking) distinction between virtue and other "so-called goods," he also finds it to raise a deep and insoluble-seeming problem, and does not develop the position so as to defend it from obvious objections, as the Stoics do.

12. *Laws* 631b–d (which distinguishes types of good) and 661b–d (which makes the point, stressed in the first *Euthydemus* passage, that true goodness is dependent on use). The *Laws* proceeds as though the *Euthydemus* problem had simply been solved. The two passages are often referred to by Middle Platonists who wish to align Plato's position as a whole with that of the Stoics. See also n. 42.

13. Here I should say a few words about my methodology, in view of the criticisms directed against my interpretation of the Stoics by Professors Cooper and Schneewind, Chapters 9 and 10, respectively, this volume. The Stoics divided philosophy into three parts: logic, physics (including metaphysics), and ethics. Different Stoics held diverging views on the proper pedagogical order for these, but all agree that ultimately they stand in mutually sustaining relationships; the whole of Stoic philosophy forms a holistic system, in which each part supports and is supported by the others. The Stoics devoted a great deal of energy to developing each of these parts in relative independence from the others; Stoic logic, for example, is a large and well-articulated system which can be mastered in its own right. Similarly with ethics; we have evidence that the Stoics explicitly distinguished the discussion of ethics on its own from discussion of it as part of Stoic philosophy as a whole. Moreover, we possess large amounts of ancient evidence of just this activity, namely, ethical discussion and debate, often with other schools. One of our three major sources, Cicero's *De Finibus*, has exactly this form. (On this issue see *The Morality of Happiness*, pp. 159–66.) I do not hold that Stoic ethics is always and only to be interpreted in this relatively independent way, merely that we should carefully distinguish the (rather large) amount of independently developed ethical theory from those passages where ethics is related to other parts of Stoic philosophy, notably metaphysics. It is wrong to focus exclusively either on the independent debates or on the passages relating ethics to metaphysics; both are part of Stoic philosophy as a whole. However, when we are comparing

Stoic ethics with other ethical theories, it is clearly legitimate to do what Cicero does, that is, to discuss the ethics without the metaphysics. We should also be careful not to read into the Stoics a modern preoccupation with ethics being founded on metaphysics, or needing it as a vital support to be a viable enterprise. Stoic philosophy is holistic, and no part of it is foundational for any other. Thus, even in the context of Stoic philosophy as a whole, ethics is not asymmetrically dependent on metaphysical claims. I thus disagree with Cooper's and Schneewind's criticisms of my interpretation of the Stoics, both because I take these two authors to focus too exclusively on the project of relating ethics to metaphysics within Stoic philosophy as a whole, and because they interpret me too narrowly in taking me to focus exclusively on the relatively independent level of ethical discussion and debate.

14. Arius Didymus ap. Stobaeus, *Eclogae* II, 79.18–80.6. I pass over complications in the theory, such as the point that there are circumstances in which normally preferred indifferents can come to be dispreferred.

15. 'Choice' is *hairesis* (*haireisthai*) while 'selection' is *eklogē* (*eklegesthai*). See Arius ap. Stobaeus, *Eclogae* II 75.1–6, 82.20–3.10, 84.24–5.1.

16. The Stoics draw a distinction, akin to Aristotle's, between the virtuous action, which may be done by an imperfect agent because of wrong or mixed motives, and the virtuous action done by a virtuous agent, who has developed a disposition of reasoning in a moral way and does not have to overcome competing motivation.

17. *NE* 1104 b 30–4. The Greek says merely that there are three things 'toward' choices and avoidances, but other passages (e.g., 1119 a 16–17) make it clear that these factors function as aims. Note that the virtuous person goes right, and the bad person wrong, about all three; it is not the case that the good and the bad share the same nonmoral reasoning, differing only about moral reasoning.

18. *NE* 1119 b 23–4.

19. Alexander of Aphrodisias later says that virtue does everything "for the sake of the *kalon qua kalon*" (*De Anima*, II 154.30–1).

20. *NE* 1105 a 26–34, 1144 a 17–20.

21. Although this connection is not spelled out, it is, I think, fairly obvious. It remains remarkable that Aristotle says so little in a positive sense about the fine in the ethical works, or about its connection with doing the virtuous action for its own sake. On the *kalon* see Christine Korsgaard, Chapter 7, Section II, this volume.

22. *Rhetoric* 1364 b 27–8.

23. *Rhetoric* 1366 a 33–5.

24. *Rhetoric* 1366 b 36–1367 a 6; cf. 1367 a 20–3, 26–7.

25. *NE* 1122 b 6–7, 1123 a 23–5.

26. *NE* 1122 b 26–9.

27. *NE* 1123 a 19–34.

28. *NE* 1122 b 6–7.

29. At least from the time of the *Republic*; I pass over the complication that earlier he seems to have regarded piety as a distinct virtue from justice.

30. The Stoic subdivisions of the virtues, for example, use terms which are artificial

255

coinages and pick out subdivisions of the virtues which are wholly defined in terms of the theory and bear little or no relation to everyday usage (often the term is a *hapax legomenon* and it is quite difficult to determine what the subvirtue is meant to be). This is totally different from Aristotle's procedure in following the lines mapped out by everyday usage.

31. Other problems arise for Aristotle's theory from the large-scale virtues; see the exchange between Terence Irwin and Richard Kraut entitled "Disunity in the Aristotelian Virtues," in *Oxford Studies in Ancient Philosophy, Supplementary Volume*, ed. Julia Annas and Robert H. Grimm (Oxford University Press, 1988), pp. 61–90.

32. The word *aretē* itself can have the meaning of 'excellence' of a general and nonmoral kind. In later authors, from the Stoics onward, we find the point made that this is a distinct sense of the word from the sense in which it is applied to the practical disposition of the person who grasps the principles of right action. (For these passages, see *The Morality of Happiness*, pp. 130–1.) The problems which I shall stress in this essay suggest that Aristotle, perhaps under the influence of ordinary usage, does not keep the two usages strictly enough apart. But this is different from the claim that he does not have the means to make the distinction in the first place.

33. It has been argued that *aretē* must mean excellence rather than moral virtue from the *ergon* argument in *NE* Book I. For Aristotle there draws an analytic connection between having an ergon and having an aretē, and there compares the human ergon, and so aretē, with examples which are clearly nonmoral. Aristotle, however, is here using clearly nonmoral examples of ergon (the sense of 'job', as with carpenter and flute player) as an analogy for the relation he wishes to point out, and indeed makes a joke of this (1097 b 28–30); there is no implication that the human ergon and corresponding aretē, the point of the passage, are to be understood as excellences of the same kind as the excellences of flute playing and working in wood.

34. This line of thought can of course be pushed further: Could it not be said that courage merely consists of the application of virtuous deliberation within a sphere of conventionally demarcated kinds of situation? This problem did in fact exercise the Stoics, and there was a debate in the school about it (on which see *The Morality of Happiness*, pp. 77–83). Any account of virtue which stresses the importance of virtuous reasoning rather than the kinds of action performed is likely to end up with a thesis of the unity, or at least reciprocity, of the virtues, and to identify them with exercises of virtuous reasoning rather than types of activity. Aristotle on the one hand commits himself in the sixth book of the *Nicomachean Ethics* to the reciprocity of the virtues, but on the other continues to identify virtues in a more commonsense way, via areas of activity and types of situation. He does not press the difficulties that the Stoics discuss – another factor which may explain his failure to distinguish sharply between moral and nonmoral virtues.

35. I have discussed this issue with regard to the Stoics in *The Morality of Happiness*, pp. 397–406. I am indebted to Terence Irwin's discussion in "Virtue, Praise and

Success: Stoic Responses to Aristotle," *Monist* 73, 1 (1990): 59–79, special issue on *Hellenistic ethics*, ed. J. Cooper.

36. The virtuous person is *katorthōtikos, NE* 1104 b 33; the verb *katorthoun* is also used. The Stoics use *katorthōma* for a virtuous act done as a virtuous person would do it.

37. Irwin, "Virtue, Praise and Success," draws out consequences for the connection of virtue with praiseworthiness.

38. See, e.g., Cicero, *Paradoxa Stoicorum* 3; Arius Didymus ap. Stobaeus, *Eclogae* II, 106.21–6.

39. See *The Morality of Happiness*, pp. 400–6. The Stoics' acceptance of the broadly shared position that virtue is a skill commits them to sticking with the idea that the virtuous person exercises a skill, even in conditions where we can intuitively attach little sense to this. Objections from the intuitive side are pressed against the Stoic position by Plutarch and Alexander of Aphrodisias, who have little trouble showing that the Stoic view is odd given our intuitive evaluation of skill in terms of its outcome.

40. *NE* 1111 b 4–6.

41. Because their theory of action permits them to say that an action has been performed in cases where we would prefer to say that only the antecedent of an action had been performed. See my *Hellenistic Philosophy of Mind*, pt. 2, chap. 4.

42. See *Laws* 697 a 10–c 2; Diogenes Laertius III 80–1 (on this see Cristina Rossitto, *Aristotele ed Altri: "Divisioni"* [Padova: Antenore 1984], pp. 135–9). There is an obvious problem, which I cannot go into here, as to the relation of this passage of the *Laws* to the earlier ones mentioned in note 12, this chapter.

43. *NE* 1098 b 9–18.

44. *Politics* 1323 a 21–38. Aristotle makes it clear in this passage that he has discussed the issue in more popular works.

45. *Magna Moralia* 1184 b 1–5. At *Eudemian Ethics* 1218 b 31–7 we find a division into two instead of three: external or in the soul. We can easily see, however, how goods of the body could be thought of as external, since they are not under the agent's control in the way that goods of the soul are, and this division seems to be a comprehensible simplification of the more common tripartition.

46. *Politics* 1323 b 7–12.

47. This is a very abbreviated and simplified account. I have laid the claim out with more detail and argument in "Prudence and Morality in Ancient and Modern Ethics," *Ethics* 105 (1995): 241–57.

48. *Grounding*, Ak. ed., p. 454.

49. Cicero, *De Finibus* III 44–45, uses the metaphors of obscuring and overwhelming, as the light of a lamp is overwhelmed by the light of the sun. (Kant uses "surpasses and eclipses" in the footnote to Ak. ed., p. 411 of the *Grounding*.)

50. The passage is at Cicero, *De Finibus* V 91–2. The image of the balance comes from Critolaus, one of the heads of Aristotle's school (see Cicero, *Tusculan Disputations* V 51).

51. Samuel Scheffler has an interesting discussion of this issue in "Overridingness,

Human Correctness, and Motivational Naturalism,'' chapter 4 of his *Human Morality* (Oxford University Press, 1992). ''One of the great themes of the *Foundations of the Metaphysics of Morals* is the incompatibility of our own prephilosophical understanding of morality with any purely naturalistic account of moral motivation: that is, with the idea that our motivations for behaving morally stem ultimately from our natural attitudes, desires, sentiments or inclinations, or from other features of our psychology. Kant believes that, rightly or wrongly, we ascribe to morality a special kind of motivational authority – a kind of authority that could not possibly have a purely naturalistic source'' (pp. 61–2). ''The fact remains, Kant thinks, that we do indeed ascribe to morality a kind of authority over our motives that is not dependent on what our natural attitudes or inclinations happen to be. If that is right, then any naturalistic account of moral motivation, including Hume's, really amounts to a denial of the existence of moral motivation as we understand it. That by itself does not imply that naturalism is wrong, only that it is inevitably skeptical or deflationary'' (pp. 63–4).

52. If this is a reputable view, why need Aristotle worry about the Stoic/Kantian alternative? Only when there is a theory which challenges this appearance and claims that it actually misrepresents the way things really are can the appearance no longer be relied upon; this is why the argumentative situation is different for Aristotle and for his later post-Stoic (and indeed post-Kantian) supporters.

V
Stoicism

9

Eudaimonism, the Appeal to Nature, and "Moral Duty" in Stoicism

JOHN M. COOPER

All the major systems[1] of moral philosophy in antiquity, including that of the early Stoics, are eudaimonist in their structure. In giving their accounts of the right way to lead a human life in general and of the reasons that there are for wanting, feeling, and doing anything in particular, they all refer ultimately to the individual agent's *eudaimonia* (happiness). Apparently following Aristotle the Stoics speak of an 'end' (*telos*)[2] of our lives, such that "everything is appropriately (*kathēkontōs*) done for the sake of it, while it is done not for the sake of anything," or again such that "everything done in life appropriately has its reference to it, while it has reference to nothing."[3] And they explain this end as "gaining happiness, which is the same as being happy."[4] They also explain it in other terms, including those of "living in agreement with nature" and "living virtuously," which they say are or come to the same thing.[5] Thus, on the Stoic theory there is for each of us some single end that it is appropriate for us to refer everything we do in life to, and this end is identical, first, with our own 'happiness' (or rather, with our gaining happiness and so living happily),[6] second, with our living in agreement with nature, and third, with our living virtuously. Now according to the Stoics the virtues, taken together with the actions that express them, are chosen, and choiceworthy, for their own sakes;[7] they are both 'productive'

This essay was first prepared for the NEH-sponsored conference at the University of Pittsburgh entitled "Duty, Interest, and Practical Reason." I thank the organizers, Stephen Engstrom and Jennifer Whiting, for giving me this opportunity, and the other participants for a very stimulating and valuable three days of discussion. My co-panelist, J. B. Schneewind, made helpful comments on the next to final version of the conference paper, and I benefited in preparing this printed version from comments by and discussion with Michael Frede, Brad Inwood, and Stephen Menn. Parts of this essay appeared in somewhat altered form in a symposium on Julia Annas's *The Morality of Happiness*, with a response by the author, in *Philosophy and Phenomenological Research* 55 (1995): 587–98.

goods, as being what generates or brings about happiness, and 'final' goods, or goods of the nature of ends, since together they "fill happiness up" and so are its parts.[8] Furthermore, insofar as living virtuously is the same as living in agreement with nature, it is – at any rate according to Chrysippus, the most important early theoretician of the Stoic school – living "without acting in any of the ways usually forbidden by the universal law,[9] that is to say by the right reasoning that goes through all things and is the same as Zeus, he being the ruler of the administration of existing things." And Diogenes Laertius, from whom I cite this, immediately adds that that amounts to "doing everything in accordance with the harmony (*sumphōnia*) of the individual's *daimōn* [guardian spirit: i.e., here, his mind] with the will of the administrator of the universe."[10] So on the Stoic theory virtuous persons act always, first, for the sake of their own happiness (referring all their actions to happiness as their single comprehensive 'end'); second, choosing virtuous acts for their own sake, as parts of their happiness; and third, choosing them as conforming to the universal law, that is, to the will of Zeus.

In what follows I want to defend the philosophical respectability of each of these three elements in the Stoic theory of the virtuous life, and of their coherence when combined within a single theory. I will be especially concerned to explain the third element, the aspect of the virtuous life that introduces something that might be compared with Kant's theory of virtuous action, and that must indeed in some indirect way be an important historical antecedent for it. (I am not competent to, and so won't, pursue such historical connections.) Kant's conception of virtue covers, in comparison with that of the Stoics and other ancient philosophers, a sharply reduced area of our lives: it deals only with what one could call the morality of right and wrong[11] – the treatment of other persons, and also the treatment of oneself insofar as it makes sense to think of having moral duties to oneself – but not with whether one is unseemly in one's liking for sex or food, or knows how to deal in a balanced and intelligent way with the stresses and strains of daily life, rather than falling into furies or depressions, or even with whether one knows and honors the value of true friendship.[12] There are deep, even deep theoretical, reasons for this limitation, to which I will allude later on. But Kant holds that virtue or morality, understood in his reduced way, involves obedience to a law, which as rational beings we each lay down to ourselves, and which consists essentially in subjecting our proposed actions to judgment from the point of view of all other rational beings, and to doing and omitting only what passes that judgment. The universal law of the Stoics is imposed by Zeus, not formally by ourselves, but it is a *rational* law – it rests on good reasons; and the Stoics hold that it is up to each of us, in the use of our own rational powers, to recognize this law's application to us and to determine its content by working out its rationale, sufficiently anyhow for our own needs in deciding what to do. The Stoics, like other Greek philosophers of their time and before, equate honoring and following Zeus with honoring and following reason. In that sense, as with Kant, this universal law is our law qua rational beings for ourselves, and not only Zeus's for us. How far is it legitimate to think that the Stoics incorporate into their ethical theory, through their notion of virtuous action as obedience to the universal law, a deontological element of a Kantian kind? In the last section of this essay I will try to say something to answer this question.

I. Eudaimonism

I said that the major Greek ethical theories, the Stoics' included, are eudaimonist in their structure. What does this mean? In *The Morality of Happiness*, Julias Annas brings much-needed illumination to this subject, though as I shall explain I think she seriously underestimates the intellectual resources available to an ethical thinker working in this tradition. I can best introduce and explain my own understanding of the structure and substance of Stoic ethical theory by referring first to her discussion. In Annas's felicitous phrase, the "point of entry for ethical reflection" in the ancient philosophical tradition is the discomfort one experiences when, as a mature or nearly mature person already having a whole set of evaluative views and fairly settled motivations in line with them, one begins to do what Socrates had famously urged we ought to do, and looks to one's life as a whole. From where one stands already, within one's life as it has developed so far, one seeks a way of bringing unity to one's life, so that one can be said to be *leading* a life, a single one, and not just living – going on from one thing to the next until one dies. Here is where the notion of a single final end for one's life comes in: as Annas suggests, it was felt that "a single final end is what is required to make sense of a single life as a whole" (p. 33). It is also where one's own happiness enters, as a way of giving some preliminary substance to the sought-for single end. The point of entry for ethics is the concern to improve your life by ordering and unifying it: ultimately, it is the concern to make your life as good as possible. One's antecedent commitments and the end that is finally settled upon may take one outside oneself, to affirm the value of objectives lying outside the confines of one's own experiences and activities. Nonetheless, the value, to the one leading the life, of leading it *with* those commitments is inevitably the focus of attention. When the Greek philosophers identify the final end with the agent's happiness, they are simply making this point explicit. As Annas rightly emphasizes, the eudaimonist orientation does not prevent an ethical theorist from developing a conception of happiness under which happy people will lead their lives on the basis of quite extensive commitments to the intrinsic value of moral action, or even to providing other people with what they need simply because they need it. If such actions make for happiness *by* being done according to those commitments, the fact that one is acting also for one's own happiness need do nothing to undermine the integrity of one's commitments and one's actions in furtherance of them. This is particularly so if one identifies happiness directly with a life made up of actions done on the basis of such commitments as those, with no determinate further conception of happiness as a value, beyond the value of such commitments themselves, together perhaps with the value of having them integrated into some unified structure along with other similarly basic values.

Given these "entry" assumptions about Greek ethical theory, how can one expect it to proceed? At the very least the search for such a unifying end and for an adequate conception of happiness will require reflection leading to some considerable integration of what antecedently will have been a disparate set of concerns, commitments, and practical attitudes. It may also lead to reordering one's existing priorities and rethinking certain of one's commitments, as the difficulty or even impossibility of fitting them together with others into a unified scheme of living, comes to light. Furthermore such reflection could conceivably lead you to drop some earlier ideas about what was valuable in life. And it could lead you to add some new values, discovered as you explore previously unnoticed implications of what you had already valued, and as you remove obstacles that earlier ideas, now rejected, posed to recognizing them as deserving such a rank. But Annas thinks that that is pretty much it – not that I wish to suggest that to get as far as that would not be to accomplish something potentially of some significance. She thinks this follows from facts about the "entry" point that I have explained: because the process of ethical reflection begins from the basis of an antecedent set of evaluational beliefs and associated motivations, aiming to bring unity to a life already begun on that basis, she thinks it is limited to arguing within and from the set of such beliefs and motivations,[13] with only such extensions or revisions as that might accomplish. At any rate she legislates, as part of what eudaimonism means or implies, that no appeal can be permitted to anything "outside" the "ethical" as constituted by this set so reflected upon, so as to justify or ground and confirm something already there, or lead to something new to be added.[14] Hence, contrary to what has usually been thought, the "appeal to nature" in an ancient ethical theory cannot – consistent with its eudaimonist character – amount to going outside ethics, so construed, in order to find reasons for believing anything of ethical significance.

But *does* it follow from the nature of the "entry point" for Greek ethical theory that its processes and results should be limited in this way? Does its commitments to eudaimonism in ethics mean that it must? I see no reason to think so. Why should a person entering upon ethical reflection in the position I have described be denied the freedom in their reflections about their life and how to bring unity to it to draw on general views, established or anyhow accepted independently of their antecedent "ethical" outlook? Why should they not use these in order to see their situation in a new light and thereby find valuable confirmation of some elements in that outlook, or grounds for believing some of the prior priorities misguided, or even grounds for believing of no importance some things previously so thought of and for believing of serious importance things not previously thought important? If one assumes that reasons for action must always be, in Bernard Williams's sense, "internal reasons," one may think that this is in fact excluded, given that these reflections are intended to give the agent reasons on which then to act in structuring and living their life, simply because of what reasons are.[15] But that only shows that any eudaimonist theory that permitted such an appeal was deeply confused and in error, not of course that none might, consistent with its being eudaimonist in character, have attempted such a thing. And on an "external" conception of reasons for action (or of some such reasons) – which there is certainly no doubt that some philosophers, like other people, have sometimes accepted – such an appeal would not by any means be precluded. Did these eudaimonist philosophers, or some of them, perhaps accept an "externalist" conception of (at least some) reasons for action?

I think both Aristotle and the Stoics did think of reasons for action in the externalist way. But without having to go into that more fundamental question I think one can see that Aristotle, surely the paradigm of a eudaimonist ethical philosopher, did engage in the sort of "outside" appeal that Annas wishes to legislate away. As Annas rightly emphasizes, it is accepted by all the ancient theorists, as part of the set of evaluational views that one brings in entering upon the philosophical enterprise, that the virtues and virtuous living are not only very good things, but things of such importance for any human being that no acceptable candidate for either the final end or happiness can fail to include them in one way or another as central, essential goods. This is impossible to miss in the ethics of Aristotle. He indicates firmly that those who have not reached the point in their upbringing where they have had experience of the essential quality of morally virtuous action, that it is "fine" or "noble" (*kalon*), and moreover prize such actions because they have it, are not capable of engaging in and learning from philosophical inquiry about ethical matters. Thus, Aristotle's listeners or readers are assumed to know in their own experience, and know in that way the value in, moral action. So it is out of the question that Aristotle should construct and present an argument, addressed to any degree to a reader who does not have this

265

knowledge (or, more noncommittally, does not see things this way), to establish that the moral virtues and morally good living do have a special value, one that is fundamentally important for a human life.

However, even people who know all this about virtue and are quite deeply committed to the truth of what they have come to experience about the value in virtuous action, can very well look to philosophical theory to confirm, on some basis that doesn't just say over again what they already know or merely expand on it a little bit, the truth of what they know through their upbringing. And it is quite clear that Aristotle offers them precisely this. The argument in *Nicomachean Ethics* I 7 leading to his first formulation of his own candidate specification of happiness or the human good contains the following thought: all animals (the same goes for plants) have a natural good, consisting in the particular kind of flourishing life that their specific natures fit them for, and this life is the life of a thing that is an excellent specimen of its kind – our common and obvious practice of speaking of some things as being good and others bad for specific kinds of living thing rests upon this fact, and brings it to light. The application of this general scheme to human beings produces the result that our good consists in a life directed by the use of our rational powers, when they are structured by their excellences, that is, by the virtues; that is what, in our case, an excellent specimen of our kind leading a flourishing life amounts to. Seeing this connection between, on the one hand, the virtuous living we have already had some experience of and already, as it were from the inside, know to value, and, on the other hand, the patterns of thought to which we are committed in dealing with and studying plants and animals – and these are of course not *ethical* patterns of thought – gives powerful confirmation, from outside ethical thought itself, of the truth of something we are committed to within it. We come to see virtuous living in a new way, one that we did not come to in our upbringing and that we need nonethical philosophical thought to reach.[16] And it enables us to say of our own ideal of virtuous living exactly what we say about the life of a fine hydrangea bush, that in it the good of the creature is achieved, and in both cases we can say this neutrally and objectively, without judging the question on the basis of needs, desires, or motivational commitments of our own, of any kind.[17] Here the appeal to human nature[18] is no self-congratulatory mere rhetorical flourish (at any rate, it is not intended by Aristotle that way – whatever a postmodern philosopher might have to say about it); it is doing real and valuable work.[19] It is a further question, of course, on which this argument is silent, whether the specific content, the specific forms of action and specific concerns, of the virtues that we already accept when we enter philosophical ethics can be given some confirmation similarly from the outside. I believe it does not occur to Aristotle to think so.

266

II. The Appeal to Nature

I think that does occur to the Stoics, however. And here I mean the so-called old Stoics, including in particular Chrysippus – and not merely the later Stoics of Imperial times, such people as Seneca, Epictetus, and Marcus Aurelius. Cicero in *On Ends* III 16 has his spokesman Cato begin his exposition of the Stoic view on the final end by discussing the initial instincts with which an animal, including of course a human being, is born. To understand fully the content and the ethical significance of this theory of what is called in Greek *oikeiōsis*, we need also to take into account the exposition of Stoic ethics in Diogenes Laertius's *Lives of Eminent Philosophers* VII, 84–131, which starts similarly with an account of the initial instincts of animals according to the Stoics. We are to understand these initial, innate instincts as goal-directed states; the Stoics assume (or think one can observe) that newborn animals have certain attachments and desires innately that show themselves immediately upon birth – these are not mere reflexes called forth for example in a human baby by pressure against its cheek that leads it to find the breast and start sucking, but an impulse *for* the food that sucking will in fact bring it. Cicero explains that these initial instincts are all directed at the preservation of the 'constitution' (Lat. *status* = Gk. *sustasis*) of the animal or else at things that in fact do serve to preserve its constitution. These are desires, based upon a liking for what it actually is – how it is in fact constituted – to preserve that into the future, for itself, and also to get such things as milk and warmth and so on that its constitution in fact needs if it is to be preserved. (Much later on, but equally as a matter of natural endowment, the Stoics say that animals experience a goal-directed impulse to care for their offspring;[20] human beings also experience in the same way an instinctual and so innate liking for knowing the truth and in general for the exercise of their rational powers in learning things, simply for its own sake, once they have developed enough to make that possible [Cicero III 17–18].)

Cicero represents the Stoics as inferring from this description of their initial natural endowment – by this time they are speaking specifically of human beings – that what newborn animals do automatically from their instincts are things they *ought* to do. He continues his exposition, after a brief digression, with the claim (¶ 20) that the things that are in accordance with nature (i.e., the things that are the objects of these initial instincts, such as milk and warmth) are things *to be taken* for their own sakes (*propter se sumenda*): they not only *are* taken – automatically, on impulse – but are such that they ought to be. Hence, they are "worth selecting" and have some positive value. Why? Not because the animal wants them or feels attracted to them – *that* doesn't constitute any reason why it ought to take them, nor

267

does it give them any value – but because in being so motivated it is in fact motivated, as follows from the assertions about the character of nature's initial endowment of an animal at birth, in ways that are (as we could loosely say) *good* for it. Suppose instead that an animal was born with instincts (goal-directed desires, remember) that were either deleterious to it, or were neither for things it needed for self-preservation nor for things that would harm it, but for some bunch of harmless frivolities (e.g., perhaps as the Stoics would think, merely with an instinctive liking for certain pleasurable sensations). In that case the Stoics would not say that it *ought* to do what it nonetheless did do, automatically and on impulse: there would be no *reason* for it to do it, even if it felt very much like doing it, as of course it would.

We can see this because Diogenes Laertius (VII 85) adds something that Cicero leaves out: an argument to show that the instincts with which nature is assumed to endow newborn animals really are ones, as Cicero also says that they are, for its good (again, I use the word 'good' loosely here). This is an argument by elimination. Assuming, presumably from observation, as I have said, that nature does endow animals with instincts, these instincts must either be for its good, or for its harm, or for neither,[21] but it is not plausible (*eikos*) that nature would either endow an animal with an instinctive disliking for itself and a liking for things that would harm or destroy it, or endow it with desires that had nothing to do with its actual needs as the organism that it is. Why is this not plausible? Plainly because, as the Stoics are assuming from the outset that we will all agree, nature is a benevolent agency. It brings animals into existence each with a particular natural constitution and a particular pattern of development into a flourishing thing of its kind, and gives it the instincts that it normally needs to further that development. The corresponding point holds for plants, too, as Diogenes Laertius (¶ 86) but not Cicero adds: these are "regulated" by nature not by instincts, but nonetheless by physical processes that are aimed at their development into a particular kind of flourishing thing.

Although it begins life acting entirely on instinct, as the other animals do (and continue to do throughout their lives), a human being gradually – during the course of a natural (and inevitable) development – comes into possession of the power of reason, that is, the power of acting *on* reasons, and no longer on instinctive impulse. Cicero continues his exposition by telling us something about the course of this development (Cicero ¶¶ 20–1). He begins by remarking that the very things he has just said are things that are "to be taken" are the objects of the first *officia* or (in Greek) *kathēkonta* – the first things that it is right to do. These are "appropriate acts," as they are often translated, following one common use of the Greek participle in nonphilosophical contexts, or else "duties," following the connotations of the Latin noun. It is worthwhile noticing that Diogenes Laertius tells us later on (VII

108 *ab init.*) that Zeno, who is said to have introduced this terminology into Stoic theory, explained it etymologically along the following lines, yielding a quite different sense from that of what is simply 'appropriate' to do: he derived it from the phrase *kata tinas hēkein;* that is, it is what "comes down on a particular person" to do, what it is your turn or your place to do.[22] So an "appropriate act" is not simply one that fits well with the circumstances in some unspecified way or because it gets you what you want; it is one that it is incumbent upon the one doing it to do, because in those circumstances it is assigned to it by its nature and by the nature of things in general, which made it the way it is.[23] If an act is "appropriate" to do and fits the circumstances, as indeed it does, that is because not only is it assigned to you by nature to do in those circumstances, but since nature acts to further the life of its creatures, doing whatever it is is "suitable" from the creature's own point of view.

With the terminology of "appropriate" or (as we can now also call them) "incumbent" acts in hand, then, Cicero can now describe the automatic, instinctive behavior already discussed, as consisting of acts of this kind. The further course of development consists in several steps by which, in effect, reason in a human being gathers its strength so as to do its natural job of "crafting the impulses" as Diogenes Laertius describes it (see below). Young persons first do what they used to do automatically and on instinct but now not in that way, but rather *because* it is "appropriate" to do it – that is, for the reason that it preserves their constitution and advances their life. It then becomes not an intermittent but a constant and fixed way of behaving to act on reasons of that kind, aiming at one's constitution and its needs as things of ultimate concern. The final stage is reached when, reflecting on what one has been doing while acting for these earlier reasons, one comes to realize that merely acting that way has tremendous appeal, that it is a mistake to think, as one has been doing, of the value of so acting in any given instance as derivative from, needed because of its presumed efficacy in achieving, the assumed value to oneself of the continuance of one's constitution or of getting whatever it was one was then acting appropriately so as to get. Such action is then seen as having an intrinsic value of its own, consisting in the fact that it is reason-directed action, where what is done is "appropriate" because it fits in with one's natural needs. In fact, this intrinsic value is seen as being of so great and unique a kind that one now withdraws, in one's thinking about the value to oneself of the objects for which one was acting previously, all qualification of them as being *good* for you to have. You now see the value of this reason-directed acting as the sole good that you can get, while the objects that it is from time to time "appropriate" for you to direct your actions toward (or away from) are now seen as having a value (or disvalue) of a totally different rank, such that having or not having them makes no

269

difference as to the totality of good or bad in your life. The objects pursued or avoided in such appropriate or incumbent action have, as one might put it, 'pursuit' or 'avoidance' value *within* reason-directed acting, but nothing more: they have *no value at all* outside it.[24]

We can understand that this is so and see what it means if we attend for a moment to the comparisons and contrasts that Cicero (III 24–5, 32) draws between wise or fully reason-directed action, and the acts of other arts. First, "wisdom" is not to be compared to 'stochastic' arts like navigation and medicine (or for that matter archery – despite his own use of it in ¶ 22).[25] Fully accomplished navigators or doctors may have it as their 'work' simply to do the best that can be done in the existing circumstances to get safely to port or to restore the patient to health, but since the latter are their *goals* they are regretful if for reasons beyond the control of their art that is not achieved: their idea was not merely to do their best (and the devil take the hindmost), but to succeed by that means, so that in such a case in some way *the art* has failed, even if the individual artist has in every way lived up to the highest professional standards. ("For wisdom involves . . . a sense of superiority to all the accidents of man's estate, but this is not the case with the other arts"; III 25.)[26] Rather, the right comparison (though itself only partial) is with the arts of dancing or of acting on the stage.[27] Just as the artistic acts of navigator or doctor are given direction by the goals of their arts, so too those of dancers and actors are given direction – not, however, from some goal lying outside the actions themselves which the performer aims to effect, but from the script and the interpretations of the director, or correspondingly from the choreographer. The goals here are simply to act or dance, so directed, in a fully artistic way. Similarly, "wise," fully rational agents, according to the Stoics, take their direction in their actions from whatever may be the natural objective to pursue at the moment, but their goal is to act 'artistically' in a thus-directed way, not actually to get anything, as the navigator or doctor as such wants to do, by acting on those directions. So there is no room for any regret or for a sense of failure of any kind in case the objectives acted for do not materialize. And, Cicero concludes, seeing one's actions and oneself as an agent in that way is the essential prior condition of learning to lead a life of consistently and fully virtuous action.

There is much in this developmental story that needs discussion, and it has been much puzzled over in the scholarly literature.[28] But the crucial point for my purposes here, and the only one I will pursue, is that because again all this happens (allegedly) by nature, and nature is a benevolent agency, we can infer immediately that not only do we live (perforce) by reasons rather than automatically implanted impulses, but this is *good* for us, and that not only do we if unperverted or not defective in some way come to *find* that reason-directed acting of the kind indicated is good for us, and indeed the *sole* good[29] – but this is *true*. In Cicero's exposition this is left implicit, but again in that of Diogenes Laertius the point is made explicitly. Continuing his account, cited earlier, of how benevolent nature endows and directs plants and animals (normally) to a life that is a flourishing one for creatures with their natural constitutions, Diogenes Laertius says (VII 86 *sub fin.*): ''And since reason has been bestowed upon the rational animals by way of a more perfect kind of management [than that merely through impulses implanted directly by nature], living in accordance with reason rightly turns out to be natural for them.[30] For [in their case] reason is added as a craftsman of impulse.'' And he goes on immediately (VII 87) to say, ''That is why in his book *On the nature of humans* Zeno said (he was the first to say this) that the end is living in agreement with nature.'' Because nature gives human beings reason as a craftsman of their impulses, the end for human beings, that is, their overall and final good – what corresponds for them to the flourishing of a plant or an animal – becomes living in agreement with nature, living on the basis not of impulses implanted in them by nature but rather of ones created by themselves through the use of their own reasoning powers, and, further, as Cicero explains, but Diogenes does not (or anyhow not here), ones created by themselves in a quite particular way – the way I described in the preceding paragraph in explaining Cicero's comparison of ''wise'' action with artistic dancing or acting. Cicero says, and Diogenes Laertius agrees, that for the Stoics that is the same as living virtuously.[31]

To assess Cicero's proposed natural progression from instinctual behavior to living ''in agreement with nature'' and the role of nature in fixing its terms, we need especially to ask how and why it should be thought 'natural' (part of being in agreement with nature) to adopt the very peculiar and certainly quite counterintuitive policy of regarding everything else besides fully rational and virtuous action as having no value except what I have called 'pursuit' or 'avoidance' value. I will argue that one cannot even begin to understand the reasons for this unless one takes into account, in conceiving the nature we are to live in agreement with, what Chrysippus says about the relation that holds between our natures as human beings and the single nature of the whole world.

Cicero omits all mention of this point in his exposition.[32] Cicero speaks of the developing rational agent as taking over from its instincts the rational pursuit of the objects at which they were aimed, and we must bear in mind that the instincts in question include not only physical self-preservation but also the instinct to love one's offspring, which is the origin (from a very young age) of the instincts of sociability. We must understand developing rational agents as also seeing that they have reasons, given the benevolence of nature's initial endowments, to care about other people as such and for their own sakes, to treat them fairly, and considerately, and humanely.

271

Let us consider the Stoic theory, as so far presented, from the point of view of those coming to the study of ethics through the "point of entry" specified by Aristotle. How, and how successfully, have the Stoics engaged such people's desire to improve their lives by listening to philosophy? As with Aristotle, they offer valuable confirmation to an agent of the rightness of his or her own commitment to the value of living virtuously: acting virtuously is the same as acting with a fully developed power of practical reason, and considerations about our human nature and the foundations within it of our true good are offered to show that acting in the latter way is at least an essential requirement for achieving our good. But in their conception of how facts about nature ground this result, the Stoics go well beyond Aristotle's very limited appeal to the good life of a member of a natural species, and therefore much farther outside the 'ethical' than does Aristotle. For them nature is a benevolent, *reasoning* agent: it plans and constitutes each kind of living thing with an eye to a specific sort of development to maturity and a particular sort of integration of life functions thereafter as its good. Nature is something *to be* followed for that reason, and it comes in as such in two places in the Stoic account of the human good. On the one hand, the material objectives for which the agent living well will act on each occasion are those that are "in accordance with nature" (*kata phusin*): they are the objects of the initial natural instincts, plus – no doubt we are to understand – obvious extensions that we can see for ourselves as we learn our way around the world and as our constitution itself expands and unfolds over the years we are growing to maturity. On the other hand, as we have seen, a particular (and quite counterintuitive) sort of rational attention to these objects is also said to be natural: this is what is referred to in the phrase 'in agreement with nature' (*homologoumenōs tē(i) phusei*) in the Stoics' most usual formulation of the *telos*.

Now the first of these two appeals to nature allows the Stoics to derive at least the rudiments of a theory of what one ought to do. In the theory of "appropriate" or incumbent acts – derived from a knowledge of how nature usually works, in the case of human and other animals, and not at all from inside the "ethical" – the Stoics offer both a confirmation of what we may have already thought at the "entry point" about what we ought to concern ourselves with, and a means of revising and extending it. (I think here especially of the famous Stoic insistence that we have duties of justice and humanity to all human beings merely as such: observation of nature gives us many bases, they think, for supposing that we were "made" for that sort of thing.) This is something, I said, that seems quite lacking in Aristotle. But it is the second appeal to nature that I want to concentrate on. What does it mean to be "living in agreement with nature"? Diogenes Laertius tells us that Cleanthes, Zeno's successor as head of the Stoic school, interpreted the

272

nature here in question simply as that of the universe as a whole – not as the nature of a human being. Chrysippus, too, understood it as the universal nature, but corrected Cleanthes on the ground that to live in agreement with human nature actually *was* to live in agreement with universal nature: ''living in agreement with nature,'' he said, is living in agreement with the universal nature and also, in particular, with human nature (Diogenes Laertius VII 89). It is important to observe that in this sequence the reference to universal nature came first, not just chronologically but even (at least in Diogenes Laertius's formulation) within Chrysippus's own explication: the end, he thought, is living in agreement with our own nature as well as with that of the universe as a whole, because it *belongs* to our human nature to be in agreement with the nature of the whole. That is why he can say also that the end is ''living in accordance with experience of what happens in the course of nature.''[33] And Diogenes Laertius in reporting this immediately adds, ''for our natures are parts of the nature of the whole.'' Thus, the experience in question is experience of what happens in the course of nature at large.

But what does happen in the course of nature that we have to have experience of if we are to live in agreement with nature? Part of this we have already seen: universal nature, through its processes of forming the world's plant and animal life, is benevolent, in the sense that for each of its creatures, universal nature establishes a coherently structured constitution and a life pattern that corresponds, which makes possible for each of them, under normal and usual conditions, a flourishing and good life. But, of course, still in the course of nature, it also frequently happens that plants or animals, or whole systems of them, are deprived of the conditions in which they *can* flourish, according to the norms laid down by nature itself for things of their different kinds. To consider only the human case, although good health is something for which the nature of our bodies normally works automatically as part of what benevolent nature wants for us, that same nature, working from outside, infects us with diseases, or causes famines and avalanches and in other such ways destroys or maims the lives that, working from inside, it is striving to advance. What do we learn from knowing this sort of thing? One could say, of course, that it must be that though nature continues to *want* things to go well for its creatures even while doing these things to them, it is just not always possible: to keep the whole thing going, which makes possible the continuance of all these marvelous life forms, sometimes some of the individuals have to be sacrificed. But that does not go far enough – not far enough, I mean, to get us to the conclusion Chrysippus wants us to reach.

If that were what one should think, one might well, in now living ''in agreement with nature,'' realize that it could not rationally be helped that one's child got cancer and died a horrible death at the age of 15: nature

273

couldn't rationally have done otherwise than to cause all that. And so one would accept the loss, as one accepts in one's own calculations the necessity to give up something one wanted – indeed, wanted very much – in order to get what overall one thinks is best. But the Stoics want us to do more than accept such things as inevitable *losses* – and this is the very core of what "living in agreement with nature" means for them. We are to think of them as no losses at all; we are not just to accept but to welcome them, and welcome them not just, I take it, as what the universe needed, but as what *we* as parts of that universe needed too. As Chrysippus said, according to Epictetus: "So long as the events coming in sequence are unclear to me I always hold to the things that are better adapted for getting things that are in accordance with nature. God himself [i.e., Zeus] has made me such as to select these. But if I knew that I was fated to get sick now I would also have an impulse toward that. After all, the foot, if it had a mind, would have an impulse toward getting muddied."[34] As we have seen, Chrysippus emphasized in this connection that our natures are parts of the nature of the whole, from which the inference apparently to be drawn is that even our 'local' advantage – what advances our individual lives – is to be measured by reference to the needs of the life of the world as a whole, just as the 'local' advantage' of the foot is rightly measured by what it needs to do *as* a foot in the life of the whole person. Even the cancer and horrible death of a child is not to be seen, once it happens, as a loss, a sacrifice that nature has called on the child's parent to accept in the interest of the whole; if the life of the whole has been advanced by that means, so has the parent's own life, since it is nothing but a part of the life of the whole.[35] So far as I can see, it is only if we think of ourselves and our lives in this way that we can see the point of the demand that living in agreement with nature (i.e., universal nature) should lead us to regard all that happens to us on a par – all the failures or successes we may have in relation to the 'material' objectives of our virtuous actions – and not to think of anything that happens to us as any better or worse than anything else that we might imagine as having happened instead. I do not see at all how one could reasonably be invited to reach that conclusion simply from within the "ethical," that is, from within our practical attitudes and our motivational set as we come to the study of philosophical ethics, plus our commitment to finding a conception of a single overall good to direct our lives by. That "ethical" starting point would include the idea that virtuous action is a crucial and indispensable value for a good human life. But I can find no pressure from within the "ethical" view we would have been brought up with that would, or that the Stoics might reasonably have thought would, lead us all by itself to this totally new way of conceiving the value of all things other than virtuous action itself.[36] The Stoics' appeal to nature as I have explained it, however much supplemented by such "ethical" considerations, is an indispensable part – indeed, the core – of their argument.

III. "Moral Duty"

With the structure of their theory now before us, what can we say about the Stoics' concept of "moral duty"? How significantly, if at all, do their eudaimonism, with its strong teleological commitments, or other features of their view, distinguish their conception of duties from that of Kant? First, as I said at the beginning of this essay, following Julia Annas, the Stoics' eudaimonism poses no obstacle at all to the moral integrity of virtuous agents. When such agents identify living virtuously with living happily, they do not have some determinate further conception of their happiness as a value, beyond that of living according to the commitments constitutive of virtuous attitudes themselves; they do not subordinate virtuous action to some other thing they know and value independently, as a means of achieving that value. On the contrary, it is the value of living virtuously itself, that is, living in agreement with nature, that they see as the basic value. Logically speaking, the identification of this with living happily is a subsequent move.

But does not this simple identification of virtuous with happy living introduce, from the opposite direction as it were, at least as great a distortion of what virtue and duty are, according to our modern conception, as would the effort to subordinate virtuous action to the pursuit of one's own happiness conceived as Kant conceives happiness? If you abolish altogether all even potential conflict between virtue and happiness, don't you remove a contrast that is essential to giving sense to what virtue and duty are? For us a dutiful life is *essentially* one requiring frequent self-denial and sacrifice of our own good to that of others. One can respond to this challenge at two levels. First, someone who accepted the Stoic outlook, and recognized in their calmer and more reflective moments that their highest good really does consist entirely in virtuous living, understood in the Stoics' way, might very well, when it came to practice, find it quite difficult to act in accordance with that vision. They might find that what that required of them was by no means what, at the moment, they most wanted to do, or most cared about. If nonetheless they found the strength of mind to do what their own happiness (= virtue) would require, this would be experienced by them as, and would in fact be, an act of self-denial, and if not precisely a sacrifice of their own good (as they saw that in doing the action), at any rate a sacrifice of what they had antecedently most wanted, most cared about, and most felt like doing. If happiness is placed on the side of virtue, there is still plenty of room for a sharp contrast between both of those things and one's perceived interests and advantage, one's material needs and welfare, one's pleasure, one's deep (nonmoral) life projects (if one puffs oneself up by thinking of one's life in such terms at all), and so on. On the Stoic view, of course, the act of such a conflicted agent, however commendable, would not be a fully virtuous one: it derived not from a permanent and deeply reasoned commitment to living in agreement with nature, but at best from a temporary and wavering acceptance of the value of doing that. On the other hand, it is also the case on the Stoic view that that sort of 'virtuous' action is in fact the best that almost any human being actually manages to produce. So one is entitled to say, for the Stoics just as much as for Kant or for us, that virtue (or rather, 'virtue' – the closest any of us actually comes to true virtue) is essentially bound up with self-denial and self-sacrifice.[37]

Second, even fully virtuous persons (so-called sages) experience virtuous action as something imposed on them by Zeus and by themselves qua rational, something that requires vigilance and discipline so that they do not follow the tendency usual for human beings to identify their perceived interests and advantage, material needs and welfare, pleasure, and nonmoral life projects as being of independent value, separate from what I have called their "pursuit" value.[38] Even if their conviction otherwise is so deeply imbedded in their minds that there is no chance at all that they will ever adopt such a mistaken view even temporarily, and they do not actively have to fight off any tendency to do that, what guarantees this success is precisely the active, forceful, and constant use of their minds in understanding things rightly. They know that in the interest of acting virtuously they often deny themselves things that can with plausibility be thought good for them: most people do think them good, and anyone, the fully virtuous person included, can readily see why, given the character of our experience of them. Moreover, even if the virtuous are so strong minded that it is certain that they will never give in to such appearances, it seems reasonable to think that they, like all other human beings, will continue to be affected by the plausible appearance of these things as if they were good. Even virtuous persons, therefore, experience their virtuous actions and outlook as requiring that they sacrifice things that they continue to be *able* to see as if they were good. They have not ceased being human beings and become gods; they experience "duty" as going against something within them, even if not against what amounts to a Kantian "inclination."

"Living in agreement with nature" as the Stoics understand it involves modeling one's thoughts in deciding on and doing one's actions, on nature's own thought in designing the world (i.e., itself), establishing the physical laws, and causing the events that happen within it. To be sure, not even a perfectly virtuous person can know the particular reasons why nature causes the events that it does – why, for example, one person falls ill when another does not. Even if a virtuous person enjoys happiness just as great as Zeus's, as Chrysippus scandalously maintained,[39] nonetheless Zeus understands what he is doing vastly more completely. So one has to accept as reasonable, and benevolent, what one often cannot know the reasons for – though, one knows, there *are* reasons, and Zeus or nature does know them. This gives emphasis to the idea that in living virtuously one lives in obedience, as Chrysippus puts it in the striking passage from Diogenes Laertius we began from, to the *koinos nomos* or the law of the universe, or universal and right reason, or the will of Zeus. This obedience involves two fundamental things: (1) acting so as to pursue or avoid the things that can be seen *normally* to accord with or go against our physical constitution and the social circumstances that naturally suit beings with that constitution, and (2) pursuing or avoiding them always with the idea that it may turn out that achieving those objectives on that occasion was not after all what we or anyone else truly needed, because it does not fit in with the needs of the whole universe of which we are organic parts.

In considering this aspect of the Stoic theory of duty one should note two points. First, the thought that in doing a virtuous act one is doing it because it is commanded by the universal law and by universal reason applies just as much, and in exactly the same way, to what one does in maintaining an appropriate diet or tending to one's daily hygiene or working hard at one's profession or behaving charmingly at a dinner party, as it does to what, according to one contemporary usage and the dominant one nowadays anyhow among philosophers, we would call *moral* decisions and actions – treating other people fairly and considerately, standing up for moral principle when that is inconvenient and one's associates or more generally one's fellow citizens would gladly override it, refusing to disobey the law even if no one will find out, or accepting financial sacrifice and personal hardship in order to serve the public good. The notion of ''duty'' among the Stoics covers a vastly wider range than it does, for example, for Kant: it covers, in fact, crucial aspects of the whole of one's life and virtually everything one does, if one is truly virtuous. So if we should choose to call all the Stoic duties *moral* duties, we should frankly admit that we are employing so widened a conception of morality as to risk losing contact with what we nowadays understand by that term.[40] Moreover, because in this theory the more private and personal side of life is lumped together with the morally right and morally wrong, without any fundamental discrimination between them, the latter, though certainly present and accounted for in the theory, do not receive the priority that moralists nowadays typically think they are entitled to. We have a deontology, perhaps, but it is not a deontology that tells us first to tend to the morally right and wrong, and only then to our private and more personal

277

concerns. It simply tells us to follow reason and not to act ever on what we might otherwise like to do, or on how the appearances of things to us might make us think it would be a good idea to act.

Second, the notion of universal reason here at work has further special features that mark it sharply off from the Kantian conception, however much it may be an important ancestor of the latter. For the Stoics, universal reason is the reason common to all human beings. But it is also, and more fundamentally, the single reason that governs the unified world as a whole. When I consult universal reason in deciding what to do – say, to do an act of justice or humanity – I do of course consult the very same ideas that any other rational human being in my situation would consult, and the very same ones that the recipient of my action, qua rational, will have in mind in considering and assessing what I am doing. But more fundamentally what I am consulting are the ideas to be found in reasoned experience of nature at large as to what that nature *intends* for me to do. There is no appeal, and no room for any appeal, to individual rational beings, such as myself, as having the power to set their own ends, or to any requirement to respect, just because it came from a free exercise of that power, any other person's preferences and decisions about what to care about in their lives. So there is no basis for attributing to the Stoics any idea of the 'rights of man' where that has at its core the idea that adult persons have an inviolable right to live as they please, so long as they don't interfere with the same right of others, and a similar right to take part equally in the establishment or authorization of public policy in their countries and communities. Since Kant's conception of universal reason as the source of moral duties has its place in a political and religious world that made human freedom and equality in precisely this sense the central moral idea, one should not fail to see that the Stoic idea of universal reason, together with its consequences for ethical theory, constitute what amounts to a different moral universe.

NOTES

1. As Julia Annas has reminded us in several recent writings, there was one exception, that of the Cyrenaics. See, e.g., *The Morality of Happiness* (New York: Oxford University Press, 1993), pp. 230, 235–6.
2. See *Nicomachean Ethics* I 2, 1094a 18–19; at I 7, 1097a 34–b 6 Aristotle identifies this end with "happiness."
3. Arius Didymus's *Epitome* of ethical theory as it occurs in Stobaeus, *Excerpts* (hereafter referred to as Arius at Stobaeus) II 7 (p. 46, lines 5–10 in C. Wachsmuth's edition [W]; Berlin, 1884–1912). The passage quoted comes not in his exposition of Stoic views "in the ethical division of philosophy" but in Arius's

general introduction, where he explains the use of the word *telos* and gives these definitions as Stoic ones. Arius's work, which unfortunately has not yet been translated into English (Julia Annas's translation for the Oxford Texts in Hellenistic Philosophy series of the portion on Stoic ethics is eagerly awaited), is one of the only three continuous, more or less comprehensive presentations of Stoic ethics to have survived from antiquity. (The other two are in Cicero, *On Ends*, Bk. III, and Diogenes Laertius, *Lives of Eminent Philosophers*, VII 84–131.)

4. Arius at Stobaeus (77, 26–7 W), within his exposition of the Stoic theories. Just above (77, 16–17 W), Arius repeats the characterization of the end, identified now as "being happy," as "that for the sake of which everything is done, while it is done but not for the sake of anything." This time he leaves off the qualification "appropriately," but that may be because he has already been speaking at length of virtue and the virtuous person, who does of course do everything in this way.

5. Diogenes Laertius VII 87 *ab init.*, attributed to Zeno; see also Arius at Stobaeus 78, 1–6 W.

6. They distinguish, quite reasonably, between 'living happily' as the predicate that we want to be true of us (our *telos* is that it shall be the case that we are living happily) and the condition of happiness as the "target" (*skopos*) that we aim at in order to bring that about: Arius at Stobaeus 77, 25–7 W. In what follows I will not take care to observe this distinction.

7. Diogenes Laertius VII 89, 127.

8. "Productive" here translates *poiētika*, "final" *telika*. See Diogenes Laertius VII 97 *ab init.* and Arius at Stobaeus 72, 3–6 W: the two passages use identical language.

9. The Greek here is *ho nomos ho koinos*, normally translated as "the law that is common (to everyone or everything)." "Universal law" (i.e., the law of the universe as a whole) seems to me to express the intended idea better; in any event we find the same adjective, *koinos*, used just below in Diogenes' text, to qualify "nature" so as to mark off the nature of the universe as a whole as opposed to human nature in particular (*phusin . . . koinēn* in 89 is a variant for *tēn tōn holōn* [*phusin*] in 88), and there translators quite rightly render it with "universal."

10. Despite the very clear and explicit evidence of Diogenes Laertius, who mentions Chrysippus by name and describes his view at some length, as a view *within* ethical theory, Julia Annas boldly seeks, in *The Morality of Happiness*, chap. 5, to deny that any such thought belonged to ethical theory as it was constructed and taught by the early Stoics – as against a metaphysical or theological addendum, within physics or metaphysics itself, showing how the ethical views already reached fit together with the conception of the cosmos as a whole; according to her, it was a later addition to the foundations of ethical theory made by Stoics of the Imperial period, such as Epictetus and Marcus Aurelius. Her chief arguments are philosophical, not textual: she does not see how the early Stoic ethical theory could be a eudaimonist theory, as it plainly claimed to be, while also relying in its account of the virtues on such an "external" standard of right action. Once one discards her too limited account of what eudaimonism is and entails (see later in this essay), one can see that early Stoic eudaimonism does not in the least speak against the appeal within Stoic

ethical theory to such a conception of Zeus's will as a universal law, conscious obedience to which is essential to virtuous action.

11. I have picked up this useful terminology from Thomas Scanlon.

12. In the *Doctrine of Virtue*, Part II of the *Metaphysics of Morals*, Kant shows how the "duties to oneself as a moral being with an animal nature" and the duties of respect for and benevolence to others may ground virtues covering some aspects of the parts of our lives here referred to. But the scope of these Kantian virtues is quite limited in comparison with the corresponding virtues of the Greek theorists, just because of their grounding in and control by these duties. For the Greeks there are many more nuanced ways of showing defects – in relation to sexuality, to the consumption of food and drink, to social occasions, to friendship – than the ones that Kant's theory permits him to take notice of. (I thank J. B. Schneewind for discussion on this point.)

13. Subjected to such pressures as may arise from (1) the acceptance of the agreed-upon formal conditions that any candidate for a 'final end' must aim to satisfy – those of finality and comprehensiveness and, perhaps less explicitly, 'self-sufficiency', adopted from Aristotle (*Nic. Eth.* I 7) (see Annas, *The Morality of Happiness*, pp. 39–42) – and in some way also (2) the most general, agreed understandings of what 'happiness' entails: it is tied closely with activity, not passivity, and yields a positive view of one's life, satisfaction with the way it is going, i.e., with the bases on which it rests and with their consequences in the conduct of one's life.

14. See Annas, *The Morality of Happiness*, pp. 161–2, in discussing the role of the appeal to "cosmic nature" in Stoic ethics.

15. See B. Williams, "Internal and External Reasons," *Moral Luck* (Cambridge University Press, 1981), pp. 101–13.

16. See further John M. Cooper, "Reason, Moral Virtue and Moral Value," M. Frede and G. Striker, eds., *Rationality in Ancient Greek Thought* (Oxford University Press: 1996), pp. 81–114.

17. It also does not involve application of any "universal" teleology, of plants and animals having been made as part of some unified grand plan, each contributing in its way to the overall good of the whole. The good of each species is judged merely on the basis of its single nature, and without assuming it was made for any further purpose.

18. Annas (*The Morality of Happiness*, p. 144) dismisses this argument from her discussion of the "appeal to nature" in Aristotle on the inadequate ground that Aristotle "does not prominently present [it] as involving nature." She apparently has in mind that the word for 'nature' does not prominently appear in his argument, but that obviously does not matter.

19. I said that Aristotle does not address his argument to any person who does not already know and value virtuous action highly. Would his argument nonetheless reasonably give such people pause, give them some reason to think they are wrong not to value it, to regret that they have not learned to appreciate the things virtuous people appreciate and to see things their way? Obviously, the argument does not attempt to convey to anyone a knowledge *of* what is so valuable about

this sort of action; so no one is being brought, through accepting the argument, thereby to know virtue and value it the way the virtuous person does. Equally obviously, the argument does not attempt to show completely nonvirtuous people that something that they already know from their own experience and find to be good and desirable is achieved especially well by the virtuous, so that they are missing out by not being virtuous on something they are already motivated to get. However, the argument operates with a conception of the good of a creature with which anyone is familiar and is not likely to feel comfortable simply dismissing, and it gives a certainly very plausible basis for saying that the good of a creature like us, corresponding to the good (= the flourishing life) of a plant, essentially involves the virtuous use of our powers of reasoning. That is enough to give even immoralists pause, if they pay attention to reason at all, and in any event it does give such people reason to think they ought to take the steps necessary (whatever those might be) to acquire virtue – whether they pay attention or not.

20. Cicero III 62–3. This is said to be the origin of all the instincts of natural sociability, which are in turn the natural psychological basis for the duties of justice and humanity. Its effects are seen already in small children, even though it is present in its primal form only when one has become a parent.

21. The assumption seems to be that on each option all the instincts are of the one character indicated: a mixed natural endowment is either not considered or thought to be ruled out on the same grounds as the third option is ruled out.

22. In explaining the intended etymology, H. G. Liddell, R. Scott, and H. S. Jones, *A Greek–English Lexicon* (Oxford University Press, 1940) (LSJ), helpfully cite s.v. *kathēkein* 2 the use of *kata* (s.v. B. 1. 3), in which Epictetus speaks (*Enchiridion* 15) of a guest at a feast who must wait quietly until the wine or whatever 'gets down to you' (*gignesthai kata se*), until it is your turn. This seems the best way of understanding what Zeno intended, in part precisely because it does not attempt to derive the participle in such a way as to make it mean directly what everyone would automatically take it to mean anyhow ('appropriate'): such a derivation is intended to reveal something that is hidden. Alternatively (but to much the same effect) we could understand, with B. Inwood and L. P. Gerson (*Hellenistic Philosophy: Introductory Readings* [Indianapolis, Ind.: Hackett, 1988], p. 140), "extending [or applying] to certain people." A. A. Long and D. N. Sedley (*The Hellenistic Philosophers* [Cambridge University Press, 1987], 59C) seem to be trying to produce the obvious derivation (not very intelligibly, either) when they give the etymology as from "to have arrived in accordance with certain persons." (I don't know why they say the etymology has not yet been satisfactorily interpreted: the proposal I have accepted was not only already in LSJ, but it or the not very different Inwood–Gerson version was in essence already well argued for by A. Dyroff, *Die Ethik der Alten Stoa* [Berlin, 1897], p. 134. Certainly the idea that *kata* in the etymology is to be understood as 'in accordance with' was shown to be wrong by Dyroff.)

23. Cicero does not mention that "appropriate acts" are done by plants as well as by animals: see Diogenes Laertius VII 107. When a plant, e.g., grows and then

unfolds its flower in the way that is normal for the kind of plant that it is, those are "appropriate acts" on its part. Presumably if, due to some abnormality, it grew in altogether the wrong way, those acts would not be "appropriate."

24. The Stoics present this final "development" as equally as "natural" as the previous ones, despite the fact that it is of course not an inevitable part of the maturation process that all but agreed cases of defective people undergo. Obviously we are not in a position to discover a "defect" in anyone who does not reach this final stage by the sort of methods we use to classify the failure of some plant to produce a fruit as due to a congenital defect or developmental anomaly. It seems best to interpret the Stoics' account of human development as intending to show how, *if* (i.e., given that) their theory of the good is correct, we could see human beings coming to grasp it by a series of steps of gradual illumination about what human life involves, each of which can seem fairly natural given its predecessors (and some of which are in fact inevitable): it is by this development that nature or Zeus has intended that we shall develop, whether or not we actually all do complete it.

25. A stochastic craft is one in which the correct performance by the craftsman does not guarantee the achievement of the craft's aim. The contrast here is with, e.g., the "crafts" of geometry and arithmetic: correct performance in these latter guarantees getting the right result, the one sought after by the art and by the artisan as such. See Gisela Striker, "Antipater, or the Art of Living," in G. Striker and M. Schofield, eds., *The Norms of Nature* (Cambridge University Press, 1986), pp. 185–204.

26. Trans. by H. Rackham in the Loeb edition (Cambridge, Mass.: Harvard University Press, 1914).

27. It seems very likely that Cicero's preference for these arts as (partial) analogues for wisdom, rather than a stochastic craft such as archery, reflects debates among the Stoics and between them and the academic skeptic Carneades in the middle and end of the second century B.C. – rather than presenting comparisons drawn by anyone of Chrysippus's generation, much less Zeno's (see Striker, "Antipater," pp. 201, 203). However, whatever its provenance, it seems clear to me that the analogy of acting and dancing is very apt for bringing out the true relationship between acting virtuously and pursuing the 'natural objective' of the moment, as this was understood by the early Stoics.

28. Among the more recent contributions, see part 1 of G. Striker, "Following Nature: A Study in Stoic Ethics," *Oxford Studies in Ancient Philosophy* 9 (1991): 1–73, and Troels Engberg-Pedersen, *The Stoic Theory of Oikeiosis* (Aarhus, Denmark: Aarhus University Press, 1990).

29. Because for the Stoics nothing can be good, strictly speaking, except rational processes carried out to perfection, I have in the preceding occasionally qualified my talk of a person's or an animal's 'good' as "loose." No nonrational animal or plant has a good strictly speaking, and our good does not include our comfort, health, etc. In what follows I will continue occasionally to speak in this loose way of a thing's good, but without encumbering the exposition with an explicit qualification to that effect.

30. The Greek is ambiguous as to the placement of the adverb translated by
    "rightly": it might, as my translation also would permit, go with the main verb
    or with the participle. The distinction does not matter for present purposes.
31. Diogenes Laertius continues the sentence last quoted, in which he cites Zeno's
    specification of the end as living in agreement with nature: "and that is living
    virtuously; for nature leads us to virtue." Cicero, who as we saw concludes his
    exposition in ¶ 21 with the claim that at the final stage of development, human
    beings come to see their final good as consisting in virtuous action, also refers
    back to this result in ¶ 26 by citing this same Zenonian specification of the end
    and saying that it was that which the developmental argument had established.
    Thus, Cicero and Diogenes come as it were each from a different direction to the
    same identification of virtuous living with living in agreement with nature. (Cic-
    ero had alluded already in ¶ 21, but indistinctly, to "agreement" as what virtuous
    action amounts to.)
32. But since he recognizes that the end we are to come to accept as the true one is
    "living in agreement with nature," and that, in fact, means for the Stoics pri-
    marily living in agreement with *universal nature* (see in my text below), he is
    silently relying on presuppositions about what that would entail. Despite this and
    the clear and explicit evidence from Diogenes Laertius about Chrysippus, Annas
    (*The Morality of Happiness*, chap. 5) wishes to exclude all reference to universal
    nature from an account of the foundations of Stoic ethical theory. Partly this is
    because she thinks that to include it would go against the order Chrysippus and
    the other older Stoics followed in expounding their philosophy: ethics preceded
    physics, and since physics is required in order to establish anything about uni-
    versal nature and its manner of working, it follows, she thinks, that ethics must
    forgo any reference to claims about those matters. She also draws on Jacques
    Brunschwig's article "On a Book-title by Chrysippus" (*Oxford Studies in An-
    cient Philosophy*, 1991, supp., pp. 81–95) to show that Chrysippus prominently
    used 'dialectical' styles of argument in his ethical writings, and that such quo-
    tations from Chrysippus by Plutarch in *On Stoic Self-contradictions*, chap. 9 as
    that "there is no other or more suitable approach to the theory of good and bad
    or to the virtues or to happiness than from universal nature and from the man-
    agement of the cosmos" (1035c) come not from ethical writings but from phys-
    ical ones. She infers that no such approach was made in ethics proper, but came
    only when at the end of the day the already-established ethical conclusions were
    permitted to be seen in the light of physics and theology. She neglects to consider
    that reliance in ethics on dialectical premises need not be restricted to premises
    about "ethical" matters, but could well include some premises indicating (in the
    rough and undetailed way that suits dialectical argument) the unity and the ra-
    tional nature of the whole cosmos and its unitary functioning. To include such
    ideas in the foundations of the ethical theory does not require a premature preview
    of the whole panoply of Stoic physics and theology, as expounded in physical
    treatises, and there is plenty of enrichment and deepening of one's ethical insights
    still to be achieved when in studying physics one learns more about these ideas
    and the scientific basis for them. As for sources for dialectical arguments (apart

from such arguments as those Chrysippus gave starting from the premise that "nothing is better than the world," see, e.g., Diogenes Laertius VII 142 *sub fin.*-143), one need only think of the arguments of Plato's *Timaeus* – appeal to these would of course count as "dialectical." Thus, when Chrysippus claims (according to Plutarch, *On Stoic Self-contradictions* 1041 e) that his theory of goods and bads is "most in harmony with life and most in contact with the preconcepts we naturally have," these preconcepts don't at all have to be only specifically *ethical* ones: preconcepts about the unity and rationality of the world-animal and so on can perfectly well be included. So the evidence that Annas cites to support her effort to exclude reference to the nature of the world as a whole from Stoic ethical theory does not in fact support it.

33. Diogenes Laertius VII 87, *kat' empeirian tōn phusei sumbainontōn zēn*; Cicero III 31: "vivere scientiam adhibentem earum rerum quae natura eveniant, seligentem quae secundum naturam et quae contra naturam sint reicientem, id est convenienter congruenterque naturae vivere."

34. Epictetus, *Discourses* II 6, 9.

35. Thus, I think that accounts such as that of F. H. Sandbach, *The Stoics* (London: Chatto & Windus, 1975), pp. 35–7, approved by Long and Sedley (*The Hellenistic Philosophers*, vol. II, p. 354), do not go far enough. Gisela Striker, "Following Nature" (see esp. pp. 10–12) is along the right lines.

36. T. H. Irwin's arguments in "Stoic and Aristotelian Conceptions of Happiness," in Striker and Schofield, eds., *The Norms of Nature*, pp. 205–44, constructed on this basis, to support the Stoic views as against those of Aristotle, are mostly very weak and tortured, and the whole effort leads, by his admission, to an entirely predictable, uneasy standoff.

37. Of course, for Kant virtue requires *real* self-sacrifice that only moral faith can allow us to think may be made up for in the end. I thank J. B. Schneewind for reminding me of this.

38. According to Galen, Chrysippus mentioned two causes to explain the fact that people generally are corrupted as they grow up and do not follow the natural development that leads to being virtuous: they learn the wrong values from what others around them say about the values of things, or else they acquire them from "the nature of things itself" (*ex autēs tōn pragmatōn tēs phuseōs*; Galen, *On the Doctrines of Hippocrates and Plato*, trans. P. De Lacy [Berlin: Academie Verlag, 1978–80], 5. 15, p. 320), glossed by Galen as "the persuasiveness of appearances" (*dia tēn pithanotēta tōn phantasiōn*, 5. 19). (This passage supports the variant reading of *pragmatōn* in place of the editors' *pragmateiōn* at Diogenes Laertius VII 89.)

39. See Arius at Stobaeus 98, 18–99, 2 W.

40. For this reason I feel very uncomfortable with Annas's uncompromising insistence that in the Stoics' and other ancient discussions of the primacy of virtue over all other values, we are getting, quite simply, theories of *morality*. See *The Morality of Happiness*, e.g. pp. 14, 452–55, and J. Annas, "Ancient Ethics and Modern Morality," *Philosophical Perspectives* 6, ed. J. Tomberlin (Atascadero, Calif.: 1992), pp. 119–36.

10

Kant and Stoic Ethics

J. B. SCHNEEWIND

Having agreed to explore teleology and deontology in Stoic and Kantian ethics, I find I am forced at the very outset to voyage between the Symplegades, the clashing rocks. On the one side there are Kantians who tell us to stop thinking of Kant as a deontologist.[1] On the other side loom the students of ancient ethics who tell us that it is a mistake to think that Stoic thought was teleological in any way that contrasts meaningfully with deontology. If we accept both these views, we should conclude that the route for my expedition is impassable. Can it be opened by fending off the rocks? Displaying a no doubt deplorable exegetical conservatism, I shall try. I begin by rejecting the position of the Kantian revisionists. I then go on to argue that ancient ethical theories are indeed teleological in contrast to something that is not so in Kant. If we can get past the clashing rocks into calmer waters, we may find ourselves rewarded with views of the significance of some of the differences between the Stoic theory of morality and Kant's.[2]

I

Teleological views are supposed to put value at the center, or the base, of morality, while deontological views put duty there. Hence, neither label cap-

I am much indebted to John Cooper for lengthy discussions of Stoicism, as well as for comments on a draft of this essay. Needless to say I have probably failed to learn much of what he tried to tell me. I owe thanks to Gisela Striker, whose essays on Stoicism I have found particularly helpful and who kept me from making a serious mistake about the doctrine. My thanks go also to the Hopkins graduate students who took my seminar on Stoic and Kantian ethics in the fall of 1993 and whose comments on an early version of this essay were acute and instructive. I benefited from the discussion in Pittsburgh throughout the symposium for which this essay was written, and from questions raised by John Simmons and Richard Rorty at the University of Virginia.

tures Kant's view. Duty for him is of course a derivative notion; but so is value. Kant explicitly allows for two kinds of goodness, or value, and gives an admirably clear account of them in the second *Critique*. Both kinds of 'good' and 'bad' on Kant's view are *relational* predicates. To be good is to be the necessary object of a will according to a rational principle. If the necessity of willing an object is conditional on a prior desire, then the object's goodness falls into the category of *das Wohl* (well-being or natural good). If an object is necessarily willed in complete independence of any desire, then its goodness falls into the category of *das Gute* (moral goodness). Necessary rational objects of aversion fall into two similar classes (V.58–60).[3]

Goodness and value, on this reading of Kant, are always explained in terms of rational willing. They cannot themselves be used as final explanations of what it is rational to will. To say this is to say that for Kant nothing possesses the kind of intrinsic value that G. E. Moore thought would belong to a beautiful world even were there no observers of it.[4] The only sort of thing that can be, as Kant says, "simply good . . . in all respects and without qualification" is the manner of acting – the maxims – of someone who acts from respect for the law (V.60).[5] This manner of acting is "simply good" because under any and all circumstances it is what is necessarily willed by anyone willing in accordance with the moral law. It is thus unconditionally good, and in that sense absolutely good, but it is not intrinsically good. When at the beginning of the *Groundwork* Kant says that the good will is unconditionally good, he is not implying that it possesses a value that is independent of the moral law. We recognize its value because, as we ultimately learn, we recognize that the law unconditionally requires maxims that make the will good. Good will does not have some other value that might provide a moral motivation different from the respect to which Kant standardly appeals.

In an important paper entitled "Kant's Morality of Law and Morality of Freedom," Paul Guyer challenges this conventional interpretation. He argues that "the fundamental but indemonstrable value of freedom itself is the heart of Kant's moral theory."[6] The categorical imperative obligates us because "it is the principle which we must follow in order to give full expression to our unique freedom in the phenomenal sphere" (G, 45). Guyer does not think that we bring about our freedom as an effect of obligatory action: "Our duty is not to create freedom but to enhance the circumstances for its exercise" (G, 64). In elaborating his conviction that "the foundation of Kant's entire moral philosophy is his belief in the absolute value of the freedom of rational beings," he speaks of conformity to the categorical imperative as that through which "this intrinsically valuable freedom can be preserved and enhanced" (G, 70). And he thinks that Kant at times considers seriously the idea that the requirement of universalizability is "necessary in order to maximize the exercise of this freedom and thus maximally realize its potential intrinsic value" (G, 71–2). These passages suggest that Guyer sees Kant as treating an increase in the display of freedom as the outcome of action that justifies requiring the actions that produce it.

Guyer does not directly challenge the kind of reading I have just sketched, nor does he try to explain how his own fits in with the passages on which that reading relies. He comes to his interpretation because he believes that Kant has not explained what motive we have for compliance with the categorical imperative. He thinks the second *Critique* "profoundly unsatisfying" because after laying down a necessary and universal law that must be formal, it says that we can comply with it "without explaining in what sense we have any *reason* to do such a thing" (G, 53). It does not explain how the moral law can motivate us by giving us a reason. The *Groundwork* likewise leaves "the underlying motivation for adhering to the moral law a mystery" (G, 57). If freedom is an absolute and intrinsic value, however, then those who possess it "provide an end . . . for the sake of which any rational being would see fit to adopt the moral law" (G, 61). The formula of the end in itself, therefore, gives Kant what he needs: not "an end which the antecedent adoption of the principle of morality could force a rational being to adopt," but "an end the intrinsic and absolute value of which would compel any rational being to adopt the principle of morality" (G, 60). Even if we can only take the absolute value of freedom as a regulative principle, it can "serve to motivate our practical behavior and to guide it towards rational coherence" (G, 85–6).

Commentators frequently find Kant's respect unsatisfactory. Perhaps this is because they assume that all action must be explained in terms solely of desire and belief. But Kant does not accept that psychological model; and it seems to me that his view of the role of respect in our motivational economy is at least not mysterious. Respect is meant to explain how we humans can respond to the constraints that we ourselves in our rational aspect impose on the goal-oriented projects proposed by ourselves as dependent sentient beings. The constraints are not themselves goal-derived, but they *have a point*. The point is to create conditions for action that we can approve of unconditionally. Our own appreciation of this point is shown in the "special joys" (*besondere Freuden*) that the moral agent feels from the effort to act as morality requires (V.117–18).

None of this, of course, shows the adequacy of Kant's account of the motive for complying with the categorical imperative. But it indicates that Kant himself did not think that some additional intrinsic kind of value was required to explain it, and that we need not, therefore, insist that he thinks that there is some intrinsic value that compels rational agents to adopt the moral law. It is worth noting that others beside Kant made the same kind of claim. Clarke, Crusius, Price, and Reid were among those attempting to develop a moral psychology allowing that we can be moved by the claims of practical rationality not only in using means to ends, but in restricting and setting ends. Kant's way of going about it is certainly unique, but the concerns to which he is responding are common to an important group of eighteenth-century philosophers.

II

Barbara Herman urges us to leave deontology behind as we read Kant.[7] Her interpretation seems intended mainly as a way of moving toward a more fully defensible Kantian ethic than we get from attributing to Kant the principle of the priority of law to good. So I read her claim that "[w]hatever it is that makes Kantian ethics distinctive, it is *not* to be found in the subordination of all considerations of value to principles of right or duty. In this sense, Kantian ethics is not a deontology" (*PMJ* 210).[8] Like Guyer, she thinks that "[w]ithout a theory of value the rationale for moral constraint is a mystery." If we do not answer the question "why?" about such constraint, we invite mere skepticism. Herman also holds that a theory of value is needed if a Kantian ethic is to enable us to deliberate successfully "in circumstances containing competing moral considerations" (*PMJ* 210–11). She fills in her second rationale in illuminating detail.[9] But she insists, rightly, that "negotiating the casuistry is not enough." The kind of defense that she thinks is needed by deontological constraints must involve us in consideration of "the place of morality in our self-conception as rational agents" (*PMJ* 212). I discuss only this part of her essay.

The value that Herman thinks Kant needs as a rationale for observing deontological constraints on action is not "some other good that this way of acting promotes or brings about." The Kantian must hold that appropriately lawful action itself has value. So we need to know "how or in what sense refraining from acting in a way that rational beings could not accept is in any way *good*" (*PMJ* 215). Herman is not asking merely about the relation of such action to the moral law. She is pushing for a deeper account of why formal lawful willing should be held to be something we can think of as basic and central to our lives as moral agents (*PMJ* 215). Unless we can see that, she thinks, we will be left wondering about the rationale for morality.

Her response is that Kant's principles of rational action themselves perform "the role a conception of value is to play in action and judgment." How can the principles of rational willing be a final end? Herman answers that "if we accept that the defining feature of ends is that they are sources of reasons that shape action, then principles can be ends" (*PMJ* 216).

Her main point, if I understand her, is that acting from reasons is itself a value whose realization in our lives is vulnerable to certain kinds of dangers, among them assault from other agents. Rational agents, Herman says, are agents who must take themselves to be, as she puts it, "acting for reasons 'all the way down.' " This is what shows that rational agents "can fully determine their actions according to reasons." They are not simply *caused* to act by their desires; desires must be adopted by the will before they become ends. And "the adoption of an end is an activity of will undertaken for a reason." Herman thinks the reason for adopting an end is always a principle. "We act," she says, "on such principles as desire satisfaction, or even this-desire satisfaction, is good. Our adoption of ends always has a principled basis" (*PMJ* 228–9). Anything that prevents our acting from reasons will violate the very possibility of our being agents of the distinctive kind that Kant thinks we are. There is thus a value inherent in compliance with the categorical imperative – the value of protecting our sense of ourselves as agents. Deontology is left behind.

Herman shows admirably how to use this reading of Kant in making the application of the categorical imperative more perspicuous. I think, however, that we cannot accept the move as Kant's own. Kant does not think that freedom is a vulnerable possession. Thorny issues are raised if it is taken to be so.[10] If our very capacity to act for reasons can be threatened, is our status as end-in-itself equally vulnerable? If there are degrees of agency, are there also degrees of being an end in itself? If I am deprived of agency can I then rightly be treated as means only? Herman does not consider these issues. Her interest lies in the extent of our ability to act for reasons.

There is a sense in which Herman is right in saying that for Kant we act for reasons all the way down. On his view what is not done from reasons is simply not a human action. Desires suggest maxims but maxims must be freely adopted if behavior ensuing from them is to count as action. But although we act for reasons, the sources of our reasons are not usually themselves reasons, or even rational. They are desires; and we do not choose our basic desires.

Here again Kant is involved with a problem that concerned many other philosophers of his time. For Kant, as for Locke and his followers, desires are nonrational causal forces varying idiosyncratically from person to person, and in any one person from time to time. Since happiness for Kant comes from satisfaction of desires, the range of components out of which we can choose to flesh out our conception of happiness is not up to us. But for Kant, as for Locke and Price and Reid, there is a difficulty concerning the choice of desires to include in the conception of happiness I decide to pursue.

Without desires I would not have my nonmoral reasons for acting. I would lack most of the reasons I have. Reason directs me to satisfy as many desires as I can without infringing on the moral law. But it cannot tell me which ones to reject from my conception of happiness unless it first privileges some whose satisfaction would be excluded by adding new ones; and it cannot tell me which desires should have this status. I can indeed refuse to act to gratify any desire I have. If the rejected desires are strong and persistent enough, that will simply leave me unhappy. I can decide to remain so, but I cannot decide desires into or out of existence, even if sometimes I can get myself to have new ones.[11]

For Kant, then, it seems, I can give reasons down to my desires but not any further. My desires are as much a part of me as my rationality, and are as essential to my being a distinctively *human* agent. They are not by themselves reasons for action, but without them my rational will could not move me in any specific direction. The self as knower requires percepts as much as concepts; and however it may be with a holy will, the human self as agent requires desires as well as the rational will. What makes human agency unique, for Kant, is not simply that it is the eruption of pure rationality into the causal order. It is rather that it is the sole point at which pure rationality can direct the part of the causal order most intimately tied to our identity. A morality that required reasons "all the way down" could not be a morality for human beings. Since the categorical imperative always requires the contribution of the desires in order to yield specific directives, it is not by itself a complete source of reasons. Hence, it does not, by Herman's own account, play the role that a conception of value plays in human agency.

The natural disarray of the passions and desires is a given in Kant's ethics, as the content of sensation is in the theoretical philosophy. The material of our lives, the substantive happiness we pursue, comes from forces we can neither create nor (as Kant eventually came to admit) eradicate.[12] Moral agency brings a kind of unity to our lives that prudential agency alone could never bring. Thus, there is a role for pure practical reason, although having and exercising it is not the whole point of our lives. If the principle of the priority of law to good encapsulates this position, then we can see why Kant need not have thought the law's claim on us mysterious. Perhaps we may call this aspect of Kant's position deontological.

III

The rocks on the other side now call for attention. Here I have in mind Julia Annas's powerfully argued views about Stoic and Kantian ethics in *The Morality of Happiness*.[13] She allows that there are important differences between the two, but the similarities as she portrays them are quite striking. Stoicism presents itself, as does all of ancient ethics, as an answer to a question any reflective person asks: "What should my life be like? . . . am I satisfied with my life as a whole, with the way it has developed and promises to continue?"

(*MH* 27, 28–9). It offers a way to happiness. But despite being cast as a morality of happiness, the Stoic theory is neither hedonistic nor egoistic nor teleological. It assigns virtue a value of a unique kind, incommensurable with any other sort of value, and it takes this value to override other kinds of value (*MH* 122–3, 171, 185). Thus, it holds that desires are to be satisfied only if virtue permits. It requires the virtuous agent to be impartial in her concern for everyone (*MH* 128, 174, 265). And it claims that virtue is constitutive of the end, not merely instrumental in achieving it (*MH* 37).

If this is not quite Kantianism, it is certainly not the kind of morality of happiness the textbooks usually find in ancient ethics. And Annas finds further similarities between Stoic and Kantian views. The Stoics make the "very Kantian" claim that whoever understands the kind of value involved in virtue also realizes that this gives "a reason to act which is different in kind from a reason that merely promotes one's own desires and projects" (*MH* 263; see also 398, 432).[14] The brave person does the brave act "just because it is brave, and not for any ulterior reason." This is the counterpart to the modern demand that the moral agent act for the moral reason, not for any ulterior reason. In each case the reason is to motivate by itself, not owing its force to "any more basic reasons." Annas adds that "in a way reminiscent of Kant, the Stoics represent the recognition of the force of a moral reason as a kind of respect for law" (*MH* 175).[15]

A further point of similarity, Annas claims, emerges more clearly in earlier than in later Stoicism: the secondary role of metaphysics. We are not required just to take our principles from nature. Nature may suggest a principle, but we must work it into a theory before we accept it. "There is an analogue here to Kant's insistence" on avoiding heteronomy (*MH* 162). Cosmic nature is not a principle within ethics for the Stoic. The content of ethics is "already established" before we get to appeal to nature (*MH* 165). Even if Stoic theology might help "the advanced student" to understand the moral point of view, "what matters for morality is already obvious before we do any metaphysics, as indeed it is for Kant" (*MH* 169n37).

Annas thus rejects the kind of contrast between ancient ethics and distinctively modern "morality" that Bernard Williams draws. She argues at length that "ancient [ethical] theories are theories of what modern moral theories are theories of" (*MH* 14; cf. 12, 47, 120ff.). Ancient thought about virtue plays the role in reflection on life that modern thought about morality plays. We can therefore usefully set one against the other. Annas seems to think that, when we do, the moderns come out looking rather badly. Leaving that issue to one side, I want to raise some questions about the commonalities that Annas sees in Stoic and Kantian thought. To do so I shall follow the Great Boyg's advice to Peer Gynt, and go round about.

IV

There is no doubt about Kant's admiration for the Stoics. Indications of agreements with them are scattered in many of his writings. They saw that the principle of morality must come from reason, and that happiness ought to be the result of virtue.[16] Their terms give the appropriate characterization of the outcome of moral strength. Virtue requires courage, to fight the monsters opposing it; moral courage constitutes honor and wisdom. "Only in its possession is a man 'free', 'healthy', 'rich', 'a king', and so forth, and can suffer no loss by chance or fate" (VI.405). Their doctrine of apathy is sound. One should never be in a state of emotional agitation, not even over one's best friend's misfortunes (VII.253; cf. VI.408–9). The Stoics point the way not only to the moral life but to the healthy one as well (VII.180). They were the best of the ancient philosophers, and "[i]n moral philosophy, we have not come any further than the ancients" (IX.32; cf. XXVII.484).

Kant's reservations about Stoicism were as pervasive as his appreciation of it. "Man fancifully exaggerates his moral capacity," Herder reports Kant as telling his class in the early 1760s,

> and sets before himself the most perfect goodness; the outcome is nonsense; but what is required of us? The Stoic's answer: I shall raise myself *above myself*, . . . rise superior to my own afflictions and needs, and with all my might be *good*, be the *image of godhood*. But how so, for godhood has no obligations, yet you certainly do. . . . Now the god departs and we are left with *man*, a poor creature, loaded with obligations. *Seneca* was an impostor, *Epictetus* strange and fanciful.[17]

Human beings can hope at most to increase in virtue, not to attain it fully, Kant thinks, but he refuses to say, with the Stoics, that without perfect virtue one is not virtuous at all. The Stoics neglect our needs, the Epicureans do not. If a Stoic moral regimen is a useful tool, it is not sufficient. In being virtuous we should have the kind of cheerful heart that Epicurus recommended. Kant rejects "monkish ascetics," as Hume did (VII.484–5). Like Descartes, Kant claims that he can reconcile the two great schools of antiquity.[18] Happiness, the satisfaction of desires, is indeed second in rank to worthiness to be happy, assured only by virtue; but it is nonetheless indispensable for needy dependent beings such as we are.

The Stoics did, of course, allow for the satisfaction of needs, allowing them to count as a secondary kind of good.[19] But Kant gives no discussion of the Stoic view of these goods. He does not try, for instance, to relate them to the goods to which we are directed by hypothetical imperatives. He is simply not interested in giving a full assessment of Stoic theory.[20] For him Stoic views are useful primarily as ways of describing his attitudes and locating his own position. Consequently his explicit comments about Stoicism do not teach us much about its relations to his philosophical ethics. We can get further by seeing what Kant thought of Leibnizian moral philosophy.

If Leibniz was not a Stoic, there are nonetheless a number of striking resemblances, some closer and some more distant, between his position and Stoicism. Like the Stoics, Leibniz is a determinist who rejects fatalism. His doctrine that all things represent all other things, however indistinctly, is a counterpart to the Stoic doctrine of the infusion of divinity in everything. He thinks our reason and God's are the same in kind. Like the Stoics he holds that the mind is all of a piece. It is its representations; the clearer and more distinct they are, the more perfect we are and the more virtuously we act. Leibniz does not accept the Stoic doctrine that virtue is an all-or-nothing affair, but he agrees in holding that virtue is a function of knowledge about the constitution of the universe. These Leibnizian views were available to Kant in the *Theodicy* and other writings.[21]

Clearly Kant disagrees with many of the points on which Leibniz and the Stoics seem to agree. Kant accepts determinism only for the phenomenal world, leaving room for freedom as noumenal, and offers a moral argument for belief in the latter. He intends the kind of freedom he defends to differ from the kind Leibniz himself thought he could defend. He denies that theoretical claims about God can be warranted, and places such rational investigation of divinity as we can carry out within morality, rather than within physics. Insofar as we are entitled to believe that we live in a rationally ordered universe, our grounds are moral. The nature of the divine order that Kant thinks us morally required to believe in is also not the same as that thought warranted either by the Stoics or by Leibniz. Here we come to a point of some importance.

Leibniz and Kant share a concern about a problem that could not have had the same meaning for the Stoics, the problem of the relation of morality to the divine will. The Stoics were no doubt aware of the dilemma put by Plato in the *Euthyphro*. But for them the issue did not carry the baggage it carries for moralists in Christian times. Voluntarism, asserted in modern times by Descartes, Hobbes, Pufendorf, King, and less overtly, by Locke, seemed to many thinkers then to be a major danger. It threatened to undermine relations between humans and God, turning him into a tyrant whom one could obey only blindly and out of fear, and toward whom one could not feel the appropriate kind of love. Since God's relations to his creation could serve as a model for the sovereign's relations to his subjects, voluntarism seemed to offer support to despotism and tyranny in earthly politics. Cumberland and Leibniz both oppose voluntarism by arguing that God is moved by his awareness of the goodness of options before him, choosing always the best. Since what we are required to do echoes what God necessarily does, both of them propound strongly consequentialist theories of morality. Like the Stoics, they think that some states of affairs are good regardless of whether they are desired or willed; and they hold that God acts to bring these about and wills that we should do so as well.

Kant, like Pufendorf, rejects the equation of Being with Goodness that Leibniz defends and comes down on the side of the voluntarist. He holds, as I have noted, that to be good is to be the object of a will. By taking the divine will to be governed by the moral law, he guards himself against the standard objections to the voluntarist thesis. Kant's God is not arbitrary, although we cannot come to any conclusion about whether he does or does not create the best of all possible worlds. We have no moral need for a decision on that point. We need think only that the divinity is just and sees to it that the increasingly virtuous become even happier. An important part of what makes it morally necessary to conceive of God in this way is the belief that nature has no necessary connection to moral worth. And for Kant, as I have said, happiness comes only from the satisfaction of natural desire, to which the Stoics give a more limited role.

Through this deliberate rejection of Leibniz, Kant in effect rejects a major aspect of Stoicism as well. The metaphysics of Stoicism is profoundly important for its ethics. Regardless of the extent to which any particular moral principle is derived from the metaphysics, Stoic metaphysics grounds at least the a priori assurance that when we act from reason as far as we can, everything of concern to us will be well.[22] Kant simply takes for granted an anti-Leibnizian, anti-Stoic acceptance of the indifference of the natural world to rational human concerns.

The indifference of the natural world to human meaning is also involved in a major disagreement between Kant and both Leibniz and the Stoics concerning the passions.[23] Plutarch tells us that the Stoics "suppose that the passionate and irrational part [of the soul] is not distinguished from the rational by any distinction within the soul's nature, but the same part of the soul (which they call thought and commanding-faculty) becomes virtue and vice as it turns around and changes in passions . . . and contains nothing irrational within itself."[24] Leibniz would not have found this objectionable. Kant would have preferred Plutarch's own view: "In us the faculty of judging and the faculty of feeling emotion are different . . . that within us which follows is different from that which it follows when persuaded, or . . . fights against when it is not persuaded."[25]

On the Stoic theory of oikeiōsis our natural development points us toward a harmonious set of desires within ourselves, leading eventually to the dominance of reason and, ideally, to full virtue.[26] We are part of the universe and can in principle become as harmonious as it is. For Leibniz, as we increase our knowledge of the divinely ordered world we cannot fail to become more harmonious ourselves, because our minds, including our pleasures and our desires, are nothing but representations of that world. The Stoics and Leibniz thus think that there is an order of goods or perfections that we have but to track to find peace and harmony. Ignorance of this real existing order is the cause of our unhappiness and disorder. If we enlighten our passions they will misrepresent good and ill less; and to the extent that they represent the values of things accurately, they will bring the order of the universe into our lives, both personal and social.

This picture of motivation gives us reason to doubt Annas's suggestion that something like respect for moral law is a central moral motive for the Stoics. For them reasons for action are all perceptions, more or less clear, of various goods or ills. They are thus commensurable. What the brave person sees when she is brave for the sake of bravery and for no ulterior reason is the goodness of being brave in that way. Even when the virtuous person is moved by the thought that Zeus directs her to act bravely, she is thinking of Zeus's directions as something it is good for her to follow. But for Kant respect is not the perception of some good. It is a unique feeling caused by being humbled by a law that we know we must follow and whose directives are incommensurable with those arising from our desires. Respect, Kant says, is that law itself "regarded subjectively as an incentive" (V.72–6). If an incentive of this kind is an essential part of Kant's deontology, then we may take a theory that lacks it or would deny it as teleological.

For Kant there is no natural harmonious order to be carried into our lives. Even if there were, the passions and desires would not carry it by representing it. On his view, the passions are not confused or indistinct representations of good or ill; they are not representations at all. They are, as in Locke and Hume, urges toward or away from various objects or states of affairs represented by the understanding. In themselves they can be neither rational nor irrational.[27] For the Stoics the thoughts embedded in desires are open to assent or dissent in virtue of their implicitly propositional nature. Leibniz's view does not differ in essentials. But for Kant, desires must generate maxims if reason is to enter as that which, in Plutarch's phrase, they are to follow. Kant says that we do not need to explain how desires and inclinations arise from pleasure, and how maxims arise from these through the cooperation of reason (IV.427). But we can see how his naturalistic theory of the passions leads him to another step away from Leibniz.

Leibniz has no need for a faculty of will that is different in kind from desire, because for him all desires are desires for more or less of the same thing, perfection or good. "The will is never prompted to action," he says, "save by the representation of the good, which prevails over the opposite representations" (T §45). When and if we reflect, whichever desire emerges as offering us the most good becomes our strongest desire, and hence our will. For Kant our desires do not all aim at objects under a common description, seeking more rather than less of the same thing. What we desire we call good, and we expect pleasure from it; but the object of our desires is not some prior goodness or abstract pleasant sensation. It is, for example, flute playing, or glory, or benefit to others. If we do not accept the view that we are moved by the strongest desire, we need to allow the existence of a different power – a will – enabling us to decide which desire to act on and which to rule out.

To explain how we can possess a will able not only to explain observable choices, but to account for the possibility of morality, Kant thinks he must invoke the whole noumenal apparatus. Morality, he thinks, requires that the self must be a free agent, not tied to the universe like a dog to a cart. We can see why he turns to the transcendental for a solution, however little it may seem to us to offer one.

V

Kant is not trying to answer questions about how one's life is going. Still less is he setting up to know better than ordinary folk where they should place their happiness. He does indeed hold that as we improve morally we can come to take satisfaction in our behavior, deriving tranquillity and even a kind of contentment from it. But such self-satisfaction is not positive enough to be more than an analog of happiness. Arising from our exercise of free will, it is something like ''the self-sufficiency which can be ascribed only to the Supreme Being'' (V.117–18). But Stoic though this sounds, it is still unlike Stoic *eudaimonia:* it leaves us with much to desire. And Kant, unlike the Stoics, thinks that when we try to help others attain happiness, we should accept their own conception of happiness, not impose ours on them.

Given Kant's view of happiness, with its deep roots in his understanding of nature, the venture that Annas says is central to ancient ethical theory does not make much sense. Kant sees regularity in the physical world, and in the operations of the mind considered as part of that world.[28] But the regularity does not include any humanly meaningful order among the impulses that are the desires and passions, even though they are part of the natural order. In the third *Critique* Kant draws a strong implication from this view. We cannot, he says, form any realizable idea of happiness, or of the complete gratification of our desires. Even if nature obeyed our every wish and our powers were unlimited, our idea of happiness is too wavering and fluctuating to allow us to attain what we think we seek. And even if we aimed at no more than satisfying ''the true wants of nature in which our species is in complete and fundamental accord,'' what we mean by happiness would remain unattainable. ''For [man's] own nature is not so constituted as to rest or be satisfied in any possession or enjoyment whatever'' (VI.430). It is not an accident that Kant never offers us a rational principle for constructing a substantive conception of happiness.

Kant allows that one might discover simple rules that add to happiness for certain kinds of people – rules about how to stage a dinner party for maximal enjoyment, for instance. But he did not propose anything like a philosophical theory that does better in guiding everyone to happiness than commonsense notions do. Kant himself remarks that among the moderns ''the concept of the highest good has fallen into disuse or at least seems to have become something secondary'' (V.64). Though he offered a view of the structure of the complete good, he did not intend to give a detailed answer to questions about how one's life might go well as a whole.

In assigning a different task to moral philosophy, Kant is not even claiming to know something important about morality that ordinary people do not know. As he says, ''Neither science nor philosophy is needed in order to know what one has to do in order to be honest and good . . . the philosopher . . . has no principle which the common understanding lacks'' (IV.404; cf. V.8n). This most un-Stoic position reflects Kant's view of the enterprise of moral philosophy.

Kant thinks it has two functions. One is simply to sort out the place of morality in the universe, and to understand what it shows us about the human mind. The theoretical task gets some urgency from a practical need. Human corruption induces us to use, among other things, bad philosophy to undermine the demands of morality. Kant explains this not by an appeal to original sin, but by the dual nature of the human constitution. Unavoidably concerned for our happiness, equally responsive to the inescapable voice of our own pure practical reason, we find in ourselves a natural dialectic that leads us to try to obfuscate the call of the latter so that we may pursue the former without limits. The problem of explaining the relations of the two voices must have been the same for Socrates as it is for us. Kant thinks that there is still work left for us to do even if the Stoics did better at dealing with that issue than any of the other ancients. Of course, he – like many another philosopher – thought that he himself had pretty much wrapped it up.

VI

If I have fended off the clashing rocks, then we can see one reason why the contrast between Kantian deontology and ancient teleology is significant. Even the Stoics are teleologists in a way that Kant is not. Kant's deontology reflects his quite modern lack of confidence in the natural world. Nothing but our powers of reason can regulate our natural inclinations and wishes so that we can act as we must if we are to live in a society of free and equal agents. Kant's theory of freedom as rooted in our transcendental nature may not seem acceptable. We may wish to replace it with a fully naturalized account of moral motivation. But he at least opened the way to a question of great importance to us. It is the question of how we are to shape our lives and our societies once we see that their structure is not imposed on us by any natural constraints. Metaphysical confidence in the rational order of nature made this a question that the Stoics could not have raised.

From here we can also see one aspect of the philosophical importance of debates about assimilating Kant to Stoicism, or to any other ancient philosophy. It concerns our approach to the history of moral philosophy. Like Annas and many others, we can approach that history with the assumption that throughout its course philosophers have all been attempting to answer the same basic question, or solve the same set of problems. We might say that just as the interaction of mind and body, or our perception of color, has always needed an explanation, so morality has always called for one. We might then think of the historian of moral philosophy as tracing different theoretical efforts to understand the domain of the moral. This might lead us to try to minimize differences between ancient and modern ethics.

I find it more useful to take another approach. We can ask whether at different times the salient questions differed. Perhaps the Stoics saw different issues facing individuals than Plato or Aristotle saw. Perhaps the problems that Grotius and Hobbes made central were problems that could not have arisen for Epictetus or Seneca. Even if we grant that there are facts about the human situation that call for some sort of norms in any society, the construal of these facts may alter drastically. It is after all our *socially meaningful* life whose facts are the concern of morality and moral philosophy. These facts are thoroughly and richly conceptualized before they come to the philosopher's attention, and the conceptualizations may be different at different times. Old ways of talking about how to live together and how to settle differences without fighting may cease to be useful under drastically altered circumstances, such as the introduction of a new religious vocabulary for discussing such matters. Moral philosophies can be viewed as sets of tools some cultures develop for coping with various deep problems in the ways we talk about or understand our common life. On that view the changes will be as important as the continuities.

Some of the essays in this volume seek commonalities between Kant and Aristotle, even when they allow for some differences. In claiming that the differences may be more revealing than the similarities, I do not mean to be implying anything about the superiority of Kant over the Stoics, still less of Aristotle. I do want to suggest that to assess the significance of what we find in the texts and arguments we need to ask what the philosophers at different times thought they were doing. If we simply assume that what they were doing was trying to solve the same "philosophical problem," we have a ready answer. But that answer does not get us down to the level of detail where we can see real history happening.

We can take the blurry notions of deontology and teleology to point, however inadequately, to profoundly different conceptions of the tasks of moral philosophers. Kant saw a world in which divisions within Christendom made an ethic centering on the highest good highly problematic. He saw, as John Cooper points out (Chapter 9, this volume), a world of contestation around rights. He saw a crumbling of the authority of old social elites, including those claiming to be the sole source of proper moral guidance for the ill-educated and poor. When he took ideas from his predecessors, he reworked them to handle issues that Aristotle and Chrysippus and Cicero could not even have formulated. By pointing out that Kant was not alone in his times in trying out a deontological view, I mean to suggest that where so many seek a radically new approach, it is worth looking for a new issue.

One might lack interest in the history of moral philosophy construed in this way. One might be interested in philosophers of the past only to the extent that their work helps us now with ours. Even so it may be important to look beyond what the old philosophers said to the situation in which they said it. We need to ask what issues they saw in their society's ways of handling private lives and personal relations. And we need to relate their philosophy to these issues. To take just one example, *eudaimonia* in ancient theory is not the same as Kantian *Glückseligkeit*. Why did Kant find it necessary to use a conception of what makes life worthwhile that differs so significantly from the conception the Greek philosophers used? Why did he think it necessary to construct a realm of the moral radically distinct from that of prudence and happiness? Answers to these questions may lead us to consider problems – such as that of rebuilding a distinctive eudaimonistic theory – that we might not otherwise have taken up. It may also lead us to question our assumptions about the problems we put at the center of our own work.

NOTES

1. Just when we began doing so is unclear. As Robert Louden points out in a forthcoming paper, Bentham used the term 'deontology' but not in the way now common. The current use seems to have been started by C. D. Broad in his 1930 commentary on Sidgwick in *Five Types of Ethical Theory*.
2. I bear in mind Brad Inwood's warning concerning overconfidence in constructing out of our multiple, often fragmentary, sources a picture of "an orthodox Stoicism teaching internally consistent doctrine, grounded on clear general principles." See his "Seneca and Psychological Dualism," in J. Brunschwig and M. Nussbaum,

J. B. SCHNEEWIND

eds., *Passions and Perceptions* (Cambridge University Press, 1993), p. 152. A similar caution is needed about treating Kant as if he never changed his mind.
3. Otherwise undesignated note and parenthetical text references are to Kant's works using the volume and page numbers of the *Gesammelte Schriften*.
4. G. E. Moore, *Principia Ethica* (Cambridge University Press, 1903), pp. 83–4. My thanks to T. E. Hill Jr. for suggesting the use of this comparison.
5. The phrase 'simply good' translates Kant's *schlechthin gut*, which Beck misleadingly translates as "absolutely good."
6. Guyer's essay is in R. M. Dancy, ed., *Kant and Critique* (Dordrecht: Kluwer Academic, 1993), pp. 43–89. Page references will be given in the text, indicated by G.
7. References to Herman are to her "Leaving Deontology Behind" in *The Practice of Moral Judgment* (Cambridge, Mass.: Harvard University Press, 1993), indicated by *PMJ*.
8. Taken literally Herman's claim is correct. Considerations of right and duty are themselves subordinate to the moral law, as are considerations of value. But I take it that Herman aims to displace the principle of the priority of law to good.
9. Guyer has a different and equally interesting program for using his theory of the value of freedom in developing a Kantian casuistry, including a politics.
10. Among them is the relation of the noumenal to the phenomenal will, since plainly – as Herman says in a footnote – we cannot interfere with noumenal freedom (*PMJ* 229n36).
11. For instance, if out of duty I make the well-being of others my end, I may come in time to feel genuine affection or love for those I decide to help.
12. Contrast *Groundwork* IV.428 with *Religion* VI.58, 28, and 36.
13. Oxford University Press, 1993; references given in the text are indicated by *MH*.
14. Earlier Annas suggests that the values involved in virtue are in fact commensurable with nonvirtue values, only they are so very much greater that it would be the height of folly to compare them (*MH* 122). However, she more frequently asserts that the kinds of value involved are incommensurable.
15. Like Guyer and Herman, Annas finds an obscurity in the modern version of this view. Ancient ethics, unlike modern, she says, "does not give up at this point" by failing to explain the source of these reasons. For ancient ethics the brave person sees that acting bravely is part of the good of her life – or, as Herman and Guyer might put it, sees a value in acting bravely (*MH* 75). There is enough similarity between ancient and modern views for Kant to lose by the comparison.
16. V.41, XVII.1402.29–31; see also V.60, and cf. *Refl.* 6630, XIX.118.
17. XXVII.67, trans. Peter Heath (from a forthcoming volume of translations of Kant's lectures on ethics).
18. For Descartes, see the letters to Queen Christina, November 20, 1647, in Cottingham et al., *Philosophical Writings of Descartes* (Cambridge University Press, 1991), vol. III, p. 325, and to Princess Elizabeth, August 18, 1645, vol. III, p. 261.
19. See A. A. Long and D. N. Sedley, eds., *The Hellenistic Philosophers* (Cambridge University Press, 1987), §58, pp. 354–7.

300

20. Kant developed his own basic ideas about morality before reading Adam Smith's *Theory of the Moral Sentiments*, but he seems to have read it in the German translation of 1770, and he evidently admired it. Smith gives a detailed account of Stoicism in his historical account of systems of moral philosophy. His discussion, in Bk. VII, ii.1, §§15–47 of the *Theory*, which is much fuller than that of any other theory he considers, is a judicious and, on the whole, favorable estimate. Kant gives no such overview of Stoicism – or of any other moral philosophy.

21. References to the *Theodicy*, given in the text by *T* and section number (§), are to the translation by E. M. Huggard, edited by Austin Farrer (LaSalle, Ill.: Open Court, 1985).

22. On these points, see John Cooper, Chapter 9, this volume.

23. 84–7 has an excellent discussion of Kant's efforts in the *Critique of Judgment* to see how far we can think away the indifference of nature.

24. See Long and Sedley, *The Hellenistic Philosophers*, vol. I, 61B.9, p. 378.

25. Plutarch, *On Moral Virtue* 449 C–D, trans. W. C. Helmbold (Loeb Classical Library, Cambridge, Mass.: Harvard University Press, 1929).

26. See Long and Sedley, *The Hellenistic Philosophers*, §57, pp. 346–50.

27. Hume gives a well-known account of what we can mean when we call a desire irrational. Kant also has an account of this (see VII.254, 265, VI.408).

28. The impossibility, as Kant saw it, of a science of psychology is not due to any lack of determinism in the temporal flow of mental happenings.

Select Bibliography

I. Primary Texts

A. Aristotle

GREEK TEXTS AND COMMENTARIES

Burnet, John. *Ethica Nicomachea*. London: Methuen, 1900.

Bywater, I. *Aristotelis Ethica Nicomachea*. Oxford University Press, 1894.

Dirlmeier, Franz. *Aristoteles, Magna Moralia*. Berlin: Akademie Verlag, 1963. German translation and commentary; no Greek text.

Gauthier, R. A., and J. Y. Jolif. *Aristote: L'Éthique à Nicomaque*. 4 vols. 2nd ed. Louvain: Universitaires de Louvain, 1970.

Mingay, R. R., and J. M. Walzer. *Aristotelis: Ethica Eudemia*. Oxford University Press, 1991.

Ross, W. D. *Aristotelis Politica*. Oxford University Press, 1957.

Stewart, J. A. *Notes on the Nicomachean Ethics*. 2 vols. Oxford University Press, 1892.

Susemihl, F. *Aristotelis Ethica Eudemia*. Leipzig: Teubner, 1883.

ENGLISH TRANSLATIONS

Aristotle: The Athenian Constitution. The Eudemian Ethics. On Virtues and Vices. Trans. H. Rackham. Rev. ed. Loeb Classical Library, 1952.

Aristotle: Eudemian Ethics, Books I, II, and VII. Trans. Michael Woods. 2nd ed. Oxford University Press, 1992.

Aristotle: Metaphysics X–XIV. Oeconomica. Magna Moralia. Trans. Hugh Tredennick and G. Cyril Armstrong. Loeb Classical Library, 1935.

Aristotle: Nicomachean Ethics. Trans. Terence Irwin. Indianapolis, Ind.: Hackett, 1985.

The Complete Works of Aristotle (Revised Oxford Translation). Ed. Jonathan Barnes. 2 vols. Princeton, N.J.: Princeton University Press, 1984.
The Nicomachean Ethics. Trans. H. Rackham. Rev. ed. Loeb Classical Library, 1934.

B. Kant

GERMAN EDITIONS

Kants gesammelte Schriften, herausgegeben von der Deutschen (formerly *Königlich Preußischen) Akademie der Wissenschaften.* 29 vols. Berlin: de Gruyter (and predecessors), 1902–.
Eine Vorlesung über Ethik. Ed. Gerd Gerhardt. Frankfurt am Main: Fischer Taschenbuch Verlag, 1990.

ENGLISH TRANSLATIONS

Anthropology from a Pragmatic Point of View. Trans. Mary J. Gregor. The Hague: Martinus Nijhoff, 1974. There is also a translation by Victor Lyle Dowdell (Carbondale: Southern Illinois University Press, 1978).
Critique of Judgment. Trans. Werner S. Pluhar. Indianapolis, Ind.: Hackett, 1987.
Critique of Practical Reason. Trans. Lewis White Beck. Indianapolis, Ind.: Bobbs-Merrill, 1956.
Critique of Pure Reason. Trans. Norman Kemp Smith. London: Macmillan, 1929.
Groundwork of the Metaphysic of Morals. Trans. H. J. Paton. New York: Harper & Row, 1964. A reprint of *The Moral Law* (London: Hutchinson, 1948). There are also translations by Lewis White Beck (New York: Macmillan, 1990) and James W. Ellington (Indianapolis, Ind.: Hackett, 1981).
Kant: Political Writings. Ed. Hans Reiss; trans. H. B. Nisbet. 2nd ed. Cambridge University Press, 1991.
Lectures on Ethics. Trans. Louis Infield. London: Methuen, 1930; Indianapolis, Ind.: Hackett, 1980.
Lectures on Philosophical Theology. Trans. Allen W. Wood and Gertrude M. Clark. Ithaca, N.Y.: Cornell University Press, 1978.
The Metaphysics of Morals. Trans. Mary Gregor. Cambridge University Press, 1991.
On History. Ed. Lewis White Beck; trans. Lewis White Beck, Robert E. Anchor, and Emil L. Fackenheim. Indianapolis, Ind.: Bobbs-Merrill, 1963.
Religion within the Limits of Reason Alone. Trans. Theodore M. Greene and Hoyt H. Hudson. La Salle, Ill.: Open Court, 1934; New York: Harper & Row, 1960.

C. The Stoics

COLLECTED SOURCES

Arnim, H. von. *Stoicorum Veterum Fragmenta.* 4 vols. Leipzig, 1903–5, 1924 (Index).
Inwood, B., and L. P. Gerson. *Hellenistic Philosophy: Introductory Readings.* Indianapolis, Ind.: Hackett, 1988.

Long, A. A., and D. N. Sedley. *The Hellenistic Philosophers*. Volume 1: *Translations of the Principal Sources with Philosophical Commentary*. Volume 2: *Greek and Latin Texts with Notes and Bibliography*. Cambridge University Press, 1987.

INDIVIDUAL TEXTS AND TRANSLATIONS

Cicero, Marcus Tullius. *De Fato. Paradoxa Stoicorum. De Partitione Oratoria.* Trans. H. Rackham. Loeb Classical Library, 1942.

Cicero, Marcus Tullius. *De Finibus Bonorum et Malorum.* Trans. H. Rackham. Rev. ed. Loeb Classical Library, 1931.

Cicero, Marcus Tullius. *De Natura Deorum. Academica.* Trans. H. Rackham. Loeb Classical Library, 1933.

Cicero, Marcus Tullius. *De Officiis.* Trans. Walter Miller. Loeb Classical Library, 1913.

Cicero, Marcus Tullius. *De Re Publica. De Legibus.* Trans. Clinton Walker Keyes. Loeb Classical Library, 1928.

Cicero, Marcus Tullius. *On Duties.* Trans. E. M. Atkins. Cambridge University Press, 1991.

Cicero, Marcus Tullius. *Tusculan Disputations.* Trans. J. E. King. Loeb Classical Library, 1960.

Diogenes Laertius. *Lives of Eminent Philosophers.* Trans. R. D. Hicks. 2 vols. Loeb Classical Library, 1925.

Epictetus. *Discourses.* Trans. W. A. Oldfather. 2 vols. Loeb Classical Library, 1925, 1928.

Epictetus. *Handbook.* Trans. Nicholas White. Indianapolis, Ind.: Hackett, 1983.

Galen. *On the Doctrines of Hippocrates and Plato.* Trans. P. De Lacy. 2 vols. Berlin: Akademie Verlag, 1978–80.

Plutarch. *On Moral Virtue.* Trans. W. C. Helmbold. Loeb Classical Library, 1929.

Plutarch. *On Stoic Self-contradictions.* Trans. Harold Cherniss. Loeb Classical Library, 1976.

Seneca. *Epistulae Morales.* Trans. Richard M. Gummere. 3 vols. Loeb Classical Library, 1917–25.

Seneca. *Moral Essays.* Trans. John Basore. 3 vols. Loeb Classical Library, 1928–35.

Stobaeus. *Eclogae.* In *Ioannis Stobaei Anthologium*. 5 vols. C. Wachsmuth and Otto Hense, eds. Berlin, 1884–1912; reprinted 1958. No English translation available.

II. Other Literature

Allan, D. J. "Aristotle's Account of the Origin of Moral Principles." *Proceedings of the XIth International Congress of Philosophy*, 12 (1953): 120–7.

Allan, D. J. "The Practical Syllogism." In S. Mansion, ed., *Author d' Aristote*. Louvain: Publications Universitaires de Louvain, 1955.

Allison, Henry E. *Kant's Theory of Freedom*. Cambridge University Press, 1990.

Annas, Julia. "Self-Love in Aristotle" (with comments by Richard Kraut). *Southern Journal of Philosophy*, supplement (1988): 1–23.

Annas, Julia. "The Hellenistic Version of Aristotle's Ethics." *Monist* 73 (1990): 80–96.

Annas, Julia. *Hellenistic Philosophy of Mind*. Berkeley: University of California Press, 1992.

Annas, Julia. "Ancient and Modern Morality." *Philosophical Perspectives* 6 (1993): 119–36.

Annas, Julia. *The Morality of Happiness*. Oxford University Press, 1993.

Annas, Julia. "Virtue as the Use of Other Goods." In T. Irwin and M. C. Nussbaum, eds., *Virtue, Love and Form: Essays in Memory of Gregory Vlastos* (pp. 53–66). Edmonton: Academic Printing and Publishing, 1994 (*Apeiron* 26, 3–4).

Annas, Julia. "Prudence and Morality in Ancient and Modern Ethics." *Ethics* 105 (1995): 241–57.

Anscombe, G. E. M. "Modern Moral Philosophy." *Philosophy* 33 (1958): 1–19. Reprinted in *The Collected Philosophical Papers of G. E. M. Anscombe*. Vol. 3: *Ethics, Religion and Politics* (pp. 26–42). Minneapolis: University of Minnesota Press, 1981.

Anscombe, G. E. M. "Thought and Action in Aristotle: What Is 'Practical Truth'?" In R. Bambrough, ed., *New Essays on Plato and Aristotle* (pp. 143–58). London: Routledge & Kegan Paul, 1965. Reprinted in *The Collected Papers of G. E. M. Anscombe*. Vol. 1: *From Parmenides to Wittgenstein* (pp. 66–77). Minneapolis: University of Minnesota Press, 1981.

Beck, Lewis White. *A Commentary on Kant's "Critique of Practical Reason."* Chicago: University of Chicago Press, 1960.

Bobonich, Christopher. "Plato's Theory of Goods in the *Laws* and *Philebus*." *Proceedings of the Boston Area Colloquium in Ancient Philosophy*, 9 (1995): 101–39

Bradley, F. H. *Ethical Studies*. 2nd ed. Oxford University Press, 1927.

Broad, C. D. *Five Types of Ethical Theory*. New York: Humanities Press, 1951. First published, London: Routledge & Kegan Paul, 1930.

Broadie, Sarah. *Ethics with Aristotle*. Oxford University Press, 1991.

Brunschwig, Jacques. "On a Book-title by Chrysippus." *Oxford Studies in Ancient Philosophy*, supplement (1991): 81–95.

Brunschwig, Jacques, and Martha Nussbaum, eds. *Passions and Perceptions*. Cambridge University Press, 1993.

Butler, Joseph. *The Works of Joseph Butler*. Ed. J. H. Bernard. 2 vols. London, 1900.

Cairns, Douglas. *Aidōs: The Psychology of Honor and Shame in Ancient Greek Literature*. Oxford University Press, 1993.

Cooper, John. "The *Magna Moralia* and Aristotle's Moral Philosophy." *American Journal of Philology* 94 (1973): 327–49.

Cooper, John. *Reason and Human Good in Aristotle*. Cambridge, Mass.: Harvard University Press, 1975.

Cooper, John. "Aristotle and the Goods of Fortune." *Philosophical Review* 94 (1985): 173–96.

Cooper, John. "Some Remarks on Aristotle's Moral Psychology." *Southern Journal of Philosophy*, supplement (1988): 25–42.

Cooper, John. "Political Animals and Civic Friendship." In Günther Patzig, ed., *Aristoteles' "Politik"* (pp. 220–41). Göttingen: Vandenhoeck & Ruprecht, 1990.

Cooper, John. "Reason, Moral Virtue and Moral Value." In M. Frede and G. Striker, eds., *Rationality in Ancient Greek Thought* (pp. 81–114) Oxford University Press, 1996.

Descartes, René. *The Philosophical Writings of Descartes.* Trans. John Cottingham, Robert Stoothoff, Dugald Murdoch, and Anthony Kenny. 3 vols. Cambridge University Press, 1984, 1985, and 1991.

Düsing, Klaus. "Das Problem des höchsten Gutes in Kants praktischer Philosophie." *Kant-Studien* 62 (1971): 5–42.

Dyroff, A. *Die Ethik der Alten Stoa.* Berlin: S. Calvary, 1897.

Engberg-Pedersen, Troels. *The Stoic Theory of Oikeiōsis.* Aarhus, Denmark: Aarhus University Press, 1990.

Engstrom, Stephen. "The Concept of the Highest Good in Kant's Moral Theory." *Philosophy and Phenomenological Research* 52 (1992): 747–80.

Engstrom, Stephen. "Kant's Conception of Practical Wisdom." *Kant-Studien,* 88 (1997): 16–43.

Flanagan, Owen, and Amélie Rorty, eds. *Identity, Character, and Morality.* Cambridge, Mass.: MIT Press, 1990.

Foot, Philippa. *Virtues and Vices.* Berkeley and Los Angeles: University of California Press, 1978.

Guyer, Paul. "Kant's Morality of Law and Morality of Freedom." In R. M. Dancy, ed., *Kant and Critique* (pp. 43–89). Dordrecht: Kluwer Academic, 1993.

Herman, Barbara. *The Practice of Moral Judgment.* Cambridge, Mass.: Harvard University Press, 1993.

Höffe, Otfried. "Universalist Ethics and the Faculty of Judgment: An Aristotelian Look at Kant." *Philosophical Forum* 25 (1993): 55–71.

Hoffman, A., ed. *Immanuel Kant: Ein Lebensbild nach Dartellungen der Zeitgenossen Jachmann, Borowski, Wasianski.* Halle: Hugo Peter, 1902.

Hume, David. *Enquiries Concerning Human Understanding and Concerning the Principles of Morals.* Eds. L. A. Selby-Bigge and P. H. Nidditch. 3rd ed. Oxford University Press, 1975.

Inwood, Brad. *Ethics and Human Action in Early Stoicism.* Oxford University Press, 1985.

Irwin, T. H. *Plato's Moral Theory.* Oxford University Press, 1977.

Irwin, T. H. "Aristotle's Conception of Morality" (with comments by Nancy Sherman). *Proceedings of the Boston Area Colloquium in Ancient Philosophy* 1 (1985): 115–50.

Irwin, T. H. "Socrates the Epicurean?" *Illinois Classical Studies* 11 (1986): 85–112.

Irwin, T. H. "Disunity in the Aristotelian Virtues" (with comments by Richard Kraut). In *Oxford Studies in Ancient Philosophy,* supplement (1988): 61–78.

Irwin, T. H. "Some Rational Aspects of Incontinence." *Southern Journal of Philosophy,* supplement (1988): 49–88.

Irwin, T. H. "Virtue, Praise and Success: Stoic Responses to Aristotle." *Monist* 73 (1990): 59–79.

Irwin, T. H. "Eminent Victorians and Greek Ethics: Sidgwick, Green and Aristotle." In B. Schultz, ed., *Essays on Sidgwick* (pp. 279–310). Cambridge University Press, 1992.

Irwin, T. H. *Plato's Ethics.* Oxford University Press, 1995.

Irwin, T. H. "Prudence and Morality in Greek Ethics." *Ethics* 105 (1995): 284–95.

Kenny, Anthony. *Aristotle on the Perfect Life*. Oxford University Press, 1992.

Korsgaard, Christine. "Two Distinctions in Goodness." *Philosophical Review* 92 (1983): 169–95.

Korsgaard, Christine. "Aristotle and Kant on the Source of Value." *Ethics* 96 (1986): 486–505.

Korsgaard, Christine. "Aristotle on Function and Virtue." *History of Philosophy Quarterly* 3 (1986): 259–79.

Korsgaard, Christine. "Kant's Formula of Humanity." *Kant-Studien* 77 (1986): 183–202.

Korsgaard, Christine. "Skepticism about Practical Reason." *Journal of Philosophy* 83 (1986): 5–25.

Korsgaard, Christine. "Kant's Analysis of Obligation: The Argument of *Foundations I*." *Monist* 72 (1989): 311–40.

Korsgaard, Christine. "Morality as Freedom." In Yirmiyahu Yovel, ed., *Kant's Practical Philosophy Reconsidered* (pp. 23–48). Dordrecht: Kluwer Academic, 1989.

Korsgaard, Christine. "Creating the Kingdom of Ends: Reciprocity and Responsibility in Personal Relations." In J. Tomberlin, ed., *Philosophical Perspectives*. Volume 6: *Ethics* (pp. 305–32). Atascadero, Calif.: Ridgeview, 1992.

Korsgaard, Christine. *Creating the Kingdom of Ends*. Cambridge University Press, 1996.

Korsgaard, Christine. *The Sources of Normativity*. Cambridge University Press, 1996.

Kraut, Richard. *Aristotle and the Human Good*. Princeton, N.J.: Princeton University Press, 1989.

Leibniz, G. W. *Theodicy*. Ed. Austin Farrer; trans. E. M. Huggard. LaSalle, Ill.: Open Court, 1985.

Louden, Robert B. "Kant's Virtue Ethics." *Philosophy* 61 (1986): 473–89.

Louden, Robert B. *Morality and Moral Theory*. Oxford University Press, 1992.

MacIntyre, Alasdair. *After Virtue: A Study in Moral Theory*. South Bend, Ind.: Notre Dame University Press, 1981.

McDowell, John. "Virtue and Reason." *Monist* 62 (1979): 331–50.

McDowell, John. "Might There Be External Reasons?" In J. E. J. Altham and Ross Harrison, eds., *World, Mind, and Ethics: Essays on the Ethical Philosophy of Bernard Williams* (pp. 68–85). Cambridge University Press, 1995.

McDowell, John. "Realism and Eudaimonism in Aristotle's Ethics." In R. Heinaman, ed., *Aristotle and Moral Realism*. London: University College Press, 1995.

McDowell, John. "Two Sorts of Naturalism." In R. Hursthouse, G. Lawrence, and W. Quinn, eds., *Virtues and Reasons: Essays in Honour of Philippa Foot* (pp. 149–79). Oxford University Press, 1995.

McDowell, John. "Some Issues in Aristotle's Moral Psychology." In S. Everson, ed., *Ethics*. Cambridge University Press, forthcoming.

Meyer, Susan Sauvé. *Aristotle on Moral Responsibility*. Oxford: Blackwell, 1993.

Mill, J. S. *Utilitarianism*. London, 1863.

Moore, G. E. *Principia Ethica*. Cambridge University Press, 1903.

Nagel, Thomas. *The Possibility of Altruism*. Princeton, N.J.: Princeton University Press, 1970.

Nietzsche, Friedrich. *On the Genealogy of Morals and Ecce Homo.* Trans. Walter Kaufmann and R. J. Hollingdale. New York: Random House, 1967.

O'Connor, David K. "Aristotelian Justice as a Personal Virtue." *Midwest Studies in Philosophy* 13 (1988): 417–27.

O'Neill (Nell), Onora. *Acting on Principle: An Essay on Kantian Ethics.* New York: Columbia University Press, 1975.

O'Neill, Onora. *Constructions of Reason: Explorations of Kant's Practical Philosophy.* Cambridge University Press, 1989.

Price, Richard. *A Review of the Principal Questions of Morals.* Ed. D. D. Raphael. Oxford University Press, 1948. A reprint of the 3rd edition, 1787.

Raphael, D. D., ed. *British Moralists.* 2 vols. Oxford University Press, 1969.

Rawls, John. "Themes in Kant's Moral Philosophy." In Eckart Förster, ed., *Kant's Transcendental Deductions* (pp. 81–113). Stanford, Calif.: Stanford University Press, 1989.

Reath, Andrews. "Kant's Theory of Moral Sensibility: Respect for the Law and the Influence of Inclination." *Kant-Studien* 80 (1989): 284–302.

Reath, Andrews. "Hedonism, Heteronomy, and Kant's Principle of Happiness." *Pacific Philosophical Quarterly* 70 (1989): 42–72.

Reich, Klaus. "Kant and Greek Ethics." *Mind* 48 (1939): 338–54, 446–63.

Reid, Thomas. *Essays on the Active Powers.* Ed. Baruch A. Brody. Cambridge, Mass.: MIT Press, 1969.

Rorty, Amélie Oksenberg, ed. *Essays on Aristotle's Ethics.* Berkeley and Los Angeles: University of California Press, 1980.

Rossitto, Cristina. *Aristotele ed Altri: "Divisioni."* Padova: Antenore, 1984.

Sandbach, F. H. *The Stoics.* London: Chatto & Windus, 1975.

Scheffler, Samuel. *Human Morality.* Oxford University Press, 1992.

Schneewind, J. B. "The Misfortunes of Virtue." *Ethics* 101 (1990): 42–63.

Schofield, Malcolm, and Gisela Striker, eds. *The Norms of Nature: Studies in Hellenistic Ethics.* Cambridge University Press, 1986.

Schopenhauer, Arthur. *The World as Will and Representation.* Trans. E. F. J. Payne. New York: Dover, 1958.

Selby-Bigge, L. A., ed. *British Moralists.* Oxford University Press, 1897.

Sidgwick, Henry. *Outlines of the History of Ethics.* 3rd ed. London: Macmillan, 1892.

Sidgwick, Henry. *The Methods of Ethics.* 7th ed. London: Macmillan, 1907.

Stewart, Dugald. *Philosophy of the Active and Moral Powers.* In *The Collected Works of Dugald Stewart.* 11 vols. Edinburgh: T. & T. Clark, 1854–60.

Striker, Gisela. "Origins of the Concept of Natural Law." *Boston Area Colloquium of Ancient Philosophy* 2 (1986): 79–94.

Striker, Gisela. "Ataraxia: Happiness as Tranquility." *Monist* 73 (1989): 97–110.

Striker, Gisela. "Following Nature: A Study in Stoic Ethics." *Oxford Studies in Ancient Philosophy* 9 (1991): 1–73.

Sullivan, Roger J. *Immanuel Kant's Moral Theory.* Cambridge University Press, 1989.

Thomas, Geoffrey. *The Moral Philosophy of T. H. Green.* Oxford University Press, 1987.

Vlastos, Gregory. *Socrates: Ironist and Moral Philosopher.* Ithaca, N.Y.: Cornell University Press, 1991.

White, Nicholas. "Conflicting Parts of Happiness in Aristotle's Ethics." *Ethics* 105 (1995): 258–83.

White, Stephen. *Sovereign Virtue.* Stanford, Calif.: Stanford University Press, 1992.

Whiting, Jennifer. "Human Nature and Intellectualism in Aristotle." *Archiv für Geschichte der Philosophie* 68 (1986): 70–95.

Whiting, Jennifer. "Impersonal Friends." *Monist* 74 (1991): 3–29.

Williams, Bernard. *Moral Luck.* Cambridge University Press, 1981.

Williams, Bernard. *Ethics and the Limits of Philosophy.* Cambridge, Mass.: Harvard University Press, 1985.

Wittgenstein, Ludwig. *Philosophical Investigations.* Trans. G. E. M. Anscombe. New York: Macmillan, 1968.

Wood, Allen, ed. *Self and Nature in Kant's Philosophy.* Ithaca, N.Y.: Cornell University Press, 1984.

Wood, Allen. "Unsociable Sociability: The Anthropological Basis of Kantian Ethics." *Philosophical Topics* 19 (1991): 325–51.

Made in the USA
San Bernardino, CA
01 May 2014